Nurturing AI-Powered HR Analytics and Virtual Reality in Employee Psychology and Workplace Happiness, Part A

Nurturing AI-Powered HR Analytics and Virtual Reality in Employee Psychology and Workplace Happiness, Part A

EDITED BY

CHANNI SACHDEVA
Lovely Professional University, India

ROHIT BANSAL
Rockford College, Australia

AND

FAZLA RABBY
Stanford Institute of Management and Technology, Australia

emerald PUBLISHING

United Kingdom – North America – Japan – India – Malaysia – China

Emerald Publishing Limited
Emerald Publishing, Floor 5, Northspring, 21-23 Wellington Street, Leeds LS1 4DL.

First edition 2026

British Library Cataloguing in Publication Data
A catalogue record for this book is available from the British Library

ISBN: 978-1-80686-126-2 (Print)
ISBN: 978-1-80686-125-5 (Online)
ISBN: 978-1-80686-127-9 (Epub)

Printed and bound by CPI Group (UK) Ltd, Croydon, CR0 4YY

Contents

About the Editors

Channi Sachdeva is pursuing a PhD in Human Resource Management at Lovely Professional University, Punjab, India. She is also serving as an Editor for the various Emerald books. Her research interests encompass artificial intelligence, technology readiness, cognitive dissonance, digital twins, virtual reality, and workplace happiness. She is working on enhancing the theory of cognitive dissonance in human resource management. She has authored several articles on public issues for prominent newspapers, including *The Tribune*, *Times of India*, and *Hindustan Times, Ludhiana*. Her research and bibliometric papers were published in Web of Science and Scopus-indexed journals, a research framework for which she received a copyright certificate from the Government of India, and also a research paper in conference proceedings published in IEEE Explorer. Taylor & Francis, Emerald, and other Scopus-indexed publishers have published her 10+ book chapters. She is a successful businesswoman based in Ludhiana, Punjab, India.

Rohit Bansal is working as an Adjunct Faculty in Rockford College, Sydney, Australia. He obtained a PhD in Management from Maharshi Dayanand University, Rohtak. With a rich experience of 18 years, he has achieved growth through robust and proactive academic initiatives. He has authored and edited many books with renowned national and international publishers, including Springer Nature, IGI Global, Scrivener-Wiley Publishing, De Gruyter, Bentham Science, etc. In addition, he has published research papers and chapters in journals of repute, including Scopus-indexed, as well as edited books. His research work is published in leading publishers like Springer, MDPI, Hindawi, IGI Global, Cell Press, De Gruyter, Elsevier, Inderscience, Wiley, etc.

Fazla Rabby is an accomplished academic and professional with a diverse background in education, management, and marketing. Holding a PhD from the University of Southern Queensland, their education includes degrees and diplomas in management, leadership, and information systems from Central Queensland University and the University of Madras. As a Teaching Academic at Macquarie University and Lecturer at Canterbury Institute of Management, Dr Rabby designs and delivers educational activities, assesses student progress, and contributes to curriculum development. Their role as Academic Director at Stanford Institute of Management and Technology highlights their leadership in stakeholder relationships, business strategies, and human resource management.

About the Contributors

Vibhuti Agrawal is currently working as a Data Analyst and Software Engineer in the Enterprise Technology division at HSBC Technology India, where she has contributed for over 2.5 years. She has worked on a variety of data-driven projects, leveraging tools such as Microsoft Power BI, Power Apps, and other Microsoft Power Platform solutions to create dashboards, automate workflows, and provide actionable insights for business decision-making. Vibhuti completed her B.Tech from Dr. A.P.J. Abdul Kalam Technical University (AKGEC), which laid the foundation for her technical expertise and analytical skills. She continues to play a key role in developing enterprise reporting solutions and data-driven applications within her organization.

Vidhi Agrawal is a Professor of Human Resource Management and Law at Ajay Kumar Garg Institute of Management, India, with over 20 years of experience in teaching and research. She holds a PhD, is an Associate Member of the Institute of Company Secretaries of India, and possesses degrees in MCom, PGDM, and LLB. She has published over 40 research papers in UGC, ABDC, and Scopus-indexed journals, and presented her work at prestigious conferences. In 2025, she edited the book *Human Resource Management and Artificial Intelligence: Automating and Optimizing Processes*, published by Routledge (Taylor & Francis). She has served as Guest Editor for Emerald's *Team Performance Management* and actively reviews for journals such as *Management Research* and MDPI's *Societies*. Recently, she received ICSSR funding for a research project on inclusive education for students with disabilities under the Vision Viksit Bharat@2047 initiative.

Ananda S. is a Doctor of Finance with over 33 years of experience in academia, research, and institutional leadership. He currently serves as Director of PG Studies, Research, and Innovation at the College of Banking and Financial Studies, Muscat. He was associated with the Goa Institute of Management and LIC Mutual Fund, India. He is an Adjunct Professor at Manipal University, India, and a Visiting Professor in Dubai, Germany, and India. He has published approximately 50 papers in reputed international journals and presented a similar number at global conferences. His research was recognized with the ICAI International Research Award 2020 (Second Best) by the Institute of Chartered Accountants of India. He has authored books on mutual funds, mergers and acquisitions, financial systems, and commercial banking, edited five Springer volumes, and serves as

Associate Editor for SAGE Publications. He has led institutional strategy, policy development, and management development programs globally.

Anitha G. holds a PhD in Marketing from Bharathiar University and is a seasoned academic professional with over 17 years of expertise in commerce, specializing in income tax, finance, and customer relationship management, and currently serves as an Associate Professor at Maharaja Institute of Management Studies. A certified Associate national cadet corps (NCC) Officer, she integrates leadership training and discipline into her academic environment, fostering holistic student development. Her scholarly contributions include numerous publications in UGC-CARE and Scopus-indexed journals, and she is also the author of a book on consumer behavior. Ethics and culture & Management International Business. Frequently invited as a resource person for faculty development programs, she has played a pivotal role in organizing national-level academic events and workshops. With a strong commitment to institutional growth, co-curricular engagement, and community outreach, she is widely recognized for her excellence in both academic and extension services, with her work continuing to impact students and professionals across academia.

Elizabeth Chacko is currently working with Christ (Deemed to be) University in Bangalore, Karnataka, India. She is a certified prevention of sexual harassment (POSH) trainer and computer-based management accounting (CBMA)-certified behavioral analyst, holding a Doctoral degree in Management with a specialization in ergonomics from Banasthali University, Rajasthan. She boasts over 16 years of dedicated experience in educating management students. She is recognized as one of the leading professors in India in July 2023 by BusinessTalkz. She is also a certified CBMA Analyst, an Inspiring Educator Award 2024 recipient, a Master Trainer – "Pride of India" Award winner under "DE&I 2024," and a proficient Mendeley expert. Her expertise spans various domains including training, ergonomics, work stress, work–life balance, diversity and inclusion, and general management.

Dina Darwish is Vice Dean, Faculty of Computer Science and Information Technology, Ahram Canadian University, Egypt. She obtained her PhD from Cairo University at 2009, Engineering Faculty. She has been as a Professor since 2020, also her special domain is artificial intelligence, and she has many publications in the following topics, including: artificial intelligence, wireless ad hoc networks, Internet of Things, Big Data analytics, blockchain applications, cloud computing applications, web technologies, intelligent systems, and others.

Azadeh Eskandarzadeh is an Instructor in fields such as marketing, business communication, and organizational behavior. She has published and co-authored various research articles and book chapters on various topics such as environmental sustainability, employee engagement, learning analytics, and educational artificial intelligence.

Yunona Gogia is an experienced higher education professional with 20 years of teaching various career colleges, business schools, and university courses in Vancouver, BC. Her professional experience includes 15 years of ownership and management of food and beverage and light industrial businesses, and 25 years of experience as a content creator, journalist, and newspaper columnist. She has co-authored articles and book chapters on topics of small business analytics and educational innovation.

Anisha P. Gopal is a Research Scholar at the Faculty of Management, SRM Institute of Science and Technology, Kattankulathur. She holds a Master of Business Administration with dual specialization in human resources and marketing. Her current Doctoral research focuses on exploring the mental health and well-being of part-time working students in Chennai's information technology sector. She has contributed to academic literature with a published book chapter in IGI Global and has received acceptance for additional chapters in edited volumes by Springer and Emerald Publishing. Her areas of academic interest include human resource management, marketing, psychology, and organizational behavior. She is committed to advancing interdisciplinary research that bridges management studies and mental health, with a particular focus on young working population.

Shashi Kant Gupta is Post-doctoral Fellow in Computer Science and Engineering at Edoxia Research University, New Castle Delaware, USA. His skills span across various areas of computer science such as artificial intelligence, machine learning, data science, cybersecurity software engineering. His work is focused on pushing the frontiers of knowledge and creating breakthrough solutions in current technology developments. He is the author of other books in the area, such as artificial intelligence and computer science. He is a coauthor of *Advances in Machine Learning Algorithms* and a contributor to several edited volumes on data analytics.

Yu Chen Hu received his PhD degree in Computer Science and Information Engineering from the Department of Computer Science and Information Engineering, National Chung Cheng University, Chiayi, Taiwan. He is a senior member of IEEE. He is also a member of Computer Vision, Graphics, and Image Processing, the Chinese Cryptology and Information Security Association, and Phi Tau Phi Society of the Republic of China. He serves as Editor of *Advances in Multimedia* (Handiwi), *Electronics* (MDPI), *IET Image Processing*, *Intelligent Automation & Soft Computing* (Tech Science Press), and *Mathematical Problems in Engineering* (Handiwi).

Ewelina Idziak is an Associate Professor at the Department of Law and Economics at Kazimierz Wielki University, Poland. She completed her PhD. She holds degrees in economic policy and strategy of companies, and also in finance and monetary policy. She also has about 20 years of strong banking background, working in very important person (VIP), small and medium enterprise (SME), and corporate departments. She also has a strong background, as she worked in global consulting and was the coordinator for international relations at the university. She is also a Financial Expert for the Polish Agency for Enterprise Development and an expert witness for the court. She is also the Associate Professor at the Faculty of Economics, Banking Department at Vilniaus, the Research Fellow in Azerbaijan State University of Economics, Women Researchers Council, and a Visiting Professor at the University of Western Macedonia in Greece. She has an experience in being the part of organizing and scientific committees.

Ferah Diba Izgi is a specialist in pedagogy and psychological counseling and is pursuing a Doctorate in Social Sciences at the University of Potsdam. She is trained in cognitive behavioral therapy (CBT), eye movement desensitization and reprocessing (EMDR), sexual therapy, and child therapy. She is the author of academic books such as *Healthy Romantic Relationships*, *Healthy Sexual Life*, *Values-Based Children's Stories*, *Mumi Loves Vegetables*, and *Let's Play Together*. In addition, she has published numerous peer-reviewed articles and book chapters in psychology, pedagogy, education, and related interdisciplinary fields.

Priah Jokhio is currently working as a Research Associate at the Case Research Center, Sukkur IBA University. She is engaged in academic research, case development, and training-related documentation, especially under initiatives like Growth for Rural Advancement and Sustainable Progress. She contributed to various capacity-building programs, such as Training of Trainers and Agripreneurship training workshops, and played an active role in event reporting and participant assessments. She is having a strong interest in project management, development research, and institutional training.

Mona Hussein Mostafa Kamel is an Assistant Professor of Human Resource Management and Organization Behaviour at McDougall Faculty of Business, University of Prince Edward Island, Cairo Campus, part of the Universities of Canada in Egypt. She values the reciprocal relationship between teaching and learning. She supports critical thinking and uses different teaching methods. She provides students with practical tools to apply in a business environment. Different teaching methods are used, such as real-world examples, case studies, and collaborative group work, to boost student engagement. She earned her PhD from the German University in Cairo. She supervises MBA students and serves as an external examiner for the MBA thesis defense at the German University in Cairo. Her research interests focus on human resources and organizational behavior.

Nilamadhab Kar, MD, DNB, DPM, FRCPsych, works in the NHS, UK, and is associated with the University of Wolverhampton. He is actively involved in mental health research along with clinical work. His research interests include stress-related mental disorders, preventative psychiatry, clinical psychopharmacology, and public mental health. He has more than 300 scientific publications, including articles, books, and chapters. Besides scientific articles, he writes newspaper columns on mental health for public education. He is the Editor of the *Journal of Geriatric Care and Research* and is on the editorial board of a few medical and literary journals (https://orcid.org/0000-0002-8801-9245).

Fatima Zahra Kherazi holds a Master's in Industrial Engineering from Sidi Mohammed Ben Abdellah University, Morocco, and is pursuing a PhD in Management Science and Engineering at Jiangsu University, China. Her research focuses on environmental sustainability, including water scarcity, ecosystem biodiversity, and the use of machine learning in addressing environmental challenges.

Pradeep Kumar is currently working as an Assistant Professor in the Department of Mathematics at Lovely Professional University, Punjab, India. He holds a Doctorate in Philosophy with a specialization in reliability theory. His research interests include system reliability analysis, multistate systems, Markov modeling, and applied mathematics engineering systems. He has published several research papers in reputed journals and has contributed significantly to the field through his work on modeling and analyzing the performance of different complex systems using probabilistic and statistical techniques.

Praveen Kumar is currently pursuing his Bachelor's degree in the School of Law at Manav Rachna University. His research area includes law and cybercrime.

Sanjeev Kumar serves as a Professor at Lovely Professional University, India. He completed Doctor of Philosophy in Hospitality Management in 2019 from Amity University, India. His research areas lie in the food service industry; his research focuses on alcoholic beverages, event management, sustainable management practices, Metaverse, machine learning, and artificial intelligence. He published more than 104 research papers, articles, and chapters in Scopus-indexed, UGC, and peer-reviewed journals and books. He participated and acted as a resource person in various national and international conferences, seminars, session chair, research workshops, and industry talks, and his work has been widely cited. He also edited more than 20 books with various international publishers such as IGI Global, Cambridge Scholars, Emerald, CABI, Bentham Science, and Taylor & Francis. He has been a reviewer of various national and international journals and also delivers guest lectures at conferences and faculty development programs.

Priya Makhija working as Associate Professor at the Center for Management Studies, JAIN (Deemed-to-be University), she has completed her MCom, MBA, MPhil, PhD, PGDHRM, and Executive Financial Data Analytics and has close to 18 years of academic work experience in the areas of teaching, research, team building, academic administration, faculty development, and research enhancement. A keen researcher, her interest areas are occupational role stress, women's growth as investors, women's leadership in higher education, enhancing the quality of higher education, and employee retention. She is writing a book for MCom level at Bangalore University and has published over 28 research papers in journals and presented her research work at various national and international conferences. She received the Prof. Indira Parikh 50 Women in Education Leaders award at the World Education Congress and the Distinguished Teacher award from MTC Education Global.

Parinita Malhotra is an instructor in the field of business studies. Her Doctorate is in Marketing with 23 years of teaching and industrial experience at national and international levels. She has delivered papers at various national and international levels, with a number of book chapters being published.

Anika Nashat Matin has received a Doctorate in Philosophy from Lovely Professional University, Punjab, India. Eventually, her field of study was integrated with tourism and marketing to form the field of destination marketing. She works as an Assistant Professor at Southeast University in Dhaka, Bangladesh. A wide variety of teaching-related learning opportunities have characterized her academic career. Over time, she has produced research that helps marketing departments in the travel and tourism industry grow. As the Secretary of the Bangladeshi UNESCO Club, she has represented her country at international conferences and demonstrated a strong commitment to her work. She has a notable background, with over 10 years of experience as a professional English news presenter for both commercial and government-owned networks. Her objectives are to educate the world and learn about the many innovative marketing and tourist strategies.

V. Mohana Sundari is an Accomplished Academician in Business Management with over 13 years of experience, currently serving as Assistant Professor at SRM Institute of Science and Technology. Holding a PhD in Human Resources with specialization in emotional intelligence and employability, she is a recognized research supervisor guiding multiple scholars. She has authored numerous research articles in Scopus and ABDC-listed journals, contributed to book chapters, and published patents. She has secured a funded project from ICSSR and been part of consultancy research. She has held key administrative roles related to accreditation and academic coordination. As a subject expert and guest speaker, she has contributed to academic boards and conferences. Her areas of expertise include human resource, marketing, entrepreneurship, digital marketing, and emotional intelligence, with a strong track record in teaching, research, and academic leadership.

Amitava Pal is the Associate Dean at the International Institute of Sports Management, which received the prestigious President's Award in 2020. A seasoned academic and industry expert, he has guided pivotal industry reports in collaboration with organizations like FICCI, ASSOCHAM, and IMC. As Training and Research Head, he guided standard operating procedures (SOPs) for the 37th National Games, Khelo India Youth Games, and Khelo India University Games. His research has been featured in leading publications, including Bonn University,

Germany, and the University of California, and he received the Best Paper Award for Sustainability in Sports. Additionally, he has mentored IIC fellows for the University of Chicago Harris School of Public Policy and spearheaded training, operation, and implementation of the computer science curriculum researched and developed at IIT Bombay, for InOpen, SINE, IIT Bombay.

Dev Panwar is currently pursuing his Bachelor's degree in Law at Manav Rachna University. His research area includes law and criminal crime.

Christoph Rasche is a Professor at the University of Potsdam, specializing in strategic management, sports economics, and professional services. After completing his Doctorate and habilitation at the University of Bayreuth, he gained experience in both academia and the consulting sector. A founding board member of GMIP, he has held visiting professorships, served on advisory boards, and contributed to leadership and management publications. He is also active in mentoring start-ups and engaging with politics, industry, and competitive sports.

Namita Rath, MA (PMIR), MBA (HR), MPhil, PhD, is an Associate Professor in Organisational Behaviour and Human Resource Management at Sri Sri University, Cuttack, India. She did her PhD in Personnel Management and Industrial Relations from Utkal University. She has over 20 years of teaching experience in business schools with bachelor's and master's programs. She has published 40 papers. Her research interests include organizational behavior, industrial relations, and talent management. She is currently guiding three doctoral candidates (https://orcid.org/0000-0002-3738-3848).

Shubhi Rathi is an Assistant Professor at the School of Business, Manipal Academy of Higher Education, Dubai, with over nine years of diverse experience spanning engineering, academics, finance, and market research. She holds a PhD. in Statistics and an MS in Financial Mathematics. As a CFA Level-II candidate, she combines her strong quantitative background with practical financial expertise. She is proficient in a range of advanced analytical tools and technologies, including MATLAB, R, Python, Power BI, Big Data technologies, and Excel, and possesses strong skills in writing and executing complex SQL queries. Her multidisciplinary experience enables her to effectively bridge the gap between quantitative analysis and real-world business applications. She has published more than 10 research articles in reputed national and international journals and actively participates in organizing and attending research conferences.

Alok Kumar Sahai is a graduate of the Indian Institute of Management Bangalore and obtained his PhD in Behavioural Finance from the National Law University Jodhpur. He was an Associate Professor in the Faculty of Management at Sri Sri University, Cuttack, and is now working as a freelance investment consultant. His research interests include behavioral finance, psychology of commodity markets, and consumer behavior. (https://orcid.org/0000-0002-8830-3131).

Ashish Saxena is an Associate Professor at the School of Business, Galgotias University, with over 17 years of experience in teaching, research, and academic administration. He holds a PhD in Commerce along with qualifications including MBA, MCom, PGDIBO, and UGC-NET in both Management and Commerce. His areas of expertise span financial accounting, cost and management accounting, financial management, security analysis, and financial institutions and services. As a dedicated educator, he is committed to fostering analytical thinking and problem-solving abilities in his students. He has authored over 20 research papers in reputed national and international journals and actively participates in academic conferences. He is also an NIIT-certified Tally trainer and has completed several NPTEL online certification courses from IITs and IIMs. Known for his productivity, efficiency, and passion for academic excellence, he continues to contribute significantly to business education and research at Galgotias University.

Sonia Najam Shaikh is pursuing a PhD in Management Science and Engineering at Jiangsu University. Also holding an MBA in Human Resource Management, she investigates the integration of human resource management with artificial intelligence and Big Data Analytic technologies, particularly the use of strategically emerging technologies in promoting organizational innovation and excellence. She actively contributes to her field by working as a peer reviewer for a number of reputable academic journals. For her current research, she analyzes the impact of technology on human resource management and the improvement of sustainable organizational performance in varying business environments.

Sudhanshu Singh is an Associate Professor at Galgotias University, India, with expertise in business analytics, blockchain, multicriteria decision-making, supply chain management, and process mining. Holding a Doctorate from NITIE, Mumbai, his research focuses on integrating data-driven and expert-driven decision-making, with publications in OPSEARCH, Springer, and international conferences like ICIPTM. He has facilitated ZED certifications for 85 micro, small and medium enterprises (MSMEs) with the Quality Council of India and led consulting for a global power transmission company. He has diverse set of experiences across multiple domains. He has spearheaded innovative projects, including establishing setting up 560 village libraries and 111 shelter home libraries in Haryana. He has developed courses on robotic process automation and machine learning at SRM Institute. A PMP-certified professional and ASQ Six Sigma Black Belt, he is proficient in Python, R, SPSS, and process mining tools like Celonis and DISCO. He actively contributes to industry–academia collaborations and smart city initiatives.

Swati Sood is a graduate of IGNOU, Bhopal, and is pursuing a PhD in Management/IT from Pacific University, Rajasthan. Presently, she is working as faculty in BIITM, Bhubaneswar, and is associated with various institutes as visiting faculty. Her research interest includes information technology, artificial intelligence, and general management (https://orcid.org/0009-0003-2141-2960).

Vishal Sood is a graduate of IMS, DAVV, Indore, and obtained a PhD in Finance from DAVV, Indore. Presently, he is a Professor in the Faculty of Management Studies at Sri Sri University, Cuttack. His research interests include behavioral finance, commodity and stock markets, general management, and human resource management. He is on the Editorial Board of ANUJAT, Ghana, and has published 70 papers in journals of repute (https://orcid.org/0000-0002-7888-4884).

Sanam Soomro is pursuing her PhD at the School of Management, Jiangsu University, Zhenjiang, China. Her research interests include artificial intelligence, human resource management, work–life balance, employee well-being, and employee performance. She is actively engaged in interdisciplinary research aimed at enhancing organizational effectiveness through innovative HR practices and technological integration. With a forward-thinking approach, she is committed to contributing to the future of work through creative, data-driven insights that support both organizational growth and human flourishing.

Syed Ahmed Salman is an accomplished academic and researcher specializing in Islamic banking, takaful, and financial innovation. Currently serving as an Associate Professor at Lincoln University College, Malaysia, he brings over a decade of expertise in teaching, research, and consultancy. He holds a PhD and Postdoctoral Fellowship from the International Islamic University Malaysia, and a Doctorate in Business Administration in Artificial Intelligence from the European Institute of Applied Sciences and Management. He has authored numerous scholarly articles and books in the domains of Islamic finance, corporate governance, and ethical insurance. He is actively engaged in several international research collaborations, with a strong focus on sustainable financial models, Shari'ah governance, and elderly care. A recipient of multiple best paper and academic excellence awards, he is also a member of several editorial boards and professional bodies, contributing significantly to thought leadership and innovation in the Islamic finance sector.

R. Thanga Kumar is an Assistant Professor and is an expert in finance and accounting with a deep passion for teaching all facets of finance. He includes practice and application of the fundamentals into corporate and cost management accounting and also his research interest lies in understanding the behavioral pattern of investment.

Neerav Verma serves as an Associate Professor and Program Chair for BBA (General, Integrated, Research with Honors) at the School of Business, Galgotias University, Greater Noida, Uttar Pradesh. He has successfully presented and published 11 research papers in national and international repute journals and also contributed one chapter to a book. He has vast experience in organizing various academic and non-academic events. He has successfully organized two faculty development programs (FDPs) one national and one international conference as organizing secretary. He has also contributed to the management education as guest speaker, conference panel chair, research thesis evaluator, paper setter, and viva expert for various business schools and universities. He has completed BA (Math – Hons.) from BHU, Varanasi, and MBA, PhD from Bundelkhand University, Jhansi. He has also completed two certifications in Business Statistics (University of Mysore) and Operations Research (IIT Madras) of NPTEL – Swayam.

Farida Virani is a distinguished professor, author, mediator, and leadership expert with over two decades of experience in human resources, behavioral sciences, and organizational development. Currently serving as Professor and Head of the MET Incubation Center, Mumbai, she has mentored thousands of students and professionals through her teaching and corporate training. A PhD in Management, she is also a CEDR-UK-certified Mediator, POSH Trainer, and award-winning educator, honored with the NFED Lifetime Achievement Award and the Teaching-Training Quality Excellence Award. She has authored books on mediation, leadership, and artificial intelligence in education, blending academic rigor with practical insights. Her work continues to inspire individuals and organizations to embrace innovation, resilience, and future-ready leadership.

Niranchana Shri Viswanathan is Assistant Professor at School of Management Studies, Sapthagiri NPS University, Bengaluru, India. Her research interests include different aspects of management in human resources, marketing, finance, and health care. She is committed to advancing business thinking and knowledge through her research into current issues facing business. She has published in other books that deal with artificial intelligence, healthcare, and human resource. She is the author of *Understanding Modern Business Strategies* and co-author of the book *The Dynamics of Organizational Behavior*.

Foreword

Rapid advances in artificial intelligence (AI), immersive technologies, and data-driven decision-making are reshaping the modern workplace. Human resource (HR) management has evolved from a largely administrative function into a strategic, analytics-driven discipline that directly influences employee psychology, well-being, and organizational sustainability. Within this context, the edited Volume 1, *Nurturing AI-Powered HR Analytics and Virtual Reality in Employee Psychology and Workplace Happiness*, offers timely and meaningful insights.

This book explores how AI-powered HR analytics and virtual reality (VR) are transforming the way human capital is understood and managed. Rather than focusing solely on efficiency and performance outcomes, the chapters emphasize human-centric dimensions, including employee psychology, engagement, learning, trust, mental well-being, and workplace happiness. This focus is particularly relevant as organizations confront challenges related to burnout, disengagement, ethical technology adoption, and the growing need for compassionate and inclusive workplaces.

AI-driven HR analytics enables organizations to move beyond traditional reporting toward predictive and prescriptive insights, offering a deeper understanding of employee behavior, motivation, and performance patterns. At the same time, VR technologies are redefining training, onboarding, leadership development, and employee well-being initiatives by providing immersive, experiential, and psychologically safe environments. When integrated thoughtfully, these technologies have the potential to enhance not only organizational effectiveness but also employee satisfaction and psychological flourishing.

A key strength of Volume 1 lies in its interdisciplinary perspective. Drawing on organizational behavior, psychology, HR management (HRM), and information systems, the contributors present robust theoretical frameworks alongside empirical evidence. The book also critically addresses ethical concerns such as data privacy, algorithmic bias, and the human implications of excessive automation.

This volume will be a valuable resource for researchers, scholars, HR practitioners, and organizational leaders seeking responsible, human-centered approaches to leveraging emerging technologies in the workplace.

Chapter 1

The Intersection of Artificial Intelligence and HR Analytics: Empowering Organization Efficiency and Workplace Optimization

Azadeh Eskandarzadeh[a], *Parinita Malhotra*[a] *and Yunona Gogia*[b]

[a] *Western Community College, Canada*
[b] *University Canada West, Canada*

Abstract

Artificial intelligence (AI) for human resource (HR) analytics is revolutionizing organization and labour force optimization and efficiency. The research examines how AI and HR analytics collaborate to transform HR paradigms through automation, predictive analytics, and personalized talent experiences. AI streamlines recruiting, performance management, talent management, and worker well-being by leveraging machine learning (ML), natural language processing (NLP), and evidence-based insights. AI streamlines talent acquisition, performance management, talent management, and worker well-being by leveraging ML, NLP, and data-driven insights. The chapter uses a systematic analysis of 37 peer-reviewed publications to show how AI can automate routine operations (resume screening, payroll processing), anticipate labour force trends (attrition, skill gap), and reduce HR biases. AI-driven HR analytics is difficult to adopt owing to ethical concerns, judgement biases, data privacy, and incumbent personnel upskilling. Fairness and responsibility need openness of AI-driven procedures and worker data security. The research shows that HR professionals need a balanced strategy that combines technology innovation with person-centered capabilities to engage in culture and talent development. Future trends, including the use of AI, blockchain, and Internet of Things (IoT) to safeguard employees' data and monitor their well-being, are also examined. Organizations require

Nurturing AI-Powered HR Analytics and Virtual Reality in Employee Psychology and Workplace Happiness, Part A, 1–17

Published under exclusive licence by Emerald Publishing Limited
doi:10.1108/978-1-80686-125-520261001

inter-disciplinary cooperation, talent upskilling, and comprehensive ethical rules to maximize AI's potential. This chapter adds to AI and HRM debates by advocating for responsible adoption that balances technological innovation with workers' and businesses' interests.

Keywords: Workforce optimization; HR analytics; employee retention; ethical AI; machine learning; data privacy

1.1. Introduction

Integration of AI in HR analytics constitutes a revolutionary shift that holds the promise to overhaul the traditional HR practice and unleash unprecedented potential in the workforce. Multi-dimensionally enabled AI with ML, NLP, and computer vision is getting rapid entries through various streams of HR and unleashing change in basic assumptions in the most valued aspect: people are managed by companies. HR analytics, long synonymous with data-centric inputs on employee performance, engagement, and retention getting turbo-charged by algorithmic dynamics fuelled by AI, able to derive insights out of humongous inputs and discern unseen patterns and forecast with unparalleled accuracy. Such integration among AI and HR analytics enables companies to break through descriptive and diagnostic analytics and draw predictive and prescriptive insights and take anticipatory decisions, and effect informed interventions. Such fusion among AI and HR analytics liberates a new avatar for data-centric human resource management (HRM) and enables companies to make decisions on things and people and be better placed in a rapid-fire business world. Potentiality of AI in easing drudgework, enabling personalized employee experience, and providing data-centric inputs is getting redefined HR professionals' role and function, and enables them to get relieved of drudgework and focus on higher-order initiatives such as people development, culture in companies, and employee well-being. Integration between AI and HR analytics provides an end-to-end solution to employee lifecycle understanding and optimization through the entire phases, such as employment and onboarding, through performance management, and offboarding. By utilizing AI-enabled tools, HR functions can ease drudgework such as resume screening and interviews and liberate HR professionals to focus on higher-order initiatives. Moreover, AI algorithms can process vast amounts of employee information, derive unseen patterns, predict future trends such as employee competency gaps, and enable the management to be proactive in specific, employee-related decisions. Such an anticipatory approach enables the company to control hazard-bearing elements, optimize allocations, and retain high-performing and motivated force. The ability of AI in processing and understanding humongous inputs allows HR to better understand dynamics in a workplace, forecast future trends, and make decisions that provide a competitive advantage. AI tools can process employee feedback, sentiments, and behaviour, unravel potential areas, and create customized interventions to improve employee well-being and work engagement. Economic impacts of AI in the workplace are mind-boggling; AI investments have multiplied the investment put in by a host of nations collectively. Such investment testifies to the transformational power of AI to drive economic growth and broaden organizational effectiveness. But inclusion of AI in HR practices also throws challenges that cannot be done away with, such as the question of ethics, the issue of data security, and reskilling the workforce. Organizations will be forced to take the challenges seriously and chalk out the strategies to mitigate the risk and ensure that the AI in HR is used ethically and responsibly. Implementation of AI in HR calls for a wholesome approach incorporating both the technological and human dimensions of the workplace.

1.2. Literature Review

Increased research interest in the HRM uses of AI finds coverage in the analysis of literature in 37 relevant articles, such that HRM use allows for improved organizational decision-making, improved processes, and improved efficiency (Sucipto, 2024). From literature analysis comes the knowledge that there exists the possibility for AI to provide decisions in real-time through algorithmically programmed computation technology intended to learn and improve, and yield better outcomes (Rodgers et al., 2022). Through this, ongoing research and practice at various organizational and other levels continue to enrich AI through the transformative potential (Dima et al., 2024). Through the automation of repetitive tasks, AI frees HR professionals to work on higher-order tasks such as talent management and organizational development.

Through recruitment and selection applications, AI expedites screening the candidates, identifies the best talents, and eradicates biases while offering a pluralistic and inclusive workplace (Madanchian, 2024). The technology allows identification of an employee better positioned in the firm by lessening keying the data manually and the likelihood of human errors. The transformational energy of AI in HRM is, then, transforming the world, as the HR activities are undertaken and how the HR professional works. AI automates the process of onboarding, individualizes the training, and offers ongoing learning chances, giving a culture of development.

Additionally, performance management deploys AI to track employee statistics, provide feedback regarding areas of concern, and uncover development opportunities to drive data-enabled decision-making and continued development. Talent management is enabled through technology to identify skills gaps, forecast future workplace demand, and craft personalized career development. Through AI, HR functions can provide evidence-based decision-making, automate HR processes, and enhance the employee experience. It must be noted, however, that such tools through AI can equally reinforce biases in the dimensions of race, gender, age, social class, and disability status.

Table 1.1 shows not only the rapid and wide spreading of AI in recruitment but also two principal benefits of using it: (1) as a potent streamlining and time-saving tool and (2) a talent-acquisition tool.

HRM practices are further transformed by AI in facilitating system and process efficiencies, advanced analytics, and facilitating the organization's value-creation

Table 1.1. AI in HR Industry Statistics.

Item	Statistical Insight
Global AI recruitment market value	$590.50 billion as of 2023
Global AI usage	88% of companies globally have been utilizing AI technology in HR
Increase in AI importance	78.9% foresee an increase in AI importance and usage in the workplace
Main reasons for using AI	A staggering 93% report significant time savings and improved efficiency, while 67% indicate cost and resource savings
Projected growth	AI recruitment is expected to grow at a CAGR of 6.17% between 2023 and 2030
Market projection	Global AI recruitment market to reach $942.3 million by 2030
Talent acquisition	24% of companies use AI to hire talented employees

Sources: Kumar (2025), Workable (2025), SRHM (2025), and CareerBuilder Survey.

process (Fenwick et al., 2024). Through AI, personalized employee experience can be delivered through personalized learning programs, career development opportunities, and benefit programs. HR professionals become more aware of the fact that HRM is not administration but a strategic business partner who builds people, culture, and compliance to obtain organizational success (Fenwick et al., 2024). Using AI allows organizations to do better in the labour market, do away with tedious work activities, and improve employees' quality of life (Rožman et al., 2023).

The AI HR solutions offer a variety of advantages, ranging from the enhancement of the effectiveness of recruitment to automating administrative tasks and creating better rapport at the workplace (Faqihi & Miah, 2023b). These span the range from the application in predictive analytics and talent search to the new advanced monitoring and tracking the sentiment and the tracking employee engagement, and utilizing the AI-enabled deployment of quick deployment support HR (Mwita & Kitole, 2025). The integrative model not only offers the best operating effectiveness functioning but also puts the HR function at a better firm structure position where it can be the data-driven arm capable of doing proactive talent management and firm development (Fenwick et al., 2024).

1.3. Impact of AI on HR Functions

AI has a bearing on several HR processes by facilitating process streamlining through automation, providing key information, and boosting efficiencies (Dima et al., 2024). AI-driven hiring software is capable of searching through huge databases of candidates to identify the ones whose skills and experience are perfectly matched to satisfying the organizational requirements. AI-driven performance management software offers customized feedback and coaching to the employees in order to empower them to grow and develop to their full potential. By streamlining mundane processes and improving decision-making processes, AI streamlines HR processes and the entire employee experience.

AI helps to improve candidate identification by broadening the coverage of recruiter activities and the identification of eligible candidates with varying levels of experience. The chatbots based on AI are capable of delivering immediate feedback to employees and allowing HR specialists to focus on longer activities. The systems based on AI even monitor employees' emotions and recognize points of difficulty sooner than when the issue is bigger. The implementations of AI in HR lead to greater efficiency, higher satisfaction of employees in their organizations, and higher organizational performance.

It brings into question data privacy and the risk of algorithmic bias with which the organizations are confronted. The biggest problem is data privacy as the AI systems are reliant on the big pools of employee data. The organizations need to be in compliance with the data protection legislation such as the general data protection regulation (GDPR) and manage the employee data in a responsible and ethical manner. The other problem is algorithmic bias; if you are training AI algorithms using biased data, then the AI algorithms will inherit the biases (Dima et al., 2024).

Table 1.2 illustrates the benefits achieved through the use of AI in HR and related to the increased efficiency of the HR function.

The organizations have to be cautious of the risk of algorithmic bias and be one step ahead in how it is managed. This is through using diversified data sets while training the algorithms, testing the algorithms on a regular basis to spot the bias, and having the final decision-making done by the HR professionals. This is an approach to embracing AI in HRM by considering the chances and the challenges. The HR units have to be very clear on what they would like to achieve and what the AI tools are capable of doing. The HR professionals have to be in a position to effectively and ethically apply the AI tools (Nyathani, 2022).

Table 1.2. The Impact of AI Automation on HR Practices.

Item	Impact
The use of AI and HR-related tasks	Approximately 25% of organizations use AI in HR
Positive outcomes in recruitment and AI	Two out of three HR professionals cite an improved process of filling the job vacancies
Increased efficiency	85% of employers who utilize AI report increased HR department efficiency

Sources: Personio (2023) and SRHM (2025).

The convergence of HRM with AI necessitates the strategic framework guided by a clear implementation plan and frequent check-ins to ensure AI-based solutions are on track with organizational goals and ideals of equity and justice. Advanced risk management enables clear rules to be set on data security and privacy and on algorithmic transparency. For HR professionals to be in a position to deploy AI to expedite processes, education and training are needed. The aim needs to be to complement human capabilities and not to replace them. For example, AI-based technologies should advance HR decision-making and the employee experience. This necessitates a broad ethical framework to deploy AI to assist HR in undertaking supervision of data governance and transparency while having the responsibility of avoiding bias and delivering equity (Prasad, 2024).

1.4. Methodology

The entire chapter hinges on the systematic literature review undertaken to find, verify, and synthesize the present body of knowledge on the convergence between HR analytics and AI. It endeavoured to critically investigate the evolution dynamics, strategic implementation, the moral dimensions, and the future trends in this dynamic field, particularly in relation to how it impacts organizational effectiveness and workforce optimization.

1.4.1. Search Strategy

A systematic searching procedure was done on various reliable academic databases to achieve a wide coverage of the literature that was applicable. The databases used for the current review were the following: Scopus and Google Scholar. The search employed a combination of key phrases and keywords, arranged in such a way that they would be capable of picking up the dominant themes in the studies. The keywords and the combinations thereof were the following:

Refer to the following keywords in context: Artificial Intelligence, HR Analytics, Workforce Optimization, Predictive Analytics, Algorithmic Bias, Ethical AI, Natural Language Processing, Data Privacy, AI in HR. The search has only been narrowed to articles published during the years 2019 through 2025 to confine the analysis to the most recent discourses and trends in the topic.

Inclusion and exclusion criteria: The literature search yielded a staggering number of articles. The quality and the degree of relevance of the literature to be included were established in the intensive screening process through the following criteria:

Inclusion criteria: research articles delivered at conferences, refereed articles, and research reviews that engage the topic areas of AI, HR analytics, and the intersection. Implementation studies on the various HR functions (recruitment, talent development, performance management, employee retention) using AI technologies. Research on the strategic imperative, future challenges and opportunities, the future trends, and the ethical dimensions that AI holds for HR.

Exclusion criteria: Blog posts, news items, opinion pieces lacking original research or comprehensive reviews; research not explicitly using AI or HR analytics; documents outside the time specified (2019–2025). Thirty-seven relevant articles, identified through this systematic procedure, formed the background literature for this review. The articles were included by their clear applicability to the research questions, research rigour, and utility for elucidating the complex interactions among AI and HR analytics. Our systematic procedure helped minimize bias and establish the validity of findings, in accordance with established protocols among similar comprehensive reviews.

1.5. The Evolving Landscape of HR Analytics in the Age of AI

The HR analytics career has evolved to go beyond reporting and descriptive statistics to predictive and prescriptive methods. The HR analytics is also complemented by the infusion of AI by delivering on high-end data analysis, pattern discovery, and predictive modelling functionality that enables the HR professionals to have a panoramic view of the dynamics of the workforce, be able to predict future patterns, and make evidence-based decisions to drive the better performance of the organization. The union of AI and HR analytics goes beyond process automation and expands human capabilities to enable the HR professionals to be more discerning and strategic in the decision-making process.

HR analytics implementation using AI completely redefines trends in talent development, trends in talent acquisition, and talent retention trends. Recruitment platforms using AI draw on the deep databases of the candidates and shortlist the individuals whose experience and skills are best aligned with the needs of the organizations (Saraswathi et al., 2023). AI-enabled performance management systems offer personalized coaching and feedback to employees and enable them to enhance performance and derive the best from themselves. AI not only automates the HR processes but also enriches the entire employee experience.

AI programs can also detect and rectify biases in HR functions, including hiring and promotion, and introduce fairness and equality, and ensure alignment with organizational values. AI can also personalize employee learning and development activities and offer individuals the skills and knowledge they need for the future. AI-enabled tools quantify employees' skills, detect skills gaps, and offer organizations the means to design personalized training interventions. Closing skills gaps and delivering personalized training helps AI develop a more skilled and adaptable workforce capable of handling future challenges. AI systems provide employees with real-time guidance and feedback on the job and help enhance employees' performance and output.

AI-enabled systems process the data of employees to identify potential threats to the welfare of employees, such as stress or burnout, and implement interventions to mitigate such risks. Insights developed using AI-fuelled HR analytics permit organizations to craft comprehensive risk profiles and establish strategic priorities for managing potential complications (Wilayat et al., 2022). AI has emerged as a tool for the enhancement of various functions of HRM and the promise of greater effectiveness and strategic alignment. However, the integration of AI in HR also presents complex questions of ethics regarding data privacy, algorithmic bias, and potential impacts on job security (Sadeghi, 2024). Such questions present the imperative for careful consideration and the development of robust frameworks for the implementation of AI in a just and responsible manner (Sadeghi, 2024). The very nature of some AI systems as having inherent opaqueness and the 'black box' problem raises questions regarding the accountability and transparency of HR decision-making and necessitates a focus on interpretable AI models (Rodgers et al., 2022). Addressing such considerations entails the existence of clear directives regarding ethics, transparent AI governance frameworks, and ongoing monitoring to mitigate risk and foster employees' trust in the implementation of AI in HR functions (Venugopal et al., 2024). The evolution of a human-centred orientation takes centre stage and gives prominence to worker welfare and happiness, and incorporates innovative and prudent steps for the implementation of technology in the company.

The future of HRM is quite different from the past since HRM is reinvigorated by AI by automating mundane tasks, rationalizing decision-making, and individualizing the experience of the employee (William et al., 2023). AI-enabled tools automate administrative tasks such as screening through CVs, interview scheduling, and payment, and give HR professionals time to spend on strategic projects (Westover, 2024). Apart from this, AI enables delivery of value to organizations by using advanced data insights and process efficiencies (Fenwick et al., 2024) and enables HR departments to function efficiently and decrease administrative tasks, and gives HR professionals time to spend on strategic priorities (George & Thomas, 2019). AI algorithms scan wide datasets on employees and find patterns and predict future trends like employee turnover or skills gaps, and give HR departments the ability to pre-empt such events. The predictive capacity enables organizations to manage future risk, rationalize future deployment of resources, and maintain a motivated and high-performing workforce. AI enables the implementation and development of customized employee experience, such as customized learning modules, career development opportunities, and customized reward packages to cater to the unique needs and preferences (Westover, 2024).

Application of AI to HR processes can revolutionize talent attraction, development, and retention. The AI-driven recruitment systems browse through voluminous candidate records databases and identify the people whose competency and experience match organizational needs. The performance enabling systems powered by AI provide one-on-one feedback and coaching to the employees and steer them towards improved performance and being better than they are capable of by themselves. Automation of routine tasks and decision-making enhancement allows simplification and the entire employee experience to be optimized.

AI enables candidate searching by broadening the scope and/search sources and by finding the best candidate through various backgrounds. Additionally, AI enables the development of chatbots that respond proactively to employees' questions, and then the employees' HR staff can focus on doing complex tasks. Additionally, the AI systems keep tracking employees' sentiment and areas requiring intervention, even before such areas become exceptionally large problems. Such uses of AI by HR enhance the efficiency rates, the employees' satisfaction rates, and the overall organizational performance.

AI not only acts as a technological tool but also as a strategic enabling tool that allows organizations to achieve their business goals. The AI improves the objectivity and effectiveness of the recruitment process and allows organizations to process the candidates more quickly and more precisely (Koman et al., 2024). The AI-enabled performance management systems provide employees with individualized feedback and coaching and help them develop and fulfil their potential. Apart from that, the AI systems also detect biases in the HR processes like recruitment and promotion and develop methodologies to minimize such biases (Sharma & Bhat, 2023), while the HR decisions are rationalizable, fair-minded, and aligned to the organization's values. This strategic alignment also compels the HR functions to be redefined and pushes the HR professionals to be more strategic business partners who can capitalize on the insights created by AI and develop evidence-based decision-making and a human-centric work culture.

1.6. Ethical Considerations and Challenges in AI-driven HRM

The addition of AI to HRM raises important ethical issues and challenges on which organizations are mandated to proactively tackle strengthening fairness, transparency, and accountability. The largest ethical problem arises from the inescapable possibility of algorithmic bias in the AI systems used on particularly strategic HR processes such as recruiting, performance appraisal, and promotion (Oman et al., 2024). The biases, if unchecked, may perpetuate existing social injustices and overtly manifest in discriminatory behaviours and consequently compromise the very foundations of diversity and inclusivity at the workplace (Akter et al., 2023). Organizations should prioritize training the AI systems on representative and diverse datasets to effectively mitigate algorithmic bias, conduct periodic audits to identify and exclude biases, and be explicit on decision-making procedures. The other related ethical problem revolves around the very real possibility of infringements in the sphere of data privacy. The AI systems entail the aggregation and processing of huge employee data and present real-world concerns with regard to the storage in safety of it, proper utilization of it, and overall safety of it. Accordingly, organizations are necessarily burdened to strictly adhere to the provisions relating to data protection and enact overarching data safety procedures to strictly preserve the confidentiality of employees. Additionally, the level of transparency given by employees on the utilization thereof cannot be undermined and accompanies the obligation to notify employees how theirs may be sought, rectified, and deleted with regard to the personal information thereof.

Moreover, the incorporation of AI in HRM raises certain very practical issues related to striking the right balance between the facilitating of automation by the AI and the distinctive and critical role of human judgement and discretion. Overreliance on the systems of AI will tend to make the workplace dehumanized in the sense that the employees will be treated as statistics and not as respected humans (Fenwick et al., 2024). The HR professionals will thus have to retain and apply their judgement, empathy, and rationality when they are confronting the process of taking decisions among employees. At their best, it is critically necessary to achieve the right balance by using the AI in the interest of streamlining processes and deriving the benefit given by the process while maintaining a human-centric HRM at its very core.

A levelling of these multi-faceted considerations and challenges to AI in HRM calls for a multi-faceted intervention. This calls for an emergence of clear guidance on ethics and adoption of stout procedures on data stewardship and widespread expenditure on developmental and training projects calibrated to HR professionals. Proactive initiative by all the stakeholders such as employees, unions, and statutory bodies is needed to extract input from diversified fractions and ensure that the AI implementation continues remaining reasonable and ethically justifiable. An emergence of the consideration of the factor of ethics at the very foundation has to bring forth the trust and ensure the AI goes on to enhance the very elementary values of fairness, clarity, and responsibility in HRM. Development and implementation of AI responsibly in HRM call for multidisciplinary endeavours by summoning in professionals in diversified arenas such as computer science, ethics, law, and HR. The multi-disciplinary endeavours bring in the multi-faceted systems like the AI systems to be technically robust and robust and plus ethically justifiable and viable in law as well. The organizations have to come up with processes of observation and evaluation and extract and correct the impending negative outcomes or wrong consequences possible if foreseen by regular observation on the AI systems. The regular observation allows an evolution in the developmental course of the deployment of AI to differing horizons and steps of the sphere of the realm of ethics and technology. The relentless evolution of the AI technologies highlights the developmental mandate on variable frameworks on the sphere of the realm of ethics that may be able to support newer forms of deployment and indefinite outcome on society in the HR sphere. Finally, incorporation of the AI algorithmic framework of decision-making on a basis of the sphere of the realm of ethics in HRM applications possibly could be in a position to provide illumining facts on how diversified strategic streams impact the decisions reached by the HR professionals (Rodgers et al., 2022). This anticipation measure facilitates detection and management of the prospective violation of the HR processes by the AI at the systemic level and facilitates developing a balanced and clearer workplace (Rodgers et al., 2022). This proscribes an effective governing architecture on HRM to facilitate incorporation of the ethical orientations on the design area by deployment and relentless implementation (Batool et al., 2025). This would involve explicit procedures on having accountability and independent monitoring in force, and periodic consideration on the ethical effects to ensure such adoption of AI is comfortable in the institution and statutory compliance. This would involve deriving explicit frameworks on having accountability in force, deployment of independent monitoring, and periodic consideration of the ethical effects to ensure adoption of AI in relation to organizational values and letter of the law. Organizations would be equally bound to develop a human-centric mindset such that the AI is developed to complement human capacity and enrich the well-being of the employees and not replace human judgement at all (Fenwick et al., 2024). Development capital in sustained adaptation and instep learning in the HR function is equally needed so that professionals are always au courant on the latest evolution in AI and the correlative considerations to ensure ethics (Batool et al., 2025). This anticipation gesture ensures that the ethical considerations become not an after-thought but are organically become imbricated in the inculcation of the AI into HRM to ensure discriminatory outcomes and injury to reputation (Bahangulu & Owusu-Berko, 2025). At the same time, the strategic deployment of the AI in HRM shifts the considerations on ethics to a fundamental restructure of the HR functions to redefinition of the traditional HR functions and activities, such that the analytic function of the AI gets leveraged towards increased strategic decision-making. This necessitates the acquisition of the new skills by the HR professionals in the areas of data science and ML and their application to the domain of ethics so that the technologies' functionalities are employed towards the well-being of the organization (Taslim et al., 2025). This type of reorientation positions the HR at the apex strategic advisor by leveraging the AI in the event of evidence-based recommendation of the talent management and the predictor analysis to the objective and plan of the workforce and the customized employee experience (Nawaz et al., 2024). This facilitates the breaking through of the mere administrative function and becomes even something even more data-driven and strategic so that it facilitates the achievement of the mission of the business (Jia & Hou, 2024). The injection of the AI essentially turns on the heels of the decision-making processes in HRM towards the data- and the predictive insight and not towards the historical trend or the gestalt or subjective analysis (Taslim et al., 2025). It induces an imperative on reassessing the HR foundation methodological frameworks to introduce the inculcation of the advanced analytics tool to derive the workforce requirements and to determine the gaps and to fine-tune the deployment of the talent. This injection facilitates the HR professionals to become engulfed in the higher-value-added strategic functions and break through even the mere administrative functions and become engulfed even deeper in the complex organizational challenges and employees' developmental (George & Thomas, 2019). Thus, HR professionals are still needed to know and be in preparation to take advantage of such technology-transforming trends redefining the organizational and workforce dynamics (Saxena, 2020). Technological innovation and AI have accelerated the very rapid evolution of the HR information system in an attempt to leverage the union of the AI and the strategic orientation in the HR functions (Madanchian & Taherdoost, 2025). This facilitates the responsive and agile HR function to take advantage of the predictive analytics to provide the proactive talent development and customized employee experience. This reorientation brings the strategic focus on upskilling and the reskilling the HR workforce to achieve the efficient functioning in the paradigm of the AI-driven worlds while keeping the human oversight at the focal point of the effective and ethical application of the AI. This strategic thinking extends to instilling the culture of innovation among the HR specialists by innovating through the assistance of the AI-driven technologies while critically examining the implications on the employee well-being and the organizational performance. In addition to this, the digitalization of the HR through the paradigmatic reorientation of the AI persists in reengineering the centuries-old processes of the recruitments by reformatting them into becoming very much swift while advancing the richness of the candidate experience (Nyathani, 2022). AI-based processes such as the computer-vision-based screening on the resumes automatically by the resume, the NLP-based screening of the job propositions and the predictive-model-based predicting of the candidate success by the success-forecasting persists in restructuring the talent discovery function by streamlining the processes and allowing an advanced quality hiring. This not only reduces the time-to-hire but minimizes the inbuilt prejudices in the initial screening rounds and develops a much diversified and inclusive talent pipeline. The capacity of the AI to sift through the haywire volume of information sets to identify the patterns and correlations persists to drive to the best positioning of the employment and the predictive identification of the probable flight risk among incumbent staffers and helps in solidifying the retention policies (Madanchian, 2024). Such analysis helps the HR units to tackle the challenges in the workforce in a much better fashion and in developing an industrious and committed employee base. Much more seriously, the injection of AI into HR processes brings final consideration and caution to the human variable in achieving a balance in the interplay of enhancement and best automation to realizing organizational performance.

1.7. Future Trends and Opportunities in AI and HR Analytics

The HR analytics and AI function continue to evolve at an extremely fast pace, and many latest trends and opportunities are upcoming that will remake human capital management. One such encouraging trend is the increased use of NLP to extract insights from unstructured data sources, for example, employee surveys, performance reviews, and social media messages (William et al., 2023). NLP algorithms extract valuable insights from the data and provide more knowledge of worker sentiment, worker engagement, and what motivates worker performance (Ravesangar & Narayanan, 2024).

Another promising future development is the development of advanced AI models that can predict employee attrition, identify high-potentials, and personalize learning and development initiatives. The predictive analytics capabilities help HR professionals respond ahead of the curve to the needs of employees, improve the level of retention, and better align talent management initiatives. The integration of AI and other technologies, such as blockchain and the IoT, also holds new promise for HRM. For instance, blockchain technology offers the option to create secure and transparent employee records, whereas IoT sensors can delineate employee security and well-being data at the workplace (Prasad, 2024). Moreover, the expansion of edge computing enables organizations to process HR data nearer the source, and this reduces latency and boosts the effectiveness of AI-centric applications. Organizations can take advantage of the technologies to enhance HR processes and employee experience and gain a competitive advantage in the talent market.

As HR analytics and AI continue to evolve, organizations will be forced to adopt a culture of innovation and experimentation to be able to realize their potential. This entails investing in research and development, collaboration with AI providers and research organizations, and the development of cross-functional teams to discover new uses and applications. Organizations should also adopt a data culture where HR professionals are enabled to leverage data and insights to help them make decisions and develop their strategies.

Moreover, organizations will be required to invest in the training and development of employees to empower the workforce to work together with the AI systems and possess the knowledge and capabilities in the fields of data analytics, AI ethics, and human–machine collaboration. Adoption of such future trends and opportunities will help organizations tap the full potential of AI and HR analytics and transform HRM practices to attain business excellence.

Reconstruction of HRM in the world of AI and big data allows innovation in management to fit new situations, including diversification of labour relations (Zhu, 2020). HR managers in the future will be using AI to forecast and check the performance at the individual level, easing recruitment and workforce planning (Hajal & Rowson, 2020). Moreover, AI has the capacity to revolutionize employee development by conceptualizing personalized learning routes, recommending personalized modules for training, and providing in-time feedback by using individual performance data; personalized development opportunities will bring greater employee involvement, skills development, and organizational success.

The growing capabilities of AI in HRM provide equal opportunities to improve worker well-being and craft a more inclusive workplace. AI-facilitated tools can process the sentiment of employees, identify burnout or stress symptoms, and provide personalized recommendations for well-being assets and interventions. Beyond this, AI provides the promise to mitigate bias in HR processes such as recruitment and performance appraisal by recognizing and addressing patterns of discrimination in the data. This function is crucial to the evolution of equitable employment practices and fairness in all HR activities (Ayanponle et al., 2022). But this transformation potential also presents extraordinary challenges, including concern about data protection and the threat of algorithmic bias, and the necessity to reduce organizational change resistance, which must be thoroughly planned and resolved to project successful implementation of AI (Madanchian & Taherdoost, 2025). Integration must be accomplished through a strategic focus on AI architectures and robust governance models to guard against potential misuse and fairly distribute outcomes for all employees (Faqihi & Miah, 2023a). Control of the challenges necessitates a multi-faceted response that includes robust ethical guidance, clear AI development processes, and recurrent dialogue among stakeholders to engender trust and support successful implementation (Venugopal et al., 2024). This includes the fostering of worker participation in the development and deployment of AI systems, potentially able to alleviate concern about job loss and deskilling, and engender a sense of ownership and collaboration. The symbiotic relationship between human and AI abilities in HR promises the potential to transform conventional paradigms by fostering a more responsive, data-centric, people-focused method of human capital administration. The transformation precipitates the necessity for proactive reexamination of HR's strategic role through extending beyond administrative functions and becoming a major driver of organizational performance through advanced analytic and intelligent automation (Fenwick et al., 2024). This transformation also precipitates the necessity for human–AI collaboration through which HR professionals leverage the tools of AI to extend capacity and permit greater strategic decision-making and personalized employee experience (Fenwick et al., 2024). This symbiotic relationship promises the unlocking of unparalleled understanding and efficiencies while presenting the complex dynamics of numerous questions about the ethical dimensions and particularly raising questions and considerations about the protection of data and algorithmic fairness, and the threat and promise of job loss. The management of the nuanced landscape entails a critical understanding of both technological ability and human-centred challenges (Charlwood & Guenole, 2022). Therefore, the future evolution of AI in HR still necessitates research on explainable AI to demystify algorithmic decisions, foster employees' and stakeholders' trust, and ensure HR practices grounded in AI are transparent, explainable, fair, and justifiable. The development of effective governance frameworks and fostering the evolution of AI in ethical considerations are important steps to contain the risk and derive the maximum benefit of utilizing AI in HRM.

1.8. Discussion

This analysis explores the larger implications of AI in the area of HRM, with an examination of the potential of change brought about by AI in this field and the related challenges. Implementation of AI is bringing about a change in the typical roles of HRM related to talent management and hiring, simultaneously giving rise to concerns about protection of data, bias in AI, and the need for collaboration between humans and AI. The use of AI in HRM is dominated by a transition described by one commentator as a 'strategic shift'.

1.9. Conclusion

The integration of AI with analytics in the field of HR is a new beginning in the management of HR, and its initial use has demonstrated the feasibility of AI, considering that it is capable of handling routine tasks such as recruitment, selection, and job description, preparing the ground for analytics including predictive training and trends analysis (Akter et al., 2023; Ayanponle et al., 2022).

It assists organizations in automating administrative tasks, providing workforce demographics, and enhancing the employee experience for better outcomes. There is a need for caution, planning, and pledges for clarity and fairness when implementing AI within HRM, according to Fenwick et al. (2024). To keep up with advancements in the field of AI, it is necessary for organizations to develop a human-centred form of AI that amplifies human capabilities, encourages trust, and promotes collaboration.

Literature emphasizes the effects of AI on HR tasks, explaining opportunities, challenges, and the roles of employees, line managers, and HR professionals (Dima et al., 2024). There are five main areas where AI affects HR tasks, including automation of tasks, better use of HR data, better use of human capabilities, the work environment, and new aspects concerning social relationships in employment (Dima et al., 2024). The changing contexts of HRM brought about by the integration of AI require readiness among all sides (Dima et al., 2024). AI promotes networked human–machine intelligence and demands a realistic understanding rather than anthropomorphic notions about its capabilities and limitations (Fenwick et al., 2024). There is a need for an active, ethic-driven reengineering of AI for achieving common prosperity, enhancing the quality and efficiency of employment, and mitigating negative effects, with active employee engagement in designing and implementing AI change in the organization. It is recommended that organizations undertake analysis of the employment impact of AI and employee engagement in implementing AI technology change in an organization because users know much about both the 'goods' and 'bads' of technology change, and AI can reduce errors and fatigue but infringe on job control, invade employee privacy, and enhance performance pressure due to increased performance accountability requirements. With a technology-driven society in today's reality, the role of AI is expedited in transforming the field of HR, with emphasis on the need for proper management of the adaptation of AI and synchronization with new technologies (Bobițan et al., 2024; Purwaamijaya & Prasetyo, 2022). AI helps with diversity and inclusion, with a need for critical skills and proper training methodologies (Morandini et al., 2023). Transdisciplinarity assists in synthesizing cognizance about AI (Morandini et al., 2023). For the execution of AI, expertise is required in the fields of data science, ML, and AI engineering technologies (Murire, 2024). For AI penetration in the field of HR, it leads to personalized engagement and growth with an emphasis on promoting inherent motivation but with some risks associated with it, including bias, violation of privacy, and potential job loss. Implementation of AI entails profound change within organizations with a need for upskilling and reskilling of employees in a participative manner. Organizational involvement is key in helping employees understand the value that can be derived from the use of AI for the employee and the organization.

References

Akter, S., Biswas, K., Vrontis, D., Cooper, C. L., & Tarba, S. Y. (2023). Mastering digital transformation in workforce management. *Production Planning & Control*, *35*(13), 1525. https://doi.org/10.1080/09537287.2023.2270465

Ayanponle, L., Okatta, C. G., & Ajiga, D. (2022). AI-powered HR analytics: Transforming workforce optimization and decision-making. *International Journal of Science and Research Archive*, *5*(2), 338. https://doi.org/10.30574/ijsra.2022.5.2.0057

Bahangulu, J. K., & Owusu-Berko, L. (2025). Algorithmic bias, data ethics, and governance: Ensuring fairness, transparency and compliance in AI-powered business analytics applications. *World Journal of Advanced Research and Reviews*, *25*(2), 1746. https://doi.org/10.30574/wjarr.2025.25.2.0571

Batool, A., Zowghi, D., & Bano, M. (2025). AI governance: A systematic literature review. *AI and Ethics*. https://doi.org/10.1007/s43681-024-00653-w

Bobițan, N., Dumitrescu, D., Popa, A. F., Sahlian, D.-N., & Turlea, I. C. (2024). Shaping tomorrow: Anticipating skills requirements based on the integration of artificial intelligence in business organizations—A foresight analysis using the scenario method. *Electronics*, *13*(11), 2198. https://doi.org/10.3390/electronics13112198

Charlwood, A., & Guenole, N. (2022). Can HR adapt to the paradoxes of artificial intelligence? *Human Resource Management Journal*, *32*(4), 729. https://doi.org/10.1111/1748-8583.12433

Dima, J., Gilbert, M., Dextras-Gauthier, J., & Giraud, L. (2024). The effects of artificial intelligence on human resource activities and the roles of the human resource triad: Opportunities and challenges. *Frontiers in Psychology, 15*. https://doi.org/10.3389/fpsyg.2024.1360401

Faqihi, A., & Miah, S. J. (2023a). Designing an AI-driven talent intelligence solution: Exploring big data to extend the TOE framework. In *Lecture notes in computer science* (p. 69). Springer Science+Business Media. https://doi.org/10.1007/978-981-99-2233-8_5

Faqihi, A., & Miah, S. J. (2023b). Artificial intelligence-driven talent management system: Exploring the risks and options for constructing a theoretical foundation. *Journal of Risk and Financial Management, 16*(1), 31. https://doi.org/10.3390/jrfm16010031

Fenwick, A., Molnár, G., & Frangos, P. (2024). Revisiting the role of HR in the age of AI: Bringing humans and machines closer together in the workplace [Review]. *Frontiers in Artificial Intelligence, 6*. Frontiers Media. https://doi.org/10.3389/frai.2023.1272823

George, G., & Thomas, D. M. R. (2019). Integration of artificial intelligence in human resource. *International Journal of Innovative Technology and Exploring Engineering, 9*(2), 5069. https://doi.org/10.35940/ijitee.l3364.129219

Hajal, G. E., & Rowson, B. (2020). The future of hospitality jobs. *Research in Hospitality Management, 10*(1), 55. https://doi.org/10.1080/22243534.2020.1790210

Jia, X., & Hou, Y. (2024). Architecting the future: Exploring the synergy of AI-driven sustainable HRM, conscientiousness, and employee engagement. *Discover Sustainability, 5*(1). https://doi.org/10.1007/s43621-024-00214-5

Koman, G., Boršoš, P., & Kubina, M. (2024). The possibilities of using artificial intelligence as a key technology in the current employee recruitment process. *Administrative Sciences, 14*(7), 157. https://doi.org/10.3390/admsci14070157

Kumar, N. (2025). *AI recruitment statistics 2025*. https://www.demandsage.com/ai-recruitment-statistics/

Madanchian, M. (2024). From recruitment to retention: AI tools for human resource decision-making. *Applied Sciences, 14*(24), 11750. https://doi.org/10.3390/app142411750

Madanchian, M., & Taherdoost, H. (2025). Barriers and enablers of AI adoption in human resource management: A critical analysis of organizational and technological factors. *Information, 16*(1), 51. https://doi.org/10.3390/info16010051

Morandini, S., Fraboni, F., Angelis, M. D., Puzzo, G., Giusino, D., & Pietrantoni, L. (2023). The impact of artificial intelligence on workers' skills: Upskilling and reskilling in organisations. *Informing Science, The International Journal of an Emerging Transdiscipline, 26*, 39. https://doi.org/10.28945/5078

Murire, O. (2024). Artificial intelligence and its role in shaping organizational work practices and culture. *Administrative Sciences, 14*(12), 316. https://doi.org/10.3390/admsci14120316

Mwita, K., M., & Kitole, F., A. (2025). *Potential benefits and challenges of artificial intelligence in human resource management in public institutions* (Vol. 3, article number 35) Springer Nature. https://doi.org/10.1007/s44282-025-00175-8

Nawaz, N., Arunachalam, H., Pathi, B. K., & Gajenderan, V. (2024). The adoption of artificial intelligence in human resources management practices. *International Journal of Information Management Data Insights, 4*(1), 100208. https://doi.org/10.1016/j.jjimei.2023.100208

Nyathani, R. (2022). AI-powered recruitment the future of HR digital transformation. *Journal of Artificial Intelligence & Cloud Computing, 1*. https://doi.org/10.47363/jaicc/2022(1)133

Oman, Z. U., Siddiqua, A., & Noorain, R. (2024). Artificial intelligence and its ability to reduce recruitment bias. *World Journal of Advanced Research and Reviews, 24*(1), 551. https://doi.org/10.30574/wjarr.2024.24.1.3054

Personio. (2025). *The impact of AI in HR*. https://www.personio.com/hr-lexicon/ai-in-hr-guide/

Prasad, B. V. (2024). *The impact of technology on human resource management: Trends and challenges*. 9746. https://doi.org/10.53555/kuey.v30i5.4635

Purwaamijaya, B., & Prasetyo, Y. (2022). The Effect of Artificial Intelligence (AI) on Human Capital Management in Indonesia. *Jurnal Manajemen dan Wirausaha. Computer Science, Business.* DOI:10.26905/jmdk.v10i2.9130

Ravesangar, K., & Narayanan, S. (2024). Adoption of HR analytics to enhance employee retention in the workplace: A review [Review]. *Human Resources Management and Services*, *6*(3), 3481. https://doi.org/10.18282/hrms.v6i3.3481

Rodgers, W., Murray, J. M., Stefanidis, A., Degbey, W. Y., & Tarba, S. Y. (2022). An artificial intelligence algorithmic approach to ethical decision-making in human resource management processes. *Human Resource Management Review*, *33*(1), 100925. https://doi.org/10.1016/j.hrmr.2022.100925

Rožman, M., Oreški, D., & Tominc, P. (2023). Artificial-intelligence-supported reduction of employees' workload to increase the company's performance in today's VUCA environment. *Sustainability*, *15*(6), 5019. https://doi.org/10.3390/su15065019

Sadeghi, S. (2024). *Employee well-being in the age of AI: Perceptions, concerns, behaviors, and outcomes*. https://doi.org/10.48550/ARXIV.2412.04796

Saraswathi, T., Karthikeyan, M., Balakrishnan, C., Nithya, T. M., Maheswari, B., & Subramanıan, R. S. (2023). Artificial intelligence in human resource management: Advancements, implications and future prospects. *International Journal on Recent and Innovation Trends in Computing and Communication*, *11*, 266. https://doi.org/10.17762/ijritcc.v11i11s.8099

Saxena, A. (2020). The growing role of artificial intelligence in human resource. *EPRA International Journal of Multidisciplinary Research (IJMR)*, *152*. https://doi.org/10.36713/epra4924

Sharma, S., & Bhat, R. (2023). *Implementation of artificial intelligence in diagnosing employees attrition and elevation: A case study on the IBM employee dataset* (p. 197). Emerald Publishing Limited eBooks. https://doi.org/10.1108/978-1-80382-027-920231010

SRHM. (2025). *Employers embrace artificial intelligence for HR*. https://www.shrm.org/topics-tools/news/employers-embrace-artificial-intelligence-hr

Sucipto, H. (2024). The impact of artificial intelligence (AI) on human resource management practices. *Deleted Journal*, *1*(1), 138. https://doi.org/10.62207/xey9mx18

Taslim, W. S., Rosnani, T., & Fauzan, R. (2025). Employee involvement in AI-driven HR decision-making: A systematic review [Review]. *SA Journal of Human Resource Management*, *23*. AOSIS. https://doi.org/10.4102/sajhrm.v23i0.2856

Venugopal, M., Madhavan, V., Prasad, R., & Raman, R. (2024). Transformative AI in human resource management: Enhancing workforce planning with topic modeling. *Cogent Business & Management*, *11*(1). https://doi.org/10.1080/23311975.2024.2432550

Westover, J. (2024). Using generative AI for strategic HR planning: How AI can elevate your people strategy. *Human Capital Leadership*, *13*(2). https://doi.org/10.70175/hclreview.2020.13.2.8

William, P., Agrawal, A., Rawat, N., Shrivastava, A., Srivastava, A. P., & Ashish. (2023). *Enterprise human resource management model by artificial intelligence digital technology*. https://doi.org/10.1109/iccakm58659.2023.10449624

Workable. (2025). *AI in hiring survey*. https://get.workable.com/ai-in-hiring-survey

Zhu, W. (2020). Reconstruction of human resource management under big data and artificial intelligence. *Journal of Physics Conference Series*, *1533*(4), 42016. https://doi.org/10.1088/1742-6596/1533/4/042016

Chapter 2

Beyond Intuition: Data-driven Hiring with AI for the Modern HR Manager

Vidhi Agrawal[a], *Yu Chen Hu*[b] *and Vibhuti Agrawal*[c]

[a]*Ajay Kumar Garg Institute of Management, India*
[b]*Tunghai University, Taiwan*
[c]*HSBC Technology, India*

Abstract

In today's competitive world, the ability to attract, assess, and acquire the right talent is not just a strategic advantage but the necessity for any business to grow, sustain, and succeed. The hiring challenge today is far more complex than ever before. Organizations must not only decide who to hire but also when to hire, why a particular skill set is needed, and how to design an efficient, fair, and future-ready hiring process. With the advent of artificial intelligence (AI)-enabled systems and Big Data analytics, human resources (HR) managers now have the opportunity to transition from intuition-based hiring to data-driven recruitment strategies. Although the AI-enabled technology has created new possibilities for HR professionals to conduct recruitment activities in a more systematic and transparent manner, but adopting AI-enabled systems has also introduced a new set of challenges, particularly for HR managers without a technical background. To get the best advantage out of AI-enabled systems, HR managers are required to develop hybrid skills that combine their core expertise of human resource management (HRM) with the foundational knowledge of data science. This chapter has explored in detail how HR managers can leverage AI and Big Data to their best advantage and can ensure more accurate hiring decisions while simultaneously enhancing candidate experience.

Keywords: Artificial intelligence; Big Data analytics in HRM; AI-driven talent acquisition; data-driven recruitment strategies; future of human resource management; digital transformation in HR

Nurturing AI-Powered HR Analytics and Virtual Reality in Employee Psychology and Workplace Happiness, Part A, 19–33

doi:10.1108/978-1-80686-125-520261002

2.1. Introduction

Recruitment is not a single decision, rather it is a series of small decisions that collectively shape the final choice. It starts with defining the role, finding candidates, screening resumes, going with interview rounds, and then finally making an offer (Vasile & Zhan, 2020).

All these steps play a crucial role in the hiring decisions. If we go with the traditional process of hiring, all these decisions were made manually and most of the decisions were based on human judgment and therefore the whole exercise was time-consuming and prone to bias (Albaroudi et al., 2024). However, in today's modernized digital era, recruitment has evolved from being a largely manual, intuition-driven process to one rooted in data, algorithms, and predictive models (Johansson & Herranen, 2019). The integration of Big Data into recruitment has unlocked the insights that were previously inaccessible. With the use of AI tools, it has become much easier to analyze things like employee turnover, drop-offs in the recruitment process, and candidates' experiences.

This revolutionary transformation has reshaped the role of the HR managers and has presented new challenges for them that demand a basic understanding of data science so that they can thrive in their roles (Agrawal et al., 2025). This new era of digitalization creates a curiosity to explore the evolution of recruitment from traditional practices to AI-driven systems. To serve the purpose, the present chapter aims to examine the integration of AI-embedded tools into various stages of the hiring process and how this change has brought new challenges for the HR managers. More specifically, the present chapter seeks to answer the following research questions:

RQ1. How has recruitment evolved in the era of AI?

RQ2. What operational and strategic benefits does AI offer that support the recruitment process?

RQ3. What are the practical challenges that HR professionals are facing in adopting AI tools?

To address these questions, the study provides a step-by-step discussion of the transition in recruitment practices and highlights various AI tools that are in use by renowned companies. The study is unique as it includes the explanation on adoption of AI at each stage of the recruitment process in layman's terms.

The study is structured into six key sections. The first section of the study emphasizes on the significance of the research and its potential contribution to existing literature. The second section offers a comparative analysis of traditional recruitment methods versus AI-driven hiring approaches. The following section delves into the integration of AI in recruitment and this section highlights both operational and strategic benefits, as well as the challenges associated with its implementation. To illustrate practical applications, the next section of this chapter presents real-world practices with the examples from leading companies that have successfully adopted AI in their hiring processes. Further, to have a detailed discussion on the future of HRM, a separate section titled "Rethinking Recruitment: A Glimpse into the Future," has been added. This section explores emerging trends and possibilities in the field of hiring. The last section of the chapter includes a summary on key insights and reflections.

2.2. Traditional Hiring Versus AI-driven Hiring

According to Okolie and Irabor (2017), the traditional recruitment involved newspaper advertisements, manual resume collection, and face-to-face interviews where intuition and subjective judgment of the panel members played key roles. Although some exceptional talent emerged with the adoption of these practices, the process was often lengthy, biased, and inefficient (Vivek, 2022). HR departments spent countless hours manually screening candidates, and final decisions were frequently influenced by unconscious bias and there was always space for perceptual distortions and biasness (Huang, 2025).

AI-driven recruitment has emerged as a powerful trend and has redefined the ways of attracting and evaluating talent (Ajunwa, 2020; Black & Van Esch, 2020; Li et al., 2021). The technologies like natural language processing (NLP), machine learning (ML), and predictive analytics have transformed the whole process of recruitment (see Halper, 2017; Sharma & Chanana, 2025; Strang & Sun, 2022). The use of AI-enabled tools can scan thousands of resumes in just a few seconds and are highly compatible in identifying the best matches based on skill sets and experience (Saxena et al., 2025). Not only that, these systems are highly efficient in predicting a candidate's future performance and retention probability (Agrawal, 2025). With the use of these tools, HR managers can reduce the burden of repetitive administrative tasks and can utilize their saved time for more strategic and human-centered aspects of their roles (Agrawal, 2025).

Fig. 2.1 highlights the journey of transition from traditional recruitment practices to AI-driven recruitment .Traditionally, identifying hiring requirements was a manual task and it was largely driven by HR personnel or department heads and most of the decisions were based on intuition and past experiences, but AI-based workforce planning tools have now enabled data-backed decision-making by analyzing organizational skill gaps, project pipelines, and historical hiring patterns and as a result has improved precision and efficiency in talent forecasting (Inaganti et al., 2021).

Once the need is identified, the next step is to create the job description (JD) and this step has also witnessed a marked improvement. Earlier, JDs were often copied from previous listings or created without much consideration for market alignment or inclusivity, which led to vague or biased descriptions (see Al-Marwai & Subramaniam, 2009; Bodnarchuk, 2012; DeLon, 1994; Switasarra & Astanti, 2021), but AI-based JD generators have improved the conventional ways of formulating JDs. In the present scenario, JDs are prepared with the use of NLP and are prepared based on the market data analysis (Saxena et al., 2025).

In the old days, jobs were advertised through newspapers or standard job boards that lacked reach and personalization, but with AI, advertisements

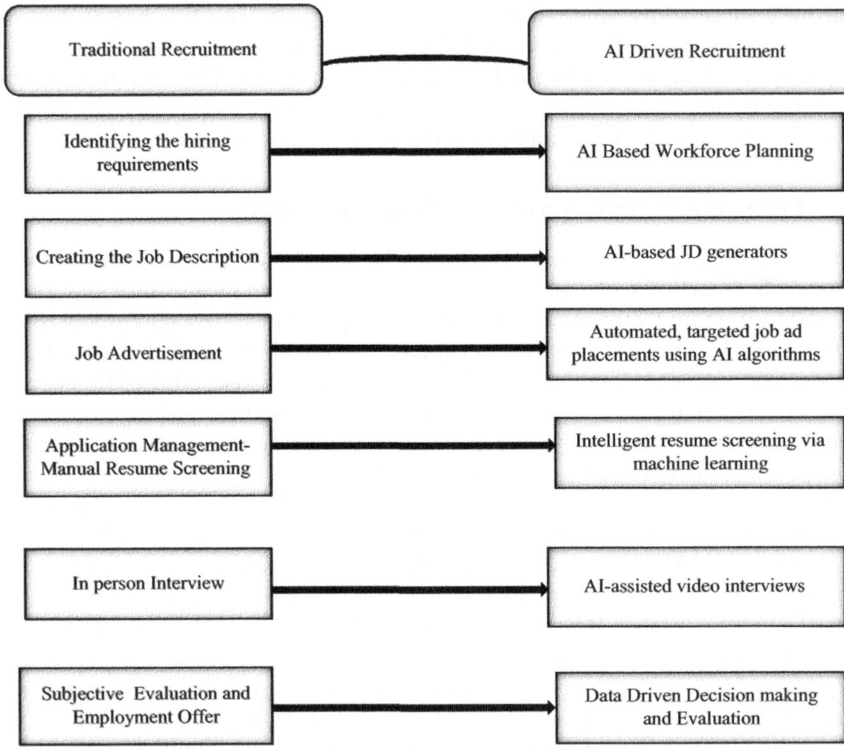

Fig. 2.1. Transition from Traditional Recruitment to AI-driven Recruitment. *Source*: Based on the author's understanding and analysis.

can now be automatically deployed to targeted digital platforms where they are most likely to reach qualified candidates. Not only that, AI-enabled algorithms are highly efficient in personalizing ad placement based on candidate behavior, search history, and platform engagement, and all these tiny steps support the system in increasing their visibility as well as application quality (Gao et al., 2023).

The next step in the recruitment process is the application management. The extensive literature on traditional recruitment systems has highlighted on the roles of HR teams like how these teams were previously engaged in tedious manual resume screening and resultant delays and inconsistencies (Aggarwal et al., 2021; Kumaresan & Premikkha, 2020). Today, intelligent resume screening tools, powered by ML, are highly effective in evaluating thousands of applications in seconds (Amro et al., 2022). These tools help reduce unconscious bias while also saving significant administrative time (Agrawal, 2025).

Finally, the interview process has also gone through improvements. In conventional traditional in-person interviews, there were more chances of subjective interpretations and interpersonal dynamics, but with AI-assisted video interviews, there are less chances of biased decisions. The AI-enabled video interviews are getting appreciation around the globe as they come up with several new insights which were inaccessible earlier. The AI-enabled video interviews works on the basis of asynchronous technologies (Suen & Hung, 2023) and are available with the advanced features like candidates behavioral and sentiment analysis, evaluation of their tone, facial expressions, and speech patterns (Alexander, 2025), and all these result in the assessment of the candidate suitability more objectively (see Fig. 2.1).

2.3. AI Integration in Recruitment: Operational and Strategic Benefits

The integration of AI into recruitment processes has brought a revolutionary change in the conventional system of hiring (Hmoud & Várallyai, 2019). This transformative shift has come up with various operational efficiencies and strategic advantages.

2.3.1. Operational Efficiencies

The hiring process usually starts with the notice of a job opening or vacancy. After that, candidates send in their applications, and resumes are looked over. Based on this assessment, shortlisted candidates are invited to a first round of interviews which is followed by a final interview with the recruiter in person. Each of the steps described plays a crucial role in the hiring process and takes a lot of time if managed without the use of automated systems.

The intervention of AI has changed the convention systems of hiring holistically. The companies like Johnson and Johnson, Intel, Accenture, Unilever are using AI tools in their recruitment systems. More specifically, if we consider the case of Johnson and Johnson, this company used the Hiredscore tool in shortlisting resumes. Academicians, practitioners, and the talent acquisition heads across the world are discussing the potential of using AI tools in the HRM function.

A growing corpus of research in the field of HRM emphasizes on the increasing role of AI in reshaping the HR practices. For instance, Heric (2018) cites a survey by Bian & Co. The results of this survey highlight that 87% of HR leaders believe digital innovation is a key driver behind the transformation of traditional HR functions. Similarly, the study conducted by Bales and Stone (2020) highlights the role of AI tools in the recruitment systems. The study discussed in detail AI tools that are in use by the popular companies like Johnson and Johnson, Intel, HP, Cisco, etc. (Bales & Stone, 2020).

According to Agrawal (2025), the integration of AI tools in recruitment systems has brought operational efficiencies and has reduced the load of routine tasks on managers. To illustrate the contribution of AI-driven recruitment let us consider an example of a big company with 500 vacancies and this company received 5,000 applications. While selecting 500 resumes manually, it took a lot of time, energy, and efforts of the HR staff, but AI-powered systems can look at and sort these resumes in only a few seconds. These tools are very good at screening and shortlisting individuals since they match their talents with the job's needs.

Therefore, AI-driven systems are far more efficient as compared to traditional manual methods.

Furthermore, AI algorithms are highly efficient in making compatibility scores. The AI-enabled tools compare the abilities listed in the JD with the applicant's real-world qualifications and experience. This kind of automation not only speeds up the hiring process but also makes it much easier for HR experts to complete their administrative tasks easily (Saxena et al., 2025). Similarly, shortlisting of resumes used to take a lot of time earlier, but now it can be done quickly with smart software that uses ML and NLP (Mhadgut et al., 2022).

Beyond resume screening and candidate shortlisting, AI tools contribute to various other operational efficiencies throughout the whole recruitment cycle. For instance, Chatbots and virtual assistants are now very useful for answering initial questions from candidates and in setting up skill tests and interviews (Uma et al., 2023). This sort of AI integration gives the HR managers a buffer from the administrative tasks and they can use their saved energy in strategic HR planning and hiring. These tools can work around the clock, seven days a week (Cancel & Gerhardt, 2019). This keeps candidates interested and gives human recruiters more time to make smart decisions. Furthermore, video interviews are conducted with the use of AI and this facilitates in hiring the best talent pool. AI-enabled video interviews are backed by asynchronous technology which is highly effective in recognizing the patterns of speech, facial expressions, and body language and therefore give employers insights that were not possible earlier with face-to-face interviews (Bales & Stone, 2020).

Another important efficiency is that AI systems are good at making real-time analytics dashboards. It helps recruiters to keep an eye on key performance indicators like applicant conversion rates, time-to-hire, and cost-per-hire (Betgeri & Chekuri, 2025). These findings help the managers to plan in advance the recruitment plans. Further, if there are a lot of jobs to be filled, AI can help predict hiring trends, help in improving sourcing strategies, and keep talent pipelines full (Inaganti et al., 2021). In this way, HR managers are able to fill the jobs in less time and with the best people. Further, AI-enabled tools also facilitate the next steps like automation of background checks (Benjamin, 2025) and onboarding paperwork (Kylliäinen, 2024). These AI-driven improvements have changed the conventional systems of hiring.

2.3.2. Strategic Benefits

Beyond operational improvements, the integration of AI in the recruitment process has also offered several strategic benefits. One of the most significant benefits is data-driven decision-making (Garcia & Adams, 2022). According to Alabi et al. (2024), AI systems may provide predictive analytics that can help HR managers in forecasting future hiring needs. Managers can evaluate talent pipeline health and can approach the best potential candidates in advance (Sainger & Irfan, 2025).

Another key advantage is reduction of biases in hiring decisions (Arduini & Beck, 2025). While traditional recruitment process was vulnerable to unconscious bias, but in AI-based recruitment process, if algorithms are designed properly, these systems can ensure hiring of best and deserving candidates with fairer evaluations systems that are based on objective data points. This practice promotes diversity, equity, and inclusion in the workplace (Houser, 2019) and adds to the goodwill of the company.

Moreover, personalized candidate experiences are also possible with AI-driven communication tools, such as chatbots and automated email follow-ups (Alex, 2025). These tools keep candidates engaged throughout the process of hiring and help them to have a smooth and transparent recruitment experience. This way, the intervention of AI results in strengthening of the employer brand and hiring of the best talent pool (Jha et al., 2024).

AI tools can also support companies in strategic workforce planning. These tools are highly effective in analyzing labor market trends, skills gaps, and internal talent mobility (Heger, 2024). These insights allow HR departments to hire the right kind of people at the right time and at the right place.

2.3.3. Challenges in Implementing AI in Recruitment

The integration of AI in HRM has transformed the traditional HR practices to data-driven HR practices, but this transition has come up with challenges. To fully leverage AI outputs, HR professionals are required to develop foundational knowledge of data science. This basic knowledge will enable them to collaborate effectively with coding teams of technocrats who design and implement algorithms which are based on the data, instructions, and departmental requirements provided by them. This adoption of AI in HRM function has also created a challenge for the managers to unlearn outdated practices and relearn new skills to compete and survive in the data-driven and digital environment.

Furthermore, the next key challenge lies in doubts about the fairness and transparency of algorithmic decisions. There are ample number of scholars who have raised concerns and are skeptical on how these systems make choices and whether the decisions driven uphold ethical standards. For instance, Black and van Esch (2020) and Ajunwa (2020) argued about the "black box" nature of algorithmic hiring and raised the questions related to authenticity and accountability.

However, despite of concerns about algorithmic fairness, many scholars state that these challenges can be overcome through proper training and collaboration between HR and technical teams. For instance, Zhang and Lee (2025) assert that with training in AI tools, HR professionals can accurately interpret AI-driven insights, and this can help in reduced misinterpretations and potential biases.

Although the mentioned challenges have created a buzz in the environment, where the users of AI are searching for the optimal solution for overcoming these challenges, we cannot deny the fact that AI solutions have markedly improved the traditional recruitment process. The new system has brought the benefits for both the hiring manager and the candidates. For instance, job seekers now possess enhanced empowerment, as AI facilitates improved access to career prospects via features like automated coaching, virtual internships, and tailored job suggestions. Similarly, hiring managers are also leveraging AI-driven systems at every stage of the recruitment process and are now able to make better decisions on hiring.

As the benefits outweigh the challenges therefore, organizations are increasingly recognizing that adopting AI in recruitment goes beyond operational efficiency. Companies like Google, Amazon, and IBM have already made significant investments in AI-based hiring tools, and now mid-sized firms have also started experiments with AI tools at a small scale.

2.4. Real-world Practices: How Leading Companies Use AI in Hiring

According to Davenport and Ronanki (2018), leading global companies are using AI more and more to improve their hiring processes because the job market is changing so quickly these days. The old ways of hiring people, which took a lot of time and were limited by human bias, are being changed by AI-driven innovations. Now the process of hiring has become faster and has enhanced the overall experience of candidates. While AI is receiving immense appreciation across the world, it creates curiosity to understand how it is actually being used. The examples from following companies demonstrate the application of AI in practice at various stages of hiring.

IBM: IBM uses AI for screening the candidates. The employment process at IBM has evolved from being centered on degrees to being based on people's skills. By utilizing systems such as Watson Recruitment the company utilizes AI to scan online profiles and resumes in order to match capabilities with job openings (Cuesta-Valiño et al., 2024).

Unilever: Unilever uses AI-driven gamified assessments in their recruitment process. Candidates participate in games based on neuroscience that assess both their cognitive and emotional characteristics. Applicants who have been shortlisted are then invited to participate in video interviews that are again analyzed with the use of AI. AI-enabled systems evaluate facial clues, speech patterns, and tone of voice, and this sort of evaluation helps Unilever to acquire the best pool of talented employees. Even with AI-enabled tools, the company has been able to reduce the time to hire new employees by 75% (Hu, 2023).

Amazon: In order to evaluate millions of applicants for positions such as warehouse associates and software developers, Amazon uses ML models. Their in-house AI systems evaluate resumes based on how well they match the job requirements and skills. Although Amazon claims that AI made their hiring system more efficient, the company faced criticism for using biased AI in 2018, which it subsequently addressed by conducting algorithmic fairness audits (Dastin, 2022).

Infosys: AI is utilized by Infosys for the purpose of workforce planning and internal hiring. In order to enable long-term strategic workforce alignment, their AI-enabled system maps the skill sets of present employees, forecasts career routes, and suggests retraining or internal shifts prior to posting job openings in the external market (Balasubramanian & Balakrishna, 2023). This kind of practice helps the company in reducing hiring costs and also enhances employee morale by providing career growth opportunities.

Hilton Hotels: Hilton Hotel Chain uses "Connie" Chatbot for managing candidate communication. The chatbot is highly efficient in responding to questions, scheduling interviews, and providing applicants with direction. Because of this, the candidate experience has been greatly improved, and the number of dropouts has decreased (Park & Son, 2025). The AI tools that are in use by the mentioned companies are presented in Table 2.1.

These real-world examples highlight how companies are deploying AI to build more efficient, inclusive, and data-driven hiring systems. With the use of skills-based screening, gamified assessments, resume parsing, or chatbot interactions, AI has proved its toil and has taken a position of catalyst for reshaping recruitment paradigms.

2.5. Rethinking Recruitment: A Glimpse into the Future

Imagine it is the year 2035 and things have changed completely. Now hiring people is no longer just about shortlisting resumes and conducting interviews. AI-powered virtual setups are capable of mimicking real-life work problems in advance and therefore candidates are required to "play" the job before they get it. These gamified tests, along with AI personality mapping, cultural fit modeling, and deep learning-based sentiment analysis, may evaluate the candidates skills and assessment results that decide whether the candidate is compatible with the job profile.

Table 2.1. Leading Companies and Their AI Tools in Recruitment.

Company	AI Application in Recruitment	AI Tool/Approach Used
IBM	Shift from degree-based to skills-based hiring with the use of AI resume screening	*Watson Recruitment* platform (AI skill-matching engine)
Unilever	Gamified assessments + AI-analyzed video interviews for early-stage screening	*Pymetrics* (for games), *HireVue* (for video analytics)
Amazon	Resume parsing at scale; internal ML-based screening models	Internal *Machine Learning Algorithms* + Resume Parsers
Infosys	Predictive workforce analytics for internal hiring and talent mobility	AI-powered *Talent Intelligence Platform* (in-house)
Hilton Hotels	Chatbot for candidate engagement, query handling, and scheduling	*Chatbot "Connie"* (custom AI for candidate experience)

Source: Compiled by the authors using publicly available company information.

The companies like IBM and Deloitte are trying out these kinds of interactive hiring experiences (Bekken, 2019). Strategic HR professionals are working on a proactive "talent intelligence" strategy (Fatol et al., 2025). This kind of practice clearly highlights that workforce analytics, AI-powered succession planning, and cross-functional skill mapping will become standard in future in most of the renowned companies (Fatol et al., 2025). So, the actual strategic benefit of AI isn't simply filling jobs; it's about building teams that are ready for the future and can handle change with strength (Hagstršm et al., 2019). Colbert et al. (2016) contended that the digital workforce of the future will be characterized not solely by automation skills but by their capacity to handle the collaborative interplay of machines and humans.

To compete with the digital environment, the function of the HR manager will become more strategic in the future. The transition will occur from reactive hiring to proactive talent planning, which will involve the utilization of real-time information and insights created by AI to facilitate internal talent mobility and reskilling of the employees which will facilitate succession planning.

In future, AI in recruiting will not only be beneficial in terms of operational efficiency, but it will also have the potential to assist HR teams in developing workforce plans that are flexible, adaptable, and forward-looking. Colbert et al. (2016) highlight the fact that the organizations that will dominate in the future are those that will be able to establish a balanced ecosystem. This ecosystem is one in which data and technology act as a supplement to human judgment rather than providing a replacement for it. Therefore, strategic HR professionals are required to look beyond automation and must concentrate on development of recruitment processes that are in line with the future of work.

One of the critical developments that will define the next phase of AI-powered hiring is personalized HRM that will be very helpful in enhancing the recruitment experience of individual candidates (Huang et al., 2023). In contrast to current job boards that give all applicants the same experience, hiring platforms of the future will be customized for each person. These systems will learn about a candidate's communication style, learning habits, and what motivates them by using NLP and behavioral analytics. This kind of information will not only help recruiters find better cultural fits, but it will also help them make better plans for hiring.

Transparent and ethical AI will also become an important part of the recruitment environment (Balasubramaniam et al., 2023). Because early AI hiring models exhibited biases that have raised concerns among the users around the world. Businesses are now putting money into explainable AI (XAI) systems. Data scientists argue that, if designed properly, these models can make it clear how choices are made, like why one resume is chosen over another, how gamified scores are calculated, and how predictive indicators are weighted. This sort of transparency will increase the trust of users in AI.

In the future, HR leaders will need to be able to talk to computers just as easily as they talk to people. Standard recruiters, data scientists, behavioral psychologists, learning and development experts, and AI ethicists will work together to make smart hiring systems. Therefore, as we move toward a future where roles change quickly and adaptability seems to be the best solution, managers need to work on building their capacity to handle these changes effectively (Agrawal, 2025).

2.6. Conclusion

HRM is an invisible function, but it is the heart of any successful business. While finance, marketing, and operations are all clearly connected to performance outcomes, HRM works in a more subtle way and affects the internal dynamics that lead to long-term success for any organization. One of the most significant developments in HRM is the move from hiring based on gut feelings and old-fashioned methods to hiring based on facts and AI. This chapter has demonstrated how AI and Big Data have enhanced operational efficiency and strategic capabilities of HR professionals. Today's HR managers are becoming data-driven strategists and are using predictive analytics for important decisions, but this revolution is mostly about people, not just technology.

Even though algorithms can rapidly and reliably screen candidates, handle huge amounts of data, and predict how well someone will fit into a company's culture, the final choice on who to hire is still very much a human one. Finding a balance between the accuracy of computers and the compassion and moral consciousness of people is both a challenge and a chance. Data scientists across the world argue that AI could get rid of unconscious bias if it is programmed carefully, but they have also warned that lack of transparency could potentially make systemic disparities worse. So, HR managers should learn how to use these technologies in a way that is fair. Because HR professionals have to both use and keep an eye on AI technologies, ethical literacy is becoming more and more vital.

IBM, Unilever, and Infosys are just a few examples of companies who are already using AI to change hiring on a large scale. These start-ups' skills-based screening, gamified assessments, and predictive talent mapping make intelligent hiring possible right now. The technology used in these successful implementations is different, and so is the way they think about AI, which they perceive as a collaborator rather than a boss. These groups are spending money on cross-functional teams, regular feedback loops, and ongoing training to make sure that AI stays in line with human values.

The research also revealed that AI has also helped in empowering employees as has made it easier for everyone to find work opportunities .Candidates are now more involved in shaping their own career paths than they used to be since the job market is so competitive. On the other hand, AI-powered hiring is helping the companies in predicting the market, planning resources more quickly, and getting real-time information about their workers. This intervention of AI has enabled HR departments to align better with organizational goals.

References

Aggarwal, A., Jain, S., Jha, S., & Singh, V. P. (2021). Resume screening. *International Journal for Research in Applied Science and Engineering Technology*, *9*(4), 66–88.

Agrawal, V. (Ed.). (2025). *Human resource management and artificial intelligence: Automating and optimizing processes*. Taylor & Francis.

Agrawal, V., Taluja, A., Sharma, S., Tomar, K., & Kumar, H. (2025). AI-powered human resource management: Redefining the future of work and workforce. In A. Sivakumar, B. Vinoth, S. Duarte Correia, & J. Valach (Eds.), *Data processing and networking: Proceedings of ICDPN 2024, Volume 2* (pp. xx–xx). Springer. https://link.springer.com/book/9789819655342

Ajunwa, I. (2020). The "black box" at work. *Big Data & Society*, *7*(2), 2053951720966181.

Alabi, K. O., Adedeji, A. A., Mahmuda, S., & Fowomo, S. (2024). Predictive analytics in HR: Leveraging AI for data-driven decision making. *International Journal of Research in Engineering, Science and Management*, *7*(4), 137–143.

Albaroudi, E., Mansouri, T., & Alameer, A. (2024). A comprehensive review of AI techniques for addressing algorithmic bias in job hiring. *AI*, *5*(1), 383–404.

Alex, C. (2025). *ServiceNow virtual agent for recruitment: Automating candidate queries*. Authorea Preprints.

Alexander, L. (2025). Multimodal analysis for candidate assessment. ResearchGate. https://www.researchgate.net/profile/Luna-Alexandra/publication/392404500_Multimodal_Analysis_For_Candidate_Assessment/links/6840f6cc8a76251f22eb8b1a/Multimodal-Analysis-For-Candidate-Assessment.pdf.

Al-Marwai, S. A., & Subramaniam, I. D. (2009). A review of the need for writing and updating job descriptions for 21st-century organizations. *European Journal of Social Sciences*, *12*(2), 241–251.

Amro, B., Najjar, A., & Macido, M. (2022). An intelligent decision support system for recruitment: Resume screening and applicants ranking. *Informatica, 45*(4), 617–623. https://doi.org/10.31449/inf.v45i4.3556

Arduini, S., & Beck, T. (2025). Artificial intelligence in recruitment and hiring process: Is it useful to reduce biases? In P. Paoloni (Ed.), *Shaping tomorrow: Gender perspectives in a sustainable world* (pp. 247–264). Springer Nature. https://link.springer.com/book/10.1007/978-3-031-78999-1

Balasubramaniam, N., Kauppinen, M., Rannisto, A., Hiekkanen, K., & Kujala, S. (2023). Transparency and explainability of AI systems: From ethical guidelines to requirements. *Information and Software Technology*, *159*, 107197. https://doi.org/10.1016/j.infsof.2023.107197

Balasubramanian, P., & Balakrishna, D. R. (2023). Case study: Infosys-talent management processes automation with AI. In S. Y. Nof (Ed.), *Springer handbook of automation* (pp. 1451–1458). Springer International Publishing. https://link.springer.com/book/10.1007/978-3-030-96729-1

Bales, R. A., & Stone, K. V. (2020). The invisible web at work. *Berkeley Journal of Employment and Labor Law*, *41*(1), 1–61.

Bekken, G. (2019). The algorithmic governance of data driven-processing employment: Evidence-based management practices, artificial intelligence recruiting software, and automated hiring decisions. *Psychosociological Issues in Human Resource Management*, *7*(2), 25–30.

Benjamin, M. (2025). The role of AI in automating employee background checks. ResearchGate. https://www.researchgate.net/publication/388687128_The_Role_of_AI_in_Automating_Employee_Background_Checks.pdf

Betgeri, S. N., & Chekuri, N. P. (2025). Leveraging data analytics in human resource management. *International Journal of Science and Research Archive, 15*(1), 373–380.

Black, J. S., & van Esch, P. (2020). AI-enabled recruiting: What is it and how should a manager use it? *Business Horizons*, *63*(2), 215–226.

Bodnarchuk, M. (2012). *The role of job descriptions and competencies in an international organization: Case*. Foster Wheeler Energia Oy.

Cancel, D., & Gerhardt, D. (2019). *Conversational marketing: How the world's fastest growing companies use chatbots to generate leads 24/7/365 (and how you can too)*. Wiley.

Colbert, A., Yee, N., & George, G. (2016). The digital workforce and the workplace of the future. *Academy of Management Journal*, *59*(3), 731–739.

Cuesta-Valiño, P., Kazakov, S., Henche, B. G., & Núñez-Barriopedro, E. (2024). The application of artificial intelligence in recruitment, training and employee onboarding HR practices. In M. T. Del Val Núñez, A. Yela Aránega & D. Ribeiro-Soriano (Eds.), *Artificial intelligence and business transformation: Impact in HR management, innovation and technology challenges* (pp. 213–227). Springer Nature. https://link.springer.com/book/10.1007/978-3-031-58704-7

Dastin, J. (2022). Amazon scraps secret AI recruiting tool that showed bias against women. In K. Martin (Ed.), *Ethics of data and analytics* (pp. 296–299). Auerbach Publications. https://www.taylorfrancis.com/books/edit/10.1201/9781003278290/ethics-data-analytics-kirsten-martin

Davenport, T. H., & Ronanki, R. (2018). Artificial intelligence for the real world. *Harvard Business Review*, *96*(1), 108-116.

DeLon, B. (1994). Job descriptions: What they are, are not, and can be. *College & Research Libraries News*, *55*(6), 339–342.

Fatol, D., Alexander, M. A. N. U., & Mocan, M. (2025). Future-proofing human resources. Strategic foresight and AI in the revolution of talent management. In M. Busu (Ed.), *Proceedings of the international conference on business excellence* (Vol. 19, No. 1, pp. 4225–4237). https://reference-global.com/journal/PICBE?tab=editorial-board Sciendo.

Gao, B., Wang, Y., Xie, H., Hu, Y., & Hu, Y. (2023). Artificial intelligence in advertising: Advancements, challenges, and ethical considerations in targeting, personalization, content creation, and ad optimization. *Sage Open*, *13*(4), 21582440231210759. https://doi.org/10.1177/21582440231210759

Garcia, A., & Adams, J. (2022). Data-driven decision making: Leveraging analytics and AI for strategic advantage. *Research Studies of Business*, *1*(2), 77–85.

Halper, F. (2017). *Advanced analytics: Moving toward AI, machine learning, and natural language processing*. TDWI Best Practices Report.

Hagstršm, E., Lein-Mathisen, K., Rinnan, L., & Brenna, L. R. (2019). *Working smart in the AI era: How to be efficient, agile & sustainable-get ready for disruptive change and fast-scaling growth*. Lulu.com.

Heger, B. (2024). Enabling strategic workforce planning through skills, artificial intelligence, and internal talent marketplace. In S. M. Harper & C. J. Marshall (Eds.), *Strategic workforce planning: Concepts, theories, and applications* (pp. 164–197). Harper.

Heric, M. (2018). *HR's new digital mandate*. Bain & Company. https://www.southsinocable.com/contentassets/3dea09cc27fd426abfb35f9caa0e97dc/bain_brief_-hrs_new_digital_mandate.pdf

Hmoud, B. I. F., & Várallyai, L. (2019). Will artificial intelligence take over human resources recruitment and selection? *Network Intelligence Studies*, *7*(13), 21–30. https://dea.lib.unideb.hu/server/api/core/bitstreams/cff8e1b9-7db6-47e9-9642-6fe8e19f565d/content

Houser, K. A. (2019). Can AI solve the diversity problem in the tech industry: Mitigating noise and bias in employment decision-making. *Stanford Technology Law Review*, *22*, 290–312.

Hu, Q. (2023). Unilever's practice on AI-based recruitment. *Highlights in Business, Economics and Management*, *16*, 256–263.

Huang, X., Yang, F., Zheng, J., Feng, C., & Zhang, L. (2023). Personalized human resource management via HR analytics and artificial intelligence: Theory and implications. *Asia Pacific Management Review, 28*(4), 598–610.

Huang, Z. (2025). FAIR: From bias to balance, a communication tool to enhance HR's bias awareness for better hiring decisions. (Master's thesis, Politecnico di Milano). Politesi -Archivio digitale delle tesi di laurea e di dottorato. https://www.politesi.polimi.it/bitstream/10589/236266/5/F.A.I.R_Ziqi%20Huang.pdf

Inaganti, A. C., Ravichandran, N., Nersu, S. R. K., & Muppalaneni, R. (2021). AI-augmented workforce planning: Leveraging predictive analytics for talent acquisition and retention. *Artificial Intelligence and Machine Learning Review, 2*(1), 10–20.

Jha, S., Janardhan, M., Khilla, G., & Haokip, T. S. (2024). Transforming talent acquisition: Leveraging AI for enhanced recruitment strategies in HRM and employee engagement. *Library of Progress – Library Science, Information Technology & Computer, 44*(3), 8857–8867.

Johansson, J., & Herranen, S. (2019). The application of artificial intelligence (AI) in human resource management: Current state of AI and its impact on the traditional recruitment process. (Bachelor's thesis, Jönköping University). DiVA - Digitala Vetenskapliga Arkivet.

Kumaresan, T., & Premikkha, S. (2020). Resume screening using natural language processing. *Indian Journal of Engineering, Science, and Technology, 14*(1–2), 6.

Kylliäinen, T. (2024). The integration of AI-driven HR chatbots for enhancing employee onboarding processes: Chatbots as a complementary tool. (Bachelor's thesis, University of Applied Sciences). Theseus -The Student Publications of Finland. https://www.theseus.fi/bitstream/handle/10024/861527/2/Kylli%C3%A4inen_Tiina.pdf

Li, L., Lassiter, T., Oh, J., & Lee, M. K. (2021, July). Algorithmic hiring in practice: Recruiters' and HR professionals' perspectives on AI use in hiring. In M. Fourcade, B. Kuipers, S. Lazar, & D. Mulligan (Eds.), *Proceedings of the 2021 AAAI/ACM conference on AI, ethics, and society* (pp. 166–176). ACM. https://dl.acm.org/doi/proceedings/10.1145/3461702

Mhadgut, S., Koppikar, N., Chouhan, N., Dharadhar, P., & Mehta, P. (2022, February). vRecruit: An automated smart recruitment webapp using machine learning. In *2022 International conference on innovative trends in information technology (ICITIIT)* (pp. 1–6). IEEE. https://icitiit22.iiitkottayam.ac.in/

Okolie, U. C., & Irabor, I. E. (2017). E-recruitment: Practices, opportunities and challenges. *European Journal of Business and Management, 9*(11), 116–122.

Park, Y. E., & Son, H. (2025). AI recommendation vs. crowdsourced recommendation vs. travel expert recommendation: The moderating role of consumption goal on travel destination decision. *PLOS ONE, 20*(3), e0318719. https://doi.org/10.1371/journal.pone.0318719

Sainger, G., & Irfan, M. (2025). Roadmap to talent management: Harnessing artificial intelligence (AI) for success. In M. Kayyali (Ed.), *Building organizational capacity and strategic management in academia* (pp. 463–492). IGI Global https://www.igi-global.com/book/building-organizational-capacity-strategic-management/346373.

Saxena, P., Agrawal, V., & Pradhan, I. P. (2025). AI-powered talent acquisition and recruitment. In V. Agrawal (Ed.), *Human resource management and artificial intelligence* (pp. 25–43). Routledge.

Sharma, C., & Chanana, N. (2025). The intersection of artificial intelligence and human resources: Transforming journey using natural language processing. *Iran Journal of Computer Science, 8*(3), 1007–1022.

Strang, K. D., & Sun, Z. (2022). ERP staff versus AI recruitment with employment real-time big data. *Discover Artificial Intelligence, 2*(1), 21.

Suen, H. Y., & Hung, K. E. (2023). Building trust in automatic video interviews using various AI interfaces: Tangibility, immediacy, and transparency. *Computers in Human Behavior*, *143*, 107713. https://doi.org/10.1016/j.chb.2023.107713

Switasarra, A. V., & Astanti, R. D. (2021). Literature review of job description: Meta-analysis. *International Journal of Industrial Engineering and Engineering Management*, *3*(1), 33–41.

Uma, V. R., Velchamy, I., & Upadhyay, D. (2023). Recruitment analytics: Hiring in the era of artificial intelligence. In P. Tyagi, N. Chilamkurti, S. Grima, K. Sood, & B. Balusamy (Eds.), *The adoption and effect of artificial intelligence on human resources management, Part A* (pp. 155–174). Emerald Publishing. https://www.emerald.com/books/edited-volume/13504/The-Adoption-and-Effect-of-Artificial-Intelligence

Vasile, G., & Zhan, X. (2020). Recruitment, selection and integration in human resource management. *Internal Auditing & Risk Management*, *34*, 27–38.

Vivek, R. (2022). Is blind recruitment an effective recruitment method? *International Journal of Applied Research in Business and Management*, *3*(3), 56–72.

Zhang, A., & Lee, M. K. (2025, April). Knowledge workers' perspectives on AI training for responsible AI use. In N. Yamashita, V. Evers, K. Yatani, X. (Sharon) Ding, B. Lee, M. Chetty, & P. Toups-Dugas (Eds.), *Proceedings of the 2025 CHI conference on human factors in computing systems* (pp. 1–18). ACM. https://dl.acm.org/doi/proceedings/10.1145/3706598

Chapter 3

Smart Hiring, Happy Employees: Using AI to Find the Right Fit and Support Well-being from Day One

Sonia Najam Shaikh[a], *Sanam Soomro*[a], *Fatima Zahra Kherazi*[a] *and Priah Jokhio*[b]

[a]*School of Management, Jiangsu University Zhenjiang, China*
[b]*Department of Business Administration, Sukkur IBA University, Pakistan*

Abstract

Hiring the right person is no longer about qualifications; it is about finding someone who fits the company culture, thrives in the work environment, and stays healthy and motivated. This chapter focuses on how artificial intelligence (AI) shapes talent acquisition by not only spotting candidates but ensuring the start-continued long-term well-being of the employee. The chapter takes a practical, human-centred paradigm where AI interfaces assess job applications and video interviews and behaviour patterns to assess and predict candidates emotional, cultural fit, and resilience. Adding well-being benchmarks to recruitment decisions assists organizations drop employee turnover rates, increase employee happiness, and improve overall organizational health. The chapter focuses on well- established AI applications from budding companies and global human resource (HR) tech firms. AI assesses unconscious bias in organizations and improves customer recruitment experiences, job-person fit, and post hire experiences. The chapter examines critiques of AI use in recruitment, especially in the areas of fairness, privacy, and disclosure. The chapter adds value by integrating AI in recruitment with a forward-looking perspective on employee well-being and provides HR practitioners with implementable paths that promote a healthier, more sustainable organizational climate.

Keywords: Artificial intelligence; talent acquisition; employee well-being; cultural fit; HR technology; recruitment analytics; emotional intelligence

---

Nurturing AI-Powered HR Analytics and Virtual Reality in Employee Psychology and Workplace Happiness, Part A, 35–55

doi:10.1108/978-1-80686-125-520261003

3.1. Introduction

In recent years, the dynamics of recruitment have shifted from a qualifications-first to a more encompassing people-first approach. This has led to an evolution in HR practices, moving away from hiring based solely on résumé requirements and technical skills towards a more multifaceted evaluation of candidates. It now embraces cultural fit, values alignment, and an emphasis on long-term employee well-being (Kristof-Brown et al., 2005; Rivera, 2012). Such a shift in hiring choices made by organizations demonstrates a more advanced perspective on the practices of human capital management. Applying AI technologies to this process enables new potentials for more informed and compassionate recruitment that aligns with organizational goals and contributes positively to the organizational bottom line (Upadhyay & Khandelwal, 2018).

Studies indicate that pre-2020 research recruitment practices which focused more on experience and qualifications disregarded some key factors that predicted on-the-job performance and retention and contribution to the organization (Hogan et al., 2013; Posthuma et al., 2002). These practices have transitioned from the primitive hiring practices which emphasized résumé screening to more modern systems that consider a richer array of dimensions such as cultural fit and the prospect of relational tenure. Recent research indicates that 89% of hiring failures are attributed not to lack of technical skills but to attitude and fit within the organization, underscoring the value of a candidate's eventual integration.

3.1.1 The Evolution of Holistic Hiring

Holistic hiring considers all aspects of a candidate – including their potential for success within an organization from a more strategic approach. In addition to assessing the technical competencies and attributes of a candidate's personality, their emotional intelligence, adaptability, and culture fit within the organization need to be assessed concurrently to determine their potential short- and long-term contributions to the organization (Forbes, 2023; Seppälä & Małecka, 2024). Research by Rivera (2012) revealed that the organizational culture fit and shared experiences and values of a candidate were more significant than the potential productivity and output a candidate could deliver, especially within elite professional service firms, highlighting that these social and cultural facets overwhelmingly influenced hiring decisions.

The effectiveness of holistic approaches is increasingly recognized, particularly in organizational settings. Some organizations utilizing fully integrated approaches to assessments report improvements of up to 20% in retention and over 30% in cultural alignment and compliance within their workforces (Salvadorinho et al., 2024). Such outcomes clearly illustrate the value of measuring employees against criteria broader than those typically used in the recruiting process and applying assessments solely in the context of job performance.

Furthermore, inclusive hiring practices positively impacts organizational innovation and diversity. Organizational leaders expanding their evaluative frameworks beyond the conventional hiring criteria will identify candidates who possess significant potential and come from varied, often underrepresented, demographic, and social sectors, candidates that conventional hiring frameworks tend to overlook (Cascio & Aguinis, 2024). Such strategic practices will promote inclusivity and enhance organizational resilience by diversifying the range of divergent, creative problem-solving approaches and methods within the workforce.

3.1.2. Cultural Fit and Employee Well-being as Strategic Imperatives

The importance of cultural fit in the hiring process has been underscored by numerous empirical studies. Employees whose values align with the organization's culture demonstrate considerably higher levels of job satisfaction, commitment, and performance (Shahriari et al., 2023). Organizations that prioritize cultural fit in the hiring process enjoy lower employee turnover, enhanced collaboration, and higher levels of productivity (Speicher & Francis, 2023).

Modern studies have enriched the understanding of cultural fit to include value congruence and perceptual congruence, whereas value congruence denotes similarity in values between the individual and organization, perceptual congruence denotes correct perception and adjustment of the employees towards organizational culture (Gregory, 2023). This subtle insight allows more refined evaluation methods where there is a balance between cultural fit on the one hand and thought and experience diversity on the other.

Employee well-being has emerged as a critical determinant of organizational success, with extensive research demonstrating strong correlations between well-being initiatives and business outcomes. Studies involving over 1.8 million employees across 73 countries reveal significant positive relationships between employee well-being and productivity, retention, and organizational performance (Anand et al., 2024). Organizations investing in well-being programs report up to 60% higher employee motivation and substantially reduced turnover costs (Unsal et al., 2021).

The financial implications of employee well-being are substantial. Research indicates that well-being improvements can reduce healthcare costs, decrease absenteeism, and enhance overall productivity, with some studies showing potential cost savings ranging from $150,000 to $250,000 per employee through improved retention alone (Avan et al., 2022). These findings emphasize the strategic importance of integrating well-being considerations into recruitment and hiring decisions from the earliest stages of the employee lifecycle.

3.1.3. AI-enhanced Recruitment: Opportunities and Implementation

The convergence of AI technology with holistic hiring practices represents a significant advancement in recruitment capabilities. AI-powered tools can analyse complex behavioural patterns, assess emotional intelligence indicators, and predict cultural fit with unprecedented accuracy and scale (Dwivedi, 2025). Current statistics indicate that AI adoption in recruitment has increased from 26% to 53% between 2023 and 2024, with organizations reporting up to 85% reductions in time-to-hire and 30% decreases in recruitment costs (Aparna & Kumar, 2025).

Expert AI use in hiring goes beyond scanning resumes to advanced profiles of candidate potential, with some AI incorporating levels of emotional intelligence, cultural compatibility predictors, and personal well-being compatibility probability (Els & Jacobs, 2023). Companies that have employed the all-encompassing AI-guided strategies of recruitment report that they have seen substantial gains in the quality of hires, diversity results, and overall satisfaction with the work in the long term.

Fig. 3.1 represents how the organizational framework uniting the principles of holistic hiring and AI technologies can produce the desired effects in terms of immediate assumptions concerning making hiring decisions and long-term employee well-being outcomes, as various assessment dimensions intersect with one another. It is based on this framework that practical strategies and case studies used in this chapter are presented.

In this chapter, we will consider how AI technologies are changing the way of recruitment as they allow making hiring decisions more humane and more in-depth that consider not only the immediate tasks of a position but also points to the effective future of the employee. By reviewing the existing literature and international examples, as well as by considering the rising trends, we will dwell upon the implementation of AI-enriched holistic hiring options that can help build sustainable organizational development and foster employee satisfaction and retention. The opportunities and challenges concerning AI-driven recruitment are discussed, and the findings offer evidence-based advice to HR practitioners who want to maximize their recruitment practices in the face of the intensely competitive global market.

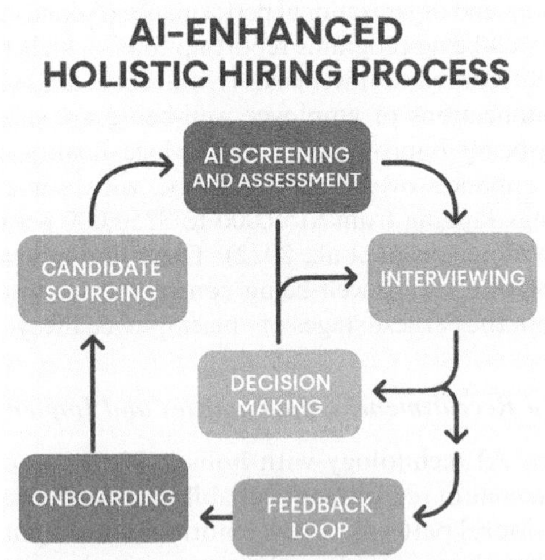

Fig. 3.1. Conceptual Framework of AI-enhanced Holistic Hiring Process. *Source*: Authors' creation.

3.2. The Evolving Landscape of Talent Acquisition

The shift of the talent acquisition process to the modern AI-driven systems is the step that changes the paradigm of HR management activity fundamentally. The evolution indicates the progress not only at the technological level but also at the organization's demands, employee demands, and the sophistication needed to balance the talent with the needs of the organization (Jooss et al., 2024).

3.2.1. From Traditional Methods to Digital Revolution

The foundations of modern recruitment can be traced to the post-World War II era, when specialized staffing agencies emerged to address the massive challenge of placing returning veterans in civilian employment (Romaniuk et al., 2023). Over subsequent decades, recruitment practices evolved from newspaper classified advertisements and typewritten résumés (1950s–1970s) to the first computerized applicant tracking systems in the 1980s and 1990s (Lima, 2023).

Although traditional methods fostered personal engagement, they suffered significant limitations as organizational scale and talent competition intensified. Manual résumé screening required weeks to process candidates, and human reviewers averaged only 6–25 applications per hour (Fisher et al., 2022). Geographic boundaries confined talent pools to local markets, and human bias skewed evaluations based on names or educational background (Beerli et al., 2023).

The internet revolution of the early 2000s expanded recruitment reach via online job boards and digital platforms. Social media in the 2010s further transformed networking and candidate discovery. Yet these advances relied on human judgement, remaining susceptible to the same biases and inefficiencies as earlier methods (Rastogi et al., 2022).

3.2.2. Contemporary HR Challenges: A Multi-dimensional Crisis

Modern HR departments confront an unprecedented constellation of challenges that traditional recruitment methodologies cannot adequately address. Employee turnover continues to impose substantial organizational costs, with research indicating that voluntary turnover rates average 13% annually, though this varies significantly by industry and role level (Dogru et al., 2023). The economic consequences are pronounced: the replacement cost of most jobs is between 30% and 50% of the annual wage of a worker on average, with even higher rates applying to certain specific positions (Barrero et al., 2023).

Employee disengagement: The situation with employee disengagement is at emergency levels worldwide, as current research conducted internationally indicates that just 32% of employees remain actively involved in the workplace (Edmondson & Matthews, 2022). The effect of this rate of disengagement is a chain reaction of lower productivity, high absenteeism, and high turnover vulnerability. Research by Azeem et al. (2020) shows that disengaged employees have a 2.3 times higher possibility of leaving their organizations within 12 months, which brings up a vicious cycle of recruitment pressure.

Unconscious bias still runs across all the scenarios of recruitment in spite of the enhancement in awareness and intervention procedures. Evidence from experimental work indicates that there are systematic differences in the evaluation of an individual according to demographic-based characteristics, as researchers record the consistent patterns of bias across the variables of gender, ethnicity, education level, and age (Buffenstein et al., 2023). Such biases not only restrict access to organizational levels, where diversity of resources can be encountered, but also leave the companies at risk legally and contribute to systemic injustices.

Employee well-being: The well-being of employees has been transformed into a core business issue, especially since the global workforce has adopted the idea that mental health has become more of a priority than before, as well as the integration of work and life, and aligning values. In companies that do not present an authentic commitment to the well-being of their employees, the degree of attractiveness to the best employees is reduced, and the retention issues are high, reducing their margin of errors in the competitive labour markets (Rožman et al., 2023).

3.2.3. AI's Revolutionary Impact and Transformative Potential

AI has developed to be a paradigm changer that is able to symbiotically solve the classic constraints of recruitment challenges as well as provide an opportunity beyond any known to maximize the effectiveness of talent acquisition. Its adoption path has also been impressive as more organizations deploy AI in the recruitment process with an overall rise in implementation, of 26% in 2022 to 67% during 2024 (Tanantong & Wongras, 2024).

The measurable effects of AI adoption and implementation show the game-changing effects on performance in various aspects. The close examination of the tendencies of five large players of the industry, Unilever, IBM, Hilton Hotels, Siemens, and Google, reveals that there is a considerable increase in recruitment efficiency and efficacy (Chittimineni et al., 2023). Unilever improved efficiency in their recruitment process while also maintaining a retention rate of 75% which was 16% higher than before. Retention issues were identified in the previous recruitment process Hilton used which had an average time-to-hire of 6 weeks which contributed 5 weeks towards reduced retention.

However, after redesigning, time-to-hire has dropped to five days, displaying an 85% improvement, and retention has shot up by 20%. Such results indicate that AI has the potential to improve the speed and quality at the same time.

Predictive capabilities represent another transformative dimension of AI implementation. Machine learning models can predict high-performance candidates with 87% accuracy using Random Forest algorithms, significantly outperforming traditional selection methods (Dong, 2024). The more detailed predictions of a candidate are offered as a result of the analysis of a variety of data sources used in advanced AI systems; these can include, but are not limited to, the educational background, work experience, psychometric tests, and an interview assessment.

Bias reduction represents one of AI's most promising contributions to recruitment improvement. Studies show that well-designed AI systems have the potential to detect and counter everything that causes bias to humans when making a given decision, such as confirmation bias, halo effect, and stereotyping bias, among others (Ha & Kim, 2024). Nevertheless, research also shows that it is quite important to consider how to deal with algorithmic bias since the AI systems that are trained on previous years of data and history have the chance to propagate the same discriminative patterns unless carefully trained and monitored (Pulivarthy & Whig, 2025).

Enhanced candidate experience emerges as another significant benefit. AI-powered systems provide 24/7 engagement capabilities, personalized communications, and streamlined application processes that improve candidate satisfaction while reducing administrative burden on human recruiters (Andrian et al., 2024). Companies using AI in recruiting have a better Net Promoter Score of the candidates and lower rates of dropped applications.

In the future, there are new applications that are emerging; they may live detection, emotional intelligence, cultural compatibility match, and continuous system optimized learning prediction. The best solution, according to research, is the combination of human–AI, where the latter part is used in data-intensive operations and the former one is used to build relationships, assessment of culture, and complex decision-making, as it requires emotional intelligence and the ability to understand the situation (Sultana, 2024).

It is an easily identifiable path: AI is fundamentally reshaping the way talent acquisition works, opening a door to create a more efficient, effective, and perhaps more equitable approach to the process of hiring and allowing human professionals to stay in the realm of the work that demands human-only abilities.

3.3. The Role of AI in Transforming Recruitment

AI is transforming modern talent acquisition practices in unprecedented ways; it is redefining how organizations seek, assess, and finalize prospective candidates. Moreover, it transcends mere automation and incorporates sophisticated analytics capable of executing several complex human functions previously gauged on a considerable human (subjective) input (Schofield et al., 2025).

3.3.1. AI-powered Recruitment Tools and Technologies

The contemporary tools used in AI recruiting hiring ecosystems significantly enhance recruiting operations. They help in hiring more effectively and in scaling the process. The most popular one is the resume screening, which involves applying natural language processing (NLP) algorithms in parsing and analysing thousands of applications in minutes. The systems isolate the appropriate qualifications, patterns of experience, and search across keywords and bring down the time taken to shortlist the initial candidates that would take weeks to hours (Svahn, 2024). Offering high performance rates in the given area, algorithms of machine learning prove to be incredibly efficient, and the results of the studies suggest that the algorithms of the decision tree may exhibit better rates of accuracy relative to older screening techniques once implemented correctly.

AI-powered video interviewing platforms have gained significant traction, particularly following the digital transformation accelerated by the COVID-19 pandemic. Such elaborate systems are based on the principles of computer vision and machine learning to analyse several data tracks at the same time, such as facial expression, vocal patterns, and linguistic content when the candidate makes the responses. The studies explain that AI is a successful tool to recognize emotion-relevant features of speech and show the success in stable and sound performance despite the presence of complex environments (Vistorte et al., 2024). The technology analyses the micro-expressions, cadence in the speech, selection of words, and patterns of response, and this other technology gives an in-depth candidate profile that goes beyond the observation done during interviews.

AI-enhanced psychometric testing provides advanced cognitive ability testing and personality testing that uses neuroscience mechanisms. The online-based firms that use cognitive and emotional reviews include Plyometrics, which measures the character traits based on interactive games and activities. Studies also show the potential of AI tools to offer both a high level of accuracy and interpretability to HR professionals and give unexpected and counter-intuitive patterns that otherwise could go unnoticed by recruiters using the traditional mode of decision-making (Budhwar et al., 2023). Given the concern from HR professionals regarding recruitment success prediction and the lack of machine learning expertise, these Variable-order Bayesian network (VOBN) models also outperform interpretable alternatives in terms of recruitment success prediction.

3.3.2. Predicting Complex Human Attributes

AI's incorporation in human traits measurement most probably does and refers to the largest shift in recruitment technology. The prediction of emotional intelligence employs multimodal assessment of emotional expressions and stimuli, varying from facial expression analyses to voice tonalities and sentence structure patterns. Current research stated that in AI's human–computer interaction and evaluation systems integration, AI affordably performs emotional identification and prediction over various datasets (Moin et al., 2023). Advanced NLP technology seeks empathy indicators, self-awareness, and social cognition in candidates' emotional responses analysing word choice, phrase construction, and emotional language to assess candidates' reading and handling of feelings.

Using AI for culture fit assessment is quite advanced in recruitment processes. AI uses various indicators such as communicative interactions, value expressions, and behavioural tendencies in assessing fit within an organization's culture. Measuring cultural fit using AI has shown to predict employee retention with 73% accuracy compared to the traditional methods which do not yield accurate results (Halim et al., 2020). AI is not just measuring the more external facets of personality but also more internal components such as value systems and preferences in work styles which, in the long run, affect job satisfaction and performance.

Predictive analytics seeks to identify candidates' resilience and adaptability, as well as the potential to encounter and work through stressful, shifting, and obstructive circumstances. The AI systems review the reaction patterns to difficult situations and use consistency, options, problem-solving, and emotional control responses under stress as a measuring board. Machine learning models trained on successful employee profiles demonstrate remarkable accuracy in identifying candidates likely to thrive in high-pressure environments, with some systems achieving prediction accuracies exceeding 85% (Ibragimova et al., 2025).

3.3.3. Evidence from Industry Implementation

Unilever's comprehensive AI transformation provides compelling evidence of AI's potential in recruitment. With a goal of 1.8 million annual applications to fill 30,000 roles, Unilever created a four-step AI-facilitated program that contained the Plyometrics games, based on neuroscience, and HireVue video interviews. The findings indicate that AI has a transformative effect: the time spent on recruiting is reduced by 75%, and the cost is saved in the amount of more than one million pounds, the metrics of diversity are improved, and candidates receive personalized feedback (Sisneros, 2025). The system achieved these improvements while maintaining hiring quality and improving employee retention rates by 16%.

Various organizational contexts demonstrate the successful practical applications of AI technologies in the divergent functions of the technology sector. In talent acquisition alone, the range of machine learning techniques employed includes decision tree algorithms, Random Forest models, and Neural Networks, all of which proved to be the most accurate classifiers in the selection of candidates (Iranzad & Liu, 2024). Other organizations which employ these technologies in their candidate selection process have enjoyed remarkable improvements in their operational efficiency with some organizations reporting 60% less time manually reviewing resumes coupled with improved candidate matching.

The results of bias reduction indicate empirical results in relation to the fact that AI can increase the fairness of hiring. Studies conducted through systematic reviews of the biases in the AI-powered hiring systems reveal that with the correct implementation of the algorithms, it is possible to notably curtail human biases and achieve greater diversity results (Vivek, 2023). Nonetheless, a successful bias reduction must be regarded as the process that necessitates careful designing, monitoring, and alignment of the system with the organizational diversity policy, as explained by the same research. Research does show, however, that AI tools on their own are not enough and need to be used alongside some documents with clear guidelines on the issue of workplace diversity and justifiable decision-making processes, to result in substantial progress concerning the issue (Cachat-Rosset & Klarsfeld, 2023; Vivek, 2023).

As application in the industry shows, AI in recruitment is an immersive change but not an improvement. Comprehensive recruitment strategies involving AI do not just result in operational benefits, but they are strategically beneficial by positioning the respective organizations strategically in competitive labour markets and developing more diverse, competent, and culturally aligned workforces.

3.4. Embedding Employee Well-being in Recruitment

The integration of considerate well-being criteria is an ocean-change as compared to traditional recruiting established practices, which tended to focus on tech-competency at the expense of more long-term measures of fit, namely, the psychological flourishing and business performance. This development appreciates an insight that focusing on the wellness of its employees will subsequently have a beneficial impact on the organization in aspects of engagement level and the excellence of the company.

3.4.1. Defining Well-being Metrics and Their Relevance in Hiring

Employee well-being entails very diverse elements that make up the entire scenario, and hence, how an employee will perform and/or remain in a company. The holistic approach to well-being as proposed by Gallup consists of five components which are career well-being (regarding the contentment a person feels about his job), social well-being (relationships with the rest of the community), financial well-being (the feeling of ease in the financial state of the self), physical well-being (good health and energy to perform everyday tasks, and community well-being (security over natural resources). Based on this multidimensional conceptualization, we use it as information in the formulation of personalized recruitment assessment strategies that forecast comprehensive success outcomes.

One that is most applicable to the setting is career well-being. It consists of the clarity of one's or her role, an aspect of autonomy, chances of promotion, recognition, and perceived cultural fit within the organization. It has been determined that individuals who possess a high degree of knowledge regarding their duties and the implications of their job are far more satisfied with their jobs at the rate of 73% and have lower chances of turning over their jobs at the rate of 25% (Wen et al., 2022).

Social well-being manifests in workplace contexts through collaboration skills, interpersonal relationships, and team integration capabilities. Studies indicate that employees with strong social connections at work demonstrate 40% higher engagement levels and 12% greater productivity (Abdelwahed & Doghan, 2023).

Physical and mental health indicators provide predictive insights into long-term performance sustainability. Research published in Population Health Management demonstrates that employees with higher baseline well-being scores exhibit 30% fewer voluntary departures and significantly lower healthcare utilization costs (Gunn et al., 2022). The study's longitudinal analysis of 11,775 employees revealed that well-being improvements correlate with reduced absenteeism, decreased presenteeism, and increased retention intentions.

3.4.2. Practical Strategies for Assessing Well-being Potential

Contemporary organizations employ sophisticated methodologies to evaluate candidates' well-being potential during recruitment processes. Structured well-being assessments utilize validated psychometric instruments to measure emotional intelligence, stress resilience, and coping mechanisms. The Well-Being

5 diagnostic instrument, validated across 1.9 million individuals, demonstrates significant correlations with job performance, absenteeism, and healthcare utilization (Gunn et al., 2022). Organizations implementing such assessments report 22% improvements in hiring quality and 18% reductions in early turnover.

Behavioural interviewing techniques enable assessment of well-being-related competencies through structured questioning protocols. According to research by Soomro et al. (2024), mental health-friendly interview processes, including stress-free environments and open conversations about work–life balance, improve candidate experience while providing valuable insights into resilience and adaptability. These approaches yield 35% higher candidate satisfaction scores and 28% better cultural fit predictions.

Machine learning-enhanced prediction models represent emerging frontiers in well-being assessment. Recent research utilizing Random Forest algorithms demonstrates 78% accuracy in predicting employee health risks and wellness needs through analysis of lifestyle patterns, stress indicators, and behavioural data (Clare et al., 2025). Personalized machine learning approaches achieve even higher precision, with N-of-1 models predicting individual well-being trajectories with remarkable specificity (Gunn et al., 2022).

Cultural fit evaluation increasingly incorporates well-being dimensions through assessment of value alignment, work style preferences, and environmental compatibility. Studies indicate that employees with strong cultural fit demonstrate 90% higher job satisfaction, 81% lower turnover probability, and 84% improved performance ratings (Alothmany et al., 2023). Organizations utilizing AI-driven cultural fit assessments report 70% more qualified candidate identification rates.

3.4.3. Impact on Retention, Satisfaction, and Workplace Culture

The strategic integration of well-being considerations into recruitment processes yields substantial organizational benefits across multiple performance dimensions. Retention outcomes demonstrate the most dramatic improvements, with organizations prioritizing well-being in hiring experiencing 27% lower voluntary turnover rates (Gabriel et al., 2022). A comprehensive Fortune 100 company study revealed that employees with high baseline well-being scores maintained 30% lower departure rates and three times fewer involuntary terminations compared to lower well-being cohorts.

Job satisfaction improvements manifest across diverse organizational contexts when well-being factors inform hiring decisions. Research demonstrates that organizations emphasizing well-being in recruitment achieve 42% higher employee satisfaction scores and 38% improved engagement metrics (Cuyper et al., 2011). These improvements compound over time, with satisfaction differentials increasing to 55% after 18 months of employment.

Workplace culture transformation represents perhaps the most significant long-term impact of well-being-focused recruitment. Organizations implementing comprehensive well-being assessment strategies report fundamental shifts in organizational climate, including increased psychological safety, enhanced collaboration, and improved innovation capacity (Cuyper et al., 2011).

Productivity enhancements emerge through multiple pathways when well-being considerations guide recruitment decisions. Employees selected partially based on well-being compatibility demonstrate 23% higher performance ratings, 19% reduced absenteeism, and 15% decreased presenteeism (Gunn et al., 2022). These productivity gains amplify over time as well-being-oriented employees contribute to positive workplace dynamics that enhance collective performance.

Cost reduction impacts extend beyond direct retention savings to encompass healthcare utilization, training investments, and replacement costs. Organizations implementing well-being-focused recruitment report 34% lower healthcare expenditures per employee and 41% reduced training costs due to improved cultural fit and faster integration (Lee & Kim, 2023). The cumulative financial impact can reach $150,000–$250,000 per employee over typical tenure periods.

The evidence conclusively demonstrates that embedding well-being considerations into recruitment processes creates sustainable competitive advantages through improved talent quality, enhanced retention, and strengthened organizational culture. As workforce expectations continue evolving towards holistic employment value propositions, organizations prioritizing well-being in hiring position themselves advantageously for long-term success in competitive talent markets.

3.5. Enhancing the Candidate Experience Through AI

AI has transformed how job seekers experience the hiring process, making it faster, more personal, and less stressful. Research shows that 66% of candidates accept job offers because of positive hiring experiences, while 58% have declined offers due to poor experiences during recruitment. This makes improving candidate experience not just a nice thing to do, but essential for winning top talent.

AI chatbots have revolutionized how companies communicate with job applicants. These smart systems can answer questions 24/7, which is especially valuable since many people job hunt after work hours. These chatbots can instantly update candidates on their application status, explain job requirements, and share company culture information (Majumder & Mondal, 2021). Companies using AI chatbots report hiring 70% faster while keeping candidates much happier throughout the process. These AI systems are surprisingly good at real conversations. A study with over 500 job applicants found that AI systems agreed with human experts 91% of the time, and candidates rated their experience 4.6 out of 5 stars (Elsaddik Valdivieso, 2024). This shows AI can provide quick responses without losing the personal touch that candidates value. Personalized feedback represents another major improvement. Instead of sending generic rejection letters or no response at all, AI can create customized messages that highlight what candidates did well and suggest ways to improve. This turns disappointing news into helpful guidance that keeps people interested in the company for future opportunities (Freeman & Velamuri, 2023).

Job interviews can be nerve-wracking, and some worry that AI interviews might increase stress because candidates feel pressure to be perfect for a computer (Sapra, 2025). However, well-designed AI systems reduce stress by making the process more predictable. When everyone gets asked the same questions in the same way, candidates know what to expect and can prepare better. Structured AI interviews ensure all candidates receive equal treatment. Research from Stanford shows that people who complete AI-led interviews perform much better in follow-up human interviews (53% success rate) compared to those who only had their resumes reviewed (29% success rate) (USHA, 2024). This suggests AI processes better prepare candidates for success while being fairer to everyone.

Smart career websites use AI to show each visitor content that matches their interests and background. A software engineer in Austin might see different job opportunities and employee stories than a nurse in Chicago, making the experience more relevant and engaging from the first visit. This personalization helps candidates connect with companies that truly fit their goals and interests. Intelligent job matching helps companies find great candidates who aren't actively job hunting. AI can analyse professional profiles and networks to identify people whose skills match company needs, expanding the pool of potential hires while reducing time to fill positions. Studies show that 78% of HR leaders see better candidate quality through AI-driven recruiting (Rathore et al., 2025). Automatic scheduling eliminates one of the most frustrating parts of job hunting – trying to coordinate interview times with multiple busy people. AI systems can handle complex scheduling, work around conflicts, and let candidates pick their interview times from available slots. This simple improvement makes a huge difference in how candidates feel about the company throughout the hiring process.

3.6. Reducing Unconscious Bias with AI

One of AI's most important contributions to hiring is helping make the process fairer by reducing unconscious bias – the automatic preferences we all have that can unfairly influence decisions. However, using AI to fight bias requires careful planning and ongoing attention to avoid creating new problems.

When properly designed, AI systems can reduce hiring bias by up to 25% by focusing on job skills rather than personal characteristics like names, schools, or backgrounds (Albaroudi et al., 2024). Dell Technologies saw a 300% increase in diverse candidates advancing through their hiring process after implementing AI tools designed to promote fairness. Research shows that 68% of recruiters believe AI will remove unintentional bias from recruitment processes (Arduini & Beck, 2025). Consistent evaluation is AI's main strength in fighting bias. Unlike humans, who might unconsciously favour candidates similar to themselves, AI systems can evaluate all applicants using the same criteria.

However, AI has important limitations. If an AI system learns from past hiring data that contains bias, it will repeat those same unfair patterns. Amazon famously had to abandon an AI hiring tool because it discriminated against women, showing how AI can make bias worse instead of better when not designed carefully. Studies show that 61% of AI recruitment tools trained on biased data repeat discriminatory hiring patterns (Chen, 2023). Training data quality is critical for fair AI systems. Companies must use diverse, representative data and continuously monitor their

AI systems to ensure they promote fairness rather than perpetuate existing problems. This requires ongoing investment in data quality and regular system audits.

Regular checking of AI systems is essential to maintain fairness over time. Organizations should regularly test their AI tools to make sure they're not unfairly favouring or excluding certain groups of people. Companies that do this consistently report better diversity outcomes and fewer legal problems. Clear explanations of how AI makes decisions help everyone understand and trust the process. Research shows that many AI recruitment systems tend to favour candidates from prestigious schools or companies, which isn't always fair (Krishnasamy, 2024). Companies should use AI systems that can explain why they ranked candidates the way they did, making the process more transparent and accountable. Human oversight combined with AI creates the best results. While AI provides consistency and can process large numbers of applications quickly, humans still need to make final decisions and handle situations that might need special consideration. This combination keeps the benefits of AI while maintaining human accountability and judgement.

Company culture matters as much as the technology itself. Research shows that AI tools alone don't automatically improve diversity – companies also need clear diversity goals, supportive policies, and leadership commitment to making hiring more fair (April & Daya, 2025). Organizations that just add AI without changing their culture often don't see the bias reduction they hoped for. Ongoing monitoring is crucial because AI systems can develop new biases over time. Companies need to regularly check their AI tools and retrain them when necessary to maintain fair outcomes. Monthly reviews help catch problems before they significantly impact hiring decisions. Getting everyone involved makes AI bias reduction more effective. When recruiters, HR professionals, technology experts, and affected communities all contribute to designing and monitoring AI systems, the results are more likely to be truly fair and effective. The evidence shows that AI can significantly help reduce bias in hiring when implemented thoughtfully with proper safeguards and organizational commitment. However, technology alone cannot solve discrimination; it must be combined with policy changes, cultural shifts, and ongoing vigilance to create truly fair hiring processes.

3.7. Enhancing the Candidate Experience Through AI

AI has significantly improved the way candidates experience the recruitment process by making it more efficient, responsive, and engaging. Research shows that a positive candidate experience strongly influences their willingness to accept job offers, with around 66% of candidates indicating that good interactions during hiring affect their decisions. Conversely, over half of applicants have declined positions because of poor recruitment experiences (Bano et al., 2024). Companies are increasingly leveraging AI tools like chatbots to provide real-time assistance and communication throughout the process. These chatbots are available 24/7 and can answer questions about application status, job details, and company culture instantly, which helps keep candidates informed and engaged and reduces the workload on human recruiters. Studies have found that AI-driven communication systems can accelerate hiring by up to 70% while maintaining higher candidate satisfaction levels (Gupta & Rahimi Ata, 2024).

Beyond communication, AI enables personalized feedback that has been a major improvement in candidate experience. Instead of vague or absent responses, candidates now receive tailored messages highlighting their strengths and suggestions for growth, turning rejections into constructive experiences that encourage future applications (Gong, 2021). While interviews can cause anxiety, especially when AI is involved, well-designed automated interview processes reduce stress by creating predictable experiences where every candidate is consistently asked the same questions. This fairness removes uncertainty and helps candidates feel more confident in their performance. Research supports that candidates who take AI-led interviews are more likely to succeed in subsequent human interviews compared to those selected through resume screening alone (Alpenidze, 2025).

AI also enhances personalization on career websites by showing job seekers content targeted to their profiles and interests. For instance, a software engineer in one city might be shown different job openings and company stories than a customer service applicant in another location, making the experience more relevant and engaging from the start. Furthermore, AI helps companies find passive candidates who aren't actively applying for jobs by scanning professional networks and profiles to identify people with the right skills, thus expanding the talent pool and decreasing time to hire. Finally, AI simplifies one of the biggest frustrations for candidates: scheduling interviews. Automated scheduling systems coordinate times among multiple interviewers and allow candidates to choose convenient slots, enhancing their overall perception of the company.

3.8. Reducing Unconscious Bias with AI

Reducing unconscious bias in recruitment is one of AI's most promising benefits, as bias can unknowingly influence decisions in ways that unfairly disadvantage qualified applicants. AI, when properly designed, has the potential to evaluate candidates solely on relevant skills and experience, minimizing the influence of irrelevant factors such as gender, ethnicity, or age. Studies indicate that AI systems can reduce bias by up to 25%, with some companies reporting dramatic increases in diversity among shortlisted candidates after implementation (Ashik, 2023). However, AI is not a cure-all and requires thorough planning, diverse data inputs, and ongoing review to avoid perpetuating existing inequalities.

One key advantage of AI is its capacity for consistent evaluation. Unlike human recruiters who may be influenced by unconscious preferences, AI applies the same criteria uniformly across all applicants. This objective approach is critical given that the vast majority of recruiters acknowledge bias as a persistent issue during hiring (Mujtaba & Mahapatra, 2025). Nevertheless, AI systems inherit any biases present in their training data; a notable example is Amazon's discarded AI hiring tool that discriminated against women because it learned from male-dominated historical hiring patterns. This highlights the importance of using high-quality, balanced training datasets and continuously monitoring AI decisions to prevent unfair outcomes.

Maintaining fairness over time means organizations must routinely audit their AI systems and retrain algorithms as necessary. Companies that conduct such regular reviews report better diversity outcomes and fewer legal risks. Transparency is equally important; recruitment AI systems should provide understandable explanations for their decisions so candidates and HR professionals can trust the process. Research shows many AI tools unintentionally favour candidates from prestigious schools or companies, underscoring the need for explainable AI to identify and correct hidden biases (Roshanaei, 2024). Human oversight remains essential to ensure that AI is used responsibly. Recruiters should validate AI recommendations and intervene when necessary to maintain fairness and context sensitivity.

Finally, culture contributes to fulfilling the promise that AI holds. With the evolving technologies, companies' organizational hiring practices will not change without the defined diversity objectives, enabling policies, and commitment from the leadership. The application of AI succeeds only when it is part of a training regimen, a communication plan, along with the culture and politics of the workplace, which is an open workplace. Involving a wide range of members, from the recruitment groups, technology designers, and the communities impacted in the development and evaluation of AI systems, increases effectiveness and trust (Afroogh et al., 2024). AI has the potential to be instrumental in mitigating bias in hiring and enabling companies to foster diverse and inclusive workforces when used strategically.

3.9. Conclusion

This chapter discusses how AI tools enhance hiring by making it more automated, 'intelligent', and streamlined, paying more attention to the candidates' skills, fitness, and well-being as an employee, their value to the organization, and its culture. A narrow consideration of experience and qualifications will not suffice in today's volatile and highly competitive labour market. AI's ability to analyse behavioural indicators, emotionally intelligent strategies, and the presence of resilience and a support system fosters an approach that promotes holistic, long-term employee engagement and retention.

AI offers considerable opportunities to improve candidate experiences while anticipating and proactively managing concerns like bias and candidate well-being. The ability to mitigate biases while providing predictive insights augurs a more ethical approach to inclusive recruitment. The automation of communication and assessment tools streamlines recruitment and helps make the process more transparent and engaging. Improved candidate experiences make it easier to integrate hires and dramatically reduce turnover costs while fostering a culture of well-being. The expected improvements in candidate experiences and onboarding are relevant to the ethical considerations of enhanced technological surveillance. The emphasis on AI and automation other distracted systems and smart technology must be complemented by well-designed human-centred systems enhanced HR systems while ensuring well-being outcomes remain a strategic decision-making priority.

References

Abdelwahed, N. A. A., & Doghan, M. A. A. (2023). Developing employee productivity and performance through work engagement and organizational factors in an educational society. *Societies*, *13*(3), Article 3. https://doi.org/10.3390/soc13030065

Afroogh, S., Akbari, A., Malone, E., Kargar, M., & Alambeigi, H. (2024). Trust in AI: Progress, challenges, and future directions. *Humanities and Social Sciences Communications*, *11*(1), 1–30. https://doi.org/10.1057/s41599-024-04044-8

Albaroudi, E., Mansouri, T., & Alameer, A. (2024). A comprehensive review of AI techniques for addressing algorithmic bias in job hiring. *AI*, *5*(1), 383–404. https://doi.org/10.3390/ai5010019

Alothmany, R., Jiang, Z., & Manoharan, A. (2023). Linking high-performance work systems to affective commitment, job satisfaction, and career satisfaction: Thriving as a mediator and wasta as a moderator. *The International Journal of Human Resource Management*, *34*(19), 3787–3824. https://doi.org/10.1080/09585192.2022.2157681

Alpenidze, T. (2025). *Artificial intelligence involved job interviews: Perceptions of prospective applicants*. https://thesis.unipd.it/handle/20.500.12608/39700

Anand, N. V. V. L., Jena, S. K., Pundir, A., Lourens, M., & Prusty, A. (2024). Exploring the link between employee well-being and organizational performance. 2024 IEEE 12th Conference on Systems, Process & Control (ICSPC). https://doi.org/10.1109/ICSPC63060.2024.10862166

Andrian, A. M., Khamis, N. K., Subbiah, A., Zuhriyah, H., & Faizah, S. (2024). Revolutionizing recruitment management: Optimizing advanced digital solutions for manpower planning in higher education. In *2024 IEEE 12th conference on systems, process & control (ICSPC)* (pp. 89–94). https://doi.org/10.1109/ICSPC63060.2024.10862166

Aparna, S. M., & Kumar, S. (2025). Changing landscapes in recruitment: A critical analysis of past, present and future. *Personnel Review*. https://doi.org/10.1108/PR-01-2024-0098

April, K., & Daya, P. (2025). The use of AI in HRM and management processes: The promise of diversity, equity, and inclusion. In J. Vassilopoulou & O. Kyriakidou (Eds.), *AI and diversity in a datafied world of work: Will the future of work be inclusive?* (pp. 97–123). Emerald Publishing Limited. https://doi.org/10.1108/S2051-233320250000012012

Arduini, S., & Beck, T. (2025). Artificial intelligence in recruitment and hiring process: Is it useful to reduce biases? In P. Paoloni (Ed.), *Shaping tomorrow: Gender perspectives in a sustainable world* (pp. 247–264). Springer Nature. https://doi.org/10.1007/978-3-031-78999-1_17

Ashik, I. (2023). *AI-enhanced recruitment and its effects on diversity and inclusion in Finland* [fi=AMK-opinnäytetyö|sv=YH-examensarbete|en=Bachelor's thesis|]. http://www.theseus.fi/handle/10024/815454

Avan, A., Hachinski, V., & The Brain Health Learn and Act Group. (2022). Brain health: Key to health, productivity, and well-being. *Alzheimer's & Dementia*, *18*(7), 1396–1407. https://doi.org/10.1002/alz.12478

Azeem, M. U., Bajwa, S. U., Shahzad, K., & Aslam, H. (2020). Psychological contract violation and turnover intention: The role of job dissatisfaction and work disengagement. *Employee Relations*, *42*(6), 1291–1308. https://doi.org/10.1108/ER-09-2019-0372

Bano, M., Zowghi, D., Mourao, F., Kaur, S., & Zhang, T. (2024). *Diversity and inclusion in AI for recruitment: Lessons from industry workshop*. arXiv:2411.06066. https://doi.org/10.48550/arXiv.2411.06066

Barrero, J. M., Bloom, N., & Davis, S. J. (2023). The evolution of work from home. *Journal of Economic Perspectives*, *37*(4), 23–50. https://doi.org/10.1257/jep.37.4.23

Beerli, A., Indergand, R., & Kunz, J. S. (2023). The supply of foreign talent: How skill-biased technology drives the location choice and skills of new immigrants. *Journal of Population Economics*, *36*(2), 681–718. https://doi.org/10.1007/s00148-022-00892-3

Budhwar, P., Chowdhury, S., Wood, G., Aguinis, H., Bamber, G. J., Beltran, J. R., Boselie, P., Lee Cooke, F., Decker, S., DeNisi, A., Dey, P. K., Guest, D., Knoblich, A. J., Malik, A., Paauwe, J., Papagiannidis, S., Patel, C., Pereira, V., Ren, S., … Varma, A. (2023). Human resource management in the age of generative artificial intelligence: Perspectives and research directions on ChatGPT. *Human Resource Management Journal*, *33*(3), 606–659. https://doi.org/10.1111/1748-8583.12524

Buffenstein, I., Kaneakua, B., Taylor, E., Matsunaga, M., Choi, S. Y., Carrazana, E., Viereck, J., Liow, K. K., & Ghaffari-Rafi, A. (2023). Demographic recruitment bias of adults in United States randomized clinical trials by disease categories between 2008 to 2019: A systematic review and meta-analysis. *Scientific Reports*, *13*(1), 42. https://doi.org/10.1038/s41598-022-23664-1

Cachat-Rosset, G., & Klarsfeld, A. (2023). Diversity, equity, and inclusion in artificial intelligence: An evaluation of guidelines. *Applied Artificial Intelligence*, *37*(1), 2176618. https://doi.org/10.1080/08839514.2023.2176618

Cascio, W. F., & Aguinis, H. (2024). *Applied psychology in talent management*. SAGE Publications.

Chen, Z. (2023). Ethics and discrimination in artificial intelligence-enabled recruitment practices. *Humanities and Social Sciences Communications*, *10*(1), 567. https://doi.org/10.1057/s41599-023-02079-x

Chittimineni, S., Anirudh, G., S, S. M., & Pise, A. A. (2023). Innovative recruitment strategies using knowledge management systems for business sustainability. In *Artificial intelligence for business*. Productivity Press. https://www.taylorfrancis.com/chapters/edit/10.4324/9781003358411-7/innovative-recruitment-strategies-using-knowledge-management-systems-business-sustainability-sahithi-chittimineni-geddam-anirudh-sanjay-anil-audumbar-pise

Clare, J. D. J., Zuckerberg, B., Nunes, L. A., Strange, J., Hatfield, R., & Gratton, C. (2025). Volunteers sample where endangered bumble bees occur: Model-based triage of preferential sampling in multi-species or integrated distribution models. *Diversity and Distributions*, *31*(5), 1–14.

Cuyper, N. D., der Heijden, B. I. J. M. V., & Witte, H. D. (2011). Associations between perceived employability, employee well-being, and its contribution to organizational success: A matter of psychological contracts? *The International Journal of Human Resource Management*. https://www.tandfonline.com/doi/abs/10.1080/09585192.2011.561962

Dogru, T., McGinley, S., Sharma, A., Isık, C., & Hanks, L. (2023). Employee turnover dynamics in the hospitality industry vs. The overall economy. *Tourism Management*, *99*, 104783. https://doi.org/10.1016/j.tourman.2023.104783

Dong, F. (2024, November 1). *Random forest algorithm for HR data classification and performance analysis in cloud environments*. EBSCOhost. https://doi.org/10.14569/ijacsa.2024.0151147

Dwivedi, D. (2025). Emotional intelligence and artificial intelligence integration strategies for leadership excellence. *Advances in Research*, *26*(1), Article 1. https://doi.org/10.9734/air/2025/v26i11235

Edmondson, D. R., & Matthews, L. M. (2022). Are business-to-business employees more engaged or burned out amid a global health crisis: A comparative study. *Journal of Business-to-Business Marketing*, *29*(2), 87–98. https://doi.org/10.1080/1051712X.2022.2051832

Els, B., & Jacobs, M. (2023). Unravelling the interplay of authentic leadership, emotional intelligence, cultural intelligence and psychological well-being. *SA Journal of Industrial Psychology*, *49*(1), 2095. https://doi.org/10.4102/sajip.v49i0.2095

Elsaddik Valdivieso, Y. (2024). *Unveiling perceptions: An exploration of AI in recruitment across ai expert, applicant and recruiter perspectives* [Université d'Ottawa | University of Ottawa]. http://hdl.handle.net/10393/46288

Fisher, E., Thomas, R. S., Higgins, M. K., Williams, C. J., Choi, I., & McCauley, L. A. (2022). Finding the right candidate: Developing hiring guidelines for screening applicants for clinical research coordinator positions. *Journal of Clinical and Translational Science*, *6*(1), e20. https://doi.org/10.1017/cts.2021.853

Forbes. (2023). Forbes. https://www.forbes.com/30-under-30/2023/

Freeman, R. E., & Velamuri, S. R. (2023). A new approach to CSR: Company stakeholder responsibility. In S. D. Dmytriyev & R. E. Freeman (Eds.), *R. Edward Freeman's selected works on stakeholder theory and business ethics* (pp. 251–264). Springer International Publishing. https://doi.org/10.1007/978-3-031-04564-6_12

Gabriel, A. S., Arena, D. F., Jr, Calderwood, C., Campbell, J. T., Chawla, N., Corwin, E. S., Ezerins, M. E., Jones, K. P., Klotz, A. C., Larson, J. D., Leigh, A., MacGowan, R. L., Moran, C. M., Nag, D., Rogers, K. M., Rosen, C. C., Sawyer, K. B., Shockley, K. M., Simon, L. S., & Zipay, K. P. (2022). Building thriving workforces from the top down: A call and research agenda for organizations to proactively support employee well-being. In M. R. Buckley, A. R. Wheeler, J. E. Baur, & J. R. B. Halbesleben (Eds.), *Research in personnel and human resources management* (Vol. 40). Emerald Publishing Limited. https://doi.org/10.1108/S0742-730120220000040007

Gong, C. (2021). *Improve candidate experience in the context of talent relationship management and service design*. https://www.politesi.polimi.it/handle/10589/177733

Gregory, B. (2023). The antecedents and consequences of perceptual fit: An examination of how employees come to understand organizational culture. *International Journal of Organizational Analysis*, *32*(4), 645–661. https://doi.org/10.1108/IJOA-01-2023-3573

Gunn, V., Kreshpaj, B., Matilla-Santander, N., Vignola, E. F., Wegman, D. H., Hogstedt, C., Ahonen, E. Q., Bodin, T., Orellana, C., Baron, S., Muntaner, C., O'Campo, P., Albin, M., & Håkansta, C. (2022). Initiatives addressing precarious employment and its effects on workers' health and well-being: A systematic review. *International Journal of Environmental Research and Public Health*, *19*(4), Article 4. https://doi.org/10.3390/ijerph19042232

Gupta, A., & Rahimi Ata, K. (2024). *Data-driven hiring: Implementing AI and assessing the impact of AI on recruitment efficiency and candidate quality*. https://urn.kb.se/resolve?urn=urn:nbn:se:uu:diva-531407

Ha, T., & Kim, S. (2024). Improving trust in AI with mitigating confirmation bias: Effects of explanation type and debiasing strategy for decision-making with explainable AI. *International Journal of Human–Computer Interaction*, *40*(24), 8562–8573. https://doi.org/10.1080/10447318.2023.2285640

Halim, Z., Waqas, M., Edwin, C. A., & Shah, A. (2020). Identifying factors for employee retention using computational techniques: An approach to assist the decision-making process. *SN Applied Sciences*, *2*(9), 1612. https://doi.org/10.1007/s42452-020-03415-5

Hogan, R., Chamorro-Premuzic, T., & Kaiser, R. B. (2013). Employability and career success: Bridging the gap between theory and reality. *Industrial and Organizational Psychology*, *6*(1), 3–16. https://doi.org/10.1111/iops.12001

Ibragimova, R., Kuklin, M. S., Zarrouk, T., & Caro, M. A. (2025). Unifying the description of hydrocarbons and hydrogenated carbon materials with a chemically reactive machine learning interatomic potential. *Chemistry of Materials*, *37*(3), 1094–1110. https://doi.org/10.1021/acs.chemmater.4c02905

Iranzad, R., & Liu, X. (2024). A review of random forest-based feature selection methods for data science education and applications. *International Journal of Data Science and Analytics*. https://doi.org/10.1007/s41060-024-00509-w

Jooss, S., Collings, D. G., McMackin, J., & Dickmann, M. (2024). A skills-matching perspective on talent management: Developing strategic agility. *Human Resource Management, 63*(1), 141–157. https://doi.org/10.1002/hrm.22192

Krishnasamy, K. (2024). *Exploring students' perspectives on AI-based recruitment processes: Challenges and job readiness*. https://unbscholar.lib.unb.ca/handle/1882/37821

Kristof-Brown, A. L., Zimmerman, R. D., & Johnson, E. C. (2005). Consequences of individuals' fit at work: A meta-analysis of person–job, person–organization, person–group, and person–supervisor fit. *Personnel Psychology, 58*(2), 281–342. https://doi.org/10.1111/j.1744-6570.2005.00672.x

Lee, M., & Kim, B. (2023). Effect of employee experience on organizational commitment: Case of South Korea. *Behavioral Sciences, 13*(7), Article 7. https://doi.org/10.3390/bs13070521

Lima, L. (2023). The commodification of job vacancies: Market practices of fee-charging employment agencies in Rio de Janeiro (1950–1975). *Sociologia & Antropologia, 13*, e210081. https://doi.org/10.1590/2238-38752022v13112

Majumder, S., & Mondal, A. (2021). Are chatbots really useful for human resource management? *International Journal of Speech Technology, 24*(4), 969–977. https://doi.org/10.1007/s10772-021-09834-y

Moin, A., Aadil, F., Ali, Z., & Kang, D. (2023, May 15). *Emotion recognition framework using multiple modalities for an effective human–computer interaction.* | EBSCOhost. https://doi.org/10.1007/s11227-022-05026-w

Mujtaba, D. F., & Mahapatra, N. R. (2025). *Fairness in AI-driven recruitment: Challenges, metrics, methods, and future directions*. arXiv:2405.19699. https://doi.org/10.48550/arXiv.2405.19699

Posthuma, R. A., Morgeson, F. P., & Campion, M. A. (2002). Beyond employment interview validity: A comprehensive narrative review of recent research and trends over time. *Personnel Psychology, 55*(1), 1–81. https://doi.org/10.1111/j.1744-6570.2002.tb00103.x

Pulivarthy, P., & Whig, P. (2025). Bias and fairness addressing discrimination in AI systems. In P. Pulivarthy, P. Whig, & P. Whig (Eds.), *Ethical dimensions of AI development* (pp. 103–126). IGI Global Scientific Publishing. https://doi.org/10.4018/979-8-3693-4147-6.ch005

Rastogi, C., Zhang, Y., Wei, D., Varshney, K. R., Dhurandhar, A., & Tomsett, R. (2022). Deciding fast and slow: The role of cognitive biases in AI-assisted decision-making. *Proceedings of the ACM on Human-Computer Interaction, 6*(CSCW1), Article 83, 1–22. https://doi.org/10.1145/3512930

Rathore, P. (Dr) S. P. S., Kaushik, P. (Dr) P., Chauhan, P. (Dr) P. S., Sharma, D. R., & Rathore, R. (2025). AI and HR 5.0: The future of recruitment. *International Journal of Environmental Sciences*, 1589–1604. https://doi.org/10.64252/wtjt1v67

Rivera, L. A. (2012). Hiring as cultural matching: The case of elite professional service firms. *American Sociological Review, 77*(6), 999–1022. https://doi.org/10.1177/0003122412463213

Romaniuk, M., Kidd, C., Banfield, M., & Batterham, P. J. (2023). Obtaining and retaining employment post military service: A qualitative analysis of challenges experienced by Australian veterans. *Journal of Employment Counseling, 60*(2), 72–88. https://doi.org/10.1002/joec.12199

Roshanaei, M. (2024). Towards best practices for mitigating artificial intelligence implicit bias in shaping diversity, inclusion and equity in higher education. *Education and Information Technologies, 29*(14), 18959–18984. https://doi.org/10.1007/s10639-024-12605-2

Rožman, M., Tominc, P., & Štrukelj, T. (2023). Competitiveness through development of strategic talent management and agile management ecosystems. *Global Journal of Flexible Systems Management, 24*(3), 373–393. https://doi.org/10.1007/s40171-023-00344-1

Salvadorinho, J., Ferreira, C., & Teixeira, L. (2024). A technology-based framework to foster the lean human resource 4.0 and prevent the great resignation: The talent management lift. *Technology in Society*, *77*, 102510. https://doi.org/10.1016/j.techsoc.2024.102510

Sapra, D. A. C. (2025). *Mastering interview skills: A comprehensive guide*. Academic Guru Publishing House.

Schofield, A., Wu, S., Bayard de Volo, T., Kuze, T., Gomez, A., & Sultana, S. (2025). "My very subjective human interpretation": Domain expert perspectives on navigating the text analysis loop for topic models. *Proceedings of ACM on Human-Computer Interact.*, *9*(1), GROUP22:1-GROUP22:30. https://doi.org/10.1145/3701201

Seppälä, P., & Małecka, M. (2024). AI and discriminative decisions in recruitment: Challenging the core assumptions. *Big Data & Society*, *11*(1), 20539517241235872. https://doi.org/10.1177/20539517241235872

Shahriari, M., Tajmir Riahi, M., Azizan, O., & Rasti-Barzoki, M. (2023). The effect of green organizational culture on organizational commitment: The mediating role of job satisfaction. *Journal of Human Behavior in the Social Environment*, *33*(2), 180–197. https://doi.org/10.1080/10911359.2022.2029789

Sisneros, K. (2025). *The impact of recruitment and selection strategies on organizational performance and employee productivity* [Doctoral Dissertations and Projects]. https://digitalcommons.liberty.edu/doctoral/6422

Soomro, R. B., Memon, S. G., Dahri, N. A., Al-Rahmi, W. M., Aldriwish, K., A. Salameh, A., Al-Adwan, A. S., & Saleem, A. (2024). The adoption of digital technologies by small and medium-sized enterprises for sustainability and value creation in Pakistan: The application of a two-staged hybrid SEM-ANN approach. *Sustainability*, *16*(17), Article 17. https://doi.org/10.3390/su16177351

Speicher, L. L., & Francis, D. (2023). Improving employee experience: Reducing burnout, decreasing turnover and building well-being. *Clinical Gastroenterology and Hepatology*, *21*(1), 11–14. https://doi.org/10.1016/j.cgh.2022.09.020

Sultana, R. (2024). *Artificial intelligence for decision making in the era of big data evolution* [SSRN Scholarly Paper No. 5056805]. Social Science Research Network. https://doi.org/10.2139/ssrn.5056805

Svahn, A. (2024). *Recruiting the new generation of computer science talent: Identifying and addressing candidate and recruiter challenges using design & AI recommendations*. KTH Royal Institute of Technology. https://urn.kb.se/resolve?urn=urn:nbn:se:kth:diva-352305

Tanantong, T., & Wongras, P. (2024). A UTAUT-based framework for analyzing users' intention to adopt artificial intelligence in human resource Recruitment: A case study of Thailand. *Systems*, *12*(1), Article 1. https://doi.org/10.3390/systems12010028

Unsal, N., Weaver, G., Bray, J. W., Bibeau, D., & Saake, G. (2021). Return on investment of workplace wellness: Evidence from a long-term care company. *Workplace Health & Safety*, *69*(2), 81–90. https://doi.org/10.1177/2165079920953052

Upadhyay, A. K., & Khandelwal, K. (2018). Applying artificial intelligence: Implications for recruitment. *Strategic HR Review*, *17*(5), 255–258. https://doi.org/10.1108/SHR-07-2018-0051

Usha, D. M. (2024). *Artificial intelligence in HR*. Archers & Elevators Publishing House.

Vistorte, A. O. R., Deroncele-Acosta, A., Ayala, J. L. M., Barrasa, A., López-Granero, C., & Martí-González, M. (2024). Integrating artificial intelligence to assess emotions in learning environments: A systematic literature review. *Frontiers in Psychology*, *15*. https://doi.org/10.3389/fpsyg.2024.1387089

Vivek, R. (2023). Enhancing diversity and reducing bias in recruitment through AI: A review of strategies and challenges. *Информатика. Экономика. Управлениеl Informatics. Economics. Management*, *2*(4), Article 4.

Wen, D., Yan, D., & Sun, X. (2022). Employee satisfaction, employee engagement and turnover intention: The moderating role of position level. *Human Systems Management*, *41*(3), 407–422. https://doi.org/10.3233/HSM-211505

Chapter 4

From Burnout to Balance: Cultivating Joy with Blockchain in High-performance Environments

Ashish Saxena[a], *Sudhanshu Singh*[a], *Neerav Verma*[a] *and Shubhi Rathi*[b]

[a]*School of Business, Galgotias University, Greater Noida, India*
[b]*Manipal Academy of Higher Education (MAHE), Dubai*

Abstract

The quick proliferation of globalisation and digital technologies has changed the modern workplace to be a continuously connected environment, which often blurs the boundary between work and personal life. Consequently, employees, especially those in technology-related roles, are increasingly exposed to stress, emotional exhaustion, and burnout. Such problems endanger not only the individuals' well-being but also the organisations' productivity, innovation culture, and employee retention. In response to these issues, we introduce a blockchain-powered employee well-being framework aimed at creating emotionally supportive and psychologically safe workplaces. The framework revolves around four fundamental pillars – value creation, interoperability, connectivity, and security and privacy (VICS) – and is enhanced through smart contracts and tokenisation. The smart contracts in the system guarantee the equitable and automatic distribution of wellness benefits, and tokenisation serves as a means of motivating positive health-related behaviours and ongoing employee engagement. One of the most important elements of the framework is that employees are allowed to own and have the authority over their personal wellness information. They can thus participate in a manner that preserves their privacy and is in line with data protection standards. The proposed framework is a departure from typical health programmes towards a transparent, trust-based, and technology-enabled ecosystem that not only makes the organisation more resilient but also helps

Nurturing AI-Powered HR Analytics and Virtual Reality in Employee Psychology and Workplace Happiness, Part A, 57–72

doi:10.1108/978-1-80686-125-520261004

to maintain the psychological and emotional well-being of the employees in the long run.

Keywords: Blockchain framework; employee well-being; workplace culture; smart contracts; tokenisation; emotional intelligence; burnout; artificial intelligence; workplace happiness; digital transformation

4.1. Introduction

In modern times, more and more employees face elevated states of stress, anxiety, and exhaustion than at any time during the past decade. The advent of the so-called digital age has substantially altered the workplace situation (Zuboff, 2019) by blurring the distinction between labour and leisure for many individuals. The so-called "always-on" culture, which emphasises consistent coding and hampers mental and physical recovery, adversely affects person's health and occupational happiness.

According to the World Health Organization (WHO, 2019), burnout is now officially recognised as an occupational phenomenon. The risks of being in a state of burnout are rising at unprecedentedly rate sweeping across different sectors. According to recent research, approximately 76% of employees (WHO, 2019) are affected by burnout at least some of the time. The three elements that highlight the state of burnout are emotional exhaustion, reduced professional efficacy, and the development of cynicism towards one's work (Gallup, 2022; Maslach & Jackson, 1981).

In view of the frequently intensifying stress in the workplace, many organisations find it challenging to attain the levels of engagement and motivation that ensure sustainable performance. Although the significance of work–life balance is recognised across the globe, the values associated with it have progressively become harder to achieve, given that overall job satisfaction, in general, has declined. This diminished manifestation leads to the higher frequency of employee dissatisfaction, feeling undervalues, and reduced feelings of engagements towards the working environment.

The core concept of the centrality of joy and fulfilment at work is increasingly being over-shadowed by growing anxiety. Situations of burnout may display visible and underlying causes that may vary significantly among employees. Traditional management interventions such as awareness programmes or flexible working hours tend to fail in addressing the deeper structural causes of distress (Maslach & Leiter, 2016). These short-term approaches focus on surface-level adjustments, rather than fundamental change. Key issues such as workload, lack of autonomy, and inequitable reward systems are still largely unresolved, continuing to erode well-being and organisational morale.

Organisations need to take proactive and disciplined steps to make real and purposeful changes. Individuals across organisational levels should work together using embedded data to plan their interventions. Their plans should be fair, clear, and act before problems show up (Tetrick & Winslow, 2015) and become difficult to handle. These plans cannot just be for branding for the outside world. They should cultivate a sense of feeling wanted and engaged for mutual benefits and organisational growth. Companies need to find out what is really causing depression and make sure their strategies include careful planning to help their employees' mental health and well-being for a long time.

Parker and Jorritsma (2020) and Edmondson (1999) have shown the importance of workers to feel safe and appreciated. Creating a secure environment for employees has the benefit of allowing them to talk openly and constructively without fear of punishment. Affording the same opportunity for meaningful and significant work is just as vital as creating a secure, productive work environment towards individual growth and organisational performance.

4.2. Literature Review

4.2.1. The Nature and Theories of Burnout

The concept of burnout was first introduced by psychologist Herbert Freudenberger in the 1970s. Observing volunteers at a free clinic, Freudenberger (1974) described burnout as a state of chronic stress leading to physical and emotional exhaustion, laying the groundwork for future research. The best indicators of burnout were imbalances between the professional and personal domains and deficiencies in social support (Stanley & Sebastine, 2023).

During the 1980s, Christina Maslach advanced the field with the Maslach Burnout Inventory (MBI), having dimensions as emotional exhaustion, depersonalisation, and reduced personal accomplishment (Maslach & Jackson, 1981). The MBI became a standardised tool, with it usage in the burnout research spreading to various professions.

The workplace continues to evolve and adapt to continually changing workforce demographics with more technological literates entering into the system than ever before. Burnout is more likely to occur in a variety of industries due to the complexity and speed of modern work life, especially in high-performance, technology-driven settings. Today's digital economies, where quick project cycles and ongoing adaptation have become the new standard, reflect these fundamental pressures of managing everyday expectations. Stress is a result of many factors covering personal, family, and organisational spaces. Stress is rarely an individual phenomenon but rather the result of structural flaws in interpersonal support systems and organisational culture (Stanley & Sebastine, 2023). Similar to technology professionals, social workers labour in emotionally taxing environments that are marked by long hours, unclear roles, and a lack of acknowledgement.

Burnout is characterised by depersonalisation (Maslach et al., 2001), implying a decreased sense of personal accomplishment, and emotional tiredness. These characteristics are now more noticeable in modern digital workplaces that in many cases provide little opportunities for planned rest and emotional recharging during the long work-hours. This further gets compounded by continuous connectivity and performance-driven cultures. Technology-intensive organisations have lot to gain from the research and body of knowledge accumulated in other environments and may provide experiential guidance to lessen the impacts.

Therefore, burnout might be reframed as an organisational sickness that results from systems prioritising efficiency above empathy – a failure of institutional design. Social workers who felt more social support (Stanley & Sebastine, 2023) from their families, coworkers, or superiors have much lower levels of burnout. This result is in line with past studies that demonstrate the critical moderating role of social support in occupational stress (Christian et al., 2011; Koeske & Koeske, 1989).

Beyond resource dynamics, we find that social and psychological factors are also critical. We discover that social and psychological aspects are equally important, in addition to resource dynamics. The concept of social exchange emphasises how crucial wholesome relationships are as the cornerstone of sustained dedication. Employees frequently grow sceptical and disengaged when they see injustice (Cropanzano & Wright, 2001). Convergence points of independence, skills, and connection are necessary for intrinsic motivation, according to the Self-Determination theory (Deci & Ryan, 2000; Meyer & Gagné, 2008). All these ideas emphasise the need for systemic explanations that can detect distress early, distribute assets equitably, and promote casual interaction – objectives that blockchain can potentially accomplish (Tapscott & Tapscott, 2016).

Understanding what causes burnout can be better explained by several key theories. The Job Demands–Resources (JD-R) model explains that burnout occurs when job demands are high and employees' resources repeatedly fall short of meeting these demands (Bakker & Demerouti, 2007; Demerouti et al., 2001). The Conservation of Resources (COR) theory further explains that stress is a reaction to the threat or actual loss of resources (Hobfoll, 2001).

4.2.2. Social and Emotional Intelligence at Workplace

Employees can share responsibilities, ask for assistance, and use group coping mechanisms in supportive social environments. On the other hand, the lack of these networks promotes emotional exhaustion and estrangement. We continue to observe and experience workplace settings within the technology-driven industries as frequently mediated by digital platforms. The skewed emphasis on task performance vis-à-vis the people managing them restricts the development of meaningful and real workplace connections. This results in a paradox wherein while technology boosts outputs, it also frequently weakens the social cohesion among participants as needed for psychological well-being.

In a bibliometric analysis on teacher burnout for the period 1970–2024, it is highlighted that little work demonstrates themes related to emotional intelligence (EI) and conflict in work-family environments (Yao & Abdullah, 2025). Individuals that have higher EI are constantly demonstrate both reduced risk taking and safe decision-making behaviours (Samu et al., 2025). EI is based upon competency and can be learned and observed. The competencies cover 'self-awareness, self-management, social awareness, and relationship management' (Goleman & Boyatzis, 2017). The concept of Social intelligence reflects the ability of a person to understand others with actions in social situations driven by wisdom (Walker & Foley, 1973). Resilience is a behavioural process that is activated through patterns of emotional and social intelligence (Liu & Boyatzis, 2021). In addition to linkage with workplace performance and recovery from stress, EI is also linked to self-regulation of daily behaviours (Kokubun et al., 2025). EI and psychological capital help employees manage emotions and relationships at work that aid in improvement of attitudes, behaviours, as well as outcomes (Tjimuku et al., 2025). Employees with higher EI are more aware of their own and others' emotions. They can manage these emotions more effectively, which helps them conserve their psychological energy and cope with stress more easily (Chen et al., 2024).

Preserving work–life balance is essential to lowering occupational burnout (Stanley & Sebastine, 2023). Significantly reduced levels of burnout were shown by respondents who reported higher work–personal life enhancement, or a belief that work enhanced personal growth. These results support the findings (Greenhaus et al., 2003), who discovered that enhanced job satisfaction and life quality result from balanced engagement in the professional and personal spheres. However, these lines are blurred in many contemporary settings due to continuous digital contact. Workers are 'at work' and 'at home' at the same time, which causes what Frone (2003) called 'work–family conflict', in which conflicting roles cause emotional stress. According to a research, burnout and family-to-work interference (PLIW) had a positive correlation (Stanley & Sebastine, 2023), indicating that emotional exhaustion is exacerbated by domain imbalance.

While adoption of digital technologies has contributed to increased burnout across organisation, they also offer opportunities for its reduction. In the subsequent section, we propose the use of blockchain technology to pause the progression and possibly reverse the journey to burnout and achieving balance in work and life.

4.2.3. Blockchain Technology and Its Administrative Applications

Management processes can be revolutionised by the use of foolproof measures provided by the blockchain technology (Nakamoto, 2008) wherein confidence in organisational systems and processes is established using its distributed, unchangeable register. There is an inbuilt digital tokenisation (verifiable assets that reflect value or recognition), intelligent agreements (autonomous accomplishment programs for independent rule automation), and zero-knowledge proofs (privacy-preserving verification procedures) (Mishra & Bhaskar, 2021; Sharples & Domingue, 2016). Transparency and impartiality in acknowledging any contribution made are ensured via creation of smart agreements, which automate encouragement distribution and contented assessment (Koul et al., 2022).

There are significant psychological ramifications to this change. According to studies, perceived autonomy and fairness are crucial protective factors against burnout (Ben-Porat & Itzhaky, 2015). Smart contracts based on behavioural analytics could, for instance, automatically allocate wellness resources, monitor workload equity, or even signal a break period. Aligned with the concept of psychological capital (PsyCap), which is a composite (Luthans et al., 2007) of self-efficacy, hope, optimism, and resilience, employing this method not only reduces management bias but also empowers individuals. Research shows that PsyCap significantly enhances employees' capacity to cope and perform under pressure (Luthans & Youssef-Morgan, 2017). These psychological constructs, when integrated into a blockchain model, have the potential to not only promote resilience and well-being but also make them quantifiable and thus, self-reinforcing, thereby broadening the domain of healthy organisational behaviour into digital architecture.

Blockchain technology can be positioned as a tool for restoring community and organisational trust by incorporating findings from this body of studies. Its distributed ledger makes it possible to record contributions and interactions in a transparent, rule-based manner, guaranteeing fairness and acknowledgement free from prejudice or partiality. In such a blockchain-based ecosystem, peer-to-peer recognition tokens are automatically issued for collaborative behaviours or acts of empathy, operationalising Stanley and Sebastine's (2023) findings on the protective effect of social support. With this method, social support – a concept that has hitherto been intangible – becomes a quantifiable and rewarding organisational consequence.

Blockchain successfully converts the culture of care into a verifiable, auditable procedure by encoding gratitude and equity into immutable smart contracts. Through intelligent agreement management, blockchain promises traceability and lowers mistakes in the blood supply chain (Singh et al., 2023). Tapscott and Tapscott (2016) discuss how open processes and fair resource distribution can be made possible by promoting trust through decentralisation. Hassan and De Filippi (2021) investigate how decentralised autonomous organisations (DAOs) can improve employee agency, which could lead to a greater equilibrium between work and life and happier employees. These results imply that by reassuring openness, even-handedness, and being empowered, cryptocurrency can address structural difficulties that lead to burnout and an unbalanced work–life schedule. These tools facilitate enterprises to develop comprehensive wellness systems rather than relying just on blockchain for administrative determinations, such identification authentication. Building on the concepts discussed, this chapter introduces a novel blockchain-based framework designed to mitigate exhaustion and promote employee well-being.

4.3. Methodology

This chapter unfolds an innovative blockchain system that aims to lessen the weariness and elevate the health condition of the user, following the ideas presented in the previous chapters. The framework combines the COR theory and the JD-R model, showing that it is very important to keep the demand–resource balance. In this system, that is, smart contracts are the mechanisms that keep the supply of resources going in a fair way, guaranteeing that the applications will not overconsume the given resources. Tokenisation is then used to recognise and reward positive actions, in line with the ERI Model's stress on fair incentives. SDT emphasises relatedness and autonomy, which are reinforced by the DAO model that makes participatory governance possible. Through the amalgamation of these ideas, the framework delivers a thorough resolution to the systemic problems that motivate the relationship between exertion and life and burnout.

Our framework is designed to help organisations support employees in moving away from burnout and towards achieving work–life balance while fostering joy at work. This framework rests on four pillars as value creation (V), interoperability (I), connectivity (C), and security and privacy (S). The VICS blockchain framework has these four pillars as environmental factors that are needed for effective operations. These are briefly explained as below.

(A) *Value creation (V):* It is a result of and also guides the development of the three pillars mentioned above to create tangible and intangible benefits for its participants.
(B) *Interoperability (I):* It is the ability of a system to integrate and operate with internal and external systems and processes.
(C) *Connectivity (C):* It is the ability of a system to connect its various components and users within and across organisational boundaries.
(D) *Security and privacy (S):* It is a fundamental requirement for users to trust the system and having control of their own data.

To work with the above fundamental pillars, a layered approach (Fig. 4.1) is proposed that has bidirectional logic over a blockchain architecture and spread across the layers. The working of each of these layers is described in the following paragraphs. The words user and employee may be used interchangeable as per situation context. The framework utilises concentric layers that consist of *identity layer, validation layer, engagement layer, and outcome layer.*

4.3.1. Identity Layer

The technical architecture of operating the VICS Blockchain framework and its interconnections across the various layers is shown in Fig. 4.2. This layer *manages*

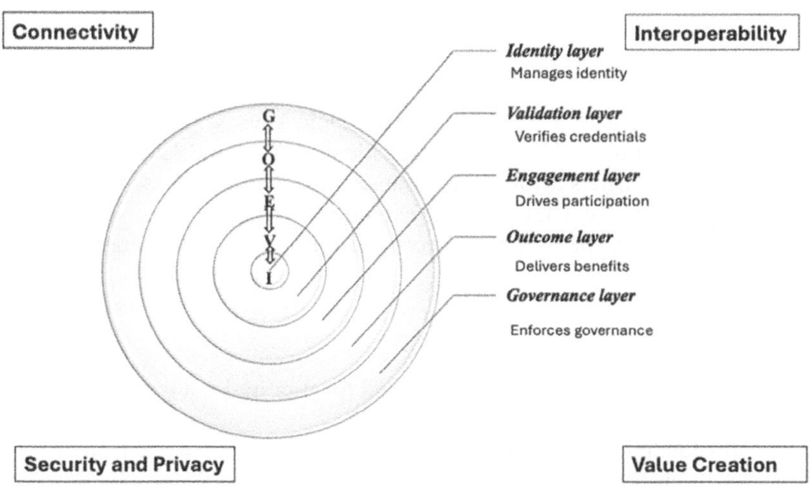

Fig. 4.1. The VICS Blockchain Framework. *Source:* Authors' view.

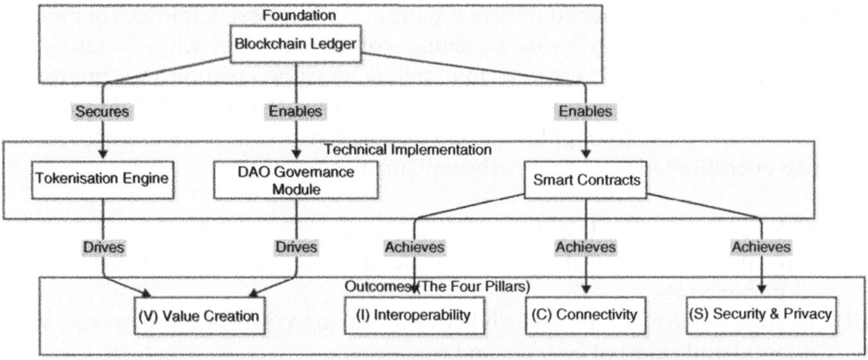

Fig. 4.2. The Technical Architecture of VICS Operating Framework. This layer is concerned with creating a permanent, user-controlled block or an anchor for the blockchain. *Source*: Authors' view.

identity transactions using institutional infrastructure and processes thereby giving employee's ownership over their profiles that is distinct from their institutional identity. A permanent, secure, and digital identity is created in this layer. Here, the blockchain ledger enables the tokenisation engine, DAO governance module, and the smart contracts.

While the *value creation* pillar is driven by the tokenisation engine and DAO governance module, the other three pillars of *interoperability, connectivity,* and *security and privacy* are driven by smart contracts. Overall, these come in a hierarchy of Foundation, Technical Implementation, and Outcomes.

It is also the *first step* wherein an employee is provided with a unique, secure, and own digital space in the enterprise system with full control of personal data.

Input:

- An employee decides to join and registers in the system.

Process:

- The system generates a pair of cryptographic keys: a private key used for authorisation, and a public key towards identification and rewards.
- The system constructs a formal transaction of creating an identity using the public key in the blockchain's public ledger.
- This transaction is permanently recorded onto the blockchain's distributed ledger.

Output:

- A decentralised identifier (DID) is created for user and is a permanent address within the system.
- The DID facilitates autonomy of user and demarcates work from personal space and well-being.

4.3.2. Validation Layer

A valuable work is also a work that is seen to reduce friction between individuals and functions and often seen to go unnoticed. The purpose of this layer is to create an official record of work that is generally or formally not noticed. Here, any valuable work that is being performed is identified and recorded in the system irrespective of whether it was formal or informal. This layer creates and signs a digital *certificate of achievement* that is linked to DID so as to make the invisible labour visible and reduce instances of burnout.

Input:

- A specific task or action performed by an employee (e.g., 'mentoring a new colleague or assisting in reducing a colleague's workload').
- Your digital address (DID) as well as the DID of the person(s) confirming the action with location and timestamps.

Process:

- The system creates a digital *certificate of achievement* that documents the actions performed and its value to individual or institution.
- This certificate is digitally signed for approval by the relevant person (e.g., person or colleague one has supported or mentored).
- Thereafter, a request to *validate action* taken is sent to the public ledger along with a linking of the signed certificate to a person's DID.

Output:

- A *validated credential record* is permanently stored as a public record proving that a user has performed a *specific* and *valuable* action.
- By this process, any previously invisible labour becomes visible making employee feel *acknowledged* and *appreciated.*
- As and when such records get updated and publicly available, the feeling of appreciation can aid in reversing the feeling of burnout that comes from feeling unappreciated.

4.3.3, Engagement Layer

This layer drives participation by acting as the system's proactive logic engine to interpret and decide information received from the *validation layer*. Smart contract *monitors ledger* and *assign rewards* based on a rulebook. It is designed to encourage the behaviours that promote better well-being and prevent burnout. This it does by creation of trusted links based on if-then logic between positive actions performed and positive consequences thereby creating motivation in users for investing in personal wellness. It aims to motivate wellness and professional growth. The emphasis is not on the total monetary value of each reward but on the *accumulation* of rewards and reward points as *acknowledgement* to contributions being made. The payment systems could be for range of reward points with *cutoff levels* for each type.

Input:

- The *validated credential record* from the *validation layer* on the blockchain.

Process:

- The system contains an automated program that is also a smart contract to constantly monitor the ledger for new validated credential records as and when they get added.
- When a new record appears, the smart contract checks it against a predefined set of rules as given in the connected rulebook. These rewards could be across diverse categories such as the following.
  - Proactively participating in a wellness session leads to a *proactive wellness* record.
  - Completing a professional growth course leads to *Growth* record.
  - Recognising and promoting a peer leads to *Kudos* record.
  - Each team member visibly acknowledged for some project leads to *Team Promotion* reward.

Output:

- The employee records are updated by an authorised reward transaction under the applicable categories with reward points and reward values.
- Each of these rewards are automated and pre-approved. It removes any uncertainty for the employee, regarding rewards being manually finalised delivered.

4.3.4. Outcome Layer

The purpose of this layer is to provide a fair and transparent distribution of value by closing the loop between an employee's contribution and their reward that is immediate, unbiased, and trustworthy. It builds *trust* through *transparent reward* delivery and only executes the commands it receives from the *engagement layer* with no decision-making power on its own. By the automated delivery of benefits, it provides tangible resource gains to offset any resource or time losses associated with stresses related to work.

Input:

- This layer generates an *authorised reward order* into the smart contract that was previously created. This contains a ready-to-execute command that issues a specific reward to a particular employee for certain category.
- This layer investigates the digitally signatures that specifies the recipient's unique address (DID) and *crosschecks* key parameters as per requirements.
- It also takes into the specific category and associated amount of the digital asset to be delivered in form of *tokens* that can be *encashed* as per certain conversion factors.

Process:

- The *outcome layer*'s smart contract first verifies the digital signature on the incoming order to ensure that it is authentic and was sent exclusively by the official *engagement layer* contract to prevent any fraudulent payouts.
- Once the signature is verified, the contract executes an internal command to allocate specified number of new tokens to the concerned employee.
- The tokens that are allocated are permanently recorded and added to the ledger showing employee's token quantity.

Output:

- The digital wallet of an employee now possesses a verified quantity of reward tokens that can be encashed as per specific provisions.

4.3.5 Governance Layer

The purpose of this layer is to layer employee's community to *collectively* design and manage the rules of the institutional wellness system to ensure that it is participatory and fair to all.

Input:

- Employees and their digital assets as reflected in the quantity of reward tokens they possess.
- A formal request through an online platform to add or modify any rules in the *engagement layer* with justification for the same.

Process:

- Initiating an online and a formal voting process after the online submitted proposal is accepted as valid and recorded on the blockchain.
- Employees cast their votes with the aid of their digital key.
- Each vote is counted and weighted by the DAO with importance given to token balance available with each of the voter.
- At the end of the voting period, the DAO contract impartially tallies all the vote transactions directly from the ledger leading to either accept or reject the proposal.

Output:

- The system rules get updated whenever there is an overall vote for change. This change to systems operational logic is automatically enforced by the blockchain itself.
- The decisions made in the *governance layer* have a direct influence on the *engagement layer* ensuring that the system evolves in a participatory way.

4.4. Some Blockchain Applications for Employee Well-being

The framework can be applied in several ways:

- *Workload management:* Smart contracts analyse real-time data to distribute tasks fairly, preventing overload and burnout.
- *Recognition and rewards:* Tokenisation incentivises behaviours like peer support or mindfulness, fostering joy and motivation.
- *Mental health support:* Blockchain secures sensitive data, enabling confidential access to support services.
- *Participatory governance:* The DAO model empowers employees to shape workplace policies, enhancing agency and work-life balance

4.5. Discussion

The application concepts and technologies of blockchain are positively influencing different domains. The application of blockchain in these two domains, which are human resources and wellness, indicates a substantial shift from the previous administrative models that were based on the discretionary trust towards the new systems that, by their very nature, integrate the concept of fairness (Tapscott & Tapscott, 2016).

We want our structure to be the one that changes the way organisations work by changing the fuzzy concept of 'trust' to one of 'accountability' that can be verified. At the core of these concepts, there is a decentralised ledger system which guarantees the continuous flow of resources and acknowledges the contributions through the transparent, automated by the rules, documented and rewarded process. The use of blockchain creates an unalterable record of who and type of assistance provided, burdens imposed or reduced, and acknowledgements received for contributions made. It also gives employees more control over their data and workplace regulations (Self-Determination and Psychological Safety) (Bakker & Demerouti, 2007; Cropanzano & Wright, 2001; Deci & Ryan, 2010; Edmondson, 1999; Hobfoll, 2001).

These structural insights (Stanley & Sebastine, 2023) directly affect organisational governance in addition to individual well-being. According to their research, social and institutional factors like supervisory support and role expectations clearly have a major impact on burnout, but demographic ones like age and marital status had no discernible effect. Emotional health is related to emotional attachments to the process as well as outcomes of work performed. Although trauma is less obvious in the technology industry, workers are negatively affected by a cognitive compassion fatigue that is marked by emotional numbness and cerebral strain that result from routine demands of customer and teamwork dynamics. This significance of managing compassion is also supported by research in the fields of social work. Secondary traumatic stress–emotional weariness brought on by sympathetic engagement is often seen to coexist with burnout (Stamm, 2002). As countermeasures to such issues, mentorship, supervision, and fostering of self-care are suggested (Stanley & Sebastine, 2023). Blockchain has potential to convert these contributions into measurable reward tokens by use of automated procedures. For instance, when worker are observed to engage in some wellness-related activities, they could earn self-care tokens that can later be converted into learning credits or vacation days. Thus, instead of being into reactive crisis management, these smart contracts-based incentives encourage proactive participation of workforce. Getting rewarded for the purpose of well-being is an idea that is similar to Fletcher and Sarkar's (2013) contention that resilience is based on flexibility and purpose. This implies that there exists a need for systemic reform that focused not just on individual coping but should also be the focus of therapies.

By decentralising decision-making, governance models using blockchain can guarantee that wellness protocols are developed through consensus rather than imposed from the top down. The collaborative supervision frameworks promoted (Kapoulitsas & Corcoran, 2015), where empowerment and shared accountability boost resilience and morale, are similar to this participatory paradigm. Furthermore, the architecture promotes a culture of continuous communication and accessibility while democratising policy-making (Hassan & De Filippi, 2021). Employees should be provided with a technology-driven platform through which they can independently and actively participate in the creation of rules and policies that regulate them. This is anticipated to increase the sense of belonging. Our framework integrates equity as a fundamental aspect of the organisational structure, thus going beyond the aspects of efficiency and safety to establish a corporate culture of a mutually supportive nature between productivity and well-being.

4.6. Conclusion

Irrespective of whether being an individual contributor or part of some group, employees seek to manage their time and energy in an optimum manner. Any contribution of theirs, no matter how small, seeks to remove any disparity among them with regard to trust and fairness. The similarities between technological companies and the social work profession show that, despite their different contexts, burnout is a result of everyone's yearning for justice, balance, and belonging.

We propose a structured solution to these disparities through the VICS blockchain paradigm, based on value creation, interoperability, connectivity, and security and privacy. The 'value creation' pillar aims at promoting psychological fulfilment (Ben-Porat & Itzhaky, 2015) through provision of tokenised rewards for non-monetary accomplishments including teamwork and mentorship. By integration and 'interoperability' of wellness platforms with human resource systems, there is an automatics transfer of well-being data bypassing any administrative bottlenecks thereby promoting organisational coherence (Allen et al., 2000). The idea of social connections constituting the foundation of well-being is reflected in 'connectivity' (Christian et al., 2011). Last but not least, the aspects of 'security and privacy' address the moral requirements of data protection. As all participating people maintain control over their personal wellness information, this removes the mistrust that discourages their involvement in mental health programmes (Stamm, 2002).

Using this novel and practical blockchain-based framework that is focused towards employee engagement, organisations can improve their employee experience. Instead of accepting burnout as an unavoidable outcome of high-pressure workplaces, they can use data-driven systems to anticipate fatigue, balance workloads, and make recognition transparent and verifiable. Groups enabled through blockchain can continue to be a supportive ecosystem that openly shares mindfulness growth, health milestones, or peer recognition in a safe way. Even more, this novel approach paves the way for a shift from short-term wellness programmes to a proactive, technology-driven model which has a positive effect on both productivity and well-being. The innovative framework exemplified here is one of the ways digital technologies and organisational theories can be combined to redesign organisations so that they become joyful and high performing without being at odds with individual productivity: in fact, they can be used to enhance it.

Overall, it provides the theoretical and empirical foundations needed for a profound reconsideration of workplace well-being by means of blockchain. Among the features that the VICS blockchain framework is expected to deliver are: trust that can be verified, decentralised care, and fair compensation. Hence, it is a shift of paradigm from very different kinds of well-being activities to transparent, self-sustaining, and inclusive mental wellness ecosystems, thus, achieving the goal of transforming burnout into a state of balance and generating happiness in high-performing environments. Additionally, this framework is also committed to the institutionalisation of social and EI as a means of safeguarding privacy during the journey towards better well-being.

References

Allen, T., Herst, D. E., Bruck, C. S., & Sutton, M. (2000). Consequences associated with work-to-family conflict: A review and agenda for future research. *Journal of Occupational Health Psychology*, *5*(2), 278–308. https://doi.org/10.1037/1076-8998.5.2.278

Bakker, A. B., & Demerouti, E. (2007). The job demands-resources model: State of the art. *Journal of Managerial Psychology*, *22*(3), 309–328.

Ben-Porat, A., & Itzhaky, H. (2015). Burnout among trauma social workers: The contribution of personal and environmental resources. *Journal of Social Work*, *15*(6), 606–620. https://doi.org/10.1177/1468017314552158

Chen, Y.-C., Huang, Z.-L., & Chu, H.-C. (2024). Relationships between emotional labor, job burnout, and emotional intelligence: An analysis combining meta-analysis and structural equation modeling. *BMC Psychology*, *12*(672). https://doi.org/10.1186/s40359-024-02167-w

Christian, M. S., Garza, A. S., & Slaughter, J. E. (2011). Work engagement: A quantitative review and test of its relations with task and contextual performance. *Personnel Psychology*, *64*(1), 89–136.

Cropanzano, R., & Wright, T. A. (2001). When a "happy" worker is really a "productive" worker: A review and further refinement of the happy–productive worker thesis. *Consulting Psychology Journal: Practice and Research*, *53*(3), 182–199.

Deci, E. L., & Ryan, R. M. (2000). The "what" and "why" of goal pursuits: Human needs and the self-determination of behavior. *Psychological Inquiry*, *11*(4), 227–268.

Demerouti, E., Bakker, A. B., Nachreiner, F., & Schaufeli, W. B. (2001). The job demands-resources model of burnout. *Journal of Applied Psychology*, *86*(3), 499–512.

Edmondson, A. C. (1999). Psychological safety and learning behavior in work teams. *Administrative Science Quarterly*, *44*(2), 350–383.

Fletcher, D., & Sarkar, M. (2013). Psychological resilience: A review and critique of definitions, concepts, and theory. *European Psychologist*, *18*(1), 12–23. https://doi.org/10.1027/1016-9040/a000124

Freudenberger, H. J. (1974). Staff burnout. *Journal of Social Issues*, *30*(1), 159–165.

Frone, M. R. (2003). Work-Family balance. *Handbook of Occupational Health Psychology*, First Edition, 143–162

Gallup. (2022). *State of the global workplace: 2022 report*. Gallup, Inc. https://www.gallup.com/workplace/349484/state-of-the-global-workplace-2022-report.aspx

Goleman, D., & Boyatzis, R. E. (2017). Emotional intelligence has 12 elements. Which do you need to work on? *Harvard Business Review*. https://hbr.org/2017/02/emotional-intelligence-has-12-elements

Greenhaus, J. H., Collins, K. M., & Shaw, J. D. (2003). The relation between work-family balance and quality of life. *Journal of Vocational Behaviour*, *63*(3), 510–531. https://doi.org/10.1016/S0001-8791(02)00042-8

Hassan, S., & De Filippi, P. (2021). Decentralized autonomous organization (DAO): Challenges and opportunities in the new governance paradigm. *Journal of Institutional Economics*, *17*(2), 1–15.

Hobfoll, S. E. (2001). The influence of culture, community, and the nested-self in the stress process: Advancing conservation of resources theory. *Applied Psychology*, *50*(3), 337–421.

Kapoulitsas, M., & Corcoran, T. (2015). Compassion fatigue and resilience: A qualitative analysis of social work practice. *Qualitative Social Work*, *14*(1), 86–101. https://doi.org/10.1177/1473325014528526

Koeske, G. F., & Koeske, R. D. (1989). Workload and burnout: Can social support and perceived accomplishment help? *Social Work*, *34*(3), 243–248.

Kokubun, K., Nemoto, K., & Yamakawa, Y. (2025). Cultural and emotional intelligence correlates with healthy lifestyles. *Acta Psychologica*, *255*, 104854. https://doi.org/10.1016/j.actpsy.2025.104854

Koul, S., Singh, S., & Verma, R. (2022). Decentralised content creation in digital learning: A blockchain concept. In T. Suring et al. (Eds.), *ICT with intelligent applications* (pp. 583–591). Springer.

Liu, H., & Boyatzis, R. E. (2021). Focusing on resilience and renewal from stress: The role of emotional and social intelligence competencies. *Frontiers in Psychology*, *12*, 685829. https://doi.org/10.3389/fpsyg.2021.685829

Luthans, F., Avolio, B. J., Avey, J. B., & Norman, S. M. (2007). Positive psychological capital: Measurement and relationship with performance and satisfaction. *Pers. Psychol. 60*, 541–72.

Luthans, F., & Youssef-Morgan, C. (2017). Psychological capital: An evidence-based positive approach. *Annual Review of Organisational Psychology and Organisational Behaviour*, *4*(1), 339–366.

Maslach, C., & Jackson, S. E. (1981). The measurement of experienced burnout. *Journal of Occupational Behaviour*, *2*(2), 99–113.

Maslach, C., & Leiter, M. P. (2016). Understanding the burnout experience: Recent research and its implications for psychiatry. *World Psychiatry*, *15*(2), 103–111.

Maslach, C., Schaufeli, W. B., & Leiter, M. P. (2001). Job burnout. *Annual Review of Psychology*, *52*(1), 397–422.

Meyer, J. P., & Gagné, M. (2008). Employee engagement from a self-determination theory perspective. *Industrial and Organizational Psychology*, *1*(1), 60–62.

Mishra, H., & Bhaskar, A. U. (2021). Blockchain in human resource management: A comprehensive review. *International Journal of Information Management Data Insights, 1*(2), 100017.

Nakamoto, S. (2008). *Bitcoin: A peer-to-peer electronic cash system* [White paper]. https://bitcoin.org/bitcoin.pdf

Parker, S. K., & Jorritsma, K. (2020). Good work design for all: Multiple pathways to making a difference. *European Journal of Work and Organizational Psychology, 29*(5), 656–676.

Samu, J., Yang, C., & Winter, S. R. (2025). Assessing the role of emotional intelligence in risk behavior across safety-critical environments: A systematic review. *Transportation Research Interdisciplinary Perspectives, 33*, 101627. https://doi.org/10.1016/j.trip.2025.101627

Stamm, B. H. (2002). Measuring compassion satisfaction as well as fatigue: Developmental history of the Compassion Satisfaction and Fatigue Test. In C. R. Figley (Ed.), *Treating compassion fatigue* (pp. 107–119). Brunner-Routledge.

Stanley, S., & Sebastine, A. J. (2023). Work-life balance, social support, and burnout: A quantitative study of social workers. *Journal of Social Work, 23*(6), 1135–1155. https://doi.org/10.1177/14680173231197930

Tapscott, D., & Tapscott, A. (2016). *Blockchain revolution: How the technology behind Bitcoin is changing money, business, and the world*. Penguin.

Tetrick, L. E., & Winslow, C. J. (2015). Workplace stress management interventions and health promotion. *Annual Review of Organizational Psychology and Organizational Behavior, 2*, 583–603.

Tjimuku, M., Atiku, S. O., & Kaisara, G. (2025). Emotional intelligence and psychological capital at work: A systematic literature review and directions for future research. *Cogent Social Sciences, 11*(1), 2443559. https://doi.org/10.1080/23311886.2024.2443559

Walker, R. E., & Foley, J. M. (1973). Social intelligence: Its history and measurement. *Psychological Reports, 33*(3), 839–864. https://doi.org/10.2466/pr0.1973.33.3.839 (Original work published 1973)

World Health Organization (WHO). (2019, May 28). *Burn-out an "occupational phenomenon": International classification of diseases*. https://www.who.int/news/item/28-05-2019-burn-out-an-occupational-phenomenon-international-classification-of-diseases

Yao, J., & Abdullah, M. N. L. Y. (2025). Five decades of teacher burnout research (1970–2024): A comprehensive bibliometric analysis. *Acta Psychologica, 259*, 105318.

Zuboff, S. (2019). *The age of surveillance capitalism*. PublicAffairs.

Chapter 5

Employees' Well-being and Mental Health Using AI: A Network Analysis of Global Literature

Namita Rath[a], *Vishal Sood*[a], *Alok Kumar Sahai*[a], *Swati Sood*[b] *and Nilamadhab Kar*[c,d]

[a]*Sri Sri University, Cuttack, India*
[b]*Pacific University, Udaipur, India*
[c]*Black Country Healthcare NHS Foundation Trust, Wolverhampton, UK*
[d]*University of Wolverhampton, Wolverhampton, UK*

Abstract

Considering the growing complexity and instability of the working environment, it is inevitable that the organisational landscape will undergo rapid change. No company or employee can escape the swift pace of change, a harsh reality that cannot be ignored. It is becoming increasingly vital to focus on the well-being and mental health of employees to ensure the success of an organisation in the current situation, which involves integrating machines and humans into the workforce. The term 'employee wellness' encompasses a broader range of aspects, including the quality of work life, job satisfaction, and the mental and emotional health of workers. To fully understand the significance of mental health and well-being in CSR activities and human resource management (HRM) initiatives, this comprehension is essential. A bibliometric analysis is performed in this study using the R package. The purpose of this analysis is to examine the contributions made by researchers and to establish connections between authors, sources, keywords, and nations. This study analyses 358 scholarly

Nurturing AI-Powered HR Analytics and Virtual Reality in Employee Psychology and Workplace Happiness, Part A, 73–94

Published under exclusive licence by Emerald Publishing Limited
doi:10.1108/978-1-80686-125-520261010

research articles published on the PUBMED website between 2015 and 2025. According to the findings, there has been very limited research conducted on the topic of how artificial intelligence (AI) impacts the mental health and well-being of workers.

Keywords: Well-being; mental health; artificial intelligence; bibliometric analysis; employees; R package

5.1. Introduction

Digital transformation, gig economy, remote work, and AI have transformed workplaces in recent decades, leading to employee well-being and mental health that have been organisational priorities throughout these transformations (Danna & Griffin, 1999; Schaufeli, 2017). Human capital's mental resilience may make or break enterprises as they need to cope with technology integration and worker adaptability (Cooper & Cartwright, 1994; Dewe & Kompier, 2008). Psychological, emotional, and occupational worker well-being has gone from a human resource (HR) concern to a crucial component of firm sustainability and productivity. AI in the workplace makes this focus more vital. AI not only increases efficiency and output, but it also causes employment instability, less human engagement, and system adaptability (Cascio & Montealegre, 2016; Makridakis, 2017). These changes cause employee stress, weariness, and cognitive overload (Brynjolfsson & McAfee, 2014; Susskind & Susskind, 2015). Companies should address the key issues and challenges of mental health in CSR, workplace design, and leadership paradigms (Harter et al., 2002; Quick et al., 2000). AI and digital automation may affect mental health without empathy and human-centred policies. A research study by Kaplan (2015), Moore (2018), and Floridi et al. (2018) focused upon using continuous algorithmic management monitoring to diminish psychological safety and autonomy. Intelligent automation has destroyed traditional jobs, affecting people's identity and job happiness (Frey & Osborne, 2017). Remote and hybrid work patterns enabled by AI-driven platforms have muddled work-life boundaries, generating stress and emotional exhaustion (Allen et al., 2015; Wang et al., 2021). Several global reports state that stress and mental health are leading cause of disability globally, exacerbated by occupational stress. The studies estimates that untreated mental health issues might cost a huge loss of $16 trillion by 2030 in terms of reduced productivity globally. This implies rethinking talent strategies and treating mental wellness as a corporate issue rather than a personal one (Grant et al., 2007).

AI may paradoxically increase employee well-being and machine learning, natural language processing, along with biometric feedback, may predict burnout, diagnose mental illness, and customise well-being solutions (Kaur et al., 2021; Wajid et al., 2025). Chatbots and AI-based virtual therapists are increasingly used for mental health counselling, particularly in HR-constrained situations (Inkster et al., 2018; Miner et al., 2016). In the process of safeguarding privacy, autonomy, and data, these interventions must be ethical (Mittelstadt et al., 2016; Winfield & Jirotka, 2018). AI, well-being, and organisational behaviour are needs of the hour, and scholarship is scattered despite its relevance. A comprehensive, network-based literature analysis is required to map the intellectual environment and identify understudied themes, important contributors, and emerging thinking patterns (Aria & Cuccurullo, 2017; van Eck & Waltman, 2010). Bibliometric analysis may indicate information distribution and academic impact by analysing co-citation networks, author collaboration, country-level trends, and keyword evolution (Donthu et al., 2021; Zupic & Čater, 2015). AI employee well-being and mental health research is extensive yet scattered across organisational psychology, HRM, computer science, and ethics. These are the sections that extensively discuss these topics' ongoing work and innovations. Traditional approaches to employee well-being focused on biological or occupational health, as given by Jahoda (1982) and Karasek (1979), whereas the modern ideas include job satisfaction, emotional resilience, and psychological capital (Luthans et al., 2007; Warr, 2007). The workplace mental health continues to affect organisational dynamics, productivity, and retention (LaMontagne et al., 2014; Schaufeli, 2017), but on the other hand, AI improves and challenges workplace well-being. AI has freed up cognitive capacity by automating boring tasks to an eventful and interesting work culture (Brynjolfsson & McAfee, 2014; Davenport & Ronanki, 2018). However, algorithmic management, predictive analytics, and robotic process automation may have psychological consequences on human knowledge and competency mapping (Möhlmann et al., 2021; Sadowski, 2019).

Ball (2010) and Moore (2018) have questioned AI's monitoring capabilities for increasing control and breaching employee autonomy in hiring, evaluation, and performance management, in contrast to the algorithmic bias and lack of transparency that make AI-based decision-making ethically challenging. Binns (2018) and Raji et al. (2020) also explain that these actions induce stress, identity risk, and job dissatisfaction (Gal et al., 2020). AI-based mental health treatments are on the rise through AI-powered chatbots, and CBT tools may detect and address mental illness in its initial stages (Fitzpatrick et al., 2017; Inkster et al., 2018). These strategies promote mental health accessibility without professionals and address issues of depersonalisation, algorithmic hallucinations, and data privacy that remain major concerns (Luxton, 2014; Mittelstadt et al., 2016; Topol, 2019). AI impacts organisational well-being through leadership, culture, and job design, resulting in transformational leadership that fosters trust and psychological safety, thus reducing the negative impacts of AI adoption (Avolio et al., 2009; Bass & Avolio, 1994). Global research indicates that job crafting and participatory design may enhance workers' well-being and control during technological changes, despite regional distinctions (Tims et al., 2013; Wrzesniewski & Dutton, 2001). Due to physical and cultural limitations, developing countries lag the USA and the UK in AI-driven mental health interventions (Sartorius, 2007; Saxena et al., 2007). Cross-national bibliometric studies demonstrate that collaborative research favours Anglophone countries, leaving low- and middle-income nations behind (Kumar et al., 2021). Gender, age, and job roles influence AI-driven wellness. Younger, tech-savvy professionals are adaptable yet prone to burnout

(Brougham & Haar, 2018; Wang et al., 2021). Women face social roles and algorithmic bias during hiring and evaluation processes (Binns et al., 2018; Criado Perez, 2019). AI may benefit mental health, but integrative, ethical, and inclusive frameworks are essential. The design of humane technology increasingly requires collaboration across neuroscience, ethics, sociology, and AI (Dwivedi et al., 2021; Floridi et al., 2018).

This study considers the R package to analyse 358 PUBMED research papers ranging from 2005 to 2025 using bibliometrics. Scholarly studies on AI-driven workplace mental health and well-being are the key results of the study. The research highlights dominating themes, academic silos, and ignored regions in this interdisciplinary confluence. Its unique contribution is mapping the global academic discourse on AI's impact on employee mental health to create integrated policy and research frameworks for future actions. Given the growing understanding of psychological capital as a performance resource (Luthans et al., 2007), the research shows how AI-enabled systems might improve human welfare. It also explores how governments and organisations have addressed the problem via cooperative research and dissemination. Global perspectives are required to encourage inclusive and sustainable AI deployment strategies that prioritise human well-being (Dwivedi et al., 2021; Nemitz, 2018). This research claims employee well-being drives company development. The study examines how AI influences workplace mental health conceptually. It bridges the gap between technological competence and psychological sustenance to make AI a workplace mental health ally.

5.2. Research Gap

Despite growing attention to employee mental health and the rise of AI technologies in the workplace, several research gaps remain. First, there is a lack of comprehensive, global bibliometric analysis that maps the interconnections between AI, mental health, and employee well-being. Most existing studies are conceptual or empirical, with a narrow regional or thematic focus. Second, while AI is recognised as both a cause and a potential solution to mental health challenges, few studies explore this duality in an integrated manner. Third, ethical concerns – such as data privacy, algorithmic bias, and the risk of dehumanising mental health interventions – are discussed in isolation, lacking interdisciplinary exploration. Fourth, there is a noticeable imbalance in research contributions across countries, with limited insights from developing economies where digital transformation is accelerating.

5.3. Research Objectives

1. To map the intellectual structure and trends in global research on AI and employee mental health.
2. To identify key authors, institutions, and countries contributing to this domain.

3. To explore thematic clusters and emerging topics in the intersection of AI, well-being, and workplace dynamics.
4. To uncover collaborative and ethical gaps and suggest future research directions.

5.4. Research Methodology

This study employs a bibliometric analysis approach using the R-based Bibliometrix package to examine the global literature on employee well-being and mental health in AI-driven work environments. The dataset consists of 358 peer-reviewed articles extracted from the PUBMED database, covering a publication tenure from 2015 to 2025. The bibliometric method is selected for its ability to quantify patterns, trends, and structures in scholarly publications, represented through network and co-citation analysis, and follows a structured procedure. First, relevant literature was extracted using Boolean keyword combinations such as 'employee well-being', 'mental health', 'AI', and 'workplace'. The dataset was refined to exclude duplicates, non-English articles, and unrelated studies. Second, bibliometric indicators, such as the most productive authors, highly cited papers, institutional affiliations, and publication sources, were calculated for analysis. Third, visual mapping techniques were employed to illustrate co-authorship networks, keyword co-occurrence, and thematic evolution. The Biblioshiny interface of the Bibliometrix package facilitated the interactive exploration of these networks. A key feature of the methodology is applying network analysis to identify centrality, density, and clustering in the domain of continuous research. This provides insights into which authors, countries, keywords, and themes dominate the discourse and where collaborative or thematic gaps exist. The analysis also includes trend mapping to detect emerging themes and declining areas of interest over time. The methodological rigour of the study is reinforced through triangulation with Scopus-based metadata, manual cross-checking, and expert validation. Ethical considerations were addressed by using publicly available data and ensuring transparent duplicability of the analysis protocol. Overall, the methodology enables a robust and holistic understanding of the intellectual landscape of employee mental health research within the AI ecosystem.

5.5. Result and Analysis

AI-based employee well-being and mental health research from 2015 to 2025 is in Table 5.1. This table helps to measure academic interest in the studied area. In the early 2000s, academic contributions were very few in investigating digital mental health interventions. Global awareness of workplace stress and the digital transformation of HR systems spiked in late 2010. The COVID-19 pandemic promoted awareness of remote work, employee welfare, and AI-driven health monitoring systems from 2019 to 2025. Academicians are becoming more conscious of technology innovation and organisational health dynamics. The table illustrates academic activity chronologically, highlighting crucial periods and proposing an exponential growth trend in the proceeding years. Real-world factors

Table 5.1. Main Information of Articles Using the R Package.

Description	Results
'MAIN INFORMATION ABOUT DATA'	
'Timespan'	2015:2025
'Sources (Journals, Books, etc)'	358
'Documents'	940
'Annual Growth Rate %'	14.68
'Document Average Age'	3.37
'Average citations per doc'	0
'References'	0
'DOCUMENT CONTENTS'	
'Keywords Plus (ID)'	2,093
'Author's Keywords (DE)'	2,093
'AUTHORS'	
'Authors'	5,650
'Authors of single-authored docs'	12
'AUTHORS COLLABORATION'	
'Single-authored docs'	13
'Co-Authors per Doc'	6.68
'International co-authorships %'	20.11
'DOCUMENT TYPES'	
'Journal Article'	358

Source: Authors' calculation.

and technology improve transdisciplinary science and its impact on employees' well-being. Fig. 5.1 shows the most important AI-based employee well-being and mental health articles, highlighting the study areas, namely psychology, computer science, management, and healthcare, which show the study's multidisciplinary nature. *The Journal of Business Research*, *Sustainability*, and *IEEE Access* are praised for spreading research in this era of industrialisation. These sites are interested in current themes like AI in employee health, health sciences, and digital innovation as a multidisciplinary approach, spreading knowledge and boosting visibility and practicality. The study helps researchers to identify journals and locate reputable fundamental material sources and to advance further in the discipline of current research.

Bibliometric theory Bradford's Law detects noteworthy scholarly articles, indicating journals that may be separated into a core group and other zones by diminishing productivity. A few articles dominate a subject's core zone literature

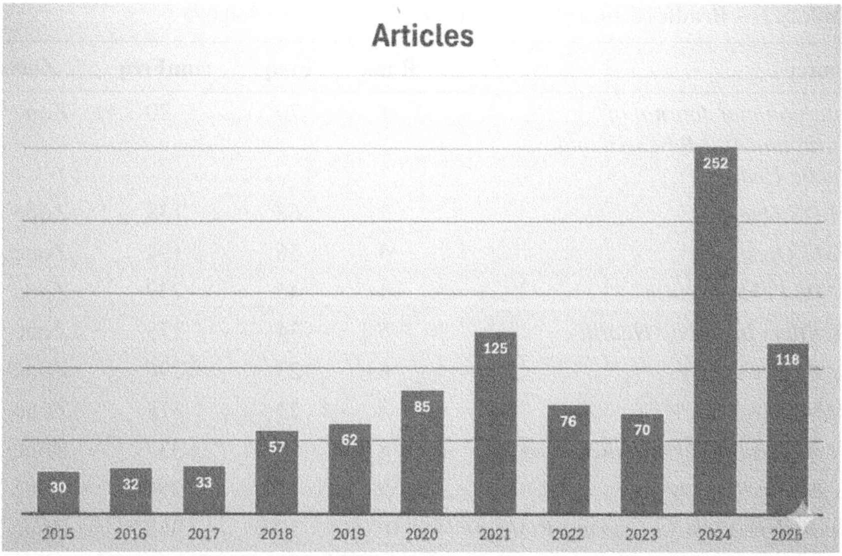

Fig. 5.1. Graphical Representation of Annual Production Using MS Excel.
Source: Authors' creation.

that tend to publish more to identify important AI and employee well-being publications (*IEEE Access, Sustainability*). This information aids literary evaluations, library collection building, and publication venue selection for optimal exposure. Lotka's Law determines field writers' publication dates. Around $1/n^2$ of authors publishing a single article produce n publications. Some writers publish numerous books but most publish one. This law describes research community production and identifies prolific writers, revealing that few researchers have consistently engaged in AI and mental health studies, as seen in Tables 5.2 and 5.3. Understanding this distribution helps find intellectual mentors and thinkers. The most referenced works in the collection show significant scholarly contributions to academia. The studied literature commonly discusses new ideas, methodologies, or conclusions that modify perceptions of AI's influence on employee mental health and well-being. The ongoing research in the field has suggested new applications like AI-driven therapeutic chatbots, predictive burnout modelling, or staff conversation sentiment analysis. Large citation counts suggest broad use in upcoming research, proving their significance towards knowledge enhancement and strengthening the field of study. These important studies give theoretical and practical foundations for future research. The materials span many nations and scenarios, demonstrating the worldwide interest in AI-driven mental health treatments and increasing the knowledge and competency of employees. This table helps researchers track major issues and gain information by listing the most essential papers and providing a literature review approach.

Table 5.4 indicates the chosen publications' authors' most active and significant institutional relationships. These institutions include top universities and

Table 5.2. Bradford's Law Calculated Using the R Package.

Source	Rank	Freq	cumFreq	Zone
International Journal of Environmental Research and Public Health	1	70	70	Zone 1
PLOS One	2	68	138	Zone 1
BMJ Open	3	56	194	Zone 1
BMC Public Health	4	45	239	Zone 1
Frontiers In Public Health	5	34	273	Zone 1
BMC Psychiatry	6	23	296	Zone 1
BMC Psychology	7	22	318	Zone 1
BMC Health Services Research	8	19	337	Zone 2
Scientific Reports	9	17	354	Zone 2
Journal of Medical Internet Research	10	14	368	Zone 2

Source: Authors' calculation.

Table 5.3. Lotka's Law Calculated Using the R Package.

Documents Written	No. of Authors	Proportion of Authors
1	5,195	0.919
2	345	0.061
3	77	0.014
4	21	0.004
5	4	0.001
6	3	0.001
7	3	0.001
8	2	0

Source: Authors' calculation.

research institutes that have published many AI, workplace mental health, and employee well-being research studies. The literature from Harvard, Oxford, and the Indian Institute of Technology suggests specialised research laboratories or multidisciplinary cooperation. North America, Europe, Asia, and Oceania are represented in organisations, suggesting worldwide interest, showcasing the need for global workplace mental health concerns and an AI-driven solution. The table is crucial for locating researchers, academic leaders, and subject specialists, along with companies with excellent technological and psychological research programmes, and collaborations on employee well-being. Table 5.5 lists the most

Table 5.4. Authors' Production Over the Years, Calculated Using the R Package.

Author	Year	Freq	TC	TCpY
Harvey SB	2018	5	0	0
Li Y	2025	4	0	0
Glozier N	2018	3	0	0
Zhang J	2024	3	0	0
Demou E	2018	2	0	0
Fear NT	2023	2	0	0
Greenberg N	2019	2	0	0
Greenberg N	2021	2	0	0
Harvey SB	2019	2	0	0
Leavey G	2016	2	0	0

Source: Authors' calculation.

Table 5.5. Most Relevant Source Publishing Articles Calculated Using R Package.

Sources	Articles
International Journal of Environmental Research and Public Health	70
PLOS One	68
BMJ Open	56
BMC Public Health	45
Frontiers in Public Health	34
BMC Psychiatry	23
BMC Psychology	22
BMC Health Services Research	19
Scientific Reports	17
Journal of Medical Internet Research	14

Source: Authors' calculation.

important AI, mental health, and employee well-being authors based on article count; their ranking emphasises prolific scholars who have consistently generated work in this area, exhibiting productivity and attention to the challenge. These writers influence research and develop new ways of collaboration with various universities operating overseas, and it might boost academic excellence.

Table 5.5 shows the authors with the highest literature citations, indicating their intellectual impact. This figure emphasises impact – how frequently particular authors are mentioned – versus chart 5, which emphasises volume. A high citation count indicates that the writers developed unique theories, hypotheses, or empirical discoveries that apply to multidimensional fields. These writers may provide the groundwork for knowledge or an approach. Their work may help integrate AI into psychological health frameworks or create data-driven organisational behaviour models. These prolific writers are well-known in their area. The problem is technological (AI) and human-centric (mental health or HR), as their citations illustrate, helps literature reviewers find reputable sources. It acknowledges notable researchers who may boost research visibility and quality. Table 5.6 illustrates AI studies on employee well-being and mental health based on the nation, and the top contributions by academic and technical nations include the USA, China, the UK, and India. In these countries, academicians have studied burnout, remote work, and computerised surveillance. Data reveals that nations with strong AI ecosystems and public health infrastructures create more literature, linking research capabilities to problem relevance. Emerging economies like Brazil and South Africa are embracing mental health digital tools, and the table also illustrates worldwide knowledge exchange and cooperation. It also helps funding agencies and governments to evaluate national research in the related field. These data points may show global engagement, regional strengths, and underrepresented research topics.

The most popular words and phrases in research articles are shown in Table 5.6, which thematically highlights AI-driven employee well-being and mental health literature themes, ideas, and focus. The terms 'mental health', 'artificial

Table 5.6. Co-words Factorial Analysis Calculated Using R Package.

	Cluster	Betweenness	Closeness	Page Rank
Cross-sectional Studies	2	4.8	0.02	0.032
Pandemics	2	2.819	0.019	0.023
Sars-Cov-2	2	2.387	0.019	0.021
Health Personnel/ Psychology	2	1.805	0.019	0.019
Covid-19	2	0.274	0.016	0.01
Covid-19/Epidemiology	2	0.107	0.015	0.01
Job Satisfaction	2	0.221	0.016	0.009
Prevalence	2	0.09	0.015	0.009
Mental Health/Statistics and Numerical Data	2	0.16	0.016	0.009
Depression/Epidemiology	2	0.188	0.015	0.009

Source: Authors' calculation.

intelligence', 'stress', 'well-being', 'workplace', 'machine learning', and 'burnout' highlight the use of technology to study and enhance mental health. AI is being used in prevention and monitoring, via terms like 'prediction', 'monitoring', and 'digital tools', which are key focus areas of various studies. Academics use word frequency data to uncover study routes and conceptual patterns to build appropriate research topics. The recurrent use of psychology, organisational studies, and computer science shows that the field blends them and prioritises employee stress, burnout, and ethical AI models for wellness, along with retention. Researchers begin or extend this area for a thematic guide and terminology.

A keyword co-occurrence network demonstrates how frequently phrases appear in the same publications. This method reveals research relationships and subject groupings, unlike frequencies, in which closely linked phrase clusters reflect domain sub-themes. For instance, 'stress', 'well-being', and 'burnout' may cluster around 'employee mental health', whereas 'machine learning', 'predictive analysis', and 'AI' may cluster around technical techniques. The network incorporates AI, HR, and psychological health assessment that help to uncover key concepts that link study domains, like 'AI', which presumably links technological and psychological issues. Co-occurrence networks describe the discipline's cognitive framework, discover new topic amalgamations, and reveal research needs. This map may help researchers position their work, examine innovative relationships (e.g., 'emotion recognition' and 'job satisfaction'), and adapt their terminology towards the contribution and advancement of academic trends.

A longitudinal topic analysis demonstrates research interests over time. Early years (2000–2010) contained 'occupational stress' and 'mental health at work', with little digital technology. The emergence of 'AI', 'deep learning', and 'predictive analytics' reveals technology in human-centric fields. Growth and maturity have led to integrated and advanced challenges such as 'digital mental health', 'AI ethics', 'employee engagement', and 'real-time monitoring' in 2019–2023. Wearable technologies, mental health applications, and business psychological safety awareness contributed to this rise. Thematic evolution analysis predicts trends and matches research ideas to emerging interests. It also describes the intellectual history of ideas and how the research field is adjusting to social and technological developments.

Table 11 displays common research subjects over the studied period and compares the themetic development as the table focuses on short-term popularity gains over significant alterations. The 2020–2021 COVID-19 epidemic increased use of 'remote work', 'mental fatigue', and 'digital surveillance'. After the pandemic, 'resilience', 'AI-driven well-being initiatives', and 'digital fatigue management' may matter. This analysis identifies urgent research needs, trending topics for special issues or conferences, funding, and citation opportunities. Employee stress and ethical AI used in various research are key themes in corporate strategy, reflecting social and economic contributions. The chart gives academics a realistic assessment of relevance and impact. It matches writers to journal and funding organisation subject areas for strategic publication.

Fig. 5.1 shows yearly scientific output from 2000 to 2023. Bar graphs show annual changes, including stasis and oscillations. The consistent rise since 2015 implies AI and mental health focus on safeguarding employees' interests. The COVID-19 epidemic and worldwide remote work shift triggered a rapid spike after 2020. The figure illustrates trends and puts the issue in socio-technological settings, demonstrating how pandemics and technological advances impact academic attention. Fig. 5.2 supplements Table 5.3 with the most prolific writers by publication count. The bar chart indicates major contributors by volume and reveals that authors from the same organisation can discover collaborative or institutional clusters. After comparing authors and identifying field research leadership using information, and help researchers to locate field-developing mentors, collaborators, and influencers.

In Fig. 5.3, a word cloud shows dataset terms and phrase frequency, and emphasises words like 'mental health', 'AI', 'employee', and 'stress', implying frequency and thematic importance. This graphic makes literary semantics plain and enjoyable. Word clouds illustrate concept significance better than tables, generating research subjects and explaining field terminology. The word cloud exhibits multidisciplinary technical (e.g., 'deep learning') and psychological (e.g., 'well-being') vocabulary. Fig. 5.4 shows data in a bar chart of key sources stating top AI-based employee well-being and mental health research is accepted and honoured globally. Bar height denotes the number of papers published for each source, resulting in technology and workplace concerns dominating *IEEE Access*, *Sustainability*, and the *Journal of Business Research*. This chart allows readers to easily compare and evaluate the main academic platforms in this discipline. It suggests high-visibility, topically relevant publications for early-career researchers and authors. The image shows how technology- and psychology-focused articles have increased the subject's multidisciplinary character. Analysing the picture reveals the publishing environment and main venues that influence academic debate on this topic.

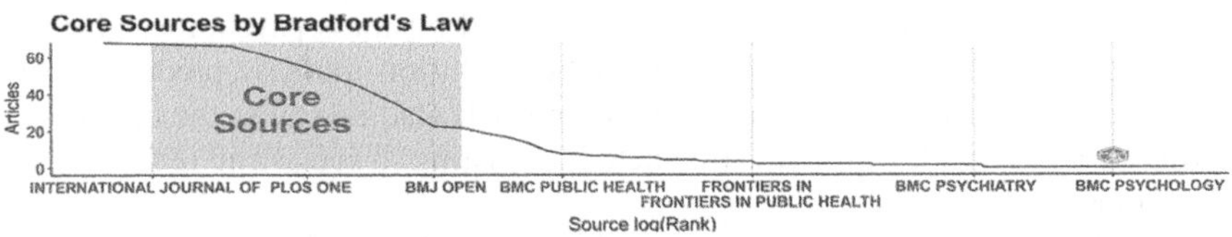

Fig. 5.2. Bradford's Law Graph Using the R Package. *Source*: Authors' creation.

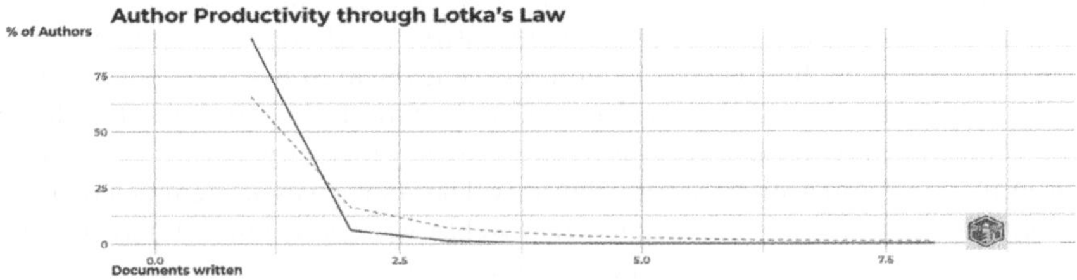

Fig. 5.3. Lotka's Law Graph Using the R Package. *Source: Authors' creation.*

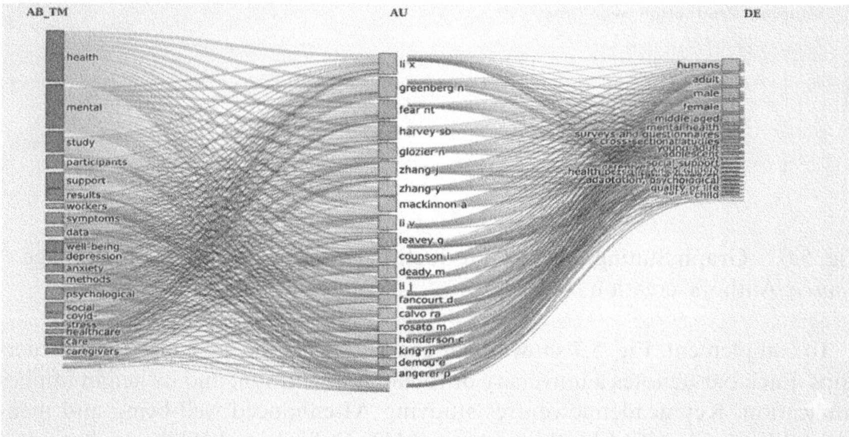

Fig. 5.4. Threefold Plot Based on Abstract (AB), Author (AU), and Keywords (DE) Using the R Package. *Source*: Authors' creation.

Fig. 5.5 is a bar graph of the most referenced works, supporting, where all bars represent documents and their heights reflect citation counts, depicting influential research. These publications frequently include foundational theory, innovative AI applications, or extensive empirical validations along with their graphical illustrations, citation patterns, and fundamental literature. A wide gap between the top one or two bars and the remainder may indicate influential articles. Scholars may locate noteworthy articles to reference or expand on in literature reviews. It also demonstrates how new books on key themes and industry changes may sell swiftly. Fig. 5.6 is a global thematic map showing country research output, and the colour-coding reveals nations by product output. Darker hues indicate more research publications, and viewers may quickly find the most studied sites using this map. We expect the USA, China, the UK, and India to lead the studied area. The chart depicts worldwide AI and employee well-being conversations, geographical discrepancies, and disadvantaged areas' advancement opportunities. This data might help policymakers, funding agencies, and global research institutes adopt cross-border cooperation strategies or invest in academically active areas.

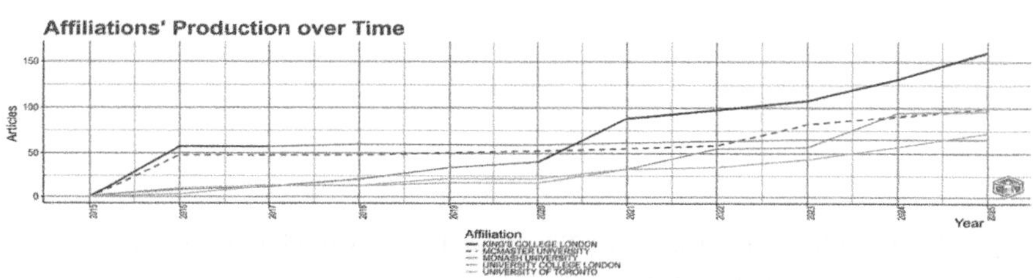

Fig. 5.5. Graph Stating Affiliations' Production over Time Using the R Package. *Source*: Authors' creation.

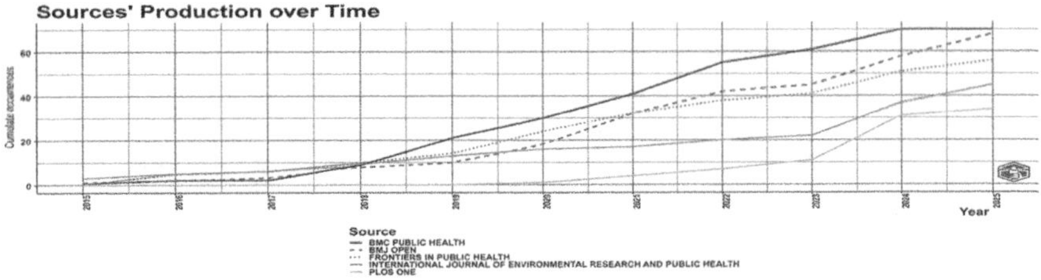

Fig. 5.6. Graph Stating Sources' Production over Time Using the R Package. *Source*: Authors' creation **Node**.

To complement, Fig. 5.7 shows a bar chart showing the most effective partnerships. Each bar denotes a university or research institution, and its height implies publication. Key academic centres studying AI-enhanced well-being and mental health are identified by this statistic. MIT, Oxford, and IITS may dominate this graphic, indicating active laboratories or research institutes in this vast topic. The picture aids academic networking, cooperation, keynote speaker and editing committee selection by identifying intellectual clusters. Fig. 5.8 depicts an author hierarchy by citation frequency from Table 5.6. Author impact comparisons are easy to understand with this bar chart and citation-based ranking indicating research quality, inventiveness, or usefulness. Fig. 5.9 depicts author-institutional cooperation using nodes formed by researchers' or organisations' contributions and edges for their partnerships. Thicker edges and nodes imply more frequent linkages, graphically measuring the academic community researching the issue sociometrically. It identifies key contributions, coordinated research groups, and solitary authors or locations. Visualisations enhance academic network transparency and inter-institutional collaboration. It uncovers regional cooperation clusters and worldwide academic partnerships. The keyword co-occurrence is shown in Fig. 5.10 which links frequency as keyword co-occurrence in texts, whereas nodes represent keywords. Network theme groups are colour-coded, featuring 'AI', 'deep learning', and 'algorithm' may be technology-focused, whereas 'stress', 'well-being', and 'burnout' may be psychological. This image illustrates topic links and assists in interdisciplinary niche discovery for mapping and gap analysis.

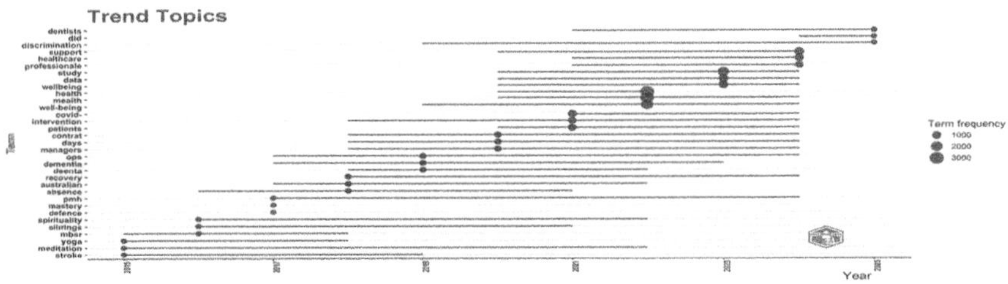

Fig. 5.7. Graph Stating the Most Trending Topic over Time Using the R Package. *Source*: Authors' creation.

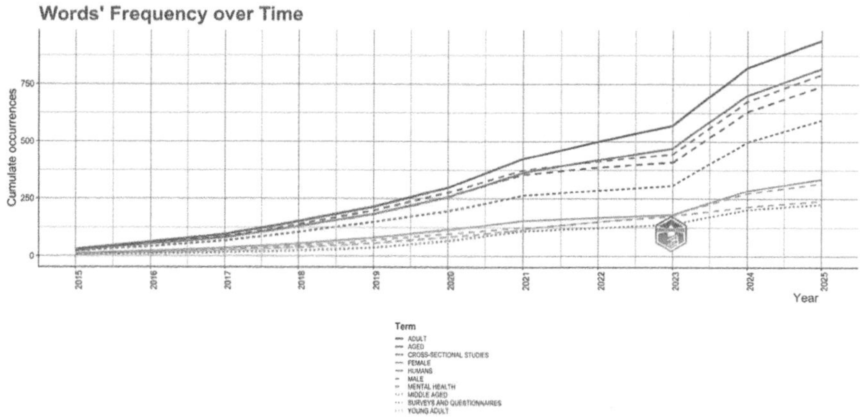

Fig. 5.8. Graph Showing Words' Frequency Calculated Using the R Package. *Source*: Authors' creation.

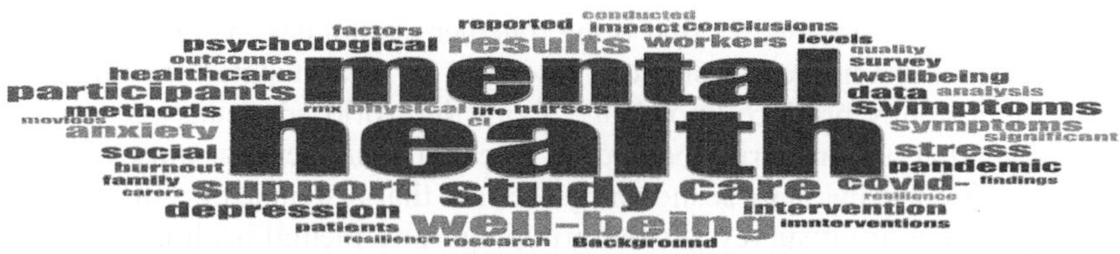

Fig. 5.9. Word Cloud Calculated Using R Package. *Source*: Authors' creation.

An in-depth, well-organised history of how research on the mental health of foreign workers has evolved over time in a world where AI is becoming more prevalent was presented in the study. Based on the findings of the research, the papers were distributed over a period. Beginning in 2015 and continuing through 2017, the pattern has gained increasing popularity. The year 2018 marked the beginning of its rapid expansion, which continued until about 2024. This trend indicates that businesses are increasingly concerned about issues such as mental health, remote work, and technology-related concerns. The mental health of employees used to be a relatively minor concern for HR, but today it is a significant strategic concern for businesses that rely on technology to communicate with one another. The reduction in 2025 is more likely to be the result of people's lack of interest in research than it is to be the result of delays in tracking. This transformation has occurred gradually over time, as shown by this graph. According to the findings of the study, major universities and health research facilities all over the globe are the only ones responsible for this progression in scientific knowledge. The University of Toronto, King's College London, and Monash University are the three most prestigious educational institutions. As they continue to work, they demonstrate how essential it

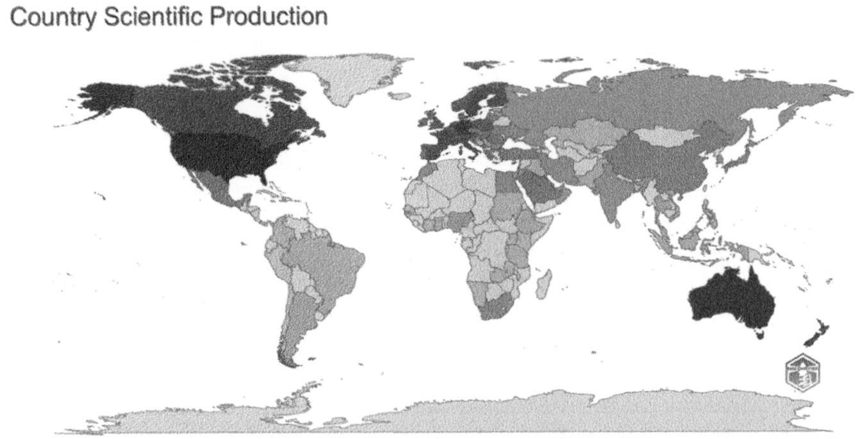

Fig. 5.10. Countries' Collaboration Map Using R Package. *Source*: Authors' creation.

is to establish robust networks that bring together mental health, employment science, and data-driven methodologies. According to what it states, the method by which we currently produce knowledge about the world advantages a select few institutions that are primarily focused on research. The fact that most of the literature is about individuals is shown by the fact that a significant portion of the research is focused on surveys, social groupings, and mental health. Researchers are primarily concerned with how AI will impact people's mental health and their day-to-day lives, rather than how it may be used in the economic world, as shown by the widespread assertion. This focused approach demonstrates that this field can handle sophisticated applications of AI, even if those applications are based on human experience. The findings of research conducted at the national level indicate that industrialised nations, such as the USA, Canada, and Australia, are the most successful in this field. In addition to having robust institutions and a substantial amount of wealth, the people in these nations place a high level of importance on their own health and safety. The figures presented here demonstrate that the field of research is both intelligent and rapidly expanding. On the other hand, it is not as extensive, does not have as many institutions, and does not make as much use of AI as others. This demonstrates that there is a need for further research to be conducted on the mental health and happiness of workers who are open to new ideas and who make use of AI.

Fig. 5.11 shows a strategy map that organises themes by centrality and density into four quadrants: motor (high centrality, low density), speciality (low centrality, high density), emerging/declining, and fundamental. While 'emotion detection' may be specialised, 'mental health' and 'AI' may dominate. Scholars use this image to evaluate subject progression and significance. It also anticipates the field's future and suggests research or integration topics. Fig. 5.11 illustrates the 2000–2010, 2011–2017, and 2018–2023 theme progression. It links keywords or clusters with lines to demonstrate how subjects get more complicated. This graphic depicts intellectual progress and a study chronology. 'Workplace stress'

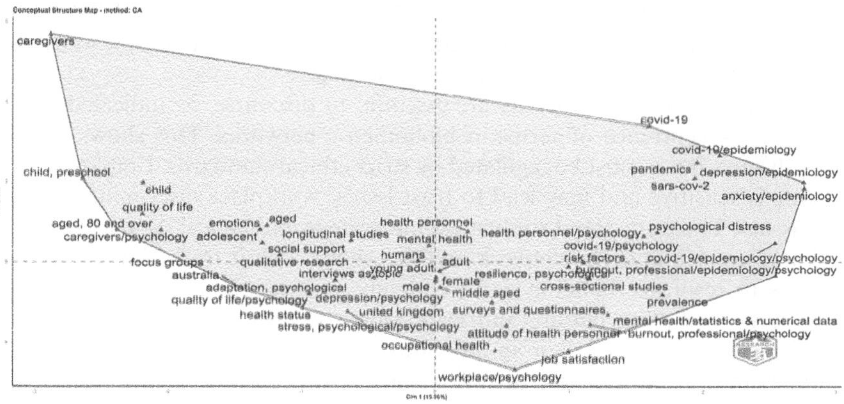

Fig. 5.11. Conceptual Structure of Factorial Map Using R Package. *Source*: Authors' creation.

might become 'digital fatigue' or 'remote work well-being'. It determines how technology and global events affect academic goals. Thus, trending themes are showcased as a heatmap, showcasing popular phrases from certain years. Post-pandemic 'AI ethics' and 'burnout detection' may surge. The graphic lets researchers rapidly find relevant subjects and connect their work to current discussions. This affects editorial choices, funding bids, and research shortages.

5.6. Interpretation

This network analysis found that AI technology has changed corporate mental health and well-being perception and management. The thematic clusters of the analysis show that research has expanded beyond psychological distress and workplace stressors to include behavioural sciences, technology, and HR strategies. The clusters favour AI-driven monitoring tools, including emotion detection, wearable devices, chatbots, and sentiment analysis, demonstrating that AI is being used in corporate health programmes. One perspective is how AI has changed mental health therapy from reactive to proactive. Traditional techniques relied on employee self-reports or visual symptoms. AI allows real-time monitoring and predictive analytics, enabling companies to intervene before modest issues become major mental health illnesses. This technological change is important in remote or mixed work contexts with little direct monitoring. Firms may now give tailored help to workers, enhancing engagement, retention, and productivity.

The centrality and density investigations of word networks show that although interest in AI for employee mental health is growing, it is still disconnected. Many fields contribute to the conversation, but findings are occasionally combined. Psychology insights are frequently not coordinated with AI system development, resulting in contextually unaware tools. Thus, the study sees this topic as promising but needs interdisciplinary collaboration to address questions. The uneven geographical distribution of research projects is noteworthy. Industrialised nations with strong technological infrastructures, such as the USA, the UK, and Europe, produce high-impact research. This suggests a worldwide AI-mental health discourse gap. Literature neglects developing countries, which may profit from scalable AI solutions. To democratise mental health technology, worldwide cooperation and capacity development are needed.

Ethical and privacy concerns are essential to discourse, as indicated by the frequent co-occurrence of terms in bibliometric networks. This shows that AI may advance, but it must be regulated by strict ethical standards. Employee mental data is sensitive and may lead to trust issues, workplace discrimination, and legal issues. Thus, any trend study must integrate technological development and ethical responsibility. The network analysis shows a shift from compliance and wellness to resilience-building and well-being as strategic organisational goals. This shifts workplace culture and leadership styles to see mental health as a business resource rather than an individual issue. AI may affect organisational attitudes and worker support on a wide scale in this scenario.

5.7. Suggestions

This network analysis suggests numerous ways to improve AI-driven employee mental health assistance research and practice. First, multidisciplinary cooperation is essential for the success of other research, followed by Psychology, AI, HRM, and ethics scholars and practitioners must collaborate to create technologically effective and human-centric solutions. This will make AI technologies technically correct, emotionally intelligent, and ethical. Second, corporations should use AI to supplement human-based mental health support systems. AI can scale and forecast, but it cannot replace empathy, trust, and judgement. AI technologies should be combined with professional counselling and peer support programmes to create a psychologically secure workplace. Third, policy frameworks must develop with technology. Transparency, informed permission, data security, and algorithmic fairness must be emphasised in mental health AI ethics regulations to develop trust and usefulness, so that organisations should co-design these platforms with workers. Fourth, the global research conversation should deliberately include underrepresented areas and industries, promoting fair access to AI-enabled mental health initiatives and motivating funding organisations, international bodies, and academic institutions to help poor nations create research capability. Finally, longitudinal and real-world AI-mental health research is needed to collaborate with current research conceptually or experimentally. Organisational case studies will provide practical insights and prove the long-term efficacy of AI-based treatments.

5.8. Conclusion

The worldwide literature on employee well-being and mental health using AI and network analysis shows an emerging yet fragmented picture where the post-COVID-19 pandemic changed workplace standards and emphasised the need for creative mental health therapies, and academic interest in this multidisciplinary topic. Research shows a move from traditional mental health frameworks to AI-augmented systems that offer predictive, preventative, and individualised therapy. The bibliometric study shows cooperation across nations, institutions, and authors, and network density supports stronger worldwide tie-ups from fundamental stress and work satisfaction research to complicated AI components like machine learning, sentiment analysis, and natural language processing. These technologies are being used in organisational systems to measure stress, forecast burnout, and provide personalised mental health care. The citation and co-citation analyses show how basic ideas and significant academics changed this area, guiding subsequent researchers. Psychology, management, information systems, and AI are merging to create new conceptual models and tools to improve worker resilience and organisational sustainability. Ethical and data privacy challenges exist despite technical advances. AI-driven mental health technologies are strong, but surveillance, consent, algorithmic bias, and data exploitation raise unanswered questions. The article emphasises the need for ethical and regulatory frameworks for mental health monitoring AI. The digital gap between nations and industries in adopting such technology might worsen employee well-being disparities.

The study maps key documents, productive nations, prolific writers, and growing field issues for useful insights. It is a comprehensive academic resource that assesses the present literature and gaps for additional study. Global study reveals that industrialised countries dominate this research participation, allowing potential for emerging nations to improve their AI for mental health research and technology. Existing research focuses on individual psychological outcomes, while organisational-level assessments are lacking. In conclusion, our network-based bibliometric approach synthesises existing research and inspires future research. AI in employee mental health is no longer futuristic, but it is rising. However, multidisciplinary cooperation, ethical integrity, technical inclusion, and supporting policy frameworks are needed to maximise its potential. The research highlights trends, difficulties, and possibilities in this expanding sector, advancing theory and practice. Organisations, politicians, and academics must co-create solutions that balance innovation with compassion to guarantee that AI improves employee well-being rather than stressing them out.

References

Allen, T. D., Golden, T. D., & Shockley, K. M. (2015). How effective is telecommuting? Assessing the status of our scientific findings. *Psychological Science in the Public Interest*, *16*(2), 40–68. https://doi.org/10.1177/1529100615593273

Aria, M., & Cuccurullo, C. (2017). Bibliometrix: An R-tool for comprehensive science mapping analysis. *Journal of Informetrics*, *11*(4), 959–975. https://doi.org/10.1016/j.joi.2017.08.007

Avolio, B. J., Walumbwa, F. O., & Weber, T. J. (2009). Leadership: Current theories, research, and future directions. *Annual Review of Psychology*, *60*, 421–449. https://doi.org/10.1146/annurev.psych.60.110707.163621

Ball, K. (2010). Workplace surveillance: An overview. *Labor History*, *51*(1), 87–106. https://doi.org/10.1080/00236561003654776

Bass, B. M., & Avolio, B. J. (1994). *Improving organizational effectiveness through transformational leadership*. SAGE.

Brougham, D., & Haar, J. (2018). Smart technology, artificial intelligence, robotics, and algorithms (STARA): Employees' perceptions of our future workplace. *Journal of Management & Organization*, *24*(2), 239–257. https://doi.org/10.1017/jmo.2017.12

Brynjolfsson, E., & McAfee, A. (2014). *The second machine age: Work, progress, and prosperity in a time of brilliant technologies*. W. W. Norton & Company.

Cascio, W. F., & Montealegre, R. (2016). How technology is changing work and organizations. *Annual Review of Organizational Psychology and Organizational Behavior*, *3*(1), 349–375. https://doi.org/10.1146/annurev-orgpsych-041015-062352

Cooper, C. L., & Cartwright, S. (1994). Healthy mind; healthy organization—A proactive approach to occupational stress. *Human Relations*, *47*(4), 455–471. https://doi.org/10.1177/001872679404700405

Criado Perez, C. (2019). *Invisible women: Exposing data bias in a world designed for men*. Abrams Press.

Danna, K., & Griffin, R. W. (1999). Health and well-being in the workplace: A review and synthesis of the literature. *Journal of Management*, *25*(3), 357–384. https://doi.org/10.1177/014920639902500305

Davenport, T. H., & Ronanki, R. (2018). Artificial intelligence for the real world. *Harvard Business Review*, *96*(1), 108–116.

Dewe, P., & Kompier, M. (2008). *Wellbeing and work: Towards a balanced agenda*. Palgrave Macmillan.

Donthu, N., Kumar, S., Mukherjee, D., Pandey, N., & Lim, W. M. (2021). How to conduct a bibliometric analysis: An overview and guidelines. *Journal of Business Research*, *133*, 285–296. https://doi.org/10.1016/j.jbusres.2021.04.070

Dwivedi, Y. K., Hughes, D. L., Ismagilova, E., Aarts, G., Coombs, C., Crick, T., Duan, Y., Dwivedi, R., Edwards, J., Eirug, A., Galanos, V., Ilavarasan, P. V., Janssen, M., Jones, P., Kar, A. K., Kizgin, H., Kronemann, B., Lal, B., Lucini, B., … Williams, M. D. (2021). Artificial intelligence (AI): Multidisciplinary perspectives on emerging challenges, opportunities, and agenda for research, practice and policy. *International Journal of Information Management*, *57*, 101994. https://doi.org/10.1016/j.ijinfomgt.2019.08.002

Fitzpatrick, K. K., Darcy, A., & Vierhile, M. (2017). Delivering cognitive behavior therapy to young adults with symptoms of depression and anxiety using a fully automated conversational agent (Woebot): A randomized controlled trial. *JMIR Mental Health*, *4*(2), e19. https://doi.org/10.2196/mental.7785

Floridi, L., Cowls, J., Beltrametti, M., Chatila, R., Chazerand, P., Dignum, V., C., Madelin, R., Pagallo, U., Rossi, F., Schafer, B., Valcke, P., & Vayena, E. (2018). AI4People—An ethical framework for a good AI society: Opportunities, risks, principles, and recommendations. *Minds and Machines*, *28*(4), 689–707. https://doi.org/10.1007/s11023-018-9482-5

Frey, C. B., & Osborne, M. A. (2017). The future of employment: How susceptible are jobs to computerisation? *Technological Forecasting and Social Change*, *114*, 254–280. https://doi.org/10.1016/j.techfore.2016.08.019

Gal, U., Jensen, T. B., & Stein, M. K. (2020). Breaking the vicious cycle of algorithmic management: A virtue ethics approach to people analytics. *Information and Organization*, *30*(2), 100301. https://doi.org/10.1016/j.infoandorg.2020.100301

Grant, A. M., Christianson, M. K., & Price, R. H. (2007). Happiness, health, or relationships? Managerial practices and employee well-being tradeoffs. *Academy of Management Perspectives*, *21*(3), 51–63. https://doi.org/10.5465/amp.2007.26421238

Harter, J. K., Schmidt, F. L., & Keyes, C. L. (2002). Well-being in the workplace and its relationship to business outcomes: A review of the Gallup studies. In C. L. Keyes & J. Haidt (Eds.), *Flourishing: Positive psychology and the life well-lived* (pp. 205–224). APA.

Inkster, B., Sarda, S., & Subramanian, V. (2018). An empathy-driven, conversational artificial intelligence agent (Wysa) for digital mental well-being: Real-world data evaluation. *JMIR mHealth and uHealth*, *6*(11), e12106. https://doi.org/10.2196/12106

Jahoda, M. (1982). *Employment and unemployment: A social-psychological analysis*. Cambridge University Press.

Kaplan, J. (2015). *Humans need not apply: A guide to wealth and work in the age of artificial intelligence*. Yale University Press.

Karasek, R. A. (1979). Job demands, job decision latitude, and mental strain: Implications for job redesign. *Administrative Science Quarterly*, *24*(2), 285–308. https://doi.org/10.2307/2392498

Kaur, P., Dhir, A., Singh, N., & Salo, J. (2021). Mapping the research landscape of artificial intelligence (AI) applications in human resource management. *Electronic Markets*, *31*(2), 215–231. https://doi.org/10.1007/s12525-020-00450-x

Kumar, S., Zafar, M. W., & Khan, A. (2021). Uncovering research trends and themes in sustainable finance: A bibliometric analysis. *Journal of Sustainable Finance & Investment*, 1–21. https://doi.org/10.1080/20430795.2021.1883989

LaMontagne, A. D., Keegel, T., Louie, A. M., Ostry, A., & Landsbergis, P. A. (2014). A systematic review of the job-stress intervention evaluation literature, 1990–2005. *International Journal of Occupational and Environmental Health*, *13*(3), 268–280. https://doi.org/10.1179/oeh.2007.13.3.268

Luthans, F., Youssef, C. M., & Avolio, B. J. (2007). *Psychological capital: Developing the human competitive edge*. Oxford University Press.

Luxton, D. D. (2014). Artificial intelligence in psychological practice: Current and future applications and implications. *Professional Psychology: Research and Practice*, *45*(5), 332–339. https://doi.org/10.1037/a0034547

Makridakis, S. (2017). The forthcoming artificial intelligence (AI) revolution: Its impact on society and firms. *Futures*, *90*, 46–60. https://doi.org/10.1016/j.futures.2017.03.006

Miner, A. S., Milstein, A., Schueller, S., Hegde, R., Mangurian, C., & Linos, E. (2016). Smartphone-based conversational agents and responses to questions about mental health, interpersonal violence, and physical health. *JAMA Internal Medicine*, *176*(5), 619–625. https://doi.org/10.1001/jamainternmed.2016.0400

Mittelstadt, B. D., Allo, P., Taddeo, M., Wachter, S., & Floridi, L. (2016). The ethics of algorithms: Mapping the debate. *Big Data & Society*, *3*(2), 2053951716679679. https://doi.org/10.1177/2053951716679679

Möhlmann, M., Zalmanson, L., Henfridsson, O., & Gregory, R. W. (2021). Algorithmic management of work on online labor platforms: When matching meets control. *MIS Quarterly*, *45*(4), 1999–2022. https://doi.org/10.25300/MISQ/2021/16488

Moore, P. V. (2018). The threat of algorithmic management: A technical fix for the human resource? *Systems Research and Behavioral Science*, *35*(4), 485–497. https://doi.org/10.1002/sres.2540

Nemitz, P. (2018). Constitutional democracy and technology in the age of artificial intelligence. *Philosophical Transactions of the Royal Society A*, *376*(2133), 20180089. https://doi.org/10.1098/rsta.2018.0089

Quick, J. C., Quick, J. D., Nelson, D. L., & Hurrell, J. J. (2000). *Preventive stress management in organizations*. American Psychological Association.

Raji, I. D., Smart, A., White, R. N., & Mitchell, M., Gebru, T., Hutchinson, B., Smith-Loud, J., Theron, D., & Barnes, P. (2020). Closing the AI accountability gap: Defining an end-to-end framework for internal algorithmic auditing. In *Proceedings of the 2020 conference on fairness, accountability, and transparency* (pp. 33–44).

Sadowski, J. (2019). When data is capital: Datafication, accumulation, and extraction. *Big Data & Society*, *6*(1), 2053951718820549. https://doi.org/10.1177/2053951718820549

Sartorius, N. (2007). Stigma and mental health. *The Lancet*, *370*(9590), 810–811. https://doi.org/10.1016/S0140-6736(07)61245-8
Saxena, S., Thornicroft, G., Knapp, M., & Whiteford, H. (2007). Resources for mental health: Scarcity, inequity, and inefficiency. *The Lancet*, *370*(9590), 878–889. https://doi.org/10.1016/S0140-6736(07)61239-2
Schaufeli, W. B. (2017). Applying the job demands-resources model. *Organizational Dynamics*, *46*(2), 120–132. https://doi.org/10.1016/j.orgdyn.2017.04.008
Susskind, R., & Susskind, D. (2015). *The future of the professions: How technology will transform the work of human experts*. Harvard University Press.
Tims, M., Bakker, A. B., & Derks, D. (2013). The impact of job crafting on job demands, job resources, and well-being. *Journal of Occupational Health Psychology*, *18*(2), 230–240. https://doi.org/10.1037/a0032141
Topol, E. (2019). *Deep medicine: How artificial intelligence can make healthcare human again*. Basic Books.
van Eck, N. J., & Waltman, L. (2010). Software survey: VOSviewer, a computer program for bibliometric mapping. *Scientometrics*, *84*(2), 523–538. https://doi.org/10.1007/s11192-009-0146-3
Wang, B., Liu, Y., Qian, J., & Parker, S. K. (2021). Achieving effective remote working during the COVID-19 pandemic: A work design perspective. *Applied Psychology*, *70*(1), 16–59. https://doi.org/10.1111/apps.12290
Wajid, A., Azam, F., & Anwar, M. (2025). Applications of artificial intelligence in mental health: A systematic literature review. *Discover Artificial Intelligence*, 5(1). https://doi.org/10.1007/s44163-025-00569-2
Warr, P. (2007). *Work, happiness, and unhappiness*. Lawrence Erlbaum Associates.
Winfield, A. F., & Jirotka, M. (2018). Ethical governance is essential to building trust in robotics and artificial intelligence systems. *Philosophical Transactions of the Royal Society A*, *376*(2133), 20180085. https://doi.org/10.1098/rsta.2018.0085
Wrzesniewski, A., & Dutton, J. E. (2001). Crafting a job: Revisioning employees as active crafters of their work. *Academy of Management Review*, *26*(2), 179–201. https://doi.org/10.5465/amr.2001.4378011
Zupic, I., & Čater, T. (2015). Bibliometric methods in management and organization. *Organizational Research Methods*, *18*(3), 429–472. https://doi.org/10.1177/1094428114562629

Chapter 6

Gamifying Workplaces: Applying AI-driven Esports and Sports Simulation Models to Boost Employee Motivation, Engagement, and Psychological Well-being

Amitava Pal[a], *Channi Sachdeva*[b], *Ewelina Idziak*[c] *and Farida Virani*[d]

[a]*Department of Management Studies, ICFAI University Jharkhand, India*
[b]*Mittal School of Business, Lovely Professional University, India*
[c]*Azerbaijan State University of Economics, Azerbaijan*
[d]*Department of HR and Behavioral Science, Institute of Management, MET Mumbai*

Abstract

As organizations undergo rapid digital transformation and the expectation evolves to a new engagement and workplace experience for the employee, it has become impossible to maintain the traditional engagement model. This chapter examines the application of gamification – an approach over two decades in the making that draws from elements of game design, sports psychology, and behavioral science – to strategically amplify workplace motivation, learning, resilience, and organizational performance. Based on well-established theories (e.g., Self-determination Theory (SDT), Flow Theory, Goal-setting Theory), the chapter elaborates the psychological processes through which gamified systems function in corporations. It also explores the rise of new technologies like AI dashboards, virtual reality (VR) simulations, and mixed reality (MR) platforms that reshape employee training, team bonding, and well-being programs. This chapter provides some pragmatic frameworks for thinking about how to architect

Nurturing AI-Powered HR Analytics and Virtual Reality in Employee Psychology and Workplace Happiness, Part A, 95–113

doi:10.1108/978-1-80686-125-520261011

systems for an inclusive, ethical, and evidence-driven gamified ecosystem, as well as some tactics for competition fatigue, language bias, and privacy issues. Case examples of relevant applications from sports, Esports, and enterprise learning models are provided throughout the chapter. The chapter concludes by proposing a phased adoption roadmap, as well as possible future developments such as blockchain-based credentials, AI-guided mentors, and sustainability-linked reward schemes. In the end, it redefines the workplace as an arena of mental gymnastics, intentional play, and flexible execution, turning gamification into a necessity rather than a gimmick in the coming of age of work.

Keywords: Behavioral psychology; employee engagement; Flow Theory; gamification; KPI alignment; organizational resilience; performance motivation; Self-determination Theory; virtual reality; workplace well-being

6.1. Introduction

We are witnessing a seismic shift in the world of work, powered by the changing workforce, automation of processes, and the younger generation's generational expectations. With Millennials and Generation Z playing an increasingly important part of the workforce (at least the global portion of the workforce), individuals are more interested in autonomy, ongoing feedback, and purposeful engagement (as opposed to hierarchical or task-oriented environments within the workplace) (Gallup, 2021). According to Frank Notohamedi, Marketing Coordinator at Flobro, this kind of generational preference has increased workplace interest in gamification – the nonscientific employment of game {{style | style}} mechanics in non-game contexts to drive engagement, provide motivation, and create a more engaging workplace.

Gamification contains inherent psychological motivators of competence, autonomy, and relatedness (the three innate needs for SDT (Deci & Ryan, 2000)) to increase the level of employee engagement (Seaborn & Fels, 2015). Using practices such as immediate feedback, incremental challenge, and progress visualization, gamified systems mimic the game design and game play of both physical and digital games and promote productivity via these repeated little victories (Hamari et al., 2014). It is hard not to notice how closely those mechanisms align with the neurobiology of motivation, particularly the dopaminergic reward system that is sensitive to expectancy, challenge, and success (Berridge & Robinson, 1998).

Gamification by itself is an already powerful tool, but with the integration of new technologies – more specifically AI and VR – its potential is skyrocketing. Thanks to AI-led dashboards that are now able to serve as individualized performance coaches, tailoring behavior-specific nudges as well as pointing to precise learning interventions (Nayal et al., 2022). In a similar vein, VR simulations are based on sports place employees in immersive and often high-impact scenarios where they hone their skills to manage stress, make decisions, and work in collaboration to solve problems. That is not to say these tools do not facilitate performance – they certainly do. However, arguably, they impact mental health and workplace contentment even more, heralding a move from task-oriented work to experience-oriented engagement.

Gamification, therefore, is not a new thing anymore, and it's no longer novelty, but a strategic methodology to incentivize productivity and emotional resilience, and to help drive long-term growth of employees. This book provides a powerful lens to rethink work – not as a string of to-do lists – but as a stimulating, purposeful, and intellectually fulfilling task.

6.2. Chapter Objective

This chapter intends to show how the principles of gamification from sports, Esports, and behavioral science have been proven as being effective in bringing order to a chaotic workplace landscape of modern organizations for engagement, motivation, learning, and organizational well-being. The book provides a cohesive framework that combines game mechanics, performance psychology, immersive technology, and ethical design to evolve conventional workspaces into experience-based, emotionally gratifying ecosystems.

At the end of the chapter, readers should be able to:

- understand the theoretical bases of gamification, such as SDT, Flow Theory, and the principles of reinforcement psychology;
- explore any of the primary game design components (points, badges, leaderboards, adaptive AI system) and their effects on motivation or learning (e.g., in-class, abroad);
- discuss the value of VR and simulations as tools for stress management, leadership training, and team building;
- identify the ethical and Fairness of gamified systems design for diversity in the workplace;
- implement a measurable and phased approach to the roll-out of gamified tools, incorporating human resource (HR) objectives, organizational key results (OKRs), and tangible Return on investment (ROI); and
- discover future-ready workplace design trends like AI mentors, digital twins, and blockchain-based credentials.

This chapter closes the loop from theory to practice. It provides its readers with food for thought and practical steps for HR leaders, corporate trainers, and L&D professionals to future-proof their organizations through smart gamification.

6.3. Literature Review

There are multiple established psychological and behavioral theories that can act as an academic underpinning for gamification in the workplace. Of the former, SDT, by Deci and Ryan, 2000, is one of the most frequently referred to, according to which there is a basic human need for autonomy, competence, and relatedness that can be fulfilled in life in general but just as much in gamified environments. Designed with intention, gamified challenges will allow choice, structured challenges, and social elements such as leaderboards and team challenges. Research in the field indicates that environments that support all three of these fundamental SDT drivers will foster sustained intrinsic motivation and even higher levels of work engagement. Also, Flow Theory, by Csikszentmihalyi (1990), is a fundamental framework describing how engaged and absorbed people are in medium and optimal challenging activity, and which conditions are required to make them so. Flow states are associated with easily accessible and explicit environmental feedback systems, immediate goal setting, and adjustable challenge vs. skill density. Because of these factors, as Sweetser and Wyeth (2005) indicate, flow states have been considered especially compatible with gamified systems, and their availability in such organic environments as sport and gaming is now being translated into work simulations and AI-based learning environments. This nurtures anticipation, task focus, met-focused endurance, and often productivity.

Additionally, Skinnerian operant conditioning, as well as what has been repeatedly referred to as nudges, appear to be seminal and seminal-adjacent to conceptual gambits in gamification due to the evidence they provide that a combination of rewards, feedback, and nudges will over time condition behavior (Department of Psychology, Harvard University, n.d.). At work environments, micro-reinforcements take the shape of perceived badges and notifications and nudges – often linked to a metric of performance – and where the aforementioned feedback loop engages the dopaminergic feedback loops with the nuances of neural loops, a concept studied to some extend as far back as in the days of gaming and sports, is now more pertinent than ever to our understanding of habit and reward development and stimulus response in work – sort of a series of digital work stimuli that all take part on the same screen.

Gamification in the pursuit of learning (e.g., corporate training modules or education platforms) emphasizes knowledge and skill acquisition. In contrast, workplace gamification is much broader in scope – targeting productivity, engagement, well-being, and collaboration across departments and utilizing AI to track goal attainment while aligning individual behavior with organizational outcome, workplace gamification seamlessly integrates with a real-time performance mechanism (Nayal et al., 2022). Learning gamification may incentivize some type of course completion, while workplace gamification incentivizes long-term behaviors such as mentoring, innovating, or working as a team. Key insights from sports psychology and Esports have stretched the conversation around how these gamified environments can help support performance and mental resilience. Feedback loop, score tracking, increasing difficulty/scoring, and scenario-based drills are part of the foundation of high-performance athletic training and are now being translated into enterprise gamification. Adaptive AI, leaderboards, and skill trees, in particular, help to keep the user fired up and progressing in esports platforms – offering potent analogs to corporate talent engagement systems (Nolte, 2022). As athletes follow "practice + feedback + reward" loops when rehearsing for competition, corporate professionals, too, can be immersed in work-reality-based challenges that help them develop emotional resilience, self-assuredness, and agility in decision-making.

6.4. Theoretical Foundations of Gamification

Gamification in the work context has its roots in behavioral science and motivational psychology. Without getting into deep academic jargon, to design meaningful, engaging, and sustainable game-based interventions for employees, one must identify the psychological theory behind the mechanisms of why gamification works. We identify the theoretical pillars that underpin gamified spaces, and the relevant literature they come from – findings particularly relevant for learning, engagement, and performance.

6.4.1. Self-determination Theory

SDT (Deci & Ryan, 1985) holds that there are three innate needs that humans strive to obtain: Autonomy (autonomous control of behavior), Competence (effectiveness), and Relatedness (social connection). Individuals will feel more engaged and alive to the extent that their needs are being satisfied.

These needs can be fulfilled with gamified workplace environments:

- where avatars can be customized or guided, or there are self-paced learning quests that allow autonomy;
- using levels, badges, and progress feedback to provide competence-related feedback; and
- increased relatedness through team missions or social leaderboards.

According to studies, gamification is based on the SDT augments participation, as well as deep learning and emotional engagement (Deci & Ryan, 2000a).

6.4.2. Flow Theory

Flow Theory: Flow Theory, by Csikszentmihalyi (1990), is the psychological state of mind where an individual is fully immersed in the task at hand, matched with a skill level that is equal to the challenge they face. Gamification, on the other hand, triggers flow states naturally when tasks are:

- clearly defined;
- appropriately challenging; and
- paired with immediate feedback.

Adaptive difficulty, progression maps, and real-time feedback loops characterize well-designed gamified systems that help get the user into this engagement zone – so that your employees remain motivated, focused, and productive.

6.4.3. Behavioral Reinforcement and Reward Systems

Based on the behavioral perspective of reinforcement from B.F. Skinner's theory of operant conditioning (Skinner, 1953) behaviors followed by rewards are more likely to be repeated. Gamification harnesses this principle using:

- positive Feedback (like badges, recognition, rewards);
- uncertain rewards (i.e., gamification with surprise or randomly awarded rewards); and
- start with feedback loops (e.g., dashboards that display improvement).

This motivates participation, but it also cultivates a routine for learning, well-being, or productivity (Werbach & Hunter, 2012).

6.4.4. Goal-setting Theory

Locke and Latham (1990) found that performance is improved from clear, specific, and challenging goals accompanied by feedback. Gamification is backed up by this theory in that it allows for:

- dynamic goal hierarchies (e.g., quests, milestones);
- graphical representation of your progress (bars/level maps, etc.); and
- social comparison (e.g., team rankings).

In those high-stakes corporate environments, this is a structured gamified approach that can be designed to increase focus and persistence.

6.4.5. Cognitive Evaluation Theory

Cognitive Evaluation Theory (CET), which is a sub-theory within SDT, states that external rewards have the potential to increase or decrease intrinsic motivation based on how they are perceived. Rewards can be undermining (if they feel controlling) or enhancing (if they support competence and autonomy). Therefore, gamification needs to be done right – reward these behaviors, but do not rely on these kinds of external motivation too heavily.

6.5. The Science of Engagement

To comprehend the influence of gamification on employee behavior, it is important to consider the science behind the concepts of motivation and engagement. So, human engagement is not a random phenomenon: some neurochemicals determine it, but the neurocognitive feedback systems are also shaped by the way a person views the challenge, reward, and their development.

6.5.1. Neurobiology of Motivation: Dopamine, Prediction, and Reward

Dopamine is a neurotransmitter that underlies the brain processes of reward-seeking and rewarding learning through predictive and feedback signals

(Berridge & Robinson, 1998), and the pathways of motivation are rooted in dopamine. Dopamine is released in anticipation of receiving a reward (and less so on receiving it), reinforcing behaviors more likely to produce a successful outcome than simply enjoying success. The anticipation machine is the basis for gamification features like earning points, maintaining streaks, and leveling up.

These systems mimic the "achievement cycle" that is prevalent in sports and games where clear goals, instantaneous feedback, and increasing challenges preserve arousal and focus (Howard-Jones, 2014). This feature could reflect these dynamics in terms of workplace settings as well, which can then be added to the training or performance monitoring tools that help the employees stay mentally active and emotionally engaged in their work.

6.5.2. Confidence-building Through Micro-successes

Gamification allows the development of micro-successes – little, small-scale successes that help people build self-efficacy gradually. Bandura (1997) posited that self-efficacy, or a belief in one's ability to succeed, affects motivation, persistence, and commitment to goals. By dividing complicated goals into smaller achievable landmarks, gamified approaches reward diligence along the way rather than just at the end. This gradual approach to mastery aids in confidence-building, which can be very helpful for new employees or employees who are shifting to a digital work environment.

6.5.3. Preventing Burnout with Gameful Design

Burnout is an increasing issue in high-pressure corporate cultures. Research has shown that gameful experiences (those which entail gaming, tracking pleasure, and choice engagement) can mitigate emotional exhaustion and depersonalization, which are two of the most well-known features of burnout (Tetrick & Winslow, 2015). Well-designed gamification uses challenge–reward balance, recovery breaks, and positive feedback loops to counter boredom and airway internal motivation at work.

In addition, Sailer et al. (2017) establish a direct correlation between the reduction of stressors, increased psychological resilience, and employees feeling as if they have the upper hand over the learning and feedback cycle and are rewarded in real-time. These results are important because hybrid or remote contexts are those where people might feel most disconnected and distanced from each other.

6.5.4. Emotional Regulation and Psychological Safety

Psychological safety predicts innovation and collaboration (Edmondson, 1999), and workplaces that juxtapose challenge with safety – low-risk simulations, missions with teammates, and structured feedback – embody this concept. Thus, gamification environments imitate such conditions; they provide instant feedback, the opportunity to try again, as well as levels of increasing difficulty that facilitate the regulation of emotion.

This structure mirrors the "safe failure" model standard to sports coaching, where participants are permitted to experiment, make mistakes, and iterate toward mastery, in an atmosphere of non-judgment. When used for corporate learning, this can not only enhance the process of skill acquisition but also build trust, peer learning, and creative problem-solving.

6.6. Gamification Mechanics in HR Systems

The use of gamification in HR systems has surpassed the stage of being merely a gimmick to attract or reward. However, today, it is seen more as a strategy vehicle that ensures employees' actions are aligned with organizational goals and at the same time enhances their motivation, engagement, and performance. Game mechanics derived from sports, video games, and behavioral psychology are being adapted into the corporate setting to assist with incentives, feedback, and learning.

6.6.1. Points, Badges, and Leaderboards

The Points, Badges, and Leaderboards (PBL) is the global standard of the gamification mechanics as they are the most widely used in gamified solutions, as they are easy to implement and appealing to the nature of humans across industries. Points quantify the activity and the progress, badges celebrate success, and the leaderboard induces social comparison – these are the components of competition to motivate people to compete healthily (Hamari et al, 2014). This is a low-level motivator appeal, particularly to the drives of recognition (Deci & Ryan, 2000) and of competence. If these are used in the right direction, PBL systems might become a safe environment facilitating course completion, enhanced performance, and/or peer collaboration.

However, studies advise not to rely on the high-rewarding incentives that are inconsistent with meaningful work. Put another way, the benefits of gamification must be woven into the fabric of feedback systems that are substantive – not shiny baubles separated from pertinent behavior (Seaborn & Fels, 2015).

6.6.2. Skill Trees, Avatar Feedback, and Achievement Paths

Skill trees, borrowed from role-playing games and Esports platforms, are a graphical representation of stacking nous. In HR, they can be visually mapped to illustrate how an employee is developing from a novice in competencies to a skilled expert (e.g., communication, data literacy, or leadership). When these mechanics are coupled with avatar-based feedback – visual indicators of their progress or mastery of skills – they increase user identification and thus motivation (Xu et al., 2017).

When well defined and visible, that clarity can reduce cognitive ambiguity around what forward means in an achieved state, and it clarifies how they can win. Particularly useful in onboarding programs or internal learning academies where a gradual learning curve can incentivize performance and course completions.

6.6.3. AI Dashboards as Performance Coaches

If we go a little technical, one of the greatest innovations that speaks of the gamified HR systems is the concept of AI-powered dashboards that function like your personal performance coaches. People are aware (and some researchers have pointed out) that these tools are built upon tracking of behavior, provide nudges and real-time behavioral prompts, and are making interventions that are highly personalized based on the data-centric conception of the person (Nayal et al., 2022). For example, if an employee consistently misses deadlines, then AI can suggest a micro-course on time management or a mentor.

These dashboards deliver feedback somewhat like performance coaches in sport, delivering constructive, unvarnished feedback along with invaluable insights. Second, they reduce reliance on periodic performance reviews, offering continuous development loops and customized paths per player, making way for timely feedback and real-time connection in the paradigm of new-age HR thought.

6.6.4. Linking Gamification with OKRs and Key Performance Indicators

To move from engagement to impact, gamification mechanics need to be closely mapped to OKRs and Key Performance Indicators (KPIs). As another example, you could attach a leaderboard for real revenue or lead conversions if you have a sales team. Along the same lines, learning platforms could award points for completing modules that map to key areas of a job, ensuring that gamified activity is aligned to strategic priorities.

Keeping this connection ensures that gamification serves not only as an engagement-boosting tactic but also as a means to influence organizational performance, accountability, and transparency directly. These are the kind of aligned systems that function as a lens through which one can see between self and accomplishment, but also represent that all are pulling their weight toward the shared captaincy.

6.7. VR/Virtually Guided Employee Training

VR in Training – modern organizations are using immersive simulations and redefining VR training to train employees on soft skills, resilience, team bonding, and much more. Unlike most e-learning and classic classroom environments, VR-based learning environments provide the person with immersive, high-risk situations to repeat practice, fail, and learn without real-world day-to-day repercussions. These are vital with stress resilience, collaborative problem-solving skills, and emotional agility, which are tailor-made for success in modern workplaces.

6.7.1. Stress Simulation, Decision-making Under Pressure, and Building Resilience

One of the most fascinating usages of VR in corporate applications is stress simulation and crisis management training. Environments such as VR enable employees to practice their emotional reactions and increase their tolerance to stress by mimicking high-stakes challenges (e.g., crisis reactions, decisions under uncertainty, and conflict management) (Cheng et al., 2021). Immersive simulations, in contrast, are dynamic, adapting to user behavior and offer virtual AI effects that enhance guidance and develop skills of self-awareness and coping skills – both workshops are tepidly traditional.

These simulators mirror some of the concepts in sports psychology, preparing athletes in high-pressure situations, and in turn acclimatizing their brains to the presence of pressure, managing their mental fortitude. Workplace training that aims to soak people with resilience not in words, but in experience, confined experience to build up the muscles of resilience (Neumann et al., 2018).

6.7.2. Sports-based Team Bonding Missions

Drawing allusion to the team-based world of traditional sport, this most recent form focuses on team-building through missions that rely on bonding in order to pass them, using VR, things like simulated obstacle courses that are impossible to complete without communicating in the virtual space or problem-solving games that require employees to work together in order to reach and unlock levels. Those are the missions that mimic the dynamics of a sports team; shared goals, delineated responsibilities, and fast decision making, fostering empathy and silos avoidance in cross-functional teams.

Cooperative VR games can not only enhance interpersonal insights but also help mitigate motivation and belonging in hybrid or distributed teams (Nørskov et al., 2021). Well, these are some very important advantages, especially during the pandemic, when physical distancing can ruin the work culture and society.

6.7.3. Cultivating Leadership, Kindness, and Emotions

VR is great for soft-skills training that traditional media struggles to replicate. This type of test could see leadership development modules place employees in situations such as managing an underperforming team or dealing with an ethical dilemma and then challenge them to make decisions and be given immediate feedback on their decisions. These scenarios are not simply a test of judgment; they are a training ground for emotional intelligence, empathy, and communication skills (Hamilton et al, 2021).

Some platforms use emotion AI, a term that refers to the design of software applications that can recognize and process human emotions, and capture verbal cues, physical expressions, and body language to monitor these behaviors, enabling people to reflect and improve over time. That suddenly differentiates it from media consumption: you can use it to tune and re-tune your emotionality, which is a vital skill set for any leader doing a high-leverage job.

6.7.4. Advantages over Passive Training Modules

Cumulative context in corporate training is a big problem when it comes to poor retention, lack of buy-in (engagement), and content not being contextualized.

Therefore, VR overcomes these limitations as experiential learning is the key principle of adult learning (Kolb, 1984). The primary explanation for VR being more effective at knowledge transfer and behavior change than other methods is that immersion of the learner in a task-oriented 3D environment enhances the attention, emotional salience, and the depth of processing (i.e., memory encoding) (Makransky & Lilleholt, 2018).

Moreover, VR leads to a higher completion rate for voluntary programs and higher levels of reported satisfaction, resulting in a practical, scalable alternative to tedious video modules or pseudo-DIGEST reading materials.

6.8. Designing Inclusive and Ethical Gamified Systems

Gamification is still going to be at the heart of digital workplace ecosystems (to read more about gamification in design, visit the page). However, now more than ever, ethical design and inclusivity are imperative. If not managed correctly, this can result in system architectures that repel certain classes of employees, unnecessary psychological pressure on some employees, and/or breach of user privacy. Organizations need to cover the diversity of user needs or preferences and design ethical guardrails in the system architecture to provide sustainable gamification that is beneficial for the well-being and performance of users.

6.8.1. Accessibility for Neurodiverse and Remote Workers

Inclusion begins with accessibility. While it is good to have gamification tools for the digitally native workforce, they may not be suitable for all employees. Not all employees are competitive by nature, nor responsive to a reward model. For instance, neurodiverse people (e.g., people with Attention-Deficit/Hyperactivity Disorder (AD/HD), autism spectrum, and learning differences) may be more or less sensitive to certain high-level qualities of environments, they may need shorter or longer cycle feedback, and they may prefer more or less social interaction (Austin & Pisano, 2017). Usability facilitates its usage. Viable is esthetically based, so it is broken into two metrics: Comfort (good) and Design (oof). It reminds you to mute hearing task reminders, as it were, and features a silent(ish) process of success, supported by tool visualizations.

Similarly, systems that rely heavily on physical presence or synchronous attendance must not make life miserable for remote and hybrid employees at the same time. These gamified platforms need the same level of accessibility across time zones and locations and provide for a parity of access through their goals, aiming to be asynchronous, missions can be done at your own pace, and accessibility through a cloud.

6.8.2. Avoiding Manipulation and Competition Fatigue

Gamification suffers an ethical paradox where system elements designed more for maximizing the time spent on an application, gamified engagement metrics, rather than well-being, drive design. Inescapable cycles of rewards and social comparison via leaderboards can create competition fatigue, particularly in already overworked employees (Zichermann & Linder, 2013). Eventually, that can cause our anxiety, make us feel less satisfied with our job, or may even burn us out.

To combat this, experts suggest mixing competitive and cooperative mechanics, offering employees an opt-out of public leaderboards, and focusing on individual growth vs. peer comparison. In ethical gamification, we steer clear of coercive incentives, prioritizing autonomy, mastery, and purpose (Deci & Ryan, 2000b).

6.8.3. Ensuring Algorithmic Fairness in AI-based Nudges

A large number of sophisticated gamified systems incorporate AI-induced nudges – automated nudges intended to promote productivity, behavior change, or learning. Though such tools can be practical, they also bring up pressing issues of algorithm fairness and bias. Legacy data folded into AI model training further bias these datasets: women still earn less than men, so if the model dials historical data and pays a lesser amount to a woman than a man, the model is going to pay the woman less simply because she is a woman (Raji & Buolamwini, 2019), furthering the negative discriminatory cycle based on gender, role or performance history.

Developers must use bias audits, varied training datasets, and transparent model logic to avoid biases and be fair. Furthermore, transparency about how nudges are created and how employees can provide feedback on them ensures a human-in-the-loop design that upholds user dignity.

6.8.4. Data Privacy, Transparency, and Consent

Gamified tracking systems amass vast amounts of behavioral data – from performance metrics to emotional responses, to screenshots and videos of our digital interactions. This demands transparent informed consent, solid data governance policies, and open usage practices to implement ethically. Employees should be trained on:

- What data is being collected?
- How it will be analyzed?
- Who will have access?
- How it will affect decisions (i.e., promotions or feedback)?

Moreover, following a principle of data minimization and GDPR-style compliance will not only foster trust but also minimize the risk of litigation. In addition, providing opt-in and opt-out options is in line with modern digital ethics ideals (Floridi et al., 2018).

6.9. Roadmap for Corporate Adoption

To make gamification a sustainable and impactful aspect of workplace strategy, organizations need more than one-off experiments; they need a roadmap.

Successful adoption needs to match business goals with behavior design and be supported by the right tech and culture. In this section, we outline a road map to incorporate gamification into HR and learning systems, enabling you to validate your impact and ROI.

6.9.1. Step-by-Step Framework for Implementation

Needs Assessment: This is preceded by an entire diagnostic phase where HR leaders assess the existing challenges, such as disengagement, high attrition, or learning gaps. Surveys, interviews, and analytics from pre-existing HR tech can reveal explicit pain points and compiled preferences of the user(s). This information is used to clarify what needs to be addressed by game mechanics (Werbach & Hunter, 2012).

Goal alignment with HR strategy: Once golden gaps are discovered, they need to be fitted to high-level HR business goals like improving onboarding processes, increasing learning retention, enhancing collaboration, or increasing employee wellness. Alignment guarantees that the game mechanics are not throwaway ideas meant to captivate players merely, but rather, the game mechanics are designed to fulfill strategic aims (Landers et al., 2015).

Game element design: Game mechanics – points, quests, leaderboards, avatars, or nudges – are tailored by organizations, based on the goals. Components can be aligned not only with the organizational culture but also with the personas being targeted. For example, introverted knowledge workers may do better with progress bars and personal goals, while sales teams may do better with leader boards and competition.

The mechanics should correspond to the principles of autodetermination theory – e-friendly autonomy, competence, and relatedness (Deci & Ryan, 2000).

Take up of tech: LMS, Dashboards, Wellness Tools: Next comes technology integration. Gamification systems can be plugged and played into the existing HR tech as follows:

- LMS for gamification of training.
- Wellness apps for health-related engagement.
- Performance dashboards for linking performance to OKR and KPI.

It reduces push-back and integrates the system into employee habits. AI-enabled platforms can provide personalized feedback, nudges for coaching, and individualized targets.

Pilot, feedback, and scale: This should be accompanied by piloting it first with a specific team or use case before full rollout. Qualitative and behavioral feedback helps refine gameplay mechanics and shed unwanted pressure. For instance, if one approaches the metrics of engagement rates, training completion, and time-on-platform as indications for grow, pause, or tweak (Sailer et al., 2017), then the design of the course can be iteratively adjusted through subsequent revisions.

This enables scaling those successful pilots across the organization, on continuous iteration cycles.

Table 6.1. Roadmap for Corporate Gamification Adoption.

Step	Stage	Key Activities	Outcomes Expected
1	Needs assessment	Identify employee engagement gaps Collect data via surveys/ HR analytics	Clear understanding of problems to solve
2	Goal alignment	Align gamification with HR goals (e.g., onboarding, learning, well-being)	Strategic clarity and focused implementation
3	Game element design	Choose game mechanics (PBL, avatars, badges) Personalize for audience	Increased engagement and motivation
4	Tech integration	Integrate with LMS, wellness apps, performance dashboards	Seamless experience and adoption
5	Pilot, feedback and scale	Run small-scale pilots Collect feedback Measure early ROI	Improved model ready for organization-wide rollout
6	ROI mapping and optimization	Track KPIs (engagement, happiness, productivity) Iterate using insights	Demonstrated business value and long-term scaling

Source: Authors' creation.

6.9.2. Mapping Gamification to Measurable ROI

Gamification is no gimmick – it has to show real ROI. Key metrics include:

- Other poll scores (pulse, Net Promoter Scores, etc.).
- Indicators of well-being (e.g., status from wellness apps, burning rate).
- Learning outcomes (completions, assessments, etc.).
- Behavioral shifts (e.g., increased collaboration, decreased absenteeism).

HR teams can justify budgets, optimize their strategies, and foster a performance culture based on both data and well-being (Burke, 2014) using dashboards that correlate gamified engagement to business KPIs. As seen in Table 6.1, the roadmap adopted for gamification.

6.10. Future Directions

Gamification is moving beyond simply a motivational element – as organizations undergo digital transformation, it becomes a strategic driver of organizational agility, inclusion, and innovation. The future will entail more advanced AI customization, immersive technologies, social contract features, and mission-driven culture development. These trends will reshape gamification to be an enabler for your employee performance, as well as your organizational values and global competencies.

6.10.1. The AI Mentor and Digital Twin

The concepts of AI-based virtual mentors and digital twins – intelligent representation of individual employees or an environment being used for plan–simulate–feedback cycles on how to do things – will influence the future of workplace gamification profoundly. Those systems will monitor personalization and behavior tracking of every individual, suggest activities to learn based on skill level, and provide a nudge in context as needed in real-time.

For instance, a digital twin of a new employee may simulate their learning curve, thereby suggesting training modules or stress coping methods depending on predicted gaps. Such models would facilitate hyper-personalized coaching that is adaptable to employee performance while maximizing learning productivity and engagement (People Dynamics, 2023).

6.10.2. MR in Hybrid Team Dynamics

With workplaces continuing to embrace the hybrid and remote models, MR – a combination of augmented reality and VR – will enable distributed teams to work in virtual immersive environments. Workers could hold strategy sessions within virtual boardrooms, compete in avatar-based team challenges, or take part in gamified wellness exercises at home.

Thus, such MR experiences will help with socializing for team bonding, boosting emotional intelligence, and increasing engagement from employees who may not meet each other physically, which will help them feel less socially isolated and more collaborative toward the same goal in life (Psico-Smart Editorial Team, 2025).

6.10.3. Gamification for Sustainability, DEI, and Culture-building

Gamification's next wave will reinforce value-based behaviors: Diversity, equity, and inclusion (DEI), sustainability, and ethical decision-making. Moreover, companies are starting to gamify these types of goals – a lower carbon footprint goal for an employee, actions of inclusive leadership, or hours volunteered, and more – and they are rewarding an employee for these behaviors that align with the values of an organization.

These systems will encourage culture-building, positive reinforcement, and translate abstract policy into concrete, daily behaviors. Leaderboards could, for example, identify departments that are doing the best job of implementing green office practices or diversity actions, thereby promoting social norms through gamified nudges (Kirchner-Krath et al., 2024).

6.10.4. Blockchain-based Badges and Portable Credentials

In order to enhance credibility and transferability, gamified achievements will become progressively stored on blockchain, allowing employees to transport their credentials (completed missions, badges earned, or competencies demonstrated) from one company to another or even one platform to another.

Badges can be built around an underlying blockchain to provide verifiable proof of soft skills like collaboration or ethical leadership that are often challenging to capture in traditional evaluations. Such transparency will ensure better alignment of hiring, talent mobility, and lifelong learning with industry needs (Grech & Camilleri, 2017).

6.11. Call to Action

Given the growing organizational challenges around engagement, retention, mental well-being, and evolving digitally to meet staff needs, gamification is no longer a futuristic experiment but an age-old imperative. HR leaders, L&D professionals, organizational psychologists, and senior managers need to take action now and reinvent what their workplace ecosystems will look and feel like by (re) designing them based on evidence-aligned gamification frameworks.

Begin with your current systems: Are employees driven from within? Is learning enjoyable and personalized? Does your feedback loop help you grow in real time? If, on the other hand, they fall short, implement micro-changes – like leaderboards, adaptive learning paths, or team missions – to spark changes in morale and performance that will be visible.

Invest in capacity-building: Collaborate with researchers, technologists, and behaviorists to co-design gamified platforms that place psychological safety and inclusive design at their core. Start rolling out some optional pilots – stress tests, incentive-driven well-being goals, AI-powered dashboards – and listen, iterate, and scale.

More importantly, shift your mindset: Gamification is not about fun at work – it is about fulfilling work needs for meaning and human-centricity. You Instinctively Evolve To Engage Because When Work Feels Like Purposeful Play, Engagement Is a Habit, Not a Mandate.

The time is now to change the narrative: Provide your teams with tools, insights, and autonomy to be successful in a world where motivation is not controlled but felt.

6.12. Conclusion

The workplace today has evolved from productivity outputs or stale management hierarchies, to experiences, emotions, and agile learning ecosystems. This chapter considered the promise of gamification, built on bricks of well-documented psychology and laminated with the varnish of technology advances, as a means of re-imagining the relationship between employees and their work, their goals, and each other.

From SDT and Flow Theory to AI dashboards and immersive VR environments, gamified workplaces are becoming environments that fulfill the psychological need for autonomy and social relatedness (per SDT) and environments that induce flow (per Flow Theory). Gamification driven by sports-like simulation, feedback loops, and reward structure can be a surefire way to keep the motivation level high, foster emotional resilience, and ensure long-term retention – the three things that no amount of training or HR system can achieve to the level of effectiveness.

However, this change needs to happen properly – inclusively, equitably, respecting data privacy, and the psychological safety of our employees. If we have a thoughtfully designed gamification strategy that is based on research, gamification is no longer a trend or a short-term solution to increase engagement. It becomes a sustainable process of having motivated, positive, and purposeful performance-oriented employees.

The following decades are looking to be more hybrid, technology-oriented, and people-centered; there is a niche between art and science but below the level of purposeful design and strategy in gamification. Gamification is not about making games as entertainment but rather about taking the motivational templates of games and creating something of substance and utility – something of substance and utility that occurs in the workplace and creates deep psychological rewards.

Declaration

We hereby declare that the content of this chapter is entirely original and has been developed without the use of any large language model (LLM) or AI-based content generation tools. The ideas, arguments, and interpretations presented are the result of independent academic inquiry and synthesis.

For the purpose of improving clarity and language quality, Grammarly was used solely as a tool for English grammar refinement and proofreading. No content was auto-generated, rephrased, or expanded using AI-based writing assistants.

References

Austin, R. D., & Pisano, G. P. (2017). Neurodiversity as a competitive advantage. *Harvard Business Review*, *95*(3), 96–103. https://hbr.org/2017/05/neurodiversity-as-a-competitive-advantage

Bandura, A. (1997). *Self-efficacy: The exercise of control*. W.H. Freeman.

Berridge, K. C., & Robinson, T. E. (1998). What is the role of dopamine in reward: Hedonic impact, reward learning, or incentive salience? *Brain Research Reviews*, *28*(3), 309–369. https://doi.org/10.1016/S0165-0173(98)00019-8

Burke, B. (2014). *Gamify: How gamification motivates people to do extraordinary things*. Routledge.

Cheng, G., Zhang, X., & Wang, Y. (2021). Enhancing resilience through virtual reality: A new paradigm for training under pressure. *Computers & Education*, *172*, 104252. https://doi.org/10.1016/j.compedu.2021.104252

Csikszentmihalyi, M. (1990). *Flow: The psychology of optimal experience*. Harper & Row.

Deci, E. L., & Ryan, R. M. (1985). *Intrinsic motivation and self-determination in human behavior*. Springer Science & Business Media. https://doi.org/10.1007/978-1-4899-2271-7

Deci, E. L., & Ryan, R. M. (2000). The “what” and “why” of goal pursuits: Human needs and the self-determination of behavior. *Psychological Inquiry*, *11*(4), 227–268. https://doi.org/10.1207/S15327965PLI1104_01

Department of Psychology, Harvard University. (n.d.). *B. F. Skinner*. Retrieved September 5, 2025, from https://psychology.fas.harvard.edu/people/b-f-skinner

Edmondson, A. (1999). Psychological safety and learning behavior in work teams. *Administrative Science Quarterly*, *44*(2), 350–383. https://doi.org/10.2307/2666999

Floridi, L., Cowls, J., Beltrametti, M., Chatila, R., Chazerand, P., Dignum, V., Luetge, C., Madelin, R., Pagallo, U., Rossi, F., Schafer, B., Valcke, P., & Vayena, E. (2018). AI4People—An ethical framework for a good AI society: Opportunities, risks, principles, and recommendations. *Minds and Machines*, *28*(4), 689–707. https://doi.org/10.1007/s11023-018-9482-5

Gallup. (2021). *State of the global workplace: 2021 report*. Gallup, Inc. https://www.gallup.com/workplace/349484/state-of-the-global-workplace-2021-report.aspx

Grech, A., & Camilleri, A. F. (2017). *Blockchain in education* [Joint Research Centre (JRC) Science for Policy Report]. Publications Office of the European Union. https://doi.org/10.2760/60649

Hamari, J., Koivisto, J., & Sarsa, H. (2014). Does gamification work? – A literature review of empirical studies on gamification. In *Hawaii International Conference on System Science* (47th ed., pp. 3025–3034). https://doi.org/10.1109/hicss.2014.377

Hamilton, D., McKechnie, J., Edgerton, E., & Wilson, C. (2021). Immersive virtual reality as a pedagogical tool in education: A systematic literature review of quantitative learning outcomes and experimental design. *Journal of Computers in Education*, *8*(1), 1–32. https://doi.org/10.1007/s40692-020-00169-6

Howard-Jones, P. A. (2014). Neuroscience and education: Myths and messages. *Nature Reviews Neuroscience*, *15*(12), 817–824. https://doi.org/10.1038/nrn3817

Kirchner-Krath, J., Dijkstra-Silva, S., Morschheuser, B., & von Korflesch, H. F. O. (2024). Gameful systems for corporate sustainability: Systematic review, conceptual framework and research agenda on gamification and sustainable employee behavior in companies. *Internet Research*. Advance online publication. https://doi.org/10.1108/INTR-06-2024-1000

Kolb, D. A. (1984). *Experiential learning: Experience as the source of learning and development*. Prentice Hall.

Landers, R. N., Bauer, K. N., & Callan, R. C. (2015). Gamification of task performance with leaderboards: A goal-setting experiment. *Computers in Human Behavior*, *71*, 508–515. https://doi.org/10.1016/j.chb.2015.08.008

Locke, E. A., & Latham, G. P. (1990). *A theory of goal setting and task performance*. Prentice Hall.

Makransky, G., & Lilleholt, L. (2018). A structural equation modeling investigation of the emotional value of immersive virtual reality in education. *Educational Technology Research and Development*, *66*, 1141–1164. https://doi.org/10.1007/s11423-018-9581-2

Nayal, M., Dwivedi, Y. K., Rana, N. P., & Alalwan, A. A. (2022). Integrating artificial intelligence into a talent management model to increase enterprise performance and employee engagement. *Frontiers in Psychology*, *13*, 998222. https://doi.org/10.3389/fpsyg.2022.998222

Neumann, D. L., Moffitt, R. L., & Thomas, P. R. (2018). A critical review of virtual reality in sport. *International Journal of Sports Science & Coaching*, *13*(4), 593–602. https://doi.org/10.1177/1747954118787493

Nolte, M. (2022). Exploring the use of gamification in enhancing employee engagement in entrepreneurial firms. *Journal of Technology in Entrepreneurship and Strategic Management*, *1*(2), 28–39. https://doi.org/10.61838/kman.jtesm.1.2.4

Nørskov, S., Mathiesen, M., & Damholdt, M. F. (2021). Enhancing team learning through VR: Exploring virtual collaboration in professional settings. *Virtual Reality*, *25*(3), 719–737. https://doi.org/10.1007/s10055-021-00488-y

People Dynamics. (2023, June–July). *Digital twin of employee – The future of people analytics*. People Dynamics. Retrieved September 5, 2025, from https://issuu.com/msgura/docs/people_dynamics_june-july-2023/s/25332693

Psico-Smart Editorial Team. (2025, March 4). *What unconventional strategies can leaders employ to harness the power of emotional intelligence in remote teams, and what studies support these approaches?* Psico-Smart Blogs. Retrieved September 5, 2025, from https://blogs.psico-smart.com/blog-what-unconventional-strategies-can-leaders-employ-to-harness-the-power-190908

Raji, I. D., & Buolamwini, J. (2019). Actionable auditing: Investigating the impact of publicly naming biased performance results of commercial AI products. In *Proceedings of the 2019 AAAI/ACM conference on AI, ethics, and society* (pp. 429–435). https://doi.org/10.1145/3306618.3314244

Ryan, R. M., & Deci, E. L. (2000a). Intrinsic and extrinsic motivations: Classic definitions and new directions. *Contemporary Educational Psychology*, *25*(1), 54–67. https://doi.org/10.1006/ceps.1999.1020

Ryan, R. M., & Deci, E. L. (2000b). Self-determination theory and the facilitation of intrinsic motivation, social development, and well-being. *American Psychologist*, *55*(1), 68–78. https://doi.org/10.1037/0003-066X.55.1.68

Sailer, M., Hense, J., Mayr, S., & Mandl, H. (2017). How gamification motivates: An experimental study of the effects of specific game design elements on psychological need satisfaction. *Computers in Human Behavior*, *69*, 371–380. https://doi.org/10.1016/j.chb.2016.12.033

Seaborn, K., & Fels, D. I. (2015). Gamification in theory and action: A survey. *International Journal of Human-Computer Studies*, *74*, 14–31. https://doi.org/10.1016/j.ijhcs.2014.09.006

Skinner, B. F. (1953). *Science and human behavior*. Macmillan.

Sweetser, P., & Wyeth, P. (2005). GameFlow: A model for evaluating player enjoyment in games. *Computers in Entertainment*, *3*(3), 1–24. https://doi.org/10.1145/1077246.1077253

Tetrick, L. E., & Winslow, C. J. (2015). Workplace stress and employee health: Challenges and opportunities for health psychology. *The Annual Review of Organizational Psychology and Organizational Behavior*, *2*, 259–289. https://doi.org/10.1146/annurev-orgpsych-032414-111341

Werbach, K., & Hunter, D. (2012). *For the win: How game thinking can revolutionize your business*. Wharton Digital Press.

Xu, B., Chen, N. S., & Chen, G. (2017). Effects of teacher role on student engagement in WeChat-based online discussions. *The International Review of Research in Open and Distributed Learning*, *18*(2). https://doi.org/10.19173/irrodl.v18i2.2603

Zichermann, G., & Linder, J. (2013). *The gamification revolution: How leaders leverage game mechanics to crush the competition*. McGraw-Hill Education.

Chapter 7

Enhancing Employee Well-being and Mental Health Through AI

Priya Makhija[a], *Elizabeth Chacko*[b], *Ananda S.*[c] *and R. Thanga Kumar*[a]

[a]*Center for Management Studies, JAIN (Deemed-to-be University), Bangalore, India*
[b]*Christ University, Bangalore, India*
[c]*Postgraduate Studies, Research & Innovation Department, College of Banking and Financial Studies, Muscat, Sultanate of Oman*

Abstract

Today's workplaces are characterized by an environment that is often detrimental to well-being, as our lives are technologically overloaded with work that leads to stress and burnout. There is growing recognition that for business to continue operating successfully and at a profit, it is important to address the mental well-being of employees. In this regard, wellness services are actively being developed and are now moving away from standard cookie-cutter solutions to solutions with a personalized, technological approach. This chapter will look at artificial intelligence (AI) and virtual reality (VR) through the theory of positive emotions (PERMA) developed by Martin Seligman to create a more holistic understanding of technological advancement in wellness. It's a qualitative case study of three companies using innovative technologies for well-being: Happily.ai, Amazon, and Deloitte. The tools of AI are applied by Amazon to assess the mood of employees and recognize early symptoms of burnout to provide quick assistance to employees in distress to keep them positive. Deloitte has utilized VR tools to assist employees with emotional resilience and stress management in a controlled, safe space. Happily.ai utilizes AI mindfulness to help employees have an improved emotional experience and build healthier workplace relationships that ultimately lead to a sense

Nurturing AI-Powered HR Analytics and Virtual Reality in Employee Psychology and Workplace Happiness, Part A, 115–132

Published under exclusive licence by Emerald Publishing Limited
doi:10.1108/978-1-80686-125-520261005

of accomplishment and connection in the long term. PERMA will provide with a theoretical backbone on technology use in workplace wellness which could help to set the stage for sustainable business decision-making more broadly, as technology continues to increase in importance for data-driven predictions.

Keywords: Employee well-being; artificial intelligence; virtual reality; workplace stress; PERMA framework; immersive therapy; psychological safety

7.1. Introduction

Workplaces are evolving since digital technologies are increasingly factoring into the realization of organizational performance, invention, and competitiveness. This is a negative factor in working and role perception of employees, daily working routines, communication, collaboration, and execution of human jobs are affected (Bailey et al., 2022). AI in the workplace has a significant impact on workers, particularly with regard to their well-being. According to a study by (Valtonen et al., 2025) instead directly affecting employee wellbeing, the use of AI has an indirect effect through work-related factors like task optimization and safety which highlights how important it is to strategically apply AI to enhance aspects of work that are important to employees in order to optimize the wellbeing benefits of AI adoption. Adoption should consequently take place since AI shows visible improvement in the areas of data security, occupational health and organizational activities, and procedures. With the right consideration, on the other hand, AI by itself can contribute to improved worker wellness and better human–AI integration on the job. Organizations must be able to evolve as a result of the increasingly stressful environment to address hybrid anxieties in the workplace and potential burnout-linked issues and consider how AI can be used to aid employee mental health and emotional resilience (Urrila et al., 2025). If AI can help an organization in identifying early signs of cognitive strain, provide those with real-time emotional support, and suggest personalized wellness interventions, then workforce managers could set aside time working with a very human touch for social interactions and comforting (Olawade et al., 2024) and this will use intelligent digital tools to increase employee satisfaction and boost company revenue (Kassa & Worku, 2025). AI development opportunities have heralded an immense potential for the businesses that take care of their employees' psychological well-being. This is to say more tailor-made, robust, exact, and cost-friendly solutions are being offered (Zirar et al., 2023), leading to companies based on innovation that have set forth to address these concerns by innovating bespoke and adaptive mental health solutions that cater to the specific needs from utilizing cutting-edge technology such as VR and AI (Thakkar et al., 2024).

At this significant confluence of mental health and technological advances, there's a lot of room for improvement, yet there are additionally challenges.

Realizing this vision would require extensive study into powered by AI behavioral health uses, responsible data governance, and efforts in strengthening human resources (HR) professionals and prospective managers in digital wellness. Additionally, businesses must maintain transparency, encourage confidence in AI, and ensure that sensitive employee data is accessed ethically (Bajwa et al., 2021).

Participation by employees, psychological wellness, work–life balance, happiness at work, and social interaction are all critical to a company's success (Urrila et al., 2025; Zirar et al., 2023). The condition of burnout strain, and impaired psychological condition can lead to higher absenteeism, turnover, and worse performance (Goetzel et al., 2014). The World Health Organization has classified workplace stress as a global epidemic and the challenges associated with it have intensified since the pandemic (*COVID-19 pandemic triggers 25% increase in prevalence of anxiety and depression worldwide*, n.d.). In light of this reality, traditional approaches to wellness are insufficient due to which AI is being employed to improve on employee well-being through the use of AI chatbots and virtual therapists who deliver real-time mental healthcare using Cognitive Behavioral Therapy and future analytics can be generated tailoring well-being recommendations by identifying signs of burnout, stress, or disengagement. AI scheduling systems nudge boundaries that benefit mental well-being and promote optimum work–life balance. Natural Language Processing algorithms monitor the well-being of organizations and personalize career development (Cronin, 2025).

The significance of employee well-being for long-term success is becoming more widely acknowledged by organizations; however, AI is transforming wellness assistance by increasing accessibility, proactivity, and customization to meet individual needs. AI-powered mental health systems provide individualized wellness advice, such as stress reduction, and sleep enhancement, by analyzing physiological, behavioral, and productivity data. Employers can take prompt action when fatigue or mental health issues are identified early, thanks to predictive analytics. Continuous care is promoted by real-time tools such as virtual assistants and AI chatbots, which provide round-the-clock assistance through data-driven insights which help AI to improve HR productivity and lessens the stigma associated while asking for assistance this kind of integrated, scalable AI solutions that blend human expertise and prediction algorithms are provided by businesses such as Kana Health (2025).

Giuntella et al. (2025) examined how German workers' health and well-being are affected by AI technology. It indicated a rise in self-reported health status and satisfaction but found no discernible benefits of AI on well-being or future worries. Nevertheless, the study had drawbacks, such as being in the early phases of the AI revolution, utilizing single-item assessments, concentrating on occupational-level indicators, and failing to generalize to young workers. Additionally, COVID-19-related variables can have an impact on the outcomes, also it is essential to put laws in place that protect employees who are at risk by offering efficient training sessions, assistance throughout technological advancements shifts in order to lessen the detrimental effects of AI on worker well-being; however, the obstacles of applying AI to mental well-being are intricate and constantly changing. Model validation, the creation of robust regulatory frameworks, constant investment in innovation, and a dedication to transparency are all necessary to realize its full potential in enhancing psychological treatment (Olawade et al., 2024; Thakkar et al., 2024). These initiatives will have a big impact on how mental health therapy develops in the future as AI technology improves, making it more moral, useful, and relatable for individuals (Giuntella et al., 2025). Strategies powered by AI require intense examination and verification processes to ensure reliability, uniformity, and efficiency. AI algorithms that have undergone extensive research and validation and they are becoming more and more popular (Sokoler, 2024; Vanhée et al., 2025) leading to be effective in enhancing mental health outcomes and it encourages openness and makes it easier for patients and doctors to comprehend the logic underlying AI-generated insights and judgments (Olawade et al., 2024).

7.2. PERMA Model

Martin Seligman, a psychologist, created the PERMA framework as a basis for human happiness. The components of well-being are summarized as follows:

- *Positive emotion*: Feeling happy, thankful, hopeful.
- *Engagement*: Being completely absorbed in or "in flow" with one's work.
- *Relationships*: Building and maintaining fulfilling and supportive social bonds.
- *Meaning*: Having a sense of direction or being part of a grand scheme.
- *Accomplishment*: Setting goals and pursuing them for self-fulfillment.

In today's hybrid and high-pressure work environment, companies worldwide are turning toward science-backed approaches to foster the well-being of their workers. Businesses that embrace PERMA thus experience a whole raft of benefits, from higher productivity to better retention; however, this model has since been expanded with the addition of four factors that extend it to organizational settings, in the form of PERMA+4, namely: Physical health, Mindset, Work environment, Economic security (Donaldson et al., 2022; van Zyl HappyBytes, 2025). This research uses a qualitative research design applying a case study method to investigate the ways in which AI-based platforms support employee mental health and well-being. The case study method is an appropriate choice as it allows for the in-depth exploration of organizational practice and experiences. Selection criteria for companies included innovation in mental health practices, integration of advanced technologies (particularly AI), and a demonstrable focus on improving employee mental well-being. Companies were chosen based on their active use of AI solutions aimed at emotional health monitoring, stress reduction, or mental health support in workplace settings.

7.3. Case Reviews

7.3.1. Case Study 1: Amazon – AI for Real-time Mood Monitoring

The growing incidence of mental wellness problems in working environments, due to rigorous work schedules and external pressures, have highlighted the pressing need for creative ways to promote workers' well-being (WHO, 2024). AI is emerging as a powerful tool with the potential to revolutionize how organizations monitor, understand, and enhance employee mental health and well-being (Bokhari et al., 2024; Tahir et al., 2024). AI's application in HR and employee well-being spans various functions, from recruitment and onboarding to performance management and personalized support (Benabou et al., 2024). In the context of well-being, AI can analyze vast datasets (e.g., communication patterns, work habits, sentiment in text) to identify early signs of stress, burnout, or disengagement, enabling proactive interventions (Mantello & Ho, 2024). Hiler (2024) highlights how AI is becoming "the next retention lever," suggesting that technologies supporting employee experience and well-being are crucial for talent management. AI-powered chatbots can provide immediate, confidential mental health support, while personalized platforms can offer resources tailored to individual needs (Fitzpatrick et al., 2017). In this chapter, we have taken few companies approaches toward well-being and mental health. The companies are Amazon, Deloitte, and Happily.

While Amazon has not explicitly marketed a system named "AI for Real-Time Mood Monitoring," its extensive use of AI to monitor employee performance, productivity, and even movements in its fulfillment centers provides a basis for discussing the potential and implications of such technology for well-being (Ye, 2022). Amazon's systems track metrics like "time off task" and fulfillment rates, which can indirectly reflect employee states like stress or fatigue (DigitalDefynd, 2025). The company has also explored AI for safety, with studies (Amazon Staff, 2023) investigating how AI and robotics can create safer and more efficient work environments, which can contribute positively to well-being by reducing physical strain. However, critical reports, such as the (Ye, 2022) analysis of Amazon's Automated Process Path Guidance and Tracking (ADAPT) system, suggest these systems are primarily geared toward maximizing efficiency, often at the expense of worker well-being, creating a high-pressure environment. Virtasant (2025) notes that AI can deeply influence corporate culture, and at Amazon, this has often been associated with a data-driven, performance-intensive environment.

While Amazon does not publicly detail AI tools specifically designed for overt emotion detection in its workforce for well-being purposes, the technologies it employs for performance and process management can be analyzed for their potential to infer emotional states or burnout risk.

Amazon employs advanced AI-driven systems like ADAPT to monitor worker productivity, task efficiency, and adherence to protocols, using data from scanners, cameras, and sensors (DigitalDefynd, 2025; Ye, 2022). While these systems do not directly assess employee mood, significant deviations in performance or increased error rates may be interpreted by AI as signs of stress, fatigue, or disengagement – early indicators of burnout. Persistent "time off task" could trigger alerts, flagging potential distress or legitimate breaks (Brady, 2024; Virtasant, 2025; Ye, 2022). In a broader context, AI is capable of sentiment analysis through internal surveys, feedback platforms, or anonymized communication data, enabling organizations to detect negative sentiment trends and shifts in morale (DigitalDefynd, 2025). While it remains unclear to what extent Amazon applies this specifically for mood tracking, the capability exists. Additionally, predictive analytics are used to identify safety risks (Amazon Staff, 2023; Brady, 2024) and such tools could potentially flag mental fatigue as a risk factor for accidents. However, it's important to emphasize that these systems are primarily designed for operational efficiency. Any insights related to emotional states or burnout risk tend to be secondary interpretations rather than core objectives, raising critical questions about their effectiveness in proactively supporting employee well-being.

AI systems are increasingly integrated into daily work routines, particularly in high-efficiency environments such as Amazon's fulfillment centers. These systems influence various facets of employee experience, from task allocation to performance monitoring. Task assignment and pacing are governed by AI algorithms, which determine the specific tasks, optimal routes, and expected speed of execution (Virtasant, 2025; Ye, 2022). Real-time instructions are communicated through handheld scanners, embedding AI into every operational step. Furthermore, AI generates continuous performance feedback loops, where workers receive updates on their output relative to algorithmically set benchmarks. These evaluations may result in direct device feedback or managerial intervention based on AI-generated alerts (Mulugeta, 2022). Surveillance technologies – cameras, sensors, and scanners – feed data into AI systems to ensure compliance with safety and procedural norms (Ye, 2022). In robotics-enabled facilities, AI systems orchestrate human–robot collaboration, requiring employees to synchronize their actions with machine rhythms (Amazon Staff, 2023). This pervasive integration not only drives efficiency but also reshapes employees' daily experiences, often intensifying workloads and reducing perceived autonomy.

Viewed through the lens of Seligman's PERMA model of well-being, the impact of such AI integration presents mixed implications (Peterson & Seligman, 2004). While AI holds the potential to support Positive Emotion through early stress detection and timely interventions (e.g., recommending breaks or flagging mental health concerns), current deployments at Amazon focus more on flagging performance deviations than on mood support (Hiler, 2024; Ye, 2022). In fact, the emphasis on continuous surveillance and efficiency can exacerbate stress and anxiety, detracting from positive emotional state (Tsujimoto et al., 2024). Although AI-led safety initiatives (Amazon Staff, 2023) may indirectly foster a sense of security, proactive emotional support remains underutilized. Thus, while AI systems significantly influence work routines, their alignment with holistic well-being frameworks like PERMA remains limited and largely incidental.

AI holds considerable potential in fostering a sense of accomplishment by supporting employees in managing workloads more effectively, identifying optimal work patterns, and offering personalized learning or upskilling opportunities (Virtasant, 2025). Such interventions can enhance mastery, streamline workflows, and improve job design by highlighting tasks that are overly demanding or inefficient, ultimately making work more manageable and meaningful (Benabou et al., 2024). Literature suggests that AI tools, when thoughtfully implemented, can contribute to better task alignment and improved process efficiency, thereby strengthening employees' perceptions of capability and achievement (Brady, 2024). In practice, Amazon's AI-driven systems emphasize productivity through mechanisms such as real-time tracking, performance analytics, and robotic support. Amazon Staff (2023) notes that such systems can make work "easier and more efficient," potentially enabling employees to focus on higher-value or more engaging tasks. However, critiques highlight that the intense productivity focus, coupled with constant surveillance, may erode the very sense of accomplishment AI is poised to support (Mulugeta, 2022; Ye, 2022). When targets are perceived as rigid or unattainable, and autonomy is limited, employees may feel disempowered or reduced to mechanical efficiency, undermining intrinsic motivation (Ye, 2022). Thus, while AI has the potential to balance productivity with personal growth, its current implementation often prioritizes output over well-being.

The integration of AI-driven systems for employee monitoring and management, particularly in high-efficiency environments like Amazon, presents a complex interplay of technological promise and human-centric concerns. A key challenge lies in privacy and surveillance, as continuous AI monitoring fosters a climate of constant oversight, leading to increased psychological pressure and behavioral inhibition (Bao et al., 2022). Algorithmic bias and fairness also pose risks, with AI tools potentially reinforcing systemic inequalities by replicating biases embedded in training data (Tavares & Ferrara, 2024). Furthermore, employee autonomy and human interaction diminish under algorithmic management, contributing to perceptions of dehumanization (Virtasant, 2025; Ye, 2022). Inferring emotional states such as stress or burnout from behavioral data remains methodologically fragile, raising questions about the accuracy and appropriateness of such detections (Mulugeta, 2022; Tavares & Ferrara, 2024). These issues are compounded by ethical dilemmas around consent, transparency, and data ownership, prompting regulatory discussions (Bao et al., 2022; Hiler, 2024; Virtasant, 2025). Paradoxically, while such systems aim to enhance performance, they may increase workplace stress and burnout (Virtasant, 2025). Outcomes observed include heightened efficiency and improved physical safety (Amazon Staff, 2023), yet these are offset by negative impacts on worker well-being, high attrition rates, and growing external scrutiny and resistance from labor and policy stakeholders (Hiler, 2024).

The potential of AI to improve employee well-being and mental health is considerable, offering opportunities for early distress detection, personalized support, and better work environments. However, Amazon's current use of AI, especially in its fulfillment centers, shows a key tension. While AI systems boost operational efficiency and potentially physical safety, their main focus seems to be on maximizing performance, often harming employee mental health, autonomy, and overall well-being. The idea of "real-time mood monitoring" for proactive support appears mainly aspirational or a future goal rather than a current, transparent strategy for broad well-being improvements at Amazon. Its alignment with the PERMA model is partial and sometimes contradictory. Although AI could support Positive Emotion and Accomplishment, its current application at Amazon, based on critical reports, often weakens these elements through excessive pressure and limited worker agency. Challenges like privacy invasion, dehumanization, and algorithmic bias are major and require careful ethical review and strong regulations (Ye, 2022). Future research should aim to develop and assess AI systems explicitly designed with employee well-being as a primary outcome, not just a side effect of efficiency efforts. Long-term studies are necessary to understand how different AI management styles impact mental health over time. Additionally, involving employees in designing and implementing AI tools – co-design – could increase acceptance and ensure these technologies genuinely promote, rather than harm, human well-being at work. Transparency from companies like Amazon about the details, purpose, and effects of their AI monitoring systems is vital for informed public and scholarly discussion.

7.3.2. Case Study 2: Deloitte – Building Resilience Through VR

Companies are changing how they think about employee happiness thanks to VR and AI as by using chatbots, data-driven insights, and predictive analytics, AI has enabled companies to provide employees personalized mental health challenges, identifying stress patterns and prescribing timely action. In contrast, VR provides a virtual, secure environment where employees can manage their emotional responses and build resilience by leveraging immersive experiences for stress relief, empathy training, and relaxation. The combination of AI and VR enables companies to support a proactive, engaging, and human-centered approach to workplace mental health. Deloitte now incorporates the use of AI and VR into its holistic training programs to contribute to employee well-being. The premise is based on mental resilience, stress reduction, and emotional regulation, while also cautioning against newer technologies that could, when misused, foster even more dysfunctional conditions than those that are observable in the context of psychological health (Raghavan Ash, 2018). This will evaluate these interventions through Seligman's PERMA model of well-being, with a distinct focus on the domains of engagement, etc. (Tsujimoto et al., 2024). Organizations are progressively checking the critical link between employee well-being, productivity, innovation, and retention (Grawitch et al., 2006). In response to this, pioneering companies venture into technological advancements. Including AI and immersive technologies like VR, to nurture supportive and resilient workplace environments. Deloitte is considered among the champions of VR for advanced soft skills training, such as emotional resilience and stress management programs (Grawitch et al., 2006; Korekar & Ray, 2025; Theunissen, 2023). Along with soft skills training (Korekar & Ray, 2025), it has systematically embedded immersive technologies into learning and development, recognizing VR's ability to deliver impactful training experience at scale. A key push toward digitally enabled employee development and well-being is facilitated by Deloitte's integration of AI and VR into learning at work. Their research, Tech Trends (2024), states that VR will be a foundational part of the workplace of the future, stating "VR is more than a novelty; it is now positioned to evolve into helpful use cases in development of leadership, onboarding and – i.e., most importantly – soft skills training" (Korekar & Ray, 2025). More and more companies are turning to VR and other immersive programs to build essential leadership and people skills. In these playful, yet serious, environments workers can rehearse tough conversations-such as giving constructive feedback or calming a heated dispute-without the usual workplace stakes. By walking through scenarios that show multiple angles and emotional states, employees gradually strengthen their emotional intelligence. Deloitte's research shows that VR learners remember more, feel surer of themselves, and put knowledge into practice faster than when they study the old-fashioned way. This hands-on, "learning by doing" spirit keeps people motivated and delivers lessons that stick longer (Hall & Hentz, 2024; Peterson & Seligman, 2004; Raghavan Ash, 2018; Tsujimoto et al., 2024).

The PERMA paradigm, which stands for Positive Emotion, Engagement, Relationships, Meaning, and Accomplishment, offers a thorough framework for comprehending well-being. Specifically, the elements of Engagement and Meaning in the PERMA model significantly align with Deloitte's use of VR for stress management, staff training, and resilience. By creating a state of flow-a moment when a person is completely wrapped up in what they are doing-immersive virtual-reality classrooms pull learners in on a deep level. Unlike traditional methods that ask students to sit back and memorize, VR training opens up the mind and senses at the same time, making lessons stick harder and keeping attention longer (Hall & Hentz, 2024; Krokos et al., 2019). Through virtual environments, Deloitte's programs allow employees to decide in real time, motivation and focus while directly relating to the "E" in PERMA through experiential learning (Deloitte, 2020; Hall & Hentz, 2024). In terms of Meaning, VR training is designed to support both personal and professional development. By focusing on emotional resilience, stress management, empathy, and inclusive leadership, the training addresses essential soft skills that are personally transformative and professionally valuable (Hall & Hentz, 2024). Learning to manage stress effectively enhances self-efficacy, while skills in empathy and collaboration foster inclusive work cultures and improve team dynamics. This dual focus provides participants with a sense of purpose and belonging, which aligns with the PERMA definition of meaning as connection to something larger than oneself (Deloitte, 2019). While Deloitte has not publicly released quantitative outcomes directly linking VR training to reduced stress levels, reported benefits from its broader immersive learning initiatives include increased learner confidence (up to 40% more than traditional methods) and reduced training time (Hall & Hentz, 2024). These factors indirectly support stress reduction by enhancing preparedness and perceived competence. Broader academic literature also supports VR's utility in mental health and skill development. Navarro-Haro et al. (2017) and Zeng et al. (2025) found VR interventions effective in reducing anxiety and stress, while Smith et al. (2020) highlighted their value in simulating high-pressure environments for healthcare professionals. Similarly, VR has shown success in enhancing empathy and communication through social skills training (Lacle-Melendez et al., 2024). Deloitte's commitment to embedding well-being into the flow of work through immersive technology signals both strategic innovation and recognition of VR's potential. However, further empirical, organization-specific data on the psychological outcomes of such initiatives would be valuable to the broader research community.

Deloitte's exploration of VR for enhancing employee well-being, particularly through resilience and stress management training, represents a forward-thinking application of immersive technology. The case demonstrates a clear understanding of VR's strengths in providing engaging, experiential learning opportunities that are difficult to replicate through other means. The alignment of these programs with key components of the PERMA model, specifically Engagement and Meaning, underscores a psychologically informed approach to employee development.

The inherent advantages of VR – realistic simulation, safe practice, potential for personalization, and fostering empathy – provide a strong theoretical basis for its effectiveness in emotional regulation and stress management training. While direct, publicly available metrics from Deloitte on stress level reduction are not extensively detailed, the firm's reported gains in learner confidence and skill application, coupled with broader academic evidence on VR's positive impact on mental health outcomes (Smith et al., 2020; Tsujimoto et al., 2024), suggest significant potential.

However, challenges such as the cost of development and deployment, ensuring equitable access, and the need for ongoing research to validate long-term impacts remain. Future research should focus on longitudinal studies within corporate settings like Deloitte to more definitively quantify the impact of VR resilience training on standardized well-being indicators, stress levels, and organizational outcomes like productivity and retention.

7.3.3. Case Study 3: Happily.ai – AI-powered Continuous Well-being Support

The rapidly expanding field of AI-driven employee well-being solutions offers promising ways to address the complexities of current workplace mental health (Espejo et al., 2023; Olawade et al., 2024). Happily.ai, a known AI-powered platform focused on employee's continuous well-being. When we look at its features and promised benefits alongside well-known well-being theories and research, it becomes clear how AI can help improve employee mental health and overall well-being. Happily.ai aims to be a comprehensive AI-powered employee experience platform focused on fostering engagement, well-being, and a positive company culture (Happily.ai, 2025a, 2025b). The platform goal is to move forward from traditional, often sporadic, initiatives related to well-being by working on continuous, data-driven support. Key features, as described by the platform, include tools for daily mood tracking, AI-driven coaching, peer-to-peer recognition, personalized feedback mechanisms, and analytics for organizational insights (Jafferi, 2025a, 2025e). The overarching goal is to proactively identify and address well-being challenges, thereby contributing to a healthier and more productive workforce (Jafferi, 2025d). This approach aligns with the growing recognition that proactive and integrated well-being strategies are more effective than reactive measures (Jafferi, 2025b, 2025e).

The daily check in system at Happily is helping to support employees and its core of the company. These brief interactions allow employees to report their mood and work engagement levels, providing real-time data on individual and collective well-being (Happily.ai, 2025a, 2025b; Jafferi, 2025a). A frequent "pulse checks" are helping in recognizing their ability to provide early warnings of declining morale or burnout, enabling timely interventions (Heaphy & Dutton, 2008; Jafferi, 2025e) and which will also suggests that regular self-reflection can enhance self-awareness, prompt help-seeking behaviors, AI-guided mindfulness coaching, delivering accessible, personalized sessions and exercises, etc. (Anantavarasilpa & Jafferi, 2022; Jafferi, 2025d). Therefore as said earlier, AI algorithms can analyze data received, sentiment and emotional, and engagement patterns to provide personalized technique, resources to employees, which is crucial for employee development and engagement (Jafferi, 2025e).

7.4. Alignment with PERMA

The PERMA model of well-being (Peterson & Seligman, 2004) conceptualizes human flourishing through five key dimensions. These elements serve as foundational components for understanding and enhancing individual well-being in organizational contexts. Emerging digital well-being platforms such as Happily.ai demonstrate potential alignment with this framework, offering practical interventions that map onto several PERMA components (Jafferi, 2025b). Positive emotions are emotional check-ins integrated into Happily.ai facilitates self-reflection on positive experiences, while mindfulness coaching is employed to enhance emotional regulation and resilience (Jafferi, 2025a, 2025d). These interventions are consistent with strategies that cultivate positive effect, a core tenet of psychological well-being (Jafferi, 2025c). Engagement is the platform supports employee engagement through personalized feedback mechanisms, continuous learning opportunities, and a psychologically safe work environment. These features align with the Job Demands-Resources model, which posits that engagement is fostered when adequate resources – such as developmental opportunities and constructive feedback – are present (Brauchli et al., 2015; Scholze & Hecker, 2024). Happily.ai explicitly promotes engagement-enhancing programs and relationships brings in social connectedness is a central element of PERMA. Happily.ai incorporates features such as peer recognition and community-building tools to facilitate interpersonal bonds (Happily.ai, 2025a, 2025b). Digital mechanisms for expressing appreciation, systems, are supported by research emphasizing the value of social support and positive relational energy in workplace well-being (Happily.ai, 2025b; Heaphy & Dutton, 2008). By ensuring timely, equitable, and transparent recognition, AI-enabled platforms can strengthen social cohesion and enhance the sense of belonging among employees (Anantavarasilpa & Jafferi, 2022). Meaning, while more indirectly addressed, Happily.ai contributes to the cultivation of meaning through stress reduction strategies and the reinforcement of a supportive organizational culture. Given the association between well-being and perceived purpose at work (Happily.ai, 2025b), tools that help individuals manage stress and feel valued may ultimately enhance the meaningfulness of their professional experiences. Accomplishment through features such as continuous feedback, progress tracking, and developmental nudges, Happily.ai can support a sense of achievement and goal attainment. These elements are essential in reinforcing an individual's perception of competence and personal growth, which are vital for sustained motivation and well-being. Overall, the integration of AI into workplace well-being platforms like Happily.ai offers promising applications of the PERMA model in organizational settings. By embedding psychological principles into digital systems, these tools can play a meaningful role in fostering holistic employee flourishing. AI-powered well-being platforms like Happily.ai don't just help individual employees, they also aim to improve the whole company culture. By sharing anonymous, big-picture data on how employees are feeling, these platforms make it easier for organizations to spot bigger problems, see what's working with their well-being programs, and create a more supportive and positive workplace (Happily.ai, 2025b; IBM, 2022). Companies focusing on investing in overall well-being initiatives improved active presence, lower attrition, and enhanced productivity (Goetzel et al., 2014; Grawitch et al., 2006). Using AI in these programs can boost their impact by making support more personal, proactive, and based on real data (Anantavarasilpa & Jafferi, 2022; Heaphy & Dutton, 2008; Jafferi, 2025d). The information obtained from Happily.ai enables organizations to develop customized workshops together with policy modifications and leadership education to resolve particular factors which harm employee well-being. The case example of Happily.ai illustrates how organizations can use AI technology to support different elements of employee well-being. The set of features within Happily.ai includes daily check-ins and personalized coaching and relationship-building tools which mirror the PERMA psychological framework and meet essential workplace requirements.

7.5. Findings: PERMA Dimension Analysis

Positive emotion: Amazon's approach to technology creates limited benefit in generating positive emotions. Although Amazon's safety AI systems create feelings of safety for a fraction of their employees inside the facilities, it is clear that the organizational design is mainly focused on their operational efficiency capacity. Deloitte: In contrast, provides means of promoting positive emotions through VR emotional regulation training intervention. Moreover, this is a proactive approach to promote positive emotions in that they are providing employees with skills to regulate and promote positive emotions. Happily.ai: Happily.ai is another organization that has an agenda focused solely on producing positive emotions, via mood tracking and mindfulness coaching. The two models of mood tracking and mindfulness coaching are intended to help employees be more aware of their moods and develop strategies to improve their overall wellness.

Engagement: Within Amazon, employee engagement primarily relates to meeting performance benchmarks. The focus on performance measures centered around productivity generates stress in the work environment that will lead to burnout and impacts the quality of employee engagement even though employees are still engaged with their work. Happily.ai has a platform that supports engagement of employees that provides awareness of employee communications and feedback on a personalized level. The platform generates engagement, thinking about employees' ability to get feedback and support, and the employee experience leads to engagement with their work and colleagues. Deloitte: Through VR training environments with immersive learning, has achieved high engagement levels among employees. VR training produces interactive design increases the depth of engagement.

Relationships: The automation focused approach of Amazon erodes connections among workers, leading to no, or minimal, workplace relationships. The opportunities for meaningful interactions hinder employees from experiencing meaningful social relationships with their coworkers. The leadership training experiences through VR-based content to employees at Deloitte serve to allow employees to develop empathy making up relationships to build workplace relationships. The training experiences support employees on better interpersonal skills. More workplace relationships are with their coworkers. Happily.ai: Happily.ai builds workplace relationships among employees by creating recognition tools available for peers. The recognition tools offer's employees a function of recognizing and applauding colleagues' contributions and perspective enhance social ties between personnel and develops a community.

Accomplishment: Amazon sense of accomplishment is strongly achieved and measurable. And although it's a good feeling when employees reach their goals, it's a fast-burning motivation that's not going to sustain anyone – especially if they feel their day-to-day doesn't contribute to broader strategies (which is often their experience). Deloitte: Deloitte's VR training promotes skill mastery and confidence, which can lead to a greater sense of accomplishment. By providing employees with opportunities to develop new skills and master existing ones, Deloitte helps them build confidence and feel a sense of achievement. Happily.ai: Happily.ai provides continuous support that encourages incremental progress and personal growth. This approach helps employees feel a sense of accomplishment as they make progress toward their goals, fostering a sense of momentum and motivation. Notably, Happily.ai demonstrates the most comprehensive alignment across PERMA dimensions, while Amazon's alignment is partial and often paradoxical – balancing high achievement demands with limited emotional support.

Innovation outcomes and emerging challenges: Changes in the way technology is utilized in different organizations are always apparent at every level, but in each situation it also presents the evidence of a successful (or unsuccessful) implementation. Amazon shows remarkable productivity increases and a modest increase in physical safety with AI-robot coordination. However, all of that is given back due to increased stress, privacy expectations from surveillance, and a lack of agency in employees – all of which leads to high employee turnover and public scrutiny. Deloitte's approach has also been effective at developing soft skills and emotional resilience – that includes greater confidence among students and the retention of related skills. Still, challenges remain around scalability, cost, and the need for longitudinal verification and confirmation of outcomes with employee mental health of all support capabilities. Thankfully situate a model that is scalable and exposes low barriers for building evaluations of employee well-being into work–life. Their reliance on data and personalization's, and social engagement, and their combination provided an example supporting workers' satisfaction and morale in organizations. Though the interventions characteristics were generally likely to be efficacious, they still need to be organizationally validated or accepted.

A continuum of shared considerations antitechnology innovation with the ethical, psychological, and cultural implications, as visiting these one at a time might also consider, implicate, or include emotional and cognitive states.

Despite using cutting-edge technologies to address employee well-being, Amazon, Deloitte, and Happily.ai's approaches show different priorities and philosophical stances, according to this cross-case study. Amazon's AI systems prioritize operational control with limited well-being benefits. Deloitte applies VR in a transformative, developmental manner. Happily.ai uses AI to promote unity among cultures while offering instant emotional encouragement. Amazon has a pragmatic but ethical ambiguous framework, Deloitte offers domain-specific depth, while Happily.ai offers the most comprehensive integration with the PERMA model. These examples demonstrate how AI and VR have the potential to revolutionize workplace mental health, but they also show how crucial deliberate design, moral leadership, and user-friendly application constitute for achieving this objective.

7.6. Conclusion

Employee happiness is more important than ever in today's ever changing digital workplace. The five fundamental elements of the PERMA framework – Positive Emotions, Engagement, Relationships, Meaning, and Accomplishment – though traditional, remain relevant, and provide a useful framework for considering how people might flourish in the workplace. Popular company's such as Amazon, Deloitte, Happily, and others, are responding to the needs for mental health in various ways, with various outcome results and perspectives. For Amazon, choices focus primarily on systems and tools to monitor productivity and performance without consideration of emotional and psychological support, even though there may be interventions that benefit performance and safety. Productivity has been prioritized and traded for things like joy, connectedness, and purpose, resulting in stress, burnout, and isolation from work and co-workers. Amazon's priority approach demonstrates the neglect of serious issues when reports focus on outcomes without considering the human aspect. Deloitte, on the other hand, takes more proactive actions in regard to mental health and wellness. It invests in a variety of training modalities and programs for strategies in skill building as it relates to leadership, stress management, and developing emotional resilience in team members. These trainings can generally align with positive emotion and engagement – two of the PERMA model's foundations – however, the format with the short training approaches and non-integration into day-to-day work practices, measures remain unclear. For example, the potential for these efforts to scale and influence the whole organization is worth noting. In a smaller organization, the workplace culture designates mental wellness a higher priority.

Employees are encouraged to attend to their own emotional health and to develop authentic connections with one another by sharing daily observations, feedback, and appreciation as a group. Emphasizing a more compassionate and encouraging environment rather than mere outputs is the crux of this. The above strategy is also in sync with the PERMA+4 framework just by virtue of linking well-being to a fresh series of attributes, thereby less aggressively defining it. PERMA+4 engineers are trained to embrace a "humane touch" by holding and affirming human moments at the office. Every model, however, has its limitations. The organization of Amazon could seem unduly inflexible and impersonal. One of the challenges may be the regular scaling up of Deloitte projects. In order to properly appreciate Happily's carefully considered approach, it still requires further longitudinal data.

It is evident from these examples that programs and tools by themselves are insufficient. In order to promote mental health, initiatives must be planned with sincere concern and an emphasis on individuals rather than just performance. Ultimately, having state-of-the-art platforms or digital systems is not the point. Making meaningful work experiences that respect psychological, social, and emotional demands is the goal. Long-term success will go to companies that see well-being as a main factor in performance rather than merely a perks.

References

Amazon Staff. (2023, October). *Amazon and MIT announce new study on impact of automation on jobs*. Amazon.

Anantavarasilpa, C., & Jafferi, T. (2022, October). *Prioritize soft skills to boost employee well-being and happiness*. Happily.Ai.

Bailey, D. E., Faraj, S., Hinds, P. J., Leonardi, P. M., & von Krogh, G. (2022). We are all theorists of technology now: A relational perspective on emerging technology and organizing. *Organization Science*, *33*(1), 1–18. https://doi.org/10.1287/ORSC.2021.1562

Bajwa, J., Munir, U., Nori, A., & Williams, B. (2021). Artificial intelligence in healthcare: transforming the practice of medicine. *Future Healthcare Journal*, *8*(2), e188–e194. https://doi.org/10.7861/fhj.2021-0095

Bao, Y., Li, W., Ye, Y., & Zhang, Q. (2022). Ethical disputes of AI surveillance: Case study of Amazon. In *Proceedings of the 2022 7th international conference on financial innovation and economic development (ICFIED 2022)* (p. 648). https://doi.org/10.2991/AEBMR.K.220307.220

Benabou, A., Touhami, F., & Demraoui, L. (2024). Artificial intelligence and the future of human resource management. In *2024 International conference on intelligent systems and computer vision (ISCV 2024)*. https://doi.org/10.1109/ISCV60512.2024.10620146

Bokhari, M. U., Yadav, G., & Zeyauddin, M. (2024). Innovating workplace mental health strategies with advanced machine learning: Application of a superior ensemble classifier for accurate stress detection in business environments. *International Journal of Information Technology (Singapore)*, 1–16. https://doi.org/10.1007/S41870-024-02332-9/METRICS

Brady, T. (2024, September). *Employees see robotics and AI's safety and career benefits, MIT study shows*. Amazon.

Brauchli, R., Jenny, G. J., Füllemann, D., & Bauer, G. F. (2015). Towards a job demands-resources health model: Empirical testing with generalizable indicators of job demands, job resources, and comprehensive health outcomes. *BioMed Research International*, *2015*, 959621. https://doi.org/10.1155/2015/959621

COVID-19 pandemic triggers 25% increase in prevalence of anxiety and depression worldwide. (n.d.). Retrieved July 1, 2025, from https://www.who.int/news/

item/02-03-2022-covid-19-pandemic-triggers-25-increase-in-prevalence-of-anxiety-and-depression-worldwide

Cronin, R. S. (2025). *AI in employee performance recruiter.com*. Unaligned Newsletter. https://www.unaligned.io/p/ai-in-employee-well-being

Deloitte. (2019, October). *Seligman's PERMA™ model: Using science to flourish at work | Deloitte Australia*. Deloitte.

Deloitte. (2020, September). *Integrating tech and well-being | Deloitte Insights*. Deloitte Insights.

DigitalDefynd. (2025). *10 ways Amazon is using AI - Case study [2025]*. DigitalDefynd.

Donaldson, S. I., van Zyl, L. E., & Donaldson, S. I. (2022). PERMA+4: A framework for work-related wellbeing, performance and positive organizational psychology 2.0. *Frontiers in Psychology*, *12*(January). https://doi.org/10.3389/fpsyg.2021.817244

Espejo, G., Reiner, W., & Wenzinger, M. (2023). Exploring the role of artificial intelligence in mental healthcare: Progress, pitfalls, and promises. *Cureus*, *15*(9), e44748. https://doi.org/10.7759/CUREUS.44748

Fitzpatrick, K. K., Darcy, A., & Vierhile, M. (2017). Delivering cognitive behavior therapy to young adults with symptoms of depression and anxiety using a fully automated conversational agent (Woebot): A randomized controlled trial. *JMIR Mental Health*, *4*(2). https://doi.org/10.2196/MENTAL.7785

Giuntella, O., Konig, J., & Stella, L. (2025). Artificial intelligence and the wellbeing of workers. *Scientific Reports*, *15*(1), 20087. https://doi.org/10.1038/S41598-025-98241-3

Goetzel, R. Z., Henke, R. M., Tabrizi, M., Pelletier, K. R., Loeppke, R., Ballard, D. W., Grossmeier, J., Anderson, D. R., Yach, D., Kelly, R. K., McCalister, T., Serxner, S., Selecky, C., Shallenberger, L. G., Fries, J. F., Baase, C., Isaac, F., Crighton, K. A., Wald, P., … Metz, R. D. (2014). Do workplace health promotion (wellness) programs work? *Journal of Occupational and Environmental Medicine*, *56*(9), 927–934. https://doi.org/10.1097/JOM.0000000000000276

Grawitch, M. J., Gottschalk, M., & Munz, D. C. (2006). The path to a healthy workplace: A critical review linking healthy workplace practices, employee well-being, and organizational improvements. *Consulting Psychology Journal*, *58*(3), 129–147. https://doi.org/10.1037/1065-9293.58.3.129

Hall, S. L., & Hentz, J. (2024, March). *The future of learning: Unleashing the potential of VR*. Deloitte.

Happily.ai. (2025a). *AI-powered employee engagement platform*. Happily.Ai.

Happily.ai. (2025b). *Your CultureOS that makes work feel like magic*. Happily.Ai.

Heaphy, E. D., & Dutton, J. E. (2008). Positive social interactions and the human body at work: Linking organizations and physiology. *Academy of Management Review*, *33*(1), 137–162. https://doi.org/10.5465/AMR.2008.27749365

Hiler, K. (2024, September). *AI: The next retention tool?*. HROToday.

IBM. (2022). *COVID-19 and the future of business*. IBM.

Jafferi, T. (2025a, March). *Using AI to tackle the workplace mental health crisis*. Happily.Ai.

Jafferi, T. (2025b, April). *Mental health in the workplace: Proven strategies*. Happily.Ai.

Jafferi, T. (2025c, April). *Top 10 employee engagement programs for success*. Happily.Ai.

Jafferi, T. (2025d, April). *Top 7 employee development programs to boost ROI*. Happily.Ai.

Jafferi, T. (2025e, May). *Top employee feedback tools for 2025 | Boost Engagement*. Happily.Ai.

Kana Health. (2025). *The role of AI in enhancing employee mental wellness programs*. https://www.kanahealth.ai/post/the-role-of-ai-in-enhancing-employee-mental-wellness-programs

Kassa, B. Y., & Worku, E. K. (2025). The impact of artificial intelligence on organizational performance: The mediating role of employee productivity. *Journal of Open Innovation: Technology, Market, and Complexity*, *11*(1), 100474. https://doi.org/10.1016/J.JOITMC.2025.100474

Korekar, G., & Ray, A. (2025, April). *Tech Trends 2025: India perspective*. Deloitte.

Krokos, E., Plaisant, C., & Varshney, A. (2019). Virtual memory palaces: Immersion aids recall. *Virtual Reality*, *23*(1), 1–15. https://doi.org/10.1007/S10055-018-0346-3/FIGURES/12

Lacle-Melendez, J., Silva-Medina, S., & Bacca-Acosta, J. (2024). Virtual and augmented reality to develop empathy: A systematic literature review. *Multimedia Tools and Applications*, *84*(11), 8893–8927. https://doi.org/10.1007/S11042-024-19191-Y/FIGURES/2

Mantello, P., & Ho, M. T. (2024). Emotional AI and the future of wellbeing in the post-pandemic workplace. *AI and Society*, *39*(4), 1883–1889. https://doi.org/10.1007/S00146-023-01639-8/METRICS

Mulugeta, H. E. (2022). Human rights issues at Amazon corporation. *Management Science and Business Decisions*, *2*(2), 19–31. https://doi.org/10.52812/MSBD.50

Navarro-Haro, M. V., López-del-Hoyo, Y., Campos, D., Linehan, M. M., Hoffman, H. G., García-Palacios, A., Modrego-Alarcón, M., Borao, L., & García-Campayo, J. (2017). Meditation experts try virtual reality mindfulness: A pilot study evaluation of the feasibility and acceptability of virtual reality to facilitate mindfulness practice in people attending a mindfulness conference. *PLoS ONE*, *12*(11). https://doi.org/10.1371/JOURNAL.PONE.0187777

Olawade, D. B., Wada, O. Z., Odetayo, A., David-Olawade, A. C., Asaolu, F., & Eberhardt, J. (2024). Enhancing mental health with artificial intelligence: Current trends and future prospects. *Journal of Medicine, Surgery, and Public Health*, *3*(April), 100099. https://doi.org/10.1016/j.glmedi.2024.100099

Peterson, C., & Seligman, M. E. P. (2004). *Character strengths and virtues: A handbook and classification*. Oxford University Press.

Raghavan Ash. (2018, December). *Immersive technologies of the new digital reality*. Deloitte Insights.

Scholze, A., & Hecker, A. (2024). The job demands-resources model as a theoretical lens for the bright and dark side of digitization. *Computers in Human Behavior*, *155*, 108177. https://doi.org/10.1016/J.CHB.2024.108177

Smith, V., Warty, R. R., Sursas, J. A., Payne, O., Nair, A., Krishnan, S., da Silva Costa, F., Wallace, E. M., & Vollenhoven, B. (2020). The effectiveness of virtual reality in managing acute pain and anxiety for medical inpatients: Systematic review. *Journal of Medical Internet Research*, *22*(11), e17980. https://doi.org/10.2196/17980

Sokoler, S. (2024). *Avoiding a crisis: How to shift from reactive to proactive EAPs*. Forbes Business Council.

Tahir, M. A., Da, G., Javed, M., Akhtar, M. W., & Wang, X. (2024). Employees' foe or friend: Artificial intelligence and employee outcomes. *Service Industries Journal*. https://doi.org/10.1080/02642069.2024.2375746;JOURNAL:JOURNAL:FSIJ19;WGROUP:STRING:PUBLICATION

Tavares, S., & Ferrara, E. (2024). Fairness and bias in artificial intelligence: A brief survey of sources, impacts, and mitigation strategies. *Sci*, *6*(1), 3. https://doi.org/10.3390/SCI6010003

Thakkar, A., Gupta, A., & De Sousa, A. (2024). Artificial intelligence in positive mental health: A narrative review. *Frontiers in Digital Health*, *6*, 1280235. https://doi.org/10.3389/FDGTH.2024.1280235/BIBTEX

Theunissen, R. (2023, December). *Tech Trends 2024: Generative AI | Deloitte Netherlands*. Deloitte.

Tsujimoto, M., Saito, T., Matsuzaki, Y., & Kawashima, R. (2024). Role of positive and negative emotion regulation in well-being and health: The interplay between positive and negative emotion regulation abilities is linked to mental and physical health. *Journal of Happiness Studies*, *25*(1–2), 1–20. https://doi.org/10.1007/S10902-024-00714-1/METRICS

Urrila, L., Siiriäinen, A., Mäkelä, L., & Kangas, H. (2025). Sense of belonging in hybrid work settings. *Journal of Vocational Behavior*, *157*, 104096. https://doi.org/10.1016/J.JVB.2025.104096

Valtonen, A., Saunila, M., Ukko, J., Treves, L., & Ritala, P. (2025). AI and employee well-being in the workplace: An empirical study. *Journal of Business Research*, *199*(July), 115584. https://doi.org/10.1016/j.jbusres.2025.115584

van Zyl HappyBytes, L. E. (2025). *The PERMA+4 framework: A new approach to well-being at work*. https://www-psychologytoday-com.cdn.ampproject.org/c/s/www.psychologytoday.com/us/blog/happybytes/202307/the-perma4-framework-a-new...1/15

Vanhée, L., Andersson, G., Garcia, D., & Sikström, S. (2025). The rise of artificial intelligence for cognitive behavioral therapy: A bibliometric overview. *Applied Psychology: Health and Well-Being*, *17*(2), e70033. https://doi.org/10.1111/APHW.70033

Virtasant. (2025, March). *Enterprise AI adoption: Insights from Amazon, SprintIT, HP by Virtasant*. Virtasant.

WHO. (2024, September). *Mental health at work*. WHO.

Ye, A. (2022, March). *Amazon's ADAPT and it's harm on workers – Data science W231 | Behind the data: Humans and values*. Blogs.Ischool.Berkeley.

Zeng, W., Xu, J., Yu, J., & Chu, X. (2025). Effectiveness of virtual reality therapy in the treatment of anxiety disorders in adolescents and adults: A systematic review and meta-analysis of randomized controlled trials. *Frontiers in Psychiatry*, *16*, 1553290. https://doi.org/10.3389/FPSYT.2025.1553290/FULL

Zirar, A., Ali, S. I., & Islam, N. (2023). Worker and workplace artificial intelligence (AI) coexistence: Emerging themes and research agenda. *Technovation*, *124*, 102747. https://doi.org/10.1016/J.TECHNOVATION.2023.102747

Chapter 8

Exploring the Role of AI and VR in Building Workplace Culture: A Bibliometric Analysis

Niranchana Shri Viswanathan[a] *and Shashi Kant Gupta*[b]

[a]*School of Management Studies, Sapthagiri NPS University, Bengaluru, India*
[b]*Department of Computer science, Edoxia Research University, New Castle, USA*

Abstract

This chapter examines how artificial intelligence (AI) and virtual reality (VR) can be leveraged to construct and enrich workplace culture. The study investigates how these technologies support the development of inclusive, engaging, and adaptive organizational environments. Using a bibliometric review of Scopus and Web of Science databases, the analysis employs VOS viewer and Biblioshiny to map co-authorship networks, keyword co-occurrences, and thematic evolution. The findings reveal five major thematic clusters: AI-enhanced employee engagement, VR-based immersive training, ethical and responsible AI use, VR-supported hybrid workplace management, and the integration of emotional intelligence through AI tools. The review highlights a growing adoption of VR for onboarding, team building, and experiential learning, while AI is increasingly used for sentiment analysis, personalization, and employee experience design. The study also identifies gaps in the existing literature, particularly the limited integration of AI and VR within broader cultural development frameworks. A key contribution of this research is its synthesis of fragmented evidence, directly linking AI and VR adoption to workplace culture transformation rather than solely operational outcomes. Emerging concepts such as AI-driven empathy development and VR-facilitated diversity

Nurturing AI-Powered HR Analytics and Virtual Reality in Employee Psychology and Workplace Happiness, Part A, 133–150

Published under exclusive licence by Emerald Publishing Limited
doi:10.1108/978-1-80686-125-520261006

training further underscore the technologies' potential. The study offers practical insights for managers, HR practitioners, and technology strategists seeking to build future-ready organizational cultures.

Keywords: AI in workplace culture; virtual reality training; organizational transformation; employee engagement technology; bibliometric analysis; future workplaces

8.1. Introduction

They're not out of touch with some history lessons; the workplace culture of today is an organism an evolving ecosystem that must remain agile and responsive in real time as countries, communities, and citizens in jobs rapidly transform. Historically, organizational culture was characterized by a strict hierarchical model, centralized in a single location, standardized throughout, and focused primarily on efficiency and control. However, the turn of the 21st century—driven by globalization and more recently by hybrid and remote working arrangements has irrevocably altered this landscape.

In the modern workplace, effective culture is defined by agility, continuous learning, and the ability to foster a sense of belonging where individuals feel safe to be themselves. Culture is no longer just about understanding formal rules and unspoken norms; organizations now recognize that building a strong and inclusive culture is essential rather than optional. This shift significantly impacts employee engagement, retention, productivity, and innovation.

As technologies continue to mature and expand in scale and scope while optimizing costs, leaders face increasing challenges in addressing the profound implications within the human dimension of work. This includes navigating evolving values, beliefs, and ways of working that collectively shape organizational culture.

8.1.1. Navigating the Technological Frontier

The objective of the current study is to conduct a systematic literature review and investigate the applications of AI and VR for creating interactive inclusive (Singh et al., 2024) and adaptive organizational settings. And our core mission is to chart the complex terrain where those powerful tools are being leveraged in building a workplace culture that thrives on its effectiveness as much as it does on its deep humanity. We want to investigate how AI can facilitate fair and unbiased decision making, personalize employee development (Liu et al., 2024) and provide insight into organizational sentiment toward promoting inclusivity This work will be an analytic process that allows us to objectively describe the state in which this scientific domain is located, showing where efforts are focused but above all emphasizing the main gaps of research perceived in technology-based organizational culture as goes through a process of scientific evolution under consideration: "time."

8.1.2. Forging a Coherent Framework and Unearthing Novel Concepts

A key contribution of this study lies in its attempt to transcend fragmented scholarly discussions by synthesizing the diverse streams of research on artificial intelligence and virtual reality into a cohesive framework aligned with the evolving trajectory of organizational culture. While existing literature has predominantly examined the application of artificial intelligence within human resource functions or the use of virtual reality in isolated training settings, the present study broadens the scope of inquiry. It critically explores the extent to which these emerging technologies shape shared values, norms, and behavioral patterns, thereby influencing workplace culture at a fundamental level.

Through a systematic examination and interpretation of these technological advancements, the study advances beyond descriptive insights and offers a more nuanced conceptual understanding of changing workplace dynamics. It is grounded in the perspective that future work environments are coevolutiony systems, wherein human cognition interacts with artificial intelligence, and physical workspaces increasingly converge with virtual environments.

Such an enriched perspective holds significant practical relevance for managers, HR practitioners, and technology strategists, as it equips them with the insights necessary to intentionally design and nurture future workplaces that are inclusive, engaging, and guided by ethical considerations.

8.2. Literature Review

The reference to the co-author of *Ten Weeks to a Better Job*™, which provides recommendations on job search strategies, appears unrelated to the core focus of this study and has therefore been omitted for clarity. Artificial Intelligence (AI) and Virtual Reality (VR) are not merely tools for improving operational efficiency; they are increasingly acting as catalysts for deeper cultural transformation within organizations.

Human capital practices go beyond typical HR transaction work. Although automating "the people stuff" has included hiring and performance management in the past (Ghobakhloo et al., 2024), AI is revolutionizing sentiment analysis to view real-time teams' mood and potential disengagement. It allows to customize even development paths, feedback, and wellness support on individual needs. But, of course, the use of AI isn't quite that straightforward, either. Further work is also needed to better understand how (Abbas et al., 2023) organizations address the ethical and privacy questions, such as those related to algorithmic bias in decision-making, employee privacy with respect to large-scale data collection and psychological well-being effects or autonomy consequences of AI (etc.). Similarly, the "extent to which workers need to acquire new skills in order to use AI tools is an area for study that merits more fine-grained analysis." There are extensive works in literature, from possibilities that AI offers, to its ethical issues and long-term impacts on trust, transparency and even the undercurrent shifts in human inter dynamics of an AI augmented space have been under researched.

The light pace of adoption is accompanied by the pivot of VR from entertainment toward super-immersive training experiences redefining onboarding and upskilling. VR has the best of both worlds: it provides higher learning retention while offering safe practicing ground for anything from technical skills to soft skills; in other words, because VR can put people into real-world-like situations, VR goes beyond just training as it is algorithms for virtual meeting spaces on which we drive remote team collaboration and bonding In a hybrid workplace emerging as the new normal. The potential of VR to foster a more empathetic and diverse work environment by applying diversity training would be especially exciting where users can walk a mile in someone else's shoes by experiencing different perspectives (Citibank & Tasleem, 2025). However, the effective application of VR solutions, the cognitive fatigue associated with extended VR use, and the hardware preferences in accessing such tools are all real issues. It is also important to learn more about the degree to which VR use leads to increased social cohesion, as opposed to isolation, especially in a hybrid approach.

The challenge is AI and VR colliding with Apple's focus on advancing the two technologies in a joined at the hip fashion. Consider AI being applied to personalize a VR training exercise on the fly with an individual users' data and learning style, or Lanyi and Withers (2020) interpreting biometric and emotional data from VR room interactions with AI providing focused feedback or assistance. This collection of strength is a strong(er) networked framework for cultural growing beyond the binary yes and no. AI-powered apps for empathy (Parnell et al., 2025) could use natural language processing to identify communication failures and then provide VR simulations that users can rehearse. Third, the psychological and sociological implications (e.g., digital fatigue, surveillance anxieties, shifts in human–human interaction patterns in AI/VR-augmented settings) should be further investigated through robust qualitative and mixed-methods research. Fourth, ethical issues – especially related to data governance; algorithmic transparency in a personalized context and the danger of a "digital divide" regarding access to these technologies – need specific academic attention so that AI and VR can be deployed responsibly. Finally, research on how AI and VR can facilitate a genuine adaptive workplace culture where organizations are able to learn how to constantly quickly respond in a world of spinning and changing environment with tech-facilitated cultural elasticity is at an embryonic stage. Such are the gaps to fill in, if firm and evidence-based guidance is desired by both managers, HR professionals, and technology strategists who want to develop a workplace that is genuinely ready in the future.

- *Research aim*: To systematically analyze how AI and VR are utilized to create more inclusive, engaging, and adaptive organizational environments.

8.2.1. Objectives and Research Questions

- *Objective 1*: To map the existing research landscape concerning the integration of AI and VR in workplace culture within the Scopus and Web of Science databases.

- *RQ1*: What are the key characteristics of the scholarly publications on AI and VR in workplace culture, including their annual trends, most influential authors, institutions, countries, and highly cited works, as found in the Scopus and Web of Science databases?
- *Objective 2*: To identify and analyze the thematic clusters and intellectual structures within the existing body of literature on AI and VR's role in workplace culture.
- *RQ2*: What are the major thematic clusters (e.g., AI-enhanced employee engagement, VR immersive training experiences) and collaborative networks that define the research on AI and VR's influence on workplace culture?
- *Objective 3*: To highlight existing research gaps and propose future research directions for the integration of AI and VR in enhancing workplace culture.
- *RQ3*: What are the key research gaps in the current literature concerning AI and VR's combined influence on workplace culture, and what promising avenues exist for future scholarly inquiry?

8.3. Conceptual Model

The Technology Enablers that reimagine the workforce culture are AI and VR, augmented reality (AR), and mixed reality (MR). However, drivers themselves do not change culture; they are mediated through, but by no means into, a further set of mediating mechanisms. It is the gift of AI to engage employees with personalized experiences and sentiment analysis; VR's nimble delivery of immersive training modules that build expertise and "muscle memory"; the ability of VR platforms to manage hybrid workplaces that can draw on enhanced connectedness and productivity across distributed teams; AI tools that boost emotional intelligence cultivate a more inclusive culture.

AI and VR are fundamental tech-based influencers of the 21st-century workplace culture. They are attenuated by the ethical use of AI, user acceptance, organizational readiness, leadership support, data security, and digital equity. These drivers work through mediating mechanisms such as AI-powered employee engagement, VR simulator training, hybrid workplace management, and emotional intelligence upgradation by AI. These technological interventions in the context of supportive organizational conditions result in positive workplace culture outcomes. This results in a number of significant outcomes, such as greater inclusivity, more engaged members of your team and a more nimble organization that can more successfully respond to some of the changing job environments and workforce expectations.

The effective functioning of these mediating processes is presumed to drive three significant Workplace Culture Outcomes: increased inclusivity (manifesting as reduced bias and high belonging), greater engagement (resulting in a highly motivated, productive workforce), and increased adaptiveness (fostering organizational agility and resilience). What is important to note here is that all this transformative process as a whole, by and large is trammeled by Moderating/Critical Factors, which are far from being a direct cause of the results but manipulate maximally the system effectiveness and value added of any techno-solution in terms of ethics. These include higher-order importance of Ethical AI Use (fairness, transparency, privacy, and trust), as well as other elements – such as user acceptance and adoption, organization readiness, strong leadership support and vision, strong data security and governance, and the critical factor to consider digital equity and access for all workers. Crucially, this holistic approach provides a systematic means to probe the complex inter-relationship of technological tool, mediating application and intended cultural output through which to reflect critically on required contextual and ethical concerns, structuring deliberation of findings and providing pointers for further work.

8.4. Methodology

Data source and search: Choose Scopus as the initial database. The definite search terms and Boolean operators were applied. Specify the date and type of your request documents. This bibliometrics, obtained through Scopus search engine, is a short summary from the AI, VR, and workplace culture horizon. The "Timespan" 2003–2025 means probably reflection on a stretch of more than 20 years, with the history and present developments in mind. The "Documents" of 305 are in 184 "Sources" (journals, books, …) with less evident but growing activity is 22.38%.

The ratio of quantities is between 2,237 "Keywords Plus (ID)" and 1,153 "Author's Keywords (DE)" Here we can read that Scopus' indexation is adding considerable value to the thematic map and is in general richer than what author assigned. A meaningful note on collaboration: 1,191 already in this area, though we already also have "Average Co-Authors per Doc" of 4.28, the fact that there are 305 documents and yet but only items show a very distributed concentration being confirmed. Its "INTERNATIONAL CO-AUTHORSHIP %" value received a score of 37.7%, indicating that the field under study is strongly international-minded and cross-disciplinary research one. "Document Types" and finally, the higher number of "article" (n = 185) and "review" papers (n = 61) underscores the focus on research papers and scholarly synthesizations which are crucial to produce a robust evidence base. Harvard Occasional papers such as "conference paper" (30) may provide evidence of vibrant academic communication and early dissemination of findings.

The bibliometric analysis covers publications from 2003 to 2025, drawing from 184 sources including journals and books. A total of 305 documents were analyzed, showing a strong annual growth rate of 22.38%, indicating increasing scholarly interest. The average document age is 1.77 years, with an average of 30.74 citations per document, reflecting high research impact. The dataset includes 35,561 references, 2,237 Keywords Plus, and 1,153 author keywords. Contributions come from 1,191 authors, with high collaboration reflected in 4.28 co-authors per document and 37.7% international co-authorships.

8.5. Data Collection and Analytical Tools

The groundwork for this bibliometric research is based on a thorough data collection process that was conducted systematically through the use of the Scopus database, which is a well-known leading abstract and citation database with wide coverage of areas of science, including the social sciences, biomedical sciences, the life sciences (such as biological, health and medical sciences), and physical sciences and the health sciences. Data were reviewed sensitively on June 22, 2025, to include the newest academic contributions during the defined timeframe (2003–2025). An iterative and thorough search was used to encompass the literature relating to AI, VR, and workplace culture. The last search string used in advanced search in the Scopus interface was:

> *((ALL(role AND of AND ai AND vr AND in AND building AND workplace) AND ALL(") ")) AND (LIMIT-TO (EXACTKEYWORD,"Virtual Reality") OR LIMIT-TO (EXACTKEYWORD,"Artificial Intelligence") OR LIMIT-TO (EXACTKEYWORD,"Workplace") OR LIMIT-TO (EXACTKEYWORD,"Virtual Reality (vr)") OR LIMIT-TO (EXACTKEYWORD,"Technology Acceptance Model") OR LIMIT-TO (EXACTKEYWORD,"Virtual Reality Technology") OR LIMIT-TO ("Bibliometrics") OR LIMIT-TO ("Web Of Science") OR LIMIT-TO (EXACTKEYWORD,"Vr") OR LIMIT-TO (EXACTKEYWORD,"Technology Acceptance") OR LIMIT-TO (EXACTKEYWORD,"Augmented Reality (ar)") OR LIMIT-TO("Bibliometric Analysis") OR LIMIT-TO("Conceptual Framework") OR LIMIT-TO (EXACTKEYWORD,"Augmented Reality") OR LIMIT-TO ("Systematic Review") OR LIMIT-TO ("Article") OR LIMIT-TO (EXACTKEYWORD,"Workers'") OR LIMIT-TO ("Technology Adoption") OR LIMIT-TO ("Systematic Literature Review"))*

This elaborate Boolean string was formulated to reach maximum sensitivity while preserving specificity, including a mix of general conceptual terms and somewhat more specific keywords in terms of the research themes and the methodological perspective on the subject matter. To maintain the academic soundness of the dataset, the search was strictly restricted to essential document types – "article," "review," "conference paper," "book," and "book chapter" – taking into consideration "retracted" and "short survey" documents. After performing this query, all found documents (305 records in total) were exported from Scopus in Comma-Separated Values format, a common format for importing references into bibliometric software, which includes metadata (i.e., titles, authors, affiliations, abstracts, keywords, years of publication, and numbers of citations). During the analytic stage, Biblioshiny was the main bibliometric software support. Biblioshiny, a user-friendly web-based GUI front end to the powerful "bibliometrix" R-package, was chosen due to its comprehensive support for science mapping and bibliometric analysis. This software enabled multiple analyses such as the production of descriptive statistics and performance indicators (annual scientific production, ranking of the most prolific authors and sources, average citations per document). Importantly, Biblioshiny also helped to conduct co-authorship network analysis to map the collaboration among authors, institutions, and countries, and to analyze the keyword co-occurrence results. The second software was used to identify and visually map broad thematic clusters and core knowledge bases in the field of studies. In addition, Biblioshiny capabilities made it possible not only to map the evolution of themes throughout time, but also to gain important insights on how research fronts have evolved and developed in the context of AI, VR, and workplace culture. The user-friendly interface would allow us to perform sophisticated bibliometric computations and visualizations, stimulating an in-depth, systematic examination of the data collected.

> *((ALL(role AND of AND ai AND vr AND in AND building AND workplace) AND ALL(") ")) AND (LIMIT-TO (EXACTKEYWORD,"Virtual Reality") OR LIMIT-TO (EXACTKEYWORD,"Artificial Intelligence") OR LIMIT-TO (EXACTKEYWORD,"Workplace") OR LIMIT-TO (EXACTKEYWORD,"Virtual Reality (vr)") OR LIMIT-TO (EXACTKEYWORD,"Technology Acceptance Model") OR LIMIT-TO (EXACTKEYWORD,"Virtual Reality Technology") OR LIMIT-TO (EXACTKEYWORD,"Bibliometrics") OR LIMIT-TO (EXACTKEYWORD,"Web Of Science") OR LIMIT-TO (EXACTKEYWORD,"Vr") OR LIMIT-TO (EXACTKEYWORD,"Technology Acceptance") OR LIMIT-TO (EXACTKEYWORD,"Augmented Reality (ar)") OR LIMIT-TO (EXACTKEYWORD,"Bibliometric Analysis") OR LIMIT-TO (EXACTKEYWORD,"Conceptual Framework") OR LIMIT-TO (EXACTKEYWORD,"Augmented Reality") OR LIMIT-TO (EXACTKEYWORD,"Systematic Review") OR LIMIT-TO (EXACTKEYWORD,"Article") OR LIMIT-TO (EXACTKEYWORD,"Workers'") OR LIMIT-TO (EXACTKEYWORD,"Technology Adoption") OR LIMIT-TO (EXACTKEYWORD,"Systematic Literature Review")))*

The year-wise distribution of publications indicates a significant growth trend in recent years. The highest number of publications was recorded in 2024 with 101 documents, followed closely by 2025 with 85 publications. A steady increase is observed from 2021 onwards, rising from 16 publications in 2021 to 49 in 2023. Earlier years show minimal research output, with sporadic publications between 2003 and 2019. This pattern highlights that scholarly interest in the field has accelerated substantially in the last five years, reflecting its growing relevance, emerging research opportunities, and increasing academic and practical significance.

This data tell a powerful story of the exploding interest in the overlap of AI, VR, and workplace culture, notably in just the last few years. The "Timespan" 2003–2025 will thus be read as a 22-year period at first instance. But focusing on the "YEAR" distribution, we see that number of publications diametrically differs between the two, even though they both seem to rank similarly. There is a sprinkling of early papers (one per year in 2003, 2006, 2008, 2013, and 2017), but the field really starts its exponential rise from 2020 onwards. This is an important observation, suggesting that the adoption of AI and VR (Chang et al., 2025) into working culture is a newly emerging and fast-growing field of academic research. This is also supported by the "Annual Growth Rate %" of 22.38%, indicating a large and consistent rise in an academic source.

The newfound boom in publications is palpable: Only 6 documents had been published in 2020, 49 in 2023 (Brauer & Vandepoele, 2025), 101 in 2024, so far 85 ones in 2025 (as of June 22, 2025). This path illuminates the pressing and emerging interest in these technologies as they become a powerful force in the transformation of organizational settings. The number of 85 documents for 2025 (not complete) already shows the research effort nowadays and the importance that is given to this field of research in the years to come. The recency of the field is indeed reflected in the "Document Average Age" of 1.77 years. It indicates that most research is very recent, which means researchers are actively working on this area and new findings are constantly being published. This "newness" of the literature is what makes a bibliometric analysis especially useful for a real-time snapshot of current research and to immediately determine areas of emerging trends and areas of lacking knowledge. It also means that whatever insights are gleaned from this dataset will be immediately useful and timely to the work.

8.6. Analysis Techniques

Describe the types of bibliometric analyses performed, such as analyzing publication trends, top authors/institutions, and mapping keyword co-occurrence for thematic clusters. It firstly maintains average citations per document of zero during the period 2003–2017, with a slight peak around 2010. This period might also coincide to the establishment or to an early phase of development of a research field, characterized by a lack of publications (potentially less connected among them) as resulting in a reduced number of citations in a short amount of time.

The trend of average citations per year reflects fluctuating but overall increasing scholarly impact over time. In the early years (2003–2008), citation averages remained very low, indicating limited visibility and emerging research activity. A noticeable rise occurs around 2013, followed by a decline until 2017. A sharp peak is observed in 2018, representing the highest average citation impact, suggesting the publication of highly influential works. Subsequent years show moderate fluctuations, with another notable increase around 2022. The decline in the most recent years is expected due to citation lag, as newer publications require time to accumulate citations.

This chart shows interesting patterns about the influence and significance of research into AI, VR, and workplace culture, across the years we analyzed for "Average Citations per Year." Clear change occurs after 2017; the average number of citations per year starts to grow with more fluctuation. The curve peak is very pronounced in 2018 where the average citations per document are close to 30. That's why the few papers from 2018 had extremely high immediate recognition and influence: so, the papers from 2018 might be papers with high impact, or maybe even ground-breaking work that attracted attention immediately. Thus, if this citation rate reflects to some extent the future impact of the most recent papers, this curve raises the issue of prospective high citation rates, in the future, of recent publications.

8.6.1. Author's Articles Production

The high proportion of common family names (Liu, Wang, Chen, and Li) suggests that in more granular studies in the future (where author disambiguation may be required), the distribution by family name may be very different in individual FBI papers, but generally these distributions indicate a dynamic and intellectually collaborative environment, rather than one with a few semi-solitary.

The authorship analysis highlights key contributors to the field based on publication output. LIU J and WANG X emerge as the most prolific authors, each contributing five articles, indicating sustained research engagement. PANDEY PK and RAMAN R follow with four publications each, reflecting strong scholarly involvement. Several authors, including CHEN M, HASANZADEH S, HUGHES L, KUMAR D, LEE S, LI H, and PAUL J, have each contributed three articles, demonstrating a broad base of active researchers. The presence of numerous authors with two publications suggests a diverse and collaborative research landscape, characterized by distributed expertise rather than dominance by a single author.

An interesting data insight on the most active authors in the field of AI, VR, and workplace culture illustrate what is, in the end, a relatively diffuse landscape of authorship. LIU J and WANG X were the most prolific authors, each with five articles, followed by PANDEY PK and RAMAN R with four articles. A significant cluster of 10 authors, namely CHEN M, HASANZADEH S, HUGHES L, KUMAR D, LEE S, LI H, MANU P, PAUL J, YANG H, and YUNUSA-KALTUNGO A, has each authored three articles, reflecting overall foundation of the active researchers. In addition, several authors have submitted two articles, possibly indicating an expanding network of researchers working in this emergent interdisciplinary field. It is probable that such prolific authors are active in the construction of evolving agendas of this highly dynamic field.

8.6.2. Affiliation Production over Time

This "Affiliations' Production Over Time" chart is an interesting visualization of institutional involvement in AI, VR, and workplace-related research, clearly showing a sharp, large increase, and a relatively new one at that. Little to no visible research output can be observed at these top institutions between 2003 and 2018.

The publication trends of leading institutional affiliations over time indicate that research output remained negligible until around 2019, after which a sharp increase is observed. Universities such as Chung-Ang University, Politecnico di Torino, the University of Manchester, and the University of Southern California demonstrate notable growth between 2020 and 2025. This surge indicates rising institutional engagement with the research domain in recent years. Variations in growth trajectories suggest differing levels of strategic focus and research capacity across institutions. Overall, the trend reflects the growing global academic involvement and institutional consolidation of research efforts in this emerging field.

This "Affiliations' Production Over Time" chart is an interesting visualization of institutional involvement in AI, VR, and workplace-related research, clearly showing a sharp, large increase, and a relatively new one at that. Little to no visible research output can be observed at these top institutions between 2003 and 2018, hence highlighting that this specific junction of technologies and cultural impact was hardly mined by leading institutions throughout this period. But then there's a drastic change around 2019–2020 that matches the overall exponential growth of trends in the field. The concomitant and concurrent rise of this research domain in several universities acknowledges the strategic importance accorded to this area of research. Chung-Ang University, Middlesex University, and The University of Manchester show a higher and steadier trend for the number of articles contributed in the past years of at least reaching or exceeding 10 articles and have a higher increase trend until 2025. Other universities such as Politecnico di Torino and the University of New South Wales also exhibit strong and increasing participation.

8.6.3. Keywords

Generated from keywords or keyword-plus terms, the word cloud creates a striking visual summary of the research landscapes, favored themes and conceptual fronts in the field of AI, VR, and workplace culture. The two most frequent terms, identified by their size, are "virtual reality" and "artificial intelligence," which clearly determine the main technological axes in the research. Closely related to this are "augmented reality" and "mixed reality," which imply a broader interest in immersive forms of technology beyond VR specifically.

The keyword word cloud highlights the dominant themes and research focus areas within the literature. "Virtual reality" emerges as the most prominent term, indicating its central role in the research domain. Closely associated keywords such as "augmented reality," "artificial intelligence," and "mixed reality" reflect the strong emphasis on immersive and intelligent technologies. Supporting themes include workplace applications, personnel training, safety training, decision-making, e-learning, and occupational health, demonstrating practical and organizational relevance. The presence of terms related to humans, gender, and age groups suggests attention to user-centered perspectives. Overall, the keyword distribution reveals an interdisciplinary research landscape integrating technology, workplace practices, and human factors.

Importantly, "workplace" also comes up as an important term that supports that the main setting of your investigation is the right one. Other apparent keywords such as "human" point toward human-centric viewpoint and also emphasize the effects to people in this technological context. Words like "adult," "male," and "female" hint at a fascination with the demographics of technology adoption and its effects on disparate user groups. Finally, the topics "personnel training," "immersive," and "e-learning" as well "safety training" show the significance of these technologies in training for skills and workplace safety. Academic terms such as "systematic literature review," "bibliometric analysis," and "review" signpost the dominance of synthesis and meta-analysis in the discipline. Terms such as "technology adoption," "decision-making," "occupational risks," and "ethical" emphasize that of the larger organizational and social implications that are being discussed. The use of "metaverses" speaks to a future-facing gaze, teasing out workspaces to come.

8.6.4. Most Cited Country

The "Most Cited Countries" is an overview of the measured national contributions to the published research on AI, VR, workplace culture, measured according to the total number of outgoing citations for articles originating in those countries.

The distribution of citations by country highlights global research impact. The UK emerges as the most cited country, with a substantially higher citation count than all others, indicating strong scholarly influence and leadership in the field. Korea follows as the second most cited country, while the USA, France, Malaysia, and Canada demonstrate moderate citation levels. China, Italy, Germany, and Australia also contribute to the citation landscape, though with comparatively lower impact. Overall, the distribution reflects a geographically diverse research base, with citation dominance concentrated in a few countries, suggesting variations in research visibility, collaboration networks, and thematic leadership across regions.

This landscape is dominated by the UK, for which the volume of their citations 3,585 is several grades above the next country on our list. This suggests that UK-originated research in this area has made the greatest impression and scholarly reputation globally. After the UK, there's quite a large distance to the next band of highly cited countries. Korea/USA/France formed the next cluster that has citation in the range of 500–600. It is succeeded by Malaysia, Canada, China, Italy, Germany, and Australia, with generally equivalent levels of citation impact, standing all in the range of 300–400. This distribution indicates that research is being carried out worldwide on the topic, but that as the time of the study, the UK was playing a prominent role in influencing the field and visibility of the work being conducted.

8.6.5. Clusters by Authors Couplings

The "Clusters by Authors Couplings" chart also generates a strategic picture of the landscape, sorting thematics according to centrality and prestige. In the "Motor Parts" upper-right quadrant, for instance, the "human" with "systematic review," and the "construction industry" areas epitomize a mature and integrated research attention, and can be interpreted as there are quite mature literature analyses in specific industrial contexts.

The author coupling analysis reveals distinct thematic clusters based on impact and centrality. High-impact, high-centrality clusters focus on metaverses, AR, VR, and systematic reviews. Emerging clusters include human–robot interaction and construction industry applications, while peripheral clusters address AI, sustainability, and information technology themes.

Likewise, "virtual reality," especially in human-oriented "e-learning," falls into this quadrant representing the mainstream and powerful position. The upper left picks up specialized but salient themes: clump around "VR," "human," "self-disclosure" (niche but significant focus on the role of VR in personal revelations). Finally, a large cluster located in the upper-right, containing "metaverses," "augmented reality," and "augmented reality technology," indicates a high-growth and highly influential research frontier that is becoming more central to the field. Taken together, the diagram provides a more vivid understanding of the intellectual topography, mapping the influential factors, niche specializations, underlying elements, and the leading-edge dynamics in the academic discussion about AI, VR, and workplace culture.

8.6.6. Visualization

This network is powerful in showing how these technologies are being considered from a human perspective with a large emphasis on applied technologies and systematic review reflective of current academic activities in leading institutions around the world.

The keyword co-occurrence network shows "virtual reality" and "human" as central nodes, strongly connected to AI, AR, safety training, construction industry, and occupational health. The dense interlinkages indicate an interdisciplinary research structure integrating immersive technologies with human-centered, workplace, and safety-focused applications.

Taken together, the included visualizations are easy-to-follow presentations of evidence for a quickly arriving and critically influencing research field that has AI, VR, and workplace culture at its core. The ACM panel of "Average Citations per Year," like the ACM of page-rank, shows a normal decreasing nature for more recent years due to the "sliding citation window," while the ACM line is also notable for its obvious leap of average citation number per paper since around the 2018–2019 year and its summits at the 2018 and the 2022–2023 years. This echoes the section of the "Affiliations Production Over Time" chart, which shows that major organizations like Chung-Ang University, Middlesex University, and The University of Manchester only started making significant contributions to this area specifically from 2019–2020, with a very fast, nearly exponential growth curve. Such simultaneous expansion of both output and effect from major global associations emphasizes the growing importance of the field and the strength of its latest substantive and research-based offerings. Coupled with this, the "Keywords Co-occurrence Network" illustrates the differing yet related "clusters" within the intellectual landscape. The red cluster is mainly composed of "virtual reality," "artificial intelligence," "e-learning," and "metaverses," representing technology applications and future scenarios.

8.6.7. Average Citations per Year

This evolution results in the 2025 period having a significant focus on "artificial intelligence," "virtual reality," "systematic review," and emerging themes including "well-being" and "economic and social effects," and thus indicating a more refined thinking about the human–technology relationship and its societal impact.

Incredible and ever-growing influence of AI, VR, and workplace culture, early works (before 2017) received low citation rates; however, a remarkable upturn of the scholarly impact started from around 2018 with distinctive peaks of average citations per document in 2018 and 2022–2023, suggesting trend-setting publication. This increasing impact ties directly to the "Affiliations' Production Over Time" plot illustrating concurrent and significant increases in academic production from notable institutions such as Chung-Ang University, Middlesex University, and The University of Manchester, immediately onwards from 2019 to 2020. It is a sign of broad and fast institutional support for this rapidly developing area. But the Thematic Evolution detailed roadmap of core concepts, the developmental path and interconnecting state between different periods. Initial themes such as "human," "e-learning," and "virtual reality" (2003–2023) turned into more sophisticated links with "augmented reality," Technology adoption," and Machine-learning" during 2024. The interrelations and time-lags visible between these plots in aggregate indicate a field of study that is not just expanding both in volume and in terms of which institutions participate but also one that is iteratively extending its intellectual attention in the direction of more advanced and stimulating research questions.

8.6.8. Cluster Analysis

Top authors are divided into five main "Clusters" according to their co-citation links that can be indicative of their thematic or intellectual relatedness in the research area of AI, VR, and workplace culture.

Cluster 1 represents foundational contributions to immersive technologies and VR applications. This cluster includes influential scholars associated with presence, immersion, and technology adoption across domains such as virtual environments and tourism. Their work continues to have a lasting impact, indicating the enduring relevance of early conceptualizations in VR research.

Cluster 2 is strongly grounded in technology acceptance and user behavior theories. It is primarily influenced by established models such as the Technology Acceptance Model (TAM) and the Unified Theory of Acceptance and Use of Technology (UTAUT), along with contributions from structural equation modeling and customer satisfaction research. This cluster emphasizes behavioral intention, user adoption, and quantitative validation techniques, which remain highly relevant in understanding AI- and VR-enabled workplace environments.

Cluster 3 reflects an emerging and rapidly evolving research domain focused on the metaverse, virtual ecosystems, and digital interaction spaces. The presence of recent scholarly contributions suggests growing interest in integrating AI and VR into education, training, and immersive digital workplaces. This cluster highlights interdisciplinary applications and future-oriented innovations. The relative newness of many of these authors (2021–2022) also indicates that this cluster is a very active and potentially newer area of research. There are authors like Mystakidis who've worked on metaverse and education, which means that this cluster would be dealing with more complicated applications of VR/AI to learning, virtual worlds, or new niche areas that are being brought to the fore. Cluster 4 represents a distinct thematic area, primarily associated with experiential learning, simulation-based environments, and applied VR use cases. However, the precise intellectual structure of this cluster requires further exploration through keyword co-occurrence and thematic mapping to better understand its research focus.

The bibliometric clustering reveals five thematic groups. Cluster 1 VR, presence, and immersive experiences. Cluster 2 focuses on technology acceptance, user satisfaction and behavioral intention models. Cluster 3 centers on metaverse concepts and digital environments. Cluster 4 highlights experiential learning and simulation. Cluster 5 concentrates on VR design, interaction and embodiment.

Cluster 5 focuses on VR design, human-computer interaction, and embodiment. It includes contributions related to user experience, virtual environment design, and psychological aspects of immersion. The recurrence of certain influential authors across multiple clusters highlights their broad and cross-cutting impact on the field, particularly in bridging theoretical and applied dimensions of VR research. Overall, the clustering structure reveals the intellectual landscape of AI and VR in workplace culture research. While some clusters emphasize foundational theories and technology adoption models, others focus on emerging applications such as the metaverse and immersive learning. Together, these clusters provide a comprehensive understanding of how AI and VR are shaping modern workplace environments.

8.7. Results and Findings

The Publication Overview shown provides a telling illustration of the rapid growth of this interdisciplinary area. From the anecdotal publications between 2003 and 2017, the steep ascent of scientific output from 2019 is impressive with a volume of 101 in year a.d. 2024 and even 85 in a.d. 2025 (stand = June-22-2025) at an extraordinary annual growth rate of +22.38%. And this unprecedented speed is new proof that AI and VR, as emerging disruptors for organizations to use and learn from are gaining momentum in academia's seal of approval. The same behavior can be observed in the "Average Citations per Year" graph which confirms a growing model of impact with peak averages near 2018 and slightly after 2022–2023, stating that last papers are adding influence to scholarship at elevated pace. Authors for productivity scale L1 U JAMA NATH and WANG Xie had the highest number (five papers each) to their credit followed by PANDEY PRAMOD Kumar and RAMAN Raghavachari (four papers each). This collaborative process is necessary to meet the complex and trans-disciplinary (AI & VR-related as well as broader issues) challenges of how AI/VR interacts with all kinds of organizational cultures in different geographical and industrial contexts. The thematic map ("Clusters by Authors Coupling") depicts such a pattern, where different groups of scientific communities including authors with diverse affiliations and backgrounds are observed to cluster together in the visual representation space on thematic topics. Some of them focus on TAMs (e.g., Cluster 2 with DAVVE) and the others go into practical application or ethical problem. The fourth category, Hybrid Workplace Management via VR looks at a developing use case in which VR increasingly alternates and complements rather than replaces real work environment or remote teams.

8.8. Discussion

Our findings strongly affirm the transformative influence of AI and VR on workplace culture, aligning with the study's goal of understanding how these technologies shape more inclusive, fluid, and responsive organizational environments. The thematic clusters identified offer detailed insights into this evolution. The cluster on *AI-Optimized Employee Engagement* indicates that AI is increasingly capable of tailoring employee experiences, enabling more responsive, personalized, and meaningful work interactions. Similarly, *VR-driven immersive training and collaboration* demonstrate how virtual environments enhance learning effectiveness, support team cohesion, and facilitate flexibility in hybrid work settings.

These insights translate into several direct practical implications for HR practitioners, managers, and technology strategists. Organizations should leverage *AI to personalize employee journeys and conduct sentiment analysis* to proactively identify and manage engagement patterns. Likewise, *VR can be deployed to scale immersive training, enable virtual collaboration rooms, and strengthen hybrid work models*. However, these implementations must be grounded in robust ethical practices. Ethical use of AI – ensuring data privacy, algorithmic fairness, and transparency – remains essential, particularly in HR processes where sensitive employee information is involved.

Although the applications of AI and VR are expanding rapidly, our analysis highlights notable gaps. Nuanced studies that integrate both technologies – for example, *AI-personalized VR training modules and VR behavioral data feeding into AI-driven empathy development programs* – remain limited. Additionally, best practices are underexplored; cultural adoption of these technologies varies widely across industries, organizational sizes, and regional contexts. Addressing these gaps is critical for developing sophisticated and responsible implementation frameworks.

8.9. Conclusion

This study demonstrates that AI and VR hold significant potential to reshape workplace culture by fostering engagement, adaptability, inclusivity, and experiential learning. The evidence underscores a growing technological shift wherein AI personalization and VR immersion increasingly complement organizational culture-building efforts. However, realizing this potential requires ethical deployment, cross-technology integration, and attention to contextual factors. Future research should focus on developing deeper theoretical models, industry-specific guidelines, and combined AI–VR frameworks that can support evidence-based and responsible cultural transformation.

8.10. Limitations and Future Directions

The bibliometric approach provides valuable insight in the shifting landscape of AI and VR for the future of workplace culture; however, we acknowledge limits that restrict generalizability as well as directing future work. First, as the study only included Scopus as the one and the only primary database with comprehensive search coverage, scholarships that were indexed in either other for comparative studies, or discipline-based repositories) could be missed. This might lead to a selection bias, as the performance of quantitative bibliographic databases may be related to their indexing policies and disciplinary areas. Furthermore, bibliometric analysis is particularly useful in terms of mapping patterns of publication outputs, collaboration and thematic structures, but it leans heavily toward quantitative (rather than qualitative depth of) indicators by design: there is no drilling down into specific information about what kinds of methodological choices different studies have made; exactly what empirical results were found or wanted to be generalized from; the details behind theoretical claims. Explanation of thematic clusters is based on keyword proximity (while strong, not nuanced to reflect the subtle argument within a paper). Furthermore, the prespecified search string, although it was deliberately designed and tested by two researchers on this theme, may also have overlooked some related literature around the perimeter if other terms were used. Finally, also because of the snapshot nature (until June 2025) of the data, most recent events in the field following the cut-off date are not included. For future research projects, observational studies need to be designed to monitor organizations over larger time frames in order to gain insight into how cultural change takes place. Finally, context-specific research is needed regarding AI and VR adoption but also how the use of these technologies affects local culture across industry sectors, organizational size, and national cultures moving beyond identification of generalizable constructs to more actionable tailored insight.

References

Abbas, A., Seo, J., Ahn, S., Luo, Y., Wyllie, M. J., Lee, G., & Billinghurst, M. (2023). How immersive virtual reality safety training system features impact learning outcomes: An experimental study of forklift training. *Journal of Management in Engineering*, *39*(1). https://doi.org/10.1061/(ASCE)ME.1943-5479.0001101

Brauer, M., & Vandepoele, L. (2025). The strength of showing weakness: Organizational supplication and investor reactions to workforce downsizing. *Journal of Management*, 1–37. https://doi.org/10.1177/01492063251339412

Chang, W.-C., Gonzalez Garcia, N. F., & Hasanzadeh, S. (2025). Deep learning-based prediction of human–robot trust dynamics in future construction using worker neuropsychophysiological responses. *Journal of Computing in Civil Engineering*, *39*(4). https://doi.org/10.1061/JCCEE5.CPENG-6302

Citibank, N. T., & Tasleem, N. (2025). *HR technology transformation and the impact of people analytics on workforce management*. *ResearchGate*. https://www.researchgate.net/

profile/Nazia-Tasleem/publication/390587245_HR_Technology_Transformation_and_The_Impact_of_People_Analytics_on_Workforce_Management/links/67f570d2e8041142a16f936a/HR-Technology-Transformation-and-The-Impact-of-People-Analytics-on-Workforce-Management.pdf

Dwivedi, Y. K., Hughes, L., Baabdullah, A. M., Ribeiro-Navarrete, S., Giannakis, M., Al-Debei, M. M., Dennehy, D., Metri, B., Buhalis, D., Cheung, C. M. K., Viglia, G., & Wamba, S. F. (2022). Metaverse beyond the hype: Multidisciplinary perspectives on emerging challenges, opportunities, and agenda for research, practice and policy. *International Journal of Information Management*, *66*, 102542. https://doi.org/10.1016/j.ijinfomgt.2022.102542

Ghobakhloo, M., Iranmanesh, M., Fathi, M., Rejeb, A., Foroughi, B., & Nikbin, D. (2024). Beyond Industry 4.0: A systematic review of Industry 5.0 technologies and implications for social, environmental and economic sustainability. *Asia Pacific Journal of Business Administration*. https://doi.org/10.1108/APJBA-08-2023-0384

Lanyi, C. S., & Withers, J. D. A. (2020). Striving for a safer and more ergonomic workplace: Acceptability and human factors related to the adoption of AR/VR glasses in Industry 4.0. *Smart Cities*, *3*(2), 289–307. https://doi.org/10.3390/smartcities3020016

Le, T.-H., & Lin, J. J. (2025). AR-enhanced near-miss incident alert system for onsite moving equipment. *Safety Science*, *191*, 106912. https://doi.org/10.1016/j.ssci.2025.106912

Liu, J., Yan, X., & Gao, W. (2024). A dualistic perspective of opportunity and risk: The impact of head-mounted augmented reality on construction onsite hazard identification of workers. *Journal of Construction Engineering and Management*, *150*(11). https://doi.org/10.1061/JCEMD4.COENG-14684

Parnell, D. R., Smith, C. S., Irving, A. N., Buhler, A. G., & Waisome, J. A. M. (2025). Augmented reality's role in addressing the US semiconductor industry's workforce demands. *Authorea*. https://doi.org/10.22541/AU.173938694.48197322

Raj, S., Sampat, B., Behl, A., & Jain, K. (2023). Understanding senior citizens' intentions to use virtual reality for religious tourism in India: A behavioural reasoning theory perspective. *Tourism Recreation Research*, *48*(6), 983–999. https://doi.org/10.1080/02508281.2023.2246735

Singh, P., Sharma, M., & Daim, T. (2024). Envisaging AR travel revolution for visiting heritage sites: A mixed-method approach. *Technology in Society*, *76*, 102439. https://doi.org/10.1016/j.techsoc.2023.102439

Chapter 9

Transforming HR with AI and VR: Key Trends, Tools, and Strategies for 2025

Anitha G.

Maharaja Agrasen Institute of Management Studies, Delhi, India

Abstract

Human resource (HR) functions are enduring a profound transformation as organizations adjust to the demands of a rapidly evolving digital landscape. This chapter looks at how artificial intelligence (AI) and virtual reality (VR) will change HR strategies in 2025, making them more efficient, personalized, and valuable from a strategic point of view. It looks at how AI may be used in hiring, managing performance, learning and development, and getting employees involved, focusing on solutions like ChatGPT, Eightfold.ai, and Workday. At the same time, the chapter talks about how VR can be used for immersive onboarding, virtual training, and simulated leadership development, showing platforms like Strivr and Talespin. The research uses data-driven insights and real-world case studies to stress the pros, drawbacks, and moral issues of using these technologies. AI and VR motivate HR work easier, morale, upskilling, and agility.

Keywords: HR digital transformation; predictive workforce analytics; immersive learning technologies; talent and recruitment innovation; personalized employee experience; remote work; future workplace

9.1. Introduction: The Future of HR – Powered by AI and VR

AI and VR are redefining the HR landscape in workplaces. HR is changing into a data-driven, employee-focused job that employs the latest technologies to find, train, and keep the best workers (Deloitte Insights, 2023; Gartner, 2024).

Nurturing AI-Powered HR Analytics and Virtual Reality in Employee Psychology and Workplace Happiness, Part A, 151–163

Published under exclusive licence by Emerald Publishing Limited
doi:10.1108/978-1-80686-125-520261007

In 2025, HR professionals will rely more and more on AI for making decisions in real time, predicting trends, and making the process of hiring better (McKinsey & Company, 2023). Through VR, organizations are renovating how organizations onboarding, training, and engaging employees through immersive learning and seamless collaboration. (XR Association & PwC, 2023).

The biggest impact is to explore the emerging trends, shaping HR's future through VR and implement these changes. The new HR strategy is to streamlining the recruitment process, along with AI-powered candidate (World Economic Forum, 2023).

9.1.1. New Trends in AI and VR in the Workplace

The combination of AI and VR is causing a significant shift in HR. Companies are developing innovative methods for hiring, training, and staff development (Gartner, 2024).

AI Trends in HRs:

- *AI automation at the initiative level*: AI Automation really helps to grow the career of employees. It helps management to stay focused on goals by automating boring tasks and making processes more efficient (McKinsey & Company, 2023).
- *Skills-based hiring*: For recruiting the candidate for the appropriate profile, AI helps to select the talent personal for the position. On a large scale automated hiring methods are getting better at giving candidates personalized encounters. (World Economic Forum, 2023).
- *Real-time decision-making by data*: To get optimize hiring, retention, and employee engagement, the real-time dashboards' data are useful for the HR professionals (Deloitte Insights, 2023).
- *Reducing preconception and promoting equality*: To reduce bias and to encourage equality, AI-powered hiring tools are being developed (Harvard Business Review, 2023).
- *Predictive trends*: AI tools are helping in predicting the trends, anticipating the attrition, and identifying the performance risks in early stage (PwC, 2024).

VR Trends in HRs:

- *Immersive onboarding practices*: To fit in the right way of company culture it provides new hires virtual office tours, fake introductions to coworkers, and hands-on activities (XR Association & PwC, 2023).
- *Training and skill-building in VR*: It provides risk-intensive businesses to develop the flexible skill development to the employees to practice high risk tasks, enhancing safety awareness, and accelerating learning. (XR Association & PwC, 2023)
- *Improvement of soft skills*: VR-based role-playing and scenario training help employees become better at communicating, leading, and resolving conflicts. Training is better when there are immediate feedback and real-life simulations (PwC, 2024).
- *Remote alliance and team building*: It has virtual conference spaces and collaboration spaces in VR that make it feel like remote teams are really together, even

though they are not. This gets people involved and makes international teams stronger (World Economic Forum, 2023).

- *Branding for employers and employees*: VR lets candidates get a feel for the job requirements and the company's culture, which makes the hiring process more interactive and informative. Companies can use VR at employment fairs or on the internet to show off their values and the environment at work, which will help them find the best employees (Gartner, 2024).

9.2. Review of Literature

9.2.1 AI and Contemporary Human Resource Management (HRM)

The growing use of AI in HRM reflects broader changes in how organizations manage people in increasingly digital environments (Society for Human Resource Management, 2023). Researchers have shown that AI is no longer limited to experimental applications but is now embedded in everyday HR activities such as hiring, performance evaluation, learning, and workforce planning. As a result, scholars have begun to examine not only the efficiency benefits of AI but also its broader implications for employees and organizational decision-making.

9.2.2. Improving HR Processes Through AI Technologies

Several studies highlight the practical value of AI in improving HR operations. Madanchian et al. (2023) reviewed existing research on AI-based HR tools and found that these technologies help organizations streamline recruitment, improve performance management, and reduce manual administrative work. Likewise, Murugesan et al. (2023) noted that AI-supported HR digitization is associated with higher productivity and more consistent HR outcomes. Together, these studies suggest that AI allows HR professionals to shift their focus from routine tasks to more strategic responsibilities.

9.2.3. Ethical and Human-centric Considerations

While efficiency gains are widely acknowledged, recent literature stresses that AI adoption in HR cannot be separated from ethical and human concerns. Fenwick et al. (2024) argue that employee trust and transparency are essential for successful AI integration. Their study points out that without clear governance and ethical safeguards, AI systems may increase perceptions of bias or unfair treatment. Similarly, Madanchian et al. (2024) examine AI use across the employee lifecycle and caution that although AI enables personalized and scalable HR solutions, unresolved ethical issues – particularly algorithmic bias – can negatively affect employee trust and organizational culture.

9.2.4. AI in Learning and Human Resource Development

The role of AI in employee learning and development has also attracted increasing attention. Ekuma (2024) reviews how AI and automation are influencing human resource development (HRD) practices and concludes that adaptive learning technologies can support skill development when implemented thoughtfully. However, the study also warns that over-reliance on automation may limit meaningful human interaction in learning environments. Supporting this view, Chowdhury et al. (2025) examine AI-enabled tools such as chatbots and virtual mentors and find that they can personalize training experiences. At the same time, the authors emphasize the importance of protecting employee data and maintaining a balance between technological support and human guidance.

9.2.5. Strategic Value of HR Analytics and Generative AI

Beyond operational improvements, recent research highlights the strategic role of AI in HR decision-making. Sharma (2025) explores AI-driven HR analytics in the IT sector and demonstrates how data-based insights strengthen workforce planning and organizational transformation. In a similar vein, Jiang (2025) discusses the growing influence of generative AI in HRM, noting its ability to support personalized decision-making and enhance HR's strategic contribution to the organization.

9.2.6. Summary and Research Gap

Overall, existing literature shows that AI has the potential to significantly reshape HRM by improving efficiency, supporting better decisions, and enabling more personalized employee experiences. However, many studies also point to unresolved challenges related to ethics, fairness, data privacy, and the quality of human–AI interaction. These concerns suggest a need for further empirical research that examines how organizations can adopt AI in HR responsibly, ensuring that technological advancement aligns with employee well-being and long-term organizational sustainability.

9.3. Combined Impact and Strategic Focus

The convergence of AI and VR in HR is creating a more agile, data-driven, and employee-centric function (World Economic Forum, 2023).. Key strategic focus areas include:

- Scaling automation and personalization across HR processes.
- Enhancing digital collaboration and communication tools for hybrid and remote workforces.
- Providing equitable access to training, career growth, and well-being resources, regardless of location.
- Using immersive technologies to foster a stronger sense of belonging and engagement among employees (see Table 9.1).

9.4. Best Tools for Creating Diagrams to Explain AI in HR

Several advanced tools make it easy to create clear, compelling diagrams for explaining AI concepts and processes in HR. Here are the top options, with features relevant to HR professionals and educators:

Table 9.1. Comparative Trends in AI and VR Innovations in HRM.

Trend Area	AI Innovations	VR Innovations
Recruitment	Automated, bias-reducing candidate screening	Virtual job previews, immersive employer branding
Onboarding	Personalized learning paths	Virtual office tours, interactive onboarding
Training and development	Predictive upskilling, personalized programs	Realistic scenario-based training, soft skills
Employee engagement	Real-time analytics, feedback mechanisms	Virtual team-building, remote collaboration
Workforce planning	Predictive analytics, talent mapping	N/A (mainly AI-driven)

Source: Author's work.

9.4.1. Piktochart AI Diagram Generator

- *AI-powered creation*: (Piktochart, n.d.) Instantly generate polished diagrams (flowcharts, org charts, process maps) by describing what you need in plain language.
- *Customization*: Adjust layouts, colors, fonts, and shapes to match your brand or presentation style.
- *HR-specific use cases*: Ideal for visualizing HR workflows, organizational structures, training processes, and competency models.
- *Ease of use*: Drag-and-drop editor, templates, and the ability to convert documents (PDF, DOCX, TXT) into diagrams automatically.

9.4.2. Creately VIZ AI Diagram Maker

- *Prompt-based generation*: Create flowcharts, mind maps, org charts, SWOT diagrams, and more using simple text prompts.
- *Collaboration*: Invite team members to co-create and edit diagrams in real-time.
- *Template library*: Access a wide range of HR-relevant templates (onboarding flows, recruitment pipelines, etc.).
- *Seamless idea transformation*: Convert mind maps to Kanban boards or expand diagrams with additional prompts.

9.4.3. Lucidchart (with AI Features)

- *Versatile diagramming*: Supports flowcharts, org charts, process diagrams, and more.
- *AI enhancements*: Some AI-powered features for auto-generating diagrams from text or data.
- *Collaboration*: Real-time editing and sharing, making it suitable for HR teams.

9.4.4. Microsoft Visio (AI-enhanced)

- *Professional diagrams*: Create detailed process charts, org charts, and workflow diagrams.
- *Integration*: Works well with Microsoft 365 suite, commonly used in HR departments.
- *AI templates*: Some AI-driven templates and auto-layout features.

9.4.5. Miro (AI-powered Visual Collaboration)

- *Collaborative whiteboard*: Ideal for brainstorming, mapping HR processes, and team workshops.
- *AI diagramming*: AI features for auto-layout and generating mind maps or workflows from prompts.

9.5. Best AI Tools for Creating Custom HR Diagrams

AI-driven diagramming tools (LinkedIn Learning, 2024) provide efficiency, adaptability, and high-quality outcomes for the creation of bespoke HR diagrams, including organizational charts, process flows, competency models, and training workflows. The premier selections, equipped with functionalities designed to meet HR requirements, are presented in the following:

9.5.1. Piktochart AI Diagram Generator

- *AI-powered Generation*: Immediately produces refined, professional diagrams from a basic textual description. Simply specify the HR process or structure you wish to illustrate (e.g., "onboarding workflow" or "HR competency model"), and the tool will generate a completely customizable diagram within seconds.
- *Customization*: Effortlessly modify layouts, colors, fonts, and shapes to align with your brand or HR presentation esthetics.
- *HR-specific templates*: Comprises templates for organizational charts, training workflows, and competence models, rendering it particularly beneficial for HR and learning and development professionals.
- *Document conversion*: Upload a PDF, DOCX, or TXT file, and the AI will transform it into a visual diagram, elucidating data-intensive HR documents into comprehensible visuals.
- *Intuitive editor*: Drag-and-drop interface for seamless modification and reorganization of diagram components.

9.5.2. Deel Engage (for Career Frameworks and Competency Matrices)

- *AI assistant*: Helps you create career frameworks, competency matrices, and development plans for all roles and levels in your organization.
- *Integrated HR visuals*: Generates career paths, skill matrices, and development plans as visual frameworks, streamlining HR strategy and communication.

9.5.3. Sembly AI (for Custom HR Analytics and Benchmarking)

- *Custom analytics diagrams*: Visualizes employee sentiment, engagement, performance mapping, and workforce planning.
- *AI-enhanced visuals*: Offers data-backed recommendations and benchmarking visuals to compare HR metrics with industry standards.

9.5.4. General-purpose AI Tools (ChatGPT, Notion AI, etc.)

- *Flexible content generation*: Tools like ChatGPT can generate the textual structure for HR diagrams (e.g., process steps, role hierarchies), which can then be imported into diagramming platforms for visualization.
- *Integration*: Notion AI and similar platforms allow you to organize HR data and generate workflows, which can be exported to visual tools.

9.5.5. AI-powered Tools for Creating and Visualizing HR Diagrams

Piktochart AI offers AI-generated and fully customizable diagrams with ready-to-use HR templates. It is especially useful for creating visually appealing organizational charts, workflow diagrams, and competency models that are easy to understand and present.

Deel Engage focuses on building AI-driven career frameworks and competency matrices. It is best suited for designing clear career paths, mapping employee skills, and aligning individual growth with organizational goals.

Sembly AI provides advanced analytics and benchmarking visuals that help translate HR data into meaningful insights. It is commonly used for visualizing employee sentiment, engagement levels, and performance patterns in a structured and data-driven manner.

ChatGPT/Notion AI supports content creation and workflow structuring. These tools are ideal for drafting the textual content behind HR diagrams, outlining processes, and organizing ideas before converting them into visual formats.

Piktochart AI stands out for its speed, HR-specific templates, and ease of customization, making it the top choice for most HR diagramming needs. For more specialized frameworks (like career paths and competency matrices), *Deel Engage* and *Sembly AI* offer tailored solutions that integrate seamlessly with broader HR strategies (see Table 9.2).

9.6. Strategic Vision for 2025

To prepare for the future of HR in 2025, the integration of AI and VR will shape the strategies that HR professionals adopt to optimize operations, improve employee experiences, and enhance decision-making (PwC, 2024; Gartner, 2024). Following are the key strategies for HR professionals to implement as they prepare for these trends in 2025.

9.6.1. Scaling AI Automation Across HR Processes

- *Strategy*: Utilize AI-driven tools to automate tedious and time-intensive HR operations, enabling HR staff to concentrate on strategic projects. Implement

Table 9.2. Key Features to Look for in an AI HR Diagram Tool.

Feature	Purpose	Benefit to HR Teams
AI-powered diagram generation	Automatically create diagrams from text or data inputs	Saves time and removes manual work from creating org charts and process flows
Customization and flexibility	Modify layouts, colors, fonts, and diagram shapes	Ensures visual consistency with company branding and adaptable to different use cases
HR-specific templates	Ready-made templates for HR scenarios like onboarding, reviews, and pipelines	Increases efficiency and aligns with HR best practices
Integration with HR systems	Connect to tools like HRIS, ATS, or payroll	Keeps diagrams updated with real-time employee or hiring data
Collaboration features	Allow teams to comment, edit, and share diagrams in real-time	Improves team alignment and speeds up decision-making
Data privacy and security	Comply with privacy laws (e.g., GDPR) and secure sensitive employee information	Protects confidential HR data and ensures compliance
Advanced analytics and reporting	Analyze data within diagrams to uncover patterns or insights	Enables data-driven decisions around talent, skills, and workforce trends
Automation capabilities	Automatically update diagrams when data or structures change	Reduces repetitive work and minimizes errors
Ease of use	Simple UI with drag-and-drop and guided onboarding	Lowers training time and increases adoption across HR teams
Bias mitigation and fairness	Embed DEI-aware AI tools in recruiting or talent management visualizations	Supports fair practices and promotes diversity and inclusion

Source: Author's work.

enterprise-scale AI automation in areas like recruitment, onboarding, performance management, and employee engagement.

- *Action steps*:
    - Implement AI-powered platforms for resume screening, talent matching, and scheduling interviews.
    - Use AI for payroll and benefits management to reduce errors and increase efficiency.
    - Introduce AI in employee performance tracking and real-time feedback mechanisms.
- *Goal*: Improve operational efficiency, reduce manual errors, and allow HR to allocate more resources to strategy rather than administration.

9.6.2. Personalizing the Employee Experience Using AI and VR

- *Strategy*: Leverage AI to create personalized experiences for recruitment, training, and career development. Integrate VR for immersive and engaging learning and onboarding processes.
- *Action steps*:
    - Implement AI algorithms that analyze candidate profiles, skills, and cultural fit to personalize recruitment and onboarding.
    - Use VR to create immersive onboarding experiences (virtual office tours, team-building exercises) for new employees.
    - Develop personalized learning paths and training modules using AI for upskilling and reskilling employees.
- *Goal*: Create a more engaging and customized experience for employees at every stage of their career, from recruitment to development and retention.

9.6.3. Making Decisions Based on Data Better

- *Strategy*: Use AI-powered dashboards and analytical tools to help you make decisions based on data in real-time in areas like hiring, keeping employees, and keeping employees engaged.
- *Steps to take*:
    - Use AI-powered HR analytics solutions to get information on trends in the workforce, employee performance, and turnover rates.
    - Predictive analytics leverages employee data to identify early signs of fatigue and disengagement, enabling organizations to proactively intervene and reduce the risk of turnover.
- *Goal*: Provide HR directors with data-driven insights and actionable information that empower them to make informed, proactive decisions for more effective employee management.

9.6.4. Bias Reduction Combines Fairness in Hiring

- *Strategy*: It effectively minimizing insensible bias in recruitment decisions by implementing AI-driven hiring processes that prioritize fairness and inclusivity.
- *Steps to take*:
  - The candidates assess the skills, experience, and qualifications, excluding demographic information through AI tools.
  - To ensure alignment with diversity, equity, and inclusion objectives we have to conduct regular evaluations of AI systems.
- *Goal*: To attract a wide range of talent and reduce bias between the employees, hiring process is used evidently.

9.6.5. Creating Development Programs and Engaging the Training Programs Using VR

- *Strategy*: In leadership programs the VR-based simulations enhance soft skills like communication and problem solving by providing employees with risk-free environment safety practice.
- *Steps to take*:
  - It provides a immersive, safe environments for employees to practice complex task through communication and problem-solving practice.
  - Use VR-based role-playing to help employees improve their soft skills in real-life situations.
- *Goal*: Enhance learning outcomes and skill acquisition by providing employees with engaging, practical, and immersive training experiences that accelerate proficiency and confidence.

9.6.6. Improving Teamwork and Collaboration at a Distance

- *Strategy*: Use VR technology to make teamwork and communication better in distant or hybrid settings. VR team-building activities can make people more interested and help teams who are separated by distance communicate better.
- *Steps to take*:
  - Set up virtual conference rooms so that remote teams may work together and talk to each other as if they were in the same room.
  - Use VR platforms for team-building events to help employees get to know each other better, work together better, and trust each other more.
- *Goal*: To improving cooperation, collaboration, and communication among teams and to sense togetherness.

9.6.7. Predicting and Addressing Workforce Gaps

- *Strategy*: By using the predictive analytics and AI to predict future trends in the workforce, find trends, identify skill shortages, and forecast talent needs.
- *Steps to take*:

  - o AI is useful to forecast the employees' data for turnover, to analyze the potential performers, and to know the future talent.
  - o In the workforce we have to bring a new plan for skill development and succession to fit with the predictable trends.

- *Goal*: To ensure HR strategies are closely associated with the company's future business needs and to manage employees transitions, and address skill deficiencies.

9.6.8. Ensuring Data Privacy and Security

- *Strategy*: To prioritize data security and compliance with regulatory standards, AI/VR tools are progressively used.
- *Steps to take*:

  - o It is compulsory to follow the data protection regulations such as general data protection pegulation (**GDPR**).
  - o It should ensure the regular security audits to safeguard sensitive employee details and maintain security.

- *Goal*: To build employee trust and confidence in AI and VR technologies, the data protection and regulatory compliance should be confirmed.

9.6.9. Enhancing Employee Well-being Through Technology

- *Strategy*: AI can help with well-being assessments by using feedback quizzes. VR can help with stress relief or mindfulness activities by giving people immersive experiences.
- *Steps to take*:

  - o To help the employees use AI-powered wellness initiatives on how employees are doing and providing them quick suggestions for how to become better.
  - o Employees capitalise on virtual reality to engage in mindfulness or relaxation exercises to help them cope with stress.

- *Goal*: Promote healthier, less stressed, and more mentally resilient employees by integrating innovative technological solutions into well-being programs.

9.7. Limitations

- Significant dependence on data quality and integrity.
- Ethical challenges to ensure fairness in algorithms, transparency, and responsible governance at scale are complex.

- Concerns over data privacy and security endure, particularly with sensitive employee information disseminated across various platforms.
- Organizational opposition stemming from inadequate technological infrastructure, insufficient AI literacy, and cultural barriers.
- Human factors emotional intelligence, relationship cultivation, and nuanced judgment may not be entirely represented or facilitated by AI and VR systems.
- The elevated expenses and technological intricacies associated with implementing VR solutions for training and onboarding may limit accessibility for certain organizations.
- Adherence to legal regulations and adjustment to local labor laws and diversity/equity requirements persist as continual challenges.
- Effective implementation necessitates change management, cross-functional collaboration, and skills development.

9.8. Suggestions

- *Visual aids*: To visually depict trends in AI versus VR within the realm of human resources use comparison charts and infographics
- *Practical applications and case studies*: Provide tangible examples or case studies demonstrating the application of AI and VR in human resources by various firms. Emphasize the return on investment (time, cost, and retention advantages) associated with the utilization of these technologies.
- *Intuitive tool comparisons*: Provide a comparative analysis of the diagramming tools, highlighting HR-specific functionalities and applications. Enumerate the advantages and disadvantages for each tool.
- *Concentrate on prospective trends*: Examine the prospective advancements of AI and VR in human resources and the trajectory of these technologies. Address ethical aspects such as AI bias and data privacy issues.
- *Employee-centric focus*: Highlight the enhancement of the employee experience using AI and VR, rather than solely work automation (e.g., VR for team cohesion, AI for individualized growth).
- *Call to Action*: Prompt HR professionals to investigate tools and interact with the information by offering resources or discussion forums.
- *Management of change*: Include a segment on change management practices to facilitate the effective adoption of AI and VR by HR departments.
- *Experiences that are interactive*: Use quizzes or polls to get readers involved and see how ready they are for AI/VR in HR.

9.9. Conclusion: Using AI and VR to Make HR Ready for the Future

Upcoming 2025, the HR technologies are implementing new hiring and onboarding to training, performance management, and employee welfare. The management can make better decisions based on data, customize their work, and make their process run more efficiently by adopting AI. It is important in today's hybrid and remote work settings to provide immersive experiences that improve learning, teamwork, and cultural unity though VR. The guidance encourages the employees to work in flexible, employee-focused, and tech-savvy HR service. The more automation is needed to create a more engaging, reasonable, and high-performing workplace. The managers must invest in regular learning and adaptability through effective transformation. The heart of deployments are data protection, ethical AI methods and, design that works completely. As HRs become a strategic partner in the success of an organization and the development of its staff, companies that use AI and VR will be in a good position to lead the way in new ideas.

HR's future isn't just digital; it's also smart, interesting, and focused on how people feel. Use this as a guide not only to deal with change but also to shape it.

References

Creately. (n.d.). *Product documentation and case studies*. Retrieved March 30 2026, from https://creately.com

Deloitte Insights. (2023). *2024 global human capital trends report*. Retrieved March 30 2026, from https://www2.deloitte.com

Gartner. (2024). *Top HR trends and priorities for 2025*. Retrieved March 30 2026, from https://www.gartner.com

Harvard Business Review. (2023). *Using AI to eliminate bias from hiring*. Retrieved March 30 2026, from https://hbr.org

LinkedIn Learning. (2024). *Workplace learning report*. Retrieved March 30 2026, from https://learning.linkedin.com

Lucidchart. (n.d.). *Product documentation and case studies*. Retrieved March 30 2026, from https://lucidchart.com

McKinsey & Company. (2023). *The state of AI in 2023: Generative AI's breakout year*. Retrieved March 30 2026, from https://www.mckinsey.com

Piktochart. (n.d.). *Product documentation and case studies*. Retrieved March 30 2026, from https://piktochart.com

PwC. (2024). *2025 workforce of the future: Human touch in a digital world*. Retrieved March 30 2026, from https://www.pwc.com

Society for Human Resource Management. (2023). *AI and the future of HR*. Retrieved March 30 2026, from https://www.shrm.org

World Economic Forum. (2023). *Future of jobs report*. Retrieved March 30 2026, from https://www.weforum.org

XR Association & PwC. (2023). *The value of XR in training*. Retrieved March 30 2026, from https://xra.org

Chapter 10

Ethical Considerations in AI and VR: Navigating Digital Copyright and Intellectual Property Rights Through a Systematic Review Approach Toward 2030

Praveen Kumar[a], *Dev Panwar*[a] *and Anika Nashat Matin*[b]

[a]*Department of Law, Manav Rachana University, India*
[b]*Southeast business School, Southeast University, Bangladesh*

Abstract

The intersection of artificial intelligence (AI) and virtual reality (VR) technologies is transforming digital ecosystems quickly, and it is providing innovative solutions in the creative, educational, and commercial worlds. However, such rapid acceleration poses unseen moral dilemmas especially in the areas of authorship, privacy, responsibility, and online proprietorship. This chapter represents the evidence-based and systematic discussion of ethical issues regarding AI and VR, with special emphasis on intellectual property rights (IPR) and law of digital copyright. Through the application of Preferred Reporting Items for Systematic Reviews and Meta-Analyses (PRISMA) framework as a means of conducting a systematic literature review (SLR), this chapter summarizes peer-reviewed studies, legal reports, and policy documents as a critical look at how current legal and ethical frameworks are adapting/not adapting to the disruptive potential of these technologies. Some of the major areas of concern are the appropriateness of AI-generated content, the legality of virtual property, the consequences of immersive user data gathering, and the renegotiation of copyright in algorithmically generated space. The chapter pinpoints

Nurturing AI-Powered HR Analytics and Virtual Reality in Employee Psychology and Workplace Happiness, Part A, 165–181

doi:10.1108/978-1-80686-125-520261008

the main gaps in the academic debate and regulation policy in forecasting ethical and legal paths in 2030, proposing the concept of interdisciplinary governance models, ethics-by-design principles, and dynamic and responsive AI–VR governance frameworks. It ends by suggesting a strong future research agenda that uses SLR and PRISMA methodologies in order to constantly evaluate and improve digital ethics standards, so that innovation is not devoid of justice, equity, and global legal standards.

Keywords: Ethical AI; virtual reality; digital copyright law; intellectual property rights; PRISMA; systematic literature review; AI-generated content, immersive technology; algorithmic governance; data privacy; 2030 technological advancements

10.1. Introduction

10.1.1. Background and Motivation

The technological revolution in the rapidly expanding number of digital technologies and especially AI and VR has resulted in the paradigm shift of how people produce, consume, and engage with digital content. AI can now be used to create complex artistic pieces, music, and literature without a human being involved, and VR can help users explore virtually recreated or completely imagined realms. AI and VR are transforming aspects of life, such as education, entertainment, medicine, and manufacturing (Kaplan & Haenlein, 2019). Nevertheless, there is a major ethical and legal dilemma that comes with this innovation. With the increasing autonomy of AI and the heightening immersion of VR, there arise issues of digital authorship, data privacy, consent, algorithmic bias, and IPR. These emerging complications usually cannot be remedied by traditional legal systems and ethical standards (Floridi & Cowls, 2020). The chapter attempts to analytically explore these issues through an evidence-based approach that is robust to inform policy development, academic research, and best practice in the industry in the future.

10.1.2. Technological Convergence of AI and VR

The synthesis of AI and VR is not only the technological one but a change of socio-cultural development. AI can deliver computational intelligence to personalize and automate virtual experiences, and VR can provide a medium of sensation to implement the intelligent decision-making in real-time situations. The synergy can be used to support applications, including AI-powered tutors in VR classrooms, algorithmic designers in immersive design platforms, and automated legal hearings with AI-assisted moderation. This convergence not only increases the benefits but poses a threat of abuse. AI-created avatars may imitate real people and, therefore, go against consent and fake identities (Cohen-Almagor, 2021).

In addition, independent actions of AI agents within the VR can lead to the outcomes whose responsibility is not established, and legal responsibility and authorship should be re-examined.

10.1.3. Scope and Purpose of the Chapter

The chapter explores the ethical and legal issues arising when AI and VR meet, specifically, in relation to digital copyright and IPR. The objective is twofold:

1. To outline the existing ethical issues and legal ambiguities with the help of an SLR strategy.
2. To predict future regulatory paths through to 2030 and give recommendations on the basis of evidence-based knowledge. Specifically, we pay attention to the law of digital copyright, AI-created content, virtual property, immersive user data aggregation, and cross-jurisdictional matters. The chapter is restricted to literature published since 2013, with the focus on peer-reviewed articles, white papers, and legal policy documents.

10.1.4. Research Questions and Objectives

The research questions that will be used in the core of this chapter are:

RQ1. What are the most important ethical concerns related to the interplay of AI and VR?

RQ2. What are the current legal (or legal non-legal) mechanisms that manage (or do not manage) AI-generated content and virtual ownership?

RQ3. What are the possible future directions that can guarantee ethical governance and legal readiness until 2030?

10.1.5. Methodological Framework: PRISMA and SLR

Such an approach is required to achieve a complete and impartial examination of the subject matter, which is why in this chapter the PRISMA framework is applied. PRISMA enables the use of a clear and reproducible evidence synthesis process, as it presents the inclusion and exclusion criteria, search tactics, and data extraction procedures. The literature used in the SLR was found in databases, including Scopus, IEEE Xplore, SSRN, and SpringerLink. The keywords to be utilized are AI and copyright, VR ethics, AI authorship, and virtual property law, ownership of AI-generated content, and IPR in immersive technology. The given approach guarantees that the discussion is informed by quality, relevant, and peer-reviewed literature only which offers a solid foundation to draw conclusions about theoretical and practical implications of the policy.

10.2. Theoretical Foundations and Conceptual Clarifications

This section provides the foundations of the discussion of the interactions between AI, VR, ethics, and the legal framework of digitalized environment. It provides explicit definitions, addresses theoretical foundations, and discusses recent shifting views of intellectual property (IP) in light of dynamically evolving technologies.

10.2.1. Defining AI and VR

AI is the ability of machines to simulate human mental activities like learning, reasoning, problem solving, and creativity (Russell & Norvig, 2021). It encompasses such subfields as machine learning, natural language processing, and computer vision. The current AI systems are not only automating the routine work but also producing creative output in the form of music, code, and art that pose new questions concerning authorship and IP. VR, in its turn, implies the production of imaginary spaces that can be engaged with and played in by users in apparently real or material means using sensory instruments such as headsets and haptic devices (Slater & Sanchez-Vives, 2016). In contrast to AI, which operates in the background, VR provides a front-end service that puts the user into digitally created realities. Collectively, AI and VR are converging to create intelligent immersions as shown in Fig. 10.1, for example, AI tutors in VR classrooms or AI-generated virtual humans in simulations.

10.2.2. Ethical Frameworks in Emerging Technologies

With the rapid development of technologies, the ethics are vital in the responsible development of innovation as the structures of law are outpaced.

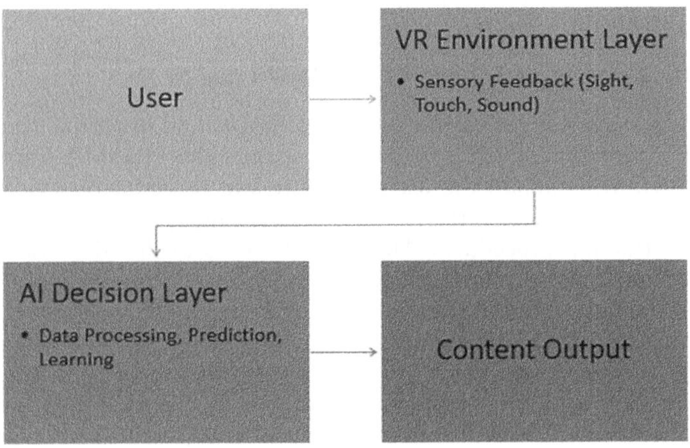

Fig. 10.1. Synergistic Interaction Between AI and VR. *Source*: Authors' creation.

The ethical principles that are most popular with regards to AI and immersive technologies are:

- *Transparency*: The systems must be understandable and explainable to the stakeholders.
- *Accountability*: It should be possible to identify the actions of or by AI.
- *Privacy and consent*: This is particularly important in the VR where personal information is gathered in the form of biometric and behavior data.
- *Fairness and reduction of bias*: AI systems are not supposed to reproduce and enhance social inequities.
- *Autonomy and human dignity*: The users should have substantive control over the technological systems.

The human-centered approach is encouraged by the ethical principles of international organizations like the High-Level Expert Group on AI, offered by the European Commission (2019), which propose an ethics-by-design approach and the dynamic regulation framework (Jobin et al., 2019).

10.2.3 IPR in the Digital Age

IPR involves the existence of laws that defend the rights of creators with regard to their inventions, designs, and works of art. These are copyrights, trademarks, patents, and trade secrets. AI has the potential to disturb IPR in the digital era because it can take on an independent creation.

The copyright law is not applied to AI-generated works in most jurisdictions, including the USA and India, unless there is a significant human intervention (WIPO, 2020). This legal gap contributes to the lack of protection and the increasing number of claims concerning ownership, particularly in such areas as automated design, synthetic media, and generative art.

10.2.4. Evolution of Digital Copyright Laws

Historically, copyright laws were created so as to safeguard tangible human-created expressions. Nevertheless, digital media and algorithmic content have changed the context. Even though the modern copyright laws were initially concentrated on books, music, and films, the latest copyright policy is now applied to streaming services, interactive media, and outputs produced by AI. There are some significant developments such as:

- In the USA, there is the Digital Millennium Copyright Act that brought about some protection of digital rights management.
- Continued debate at WIPO and UNESCO to revise laws on copyright to accommodate machine-generated content and transnational law enforcement.

Regardless of such progress, laws do not keep pace with innovations, particularly in such spheres as deepfakes, virtual assets, and non-fungible tokens (NFTs).

These advances indicate why the world must urgently come to a consensus and adopt technological neutrality in legislation (Gervais, 2021).

10.2.5. Algorithmic Content Creation and Challenges to Traditional Authorship

Probably the most disruptive element of AI in the artistic world is that algorithms are capable of creating content on their own. The classic understanding of creativity, originality, and ownership is being rebranded with AI-generated novels and paintings, voice imitation, and artificial video creation. Key concerns include:

- *Economic value*: Is there a need to have AI-created works to bring royalties or licensing fees?
- *Moral rights*: Does a machine have the right to violate the right of a human being to integrate or reputation? Naruto v. is one of a number of court cases.

This debate has been informed by Slater case (about the authorship of a photograph by an animal) but not AI-specific. The majority of legal frameworks are still wary of awarding the copyright to non-humans and, therefore, AI-generated content is in a legal grey zone.

10.3. Methodology: SLR Using PRISMA

That is why this chapter employs the SLR methodology that is based on the PRISMA 2020 guidelines to guarantee the objectivity, reproducibility, and credibility of the findings regarding the ethical and legal implications of AI and VR. The SLR method allows pooling of the quality research data to define gaps, evaluate trends, and make evidence-based recommendations.

10.3.1. Research Design and Selection Criteria

The study utilized a qualitative SLR paradigm where legal, ethical, and policy-related articles that discussed the interchange of AI and VR were used. The design had five important steps which included:

1. *Research question(s) definitions*: What are the significant ethical issues raised by AI–VR convergence?

    - What is the redefinition of copyright and IP through emerging new technologies?

2. *Database selection*: Primary academic databases: Scopus, IEEE Xplore, SpringerLink, SSRN, and ScienceDirect. Supplementary databases: legal sources, Google Scholar, Web of Science, and WIPO Lex.

3. *Search string construction*:

    - Such Boolean phrases as: "AI AND VR" AND "ethics" AND "intellectual property" AI and VR and copyright law.

4. *Prominence of peer-reviewed sources*: Only theoretical articles, judicial commentaries, official policy documents, and official white papers were taken into account.
5. *Time frame*:

    - The articles that were published in 2013–2024 to discuss the latest and the most topical developments.

10.3.2. Inclusion and Exclusion Parameters

The inclusion and exclusion criteria were well-defined to provide the necessary methodological rigor.

This is because the transparent filtering of the research will only consider the most pertinent and rigorous studies to inform the review.

10.3.3. Data Collection Process

Search and selection of literature were performed in accordance with the PRISMA protocol: identification, screening, eligibility, and inclusion in four phases.

1. *Identification*:

    - The first search resulted in 1,138 records.

2. *Screening*:

    - Upon removal of the duplicates (232 duplicates), 906 records remained.

3. *Eligibility*:

    - Abstract and title review screened off 541 articles.

4. *Inclusion*:

    - Three hundred and sixty-five full-text articles have been evaluated, and the last thing is that 92 studies were incorporated in the qualitative synthesis.

10.3.4. PRISMA Flow Diagram and Justification

PRISMA (Fig. 10.2) framework helps to improve transparency by clarifying the pathway of decisions on identifying and finally including. It avoids bias during the selection process and allows the studies not used to be tracked and reasonably excluded (Moher et al., 2009). This systematic documentation is also consistent with the best practices in interdisciplinary research that touches upon ethics, law, and technology.

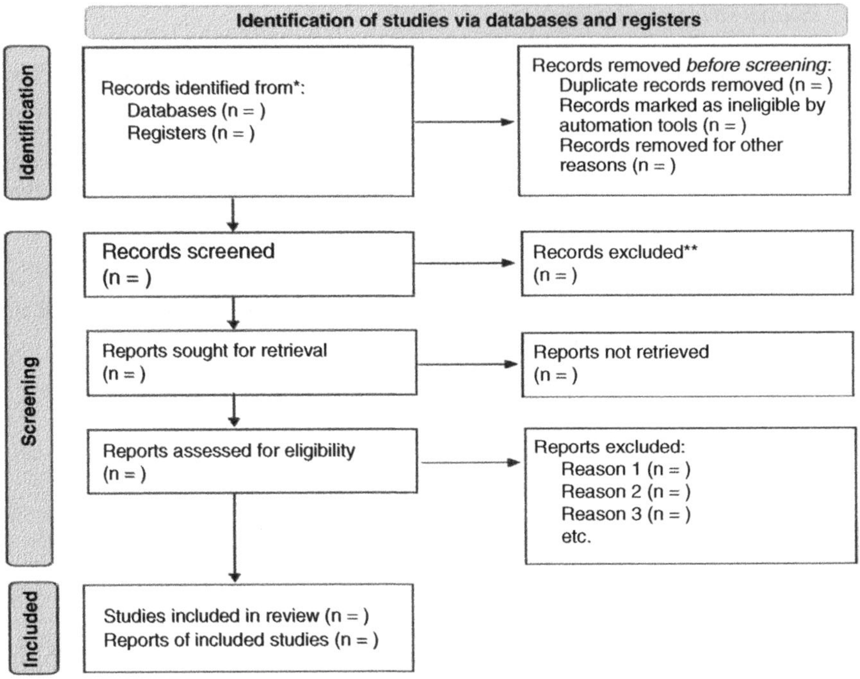

Fig. 10.2. PRISMA 2020 Flow Diagram.

10.3.5. Data Synthesis and Thematic Analysis

A narrative synthesis method was used to analyze the 92 studies included. A qualitative method of coding was used which allows one to detect recurring themes with the help of NVivo program. Topical categories were formed inductively according to dominance and interdisciplinarity.

It is based on this thematic deconstruction that the analytical elements of the chapter and policy recommendations are informed, keeping them grounded on a sound academic consensus and legal precedence.

10.4. Key Ethical and Legal Challenges in AI–VR Integration

The combination of AI and VR technologies means that, in addition to opportunities of enormous dimensions, a multitude of ambiguous legal and ethical issues arise. Such difficulties are frequently out of the scope of the conventional regulatory framework, and it requires a multidisciplinary approach to deal with law, ethics, and technology. The most urgent of these issues are considered in this section.

10.4.1. Legitimacy of AI-generated and VR-based Content

One of the main legal issues in the sphere of AI–VR is the validity and originality of machine-generated content. The current copyright regulation presupposes that originality and humanity are the conditions of protection (Gervais, 2021). But with the current development of AI systems that automatically create music, art, literature, and even software code, the legal concept of an author is being shaken. These issues are enhanced in VR because of interactive and dynamic content production. As an example, an AI non-player character can generate new narrative directions by interaction with the user. Should these narrative developments be subject to copyright law?

Courts do not consider copyright without a human author, which creates regulatory loopholes that pose a threat to creators and users of immersive media (WIPO, 2020).

10.4.2. Ownership and Authorship in Immersive Digital Environments

The erosion of virtual and physical space has brought new unanswered questions concerning the ownership of the digital. Objects like virtual real-estate, fashion, and even tools, and even user-created avatars, are exchanged, possessed, and even patented (Yoo & Kim, 2022). But there is confusion in the sense of:

- Is user-generated content in platforms such as Metaverse legally owned by anyone?
- Is it possible to patent or have a copyright on a virtual object that was generated by an AI under user direction?
- What is joint ownership when more than one agent, both human and non-human, operates?

This ambiguity may lead to users losing rights to their digital works without realizing it, and it is often the case because platform End-User License Agreements are usually vague (Mendis & Kretschmer, 2021).

10.5. IP and Copyright Dilemmas

10.5.1. Case Studies of AI-generated Works and IPR Disputes

Among the most visible questions of present-day IPR jurisprudence, there is the question of whether AI-generated content should be entitled to protection under the current legal frameworks. To highlight, in the case of the well-known DABUS, an AI system called DABUS was registered as the inventor in patent applications filed in the USA, the UK, and the EU. The original rejection of all three jurisdictions was based on the need to have human inventorship (Abbot, 2020). Equally, Stephen Thaler, who filed the applications, was not granted copyright protection in the USA for one of his works that he asserted, which was independently generated by AI (USPTO, 2022). These cases are examples of the absence of the consensus on the issue of the possibility of non-human creators to possess IPR worldwide.

10.5.2. Virtual Assets and Digital Property Rights

The new challenges to the traditional property law are virtual properties such as NFT art and VR real estate. The assets can be of real-world economic value, and they can be legally different in different jurisdictions (Koulu, 2022). For instance:

- NFTs challenge the concept of transferability of copyright.
- VR products and lands will be coded and exchanged in the real world.

10.5.3. Cross-border Jurisdictional Complexities

The VR world exists within the non-physical digital space. It becomes hard to establish the jurisdiction when a copyright violation is committed in a universal multi-player VR world (e.g., when the person is impersonating a character under copyright).

Key challenges:

- The clashes of the laws on data protection (e.g., GDPR vs CCPA).
- The dissimilarity in definition of authorship and originality.
- From equal treatment on enforcement and takedown procedures.

The international flows of data also contribute to these problems, and international treaties or unified frameworks are required (WIPO, 2020).

10.5.4. Existing Legal Frameworks: Gaps and Inconsistencies

The traditional IP frameworks (e.g. TRIPS Agreement, Berne Convention) fail to accommodate:

- Non-human creators.
- Real-time/interactive generative processes.
- Co-created content of multiple layers.

Most of the laws are reactive and not proactive by following the old understanding of the law to apply to non-traditional productions.

10.5.5. Comparative Analysis: EU, USA, and Indian IPR Approaches

- *EU*: It focuses more on moral rights and originality but limits IP to human creators (European Parliament, 2020).
- *USA*: Is concerned with the originality test; AI-generated works do not qualify to receive a copyright unless human input is present (USPTO, 2022).

- *India*: Adheres to the Berne Convention; courts are rather hesitant to accept the machine authorship (NITI Aayog, 2021). These comparative models indicate the disintegration of the global AI-IP policy which poses uncertainty to the cross-border stakeholders.

10.6. Regulatory and Governance Models: Toward 2030

AI and VR have ethical and legal consequences that require proactive governance structures that are interdisciplinary and harmonized at an international scale. The current regulatory models are reactive and jurisdiction based, AI–VR ecosystem is dynamic, decentralized, and borderless. In this section, the researcher describes the future forms of governance in line with the ethical demands and legal intricacies of new immersive technologies.

10.6.1. Ethics-by-Design and Compliance-by-Architecture

The principle of ethics-by-design, which states that such ethical principles like transparency, fairness, and user dignity should be actively integrated into AI and VR system architecture, is the core idea of the topic under discussion. This method will require the developers and system architects to incorporate ethical considerations when conceptualizing and coding. Compliance-by-architecture goes hand in hand with this, with legal rules and regulatory protection built into the infrastructure of the system. For instance:

- VR platforms can have data minimization principles hardcoded.
- AI algorithms can be used to ensure access controls in order to safeguard sensitive content.
- The automation of log management can be used to provide accountability audit trails.

The early incorporation of ethical and legal concerns into the pipeline will reduce the harm and make technology social good and within the law.

10.6.2. Interdisciplinary Regulatory Approaches

Due to the complexity and fluidity of AI–VR technologies, their regulation should be based on a variety of disciplinary viewpoints. The matter of implications cannot be fully covered by only one field law, engineering, ethics, or sociology.

Similar to Cath (2018), the creation of the so-called technology governance ecosystems, which involve a variety of stakeholders, is the way to have more inclusive, reflexive, and scalable regulatory frameworks.

10.6.3. Dynamic Licensing for AI and VR Content

Conventional IP licenses do not fit any real-time, collaboratively created or algorithmically generated content. Since AI is a dynamic content creator, and VR worlds are a collaborative editing platform, its licensing is required to be no less dynamic or transactional. Emerging solutions:

- *Real-time licensing*: Immediately provides or blocks access to the right to use depending on the circumstances (e.g., time, region, co-creators).
- *Smart contracts*: Self-executable contracts written on blockchain in order to automate the licensing, payments, and attribution.

Example use cases: A virtual theater performance, co-performed by human actors and AI scripts, dynamically licensed in the process of real-time streaming.

- NFTs containing words to represent the derivative works, which will not allow unauthorized remixing in the metaverse. These are licensing models that offer transparency and scalability to distributed and co-owned digital assets (Gervais, 2021).

10.6.4. Emerging Standards and Global Collaborations

Enhanced standardization and interoperability international organizations understand the cross-border aspect of AI and VR and are promoting it. Cooperative systems promote both consistency and legal and ethical coherence. Shared goals:

- International understanding of authorship, consent, data ownership.
- AI and immersive experiment regulatory sandboxes.
- Capacity-building of ethical compliance in Third World countries. It is these collaborations that make the foundation of digital legal harmonization and is key to having a truly global approach to immersive ethics and rights.

10.7. Discussion

The systematic review and thematic synthesis conducted in this chapter demonstrate that there is a dynamic and complex nature of the intersection of AI, VR, and IP governance. On the one hand, the potential of these technologies to transform is quite obvious, but on the other hand, there is a lot of legal and ethical vulnerability caused by uncontrolled proliferation. This part will provide a critical debate on major findings, stakeholder roles, balancing between innovation and regulation, and the need of public education.

10.7.1. Synthesis of Systematic Findings

The PRISMA methodology SLR presented three themes that have been repeatedly identified in the corpus:

- *Legal inadequacy*: The existing IP regulations were discovered to be poorly configured to radicalize AI-generated and VR-mediated content especially in cases where there is no obvious human authorship.

- *Ethical ambiguity*: The issues of data privacy, user consent, and algorithmic fairness are further intensified in immersive settings where passive data acquisition on an emotional, biometric, and behavioral level is performed (Slater & Sanchez-Vives, 2016).
- *Policy lag*: Technological change is fast and quick, but the legislative and regulatory process can keep up with it, posing a gap in governance (WIPO, 2020). These themes underscore the pressing need to have normative frameworks that are responsive to the present and also resistant to future disruptive events.

10.7.2. The Role of Legal Scholars, Technologists, and Policymakers

The multi-dimensional issues of AI and VR cannot be resolved without the concerted efforts of legal representatives, computer scientists, ethicists, and policymakers. Their duty can be broadly defined as follows.

10.7.3. Innovation Versus Regulation: Striking a Balance

One of the continuing conflicts in technology governance is that of tradeoff between regulation and creative freedom. Excessive regulation may:

- Deter innovation.
- Impose compliance burdens.
- Slow time-to-market of AI–VR applications. On the other hand, lack of sufficient regulation may lead to:
- Misuse of personal information and the theft of IP.
- Deepfakes: reputational and economic harm.

The idea that the OECD (2021) promotes is agile governance, which is a concept that suggests modular, adaptive, and stakeholder-co-created policies. Regulatory agility enables changes with the changes in technologies without straining innovation.

10.7.4. Public Awareness and Ethical Literacy

One of the principles that are promoted by the OECD (2021) is that of agile governance, which implies the use of a policy that is modular, adaptive, and co-created with stakeholders. Regulatory agility enables changes because even the most advanced regulations will not work without the ethical literacy of the population. The masses should be prepared to know:

Their privileges in virtual worlds.

- Threats of information disclosure and manipulation of the algorithms.
- Implications of AI-generated content on privacy, authorship, and fairness. Ethical Literacy Recommendations of policy:

1. *Public Campaigns*: Demystify deepfakes, bias, and ownership with the help of social media, virtual space, and influencer partnerships.

2. *Digital Rights Clinics*: Provide citizens with an opportunity to find legal and technical advice on their rights in the metaverse or in immersive applications.

UNESCO (2022) goes as far as indicating that education is the key factor in instilling trust in AI systems, and consequently, the creation of informed digital citizens. Without hampering creativity, technologies develop.

10.8. Future Research Agenda

With the current levels of AI and VR technologies developing exponentially, the legal and ethical scholarship of the two technologies must shift their perspectives on the technologies to be proactive and anticipatory. The regulatory ecosystem of the future must be future-proof and heavily research-intensive, interdisciplinary, and recursive. This part highlights key loopholes, suggests monitoring systems, incorporates novelty in the methodologies, and assigns the stakeholder-specific tasks to help frame the ethical application of immersive and intelligent systems to 2030 and beyond.

10.8.1. Identified Gaps in Existing Literature

Although there is an overall increase in discussion of the integration of AI and VR, gaps in the academic coverage remain. The SLR which was conducted with the help of PRISMA shows that there is no sustained, comparative, and global research.

10.8.2. Proposed Frameworks for Continuous Monitoring

It is not enough to develop policy once in AI–VR changing ecosystems. Ongoing and repeated testing has to be the order of the day. This will be done in the following ways:

1. AI–VR Ethics Surveillance Committee. Teams and commissions of ethicists, technologists, legal scholars, and users.

    - Responsible to evaluate the new cases of use, raise ethical risk warnings, and consult governments and other regulators in the industry.

2. Regulatory Reviews based on PRISMA.

    - Not only academic use PRISMA-SLR but also governmental and legislative audit of the effectiveness of new policies.
    - About annual reports on the State of Immersive Ethics. Encourage reports with a synthesis of evidence derived out of the world-wide body of legal and technical literature.

10.8.3. Integrating PRISMA-SLR in Ongoing Legal-Tech Research

Conventionally, the basis of legal changes has been case-law, expert consultations or the general populace. Nevertheless, due to the dynamism and rapid development of AI-VR systems, PRISMA-based SLRs need to be at the core of:

- Government drafted whitepapers and bills.
- Academic and think tank papers, which affect regulation. These evidence-based practices guarantee coherence, transparency, and scientific validity of policy in law reform, and are replacing anecdotal or reactive governance.

10.9. Conclusion

AI and VR have a prophetic intersection point in the digital transformation of society. Such technologies can transform creativity, change the way people interact, and transform whole industries. However, with this change, there are complicated moral issues, regulatory ambiguities, and IP scandals that the current legal framework could not adequately handle. These challenges have been methodically discussed in this chapter in terms of a PRISMA-based literature review, relevant trends upcoming, and possible actionable routes to take to negotiate the ethical and legal landscape to 2030. Along with the continued development of AI and the VR technologies, the development of governance mechanisms, the law, and the values of society also has to evolve.

10.9.1. Summary of Key Insights

- AI and VR are transforming the very concept and idea of authorship, ownership, and user agency particularly with non-human agents playing a role in creating content.
- Relevant IP regulations are outmoded and divided and cannot serve the evolving as well as co-created as well as algorithmically produced material that is immersive in nature. Ethical issues like data privacy, algorithmic bias, and emotional manipulation are also exacerbated by VR because it is high-fidelity sensory and because behavioral tracking is always at high fidelity.
- There is no international regulatory harmonization, and jurisdiction sources are lacking to regulate and enforce that in the virtual space.

10.9.2. Ethical Imperatives for the AI–VR Future

The future of the AI and VR is not simply a technological one, but in fact, it is very human. As much as automation, realism, and personalization will keep on improving, the same should be applied to our ethical values like:

- *Human dignity*: Safeguarding people against hyper automation or digital impersonation.

- *Creativity and originality*: An appreciation of human expression and a sensible use of AI help.
- *Equity and inclusion*: It is important that these technologies can benefit other people besides the digitally privileged. Ethics-by-design approach is no longer a choice but a prerequisite of trust and legitimacy in the AI–VR system.

10.9.3. Legal Preparedness for 2030

To move to technology-reactive to technology-proactive governance, legal systems should defining core IP constructs and redefining core IP constructs to incorporate algorithmic collaboration and non-human agency.

- Adopt dynamic licensing models and content registries, which are compatible with real-time and immersive settings. Facilitate international legal harmonization: Treaties, model laws, and charters of digital ethics.

Regulatory sandboxes – Promote the use of AI–VR policies in regulatory sandboxes by encouraging experimentation and establishing precedents prior to its widespread implementation. It is not only to control risk but also to make responsible innovations that would be in line with democratic values and global justice.

References

Abbot, R. (2020). *The reasonable robot: Artificial intelligence and the law*. Cambridge University Press.

Cath, C. (2018). Governing artificial intelligence: Ethical, legal and technical opportunities and challenges. *Philosophical Transactions of the Royal Society A*, *376*(2133), 20180080.

Cohen-Almagor, R. (2021). Digital ethics: Artificial intelligence and virtual reality. *AI & Society*, *36*(3), 567–578. https://doi.org/10.1007/s00146-021-01184-w

European Commission. (2019). *Ethics guidelines for trustworthy AI*. https://digital-strategy.ec.europa.eu

European Parliament. (2020). *Intellectual property rights for the development of artificial intelligence technologies*. https://www.europarl.europa.eu/

Floridi, L., & Cowls, J. (2020). A unified framework of five principles for AI in society. *Harvard Data Science Review*, *1*(1). https://doi.org/10.1162/99608f92.8cd550d1

Gervais, D. (2021). The machine as author. *Iowa Law Review*, *105*(5), 2053–2105.

Jobin, A., Ienca, M., & Vayena, E. (2019). The global landscape of AI ethics guidelines. *Nature Machine Intelligence*, *1*(9), 389–399. https://doi.org/10.1038/s42256-019-0088-2

Kaplan, A., & Haenlein, M. (2019). Siri, Siri, in my hand: Who's the fairest in the land? On the interpretations, illustrations, and implications of artificial intelligence. *Business Horizons*, *62*(1), 15–25. https://doi.org/10.1016/j.bushor.2018.08.004

Koulu, R. (2022). Virtual property law in the Metaverse: Challenges and opportunities. *Journal of Law & Digital Society*, *3*(1), 15–35.

Mendis, D., & Kretschmer, M. (2021). Ownership of user-generated content in the age of artificial intelligence. *European Intellectual Property Review*, *43*(2), 81–91.

Moher, D., Liberati, A., Tetzlaff, J., Altman, D. G., & The PRISMA Group. (2009). Preferred reporting items for systematic reviews and meta-analyses: The PRISMA statement. *PLoS Med*, *6*(7), e1000097. https://doi.org/10.1371/journal.pmed.1000097

NITI Aayog. (2021). *Responsible AI: Strategy for India*. https://niti.gov.in/

OECD. (2021). *OECD framework for the governance of AI*. https://www.oecd.org/

Russell, S., & Norvig, P. (2021). *Artificial intelligence: A modern approach* (4th ed.). Pearson Education.

Slater, M., & Sanchez-Vives, M. V. (2016). Enhancing our lives with immersive virtual reality. *Frontiers in Robotics and AI*, *3*, 74. https://doi.org/10.3389/frobt.2016.00074

UNESCO. (2022). *Recommendation on the ethics of artificial intelligence*. https://unesdoc.unesco.org/

USPTO. (2022). *Guidance on AI and patent inventorship*. https://www.uspto.gov/

WIPO. (2020). *Artificial intelligence and intellectual property policy*. World Intellectual Property Organization.

Yoo, Y., & Kim, Y. (2022). Property rights in the Metaverse: Legal frameworks and challenges. *Journal of Law, Innovation & Technology*, *14*(1), 56–78.

Chapter 11

Transforming HR with AI: Opportunities, Challenges, and Ethical Considerations

Mona Hussein Mostafa Kamel

McDougall Faculty of Business, University of Prince Edward Island, UPEI, Cairo Campus, Egypt

Abstract

Artificial intelligence (AI) is rapidly changing how business processes are managed. Human resource (HR) functions are among the areas most significantly impacted by AI tools. The use of AI shifts the role of HR from being traditional and administrative to being more strategic, supporting decisions, and enhancing efficiency, while improving employee experience. The successful adoption of AI requires an effective strategic plan that aligns the organization's plans with HR goals and objectives. AI tools automate administrative HR functions, reducing time consumption and supporting areas such as applicant screening, recruitment, and learning. In recruitment, it provides resume screening and evaluates candidates, thus saving time and reducing biases during the screening process. Although AI tools are highly effective, organizations face several challenges in adopting and operating them. This chapter addresses various challenges that organizations encounter and offers guidance on how to overcome them. The chapter will highlight various real-world organizations that utilize AI tools across multiple HR functions. Moreover, the chapter will discuss ethical considerations when applying AI tools and provide guidelines on how HR professionals' roles are changing, highlighting successful change management techniques and infrastructure to achieve a successful technological shift.

Keywords: Artificial intelligence; human resources; talent management; data-driven decisions; HR professional roles; ethical AI; strategic HR

Nurturing AI-Powered HR Analytics and Virtual Reality in Employee Psychology and Workplace Happiness, Part A, 183–197

Published under exclusive licence by Emerald Publishing Limited
doi:10.1108/978-1-80686-125-520261009

11.1. Introduction: The AI Revolution in HRs

AI is significantly impacting various HR functions, including recruitment, performance appraisal, and screening, as well as providing analytics and data analysis to support informed decisions. This chapter provides an overview of the various applications of AI in HR functions, including benefits, challenges, ethical considerations, and the changing role of HR professionals. Moreover, it will include various case studies of companies applying AI in human resource management (HRM).

AI refers to computer systems capable of performing tasks that typically require human intelligence. In the context of HR, this encompasses various forms of AI, including machine learning, natural language processing, and generative AI. Additionally, AI analytics support workforce planning and informed strategic HR decisions by providing insights from large datasets (Budhwar et al., 2022; Malik et al., 2020; Qamar et al, 2021; Žibret, 2024). AI also enables HR to develop personalized learning and skills development plans for employees, allowing HR professionals to become strategic partners in employee growth (Muridzi et al., 2024; Nyathani, 2023b). Furthermore, AI enhances candidate sourcing, screening, and shortlisting by reducing bias and increasing objectivity through automated tools and predictive analytics (Jatobá et al., 2023; Pan & Froese, 2023; Žibret, 2024).

11.2. The Benefits of AI in HR

AI supports the HR function in several activities, including recruitment, planning, and enhancing diversity, by analyzing employee data records and organizational records, which informs HR strategies (Natarajan et al., 2024; Stone et al., 2024). AI implementation in HR offers numerous benefits, including increased efficiency, improved decision-making, a better employee experience, and fewer errors.

- *Increased efficiency*: AI automates repetitive administrative tasks and time-consuming tasks such as data entry, interview screening, resume screening, and payroll processing. Thus, allowing HR professionals to be engaged in more strategic activities and focus on initiatives that support organizational growth and employee well-being (Huang & Lin, 2025; Wamba-Taguimdje et al., 2020).
- *Improved decision-making*: AI supports HR leaders' decision-making process by using predictive analysis to provide more accurate decisions in several areas, such as recruitment, performance management (PM), and workforce planning. For instance, AI tools can be used in workforce planning to forecast staffing needs and identify potential skills gaps within the organization (Baabdullah, 2024; Madhumita et al., 2024).
- *Reductions of errors and improved accuracy*: Decisions will be based on quantitative data from analysis of employee and company records. This will reduce errors and support the decision-making process, thus achieving the desired results (Baabdullah, 2024; Madhumita et al., 2024). I will reduce errors in administrative areas, such as data management and payroll processing. Thus,

using AI will reduce the liability of making costly mistakes (Budhwar et al., 2022; Malik et al., 2022; Pereira et al., 2023).

- *Enhanced employee experience and engagement*: AI helps provide a customized employee experience in functions such as onboarding and training, tailored to individual capabilities and requirements. AI utilizes historical data about employees, including performance, output, and work patterns, to provide suggestions for improving employee performance. Those suggestions can support work–life balance, enhance employee commitment and well-being, and prevent turnover. AI provides tools to collect information and data from employees through surveys and chatbots, gathering feedback that enables analysis and informs any required action or decision. Additionally, AI facilitates connections among team members by providing automated scheduling systems and recognition programs, thereby reducing the administrative burden on HR professionals (Madhumita et al., 2024; Malik et al., 2022;; Subhadarshini et al., 2024).

11.3. Applications and Benefits of AI in HRM Function

11.3.1. Applications and Benefits of AI in Talent Acquisition and Recruitment

AI is applied in talent management for acquiring and selecting candidates, utilizing various tools and techniques. AI tools can provide analysis of candidate records across various platforms, including LinkedIn and internal employee records. Accordingly, talent acquisition is enhanced by increasing efficiency, reducing costs, enhancing the candidate's experience, and supporting informed decision-making.

1. *Efficiency and speed in processing applicants*: The use of Applicant Tracking Systems (ATS) that filter and rank candidates based on specific qualifications. The ATS utilizes relevant keywords, qualifications, and experience to analyze resumes and applications, identifying the most qualified candidates (Marinakou et al., 2024).
2. *Cost-effectiveness*: automating resume screening reduces recruiters' administrative workload, allowing them to focus on more strategic tasks (Tay et al., 2024). This results in lower administrative costs and time savings for organizations, leading to improved performance and productivity.
3. *Improving candidate experience*: This involves utilizing AI tools, such as chatbots and automated communication systems, to enhance engagement by addressing frequently asked questions, thereby improving the overall candidate experience. These tools offer quick responses to inquiries, which positively impact the company's reputation as an employer (Albert, 2019).
4. *Data-driven decision-making*: AI supports objective hiring by using predictive and talent analytics. This enhances the talent matching process and helps reduce human bias. The system can be used to show candidates with the required qualifications and skills, allowing HR professionals to base their decisions solely on a candidate's abilities and experience (Faqih et al., 2024; George et al., 2024). For example, AI can be used in pre-employment

assessments and in analyzing video interviews. Machine learning algorithms can evaluate candidates based on body language, responses, and speech patterns during video interviews. However, human judgment remains essential to assess culture-fit and overall personality. AI is also helpful in analyzing industry salary data and pay structures to help determine competitive and fair salaries. This enables HR professionals to identify pay gaps and develop a more effective compensation strategy within the organization (Arora & Mittal, 2024; Bharadwaj, 2024; Kadirov Shakirova et al., 2024; Kaushal et al., 2023).

11.3.2. Applications and Benefits of AI in Learning and Development

AI plays a significant role in enhancing learning and development in organizations. Personalized learning experience is enhanced through several ways by customizing content, delivery methods, and assessments (Bhatt & Muduli, 2023).

1. *Personalizing content*: It is achieved by customizing content, delivery methods, and assessments (Bhatt & Muduli, 2023). AI is used to identify skill gaps and provide personalized learning objectives and training content. This personalized approach provides better employee engagement and knowledge retention, leading to a more skilled workforce. AI-powered learning management systems can adjust the difficulty of content based on a learner's performance, ensuring that employees are challenged but not overwhelmed, thereby optimizing the learning process (Bhatt & Muduli, 2023). Moreover, AI can provide scalable and on-demand support for employees, complementing traditional methods and making employee development more accessible (Kaushal et al., 2023; Malik et al., 2022).
2. *Automation of content*: AI technologies automate the creation of learning materials by providing practice exercises, converting content into different formats, offering real-time feedback, and supporting large-scale training. This makes learning quicker, more accurate, and cost-effective (Bhandare, 2024; Bhatt & Muduli, 2023; Tang et al., 2023). It significantly reduces the time and resources needed for content development, allowing learning and development teams to focus on strategy and instructional design.
3. AI tools promote collaborative learning environments by supporting peer learning, enhancing communication, and facilitating cooperative activities (Msambwa et al., 2025). AI-powered adaptive assessment tools offer real-time feedback and interventions, enabling learners to pinpoint errors and improve their performance (Bhatt & Muduli, 2023; Ejjami, 2024). AI-driven coaching and mentoring platforms offer personalized feedback and guidance to employees, serving as virtual tutors and assistants to support their professional development (Ejjami, 2024).

11.3.3. Applications and Benefits of AI in Employee Onboarding

AI offers numerous applications for streamlining and improving the employee onboarding process. AI-driven platforms can automate a variety of administrative tasks, including completing paperwork, setting up new employee accounts, and delivering compliance training. This enables HR professionals to focus more on cultural integration and building relationships with new hires (Madanchian, 2024; Okatta et al., 2024; Tyagi et al., 2023). Continuous improvement of the onboarding process involves collecting and analyzing feedback from new hires about their experience to identify areas for enhancement. AI allows organizations to efficiently onboard large numbers of employees, particularly in remote or hybrid work environments (Madanchian, 2024). Additionally, AI-driven systems can tailor onboarding content to meet employees' specific needs, skills, and learning styles, resulting in improved engagement and knowledge retention (Madanchian, 2024; Okatta et al., 2024; Tyagi et al., 2023).

AI-powered chatbots and virtual assistants offer instant answers and guidance to new hires, improving their experience and reducing confusion during onboarding (Tyagi et al., 2023). The availability of AI support around the clock can significantly decrease anxiety and enhance employee experience by providing immediate information about company benefits, policies, and job responsibilities.

11.3.4. Applications and Benefits of AI in PM

PM in organizations is shaped by AI tools, which offer new ways to assess, develop, and motivate employees. PM in organizations is influenced by AI tools, which provide new tools for evaluating, developing, and motivating employees. The integration of AI into PM systems leads to overcoming traditional methods' limitations, such as subjectivity, infrequent feedback, and inefficiency (Natarajan et al., 2024; Stone et al., 2024).

AI will support performance reviews by being evidence-based instead of a subjective process. AI will analyze employees' strengths and determine areas that require development. This process involves tracking employee performance records and determining key performance indicators. AI will provide feedback and personalized recommendations that will help employees improve and align with organizational goals (Madhumita et al., 2024; Nyathani, 2023a; Subhadarshini et al., 2024; Varma et al., 2024).

AI technologies support PM by enabling better decision-making. AI can support the goal-setting process by providing recommendations that consider past performance and industry conditions and align individual goals with organizational objectives (Zawada, 2024). As a result, improved efficiency, productivity, and the ability to detect and address issues proactively have been achieved (Huang & Lin, 2025; Madhumita et al., 2024; Natarajan et al., 2024; Wamba-Taguimdje et al., 2020).

Additionally, AI tools are utilized to identify employee strengths, weaknesses, and potential retention risks by analyzing various data points and employing predictive analytics to forecast turnover. This early identification allows HR to implement proactive strategies to engage and retain valuable employees (Zawada, 2024).

11.4. The Evolving Role of HR Professionals in an AI-driven World

The increasing adoption of AI in HR is fundamentally changing the roles and responsibilities of HR professionals. By automating many administrative tasks, HR professionals can focus on strategic activities such as talent management, development, communication, and employee engagement, as well as strategic planning. This will facilitate the business partner's contribution to achieving organizational goals.

HR professionals are required to develop new skills and competencies to effectively manage AI tools, such as data analytics and AI management, and to learn about the associated ethical concerns. HR professionals must develop teamwork skills with AI experts and be able to interpret insights generated from AI tools. Continuous learning and upskilling will be crucial for HR professionals to remain relevant and practical in an AI-driven world.

11.5. Current Trends and the Future of AI in HR

The landscape of AI in HR is continuously evolving, with several key trends shaping its present and future, as shown in Fig. 11.1.

- *Rising adoption of generative AI*: HR professionals are utilizing generative AI to enhance various HR activities and automate administrative tasks. HR professionals are using generative tools in areas such as creating job descriptions, preparing training materials, and writing HR policies. Generative AI delivers high-quality, text-based content tailored to specific needs, becoming an essential tool for enhancing the efficiency of HR operations.
- *Emergence of AI agents*: AI agents are tools that can perform actions and engage in HR-related tasks. Those tools act in the form of bots that can monitor employees' productivity, provide career development opportunities, and assist candidates through the hiring and onboarding process. AI agents will support HR by taking on more active and important roles and responsibilities within HR functions.
- *Skills-based HR*: HR is increasingly focusing on employees' skills instead of traditional job roles. AI plays a vital role in identifying and matching employee skills with organizational needs. AI tools can detect skills gaps and help align workforce capabilities with changing business goals, making workforce management more adaptable and responsive.

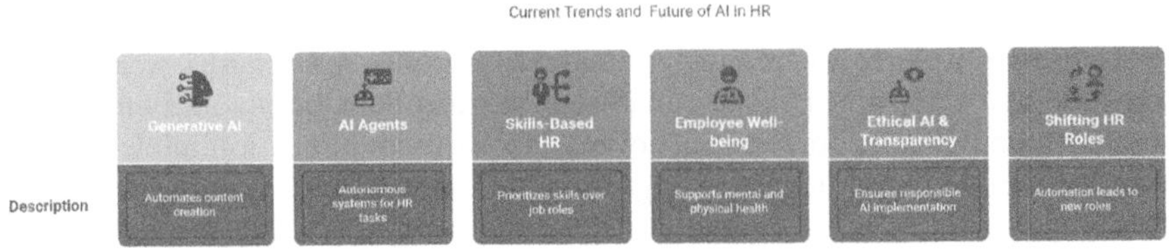

Fig. 11.1 Current Trends and Future of AI in HR. *Source*: Author's creation.

- *Integration of AI for employee well-being*: AI supports and monitors employee well-being, covering both mental and physical health. It can track employee sentiment, provide personalized wellness advice, and suggest ways to improve work–life balance. This suggests a growing awareness of the importance of employee well-being for overall engagement and productivity (Žibret, 2024).
- *Ethical AI and transparency*: The importance of ethics and transparency is increasing. There is a growing emphasis on developing and deploying AI in an ethical, transparent, and responsible way. New laws and standards for the ethical use of AI in HR are emerging, highlighting the need to build trust and ensure responsible AI usage in the workplace.
- *Shifting roles and redesigning jobs in HR*: The automation of routine tasks through AI is causing a significant change in the roles and responsibilities of HR professionals. The use of AI leads to the creation of new, more specialized roles within HR teams, such as HR technologists and AI experts. HR professionals need to develop new skills in areas like data analysis, AI management, and strategic thinking to effectively navigate this changing environment (Okatta et al., 2024).
- Successful implementation requires strategic frameworks, change management, and alignment with organizational goals (Jatobá et al., 2023; Malik et al., 2022; Muridzi et al., 2024).

11.6. Challenges and Considerations

Several challenges are facing the successful adoption of AI technology within HR functions, including the need for human insights, ethical and privacy concerns, implementation complexity, and the performance expectations of employees toward AI adoption.

While AI offers significant benefits, implementing it in HR also presents challenges and limitations that organizations must manage.

- *Resistance to change and lack of trust*: Introducing AI into HR can face opposition from both employees and HR professionals. Employee resistance often arises from concerns such as job displacement, a limited understanding of AI's capabilities, or worries about data privacy and security. Organizations should foster awareness and trust in AI tools through various efforts, such as being transparent about their decision-making processes and the operation of AI systems. Raising awareness about AI tools can be supported by effective change management strategies, including comprehensive training programs, clear communication of AI benefits, and involving employees in the implementation process to ensure the successful adoption of AI in HR.
- *Cost of implementation and maintenance*: Implementing and maintaining advanced AI solutions in HR can significantly impact performance and is considered a substantial financial investment. Unfortunately, it requires infrastructure, software licenses, and hiring skilled personnel to operate the systems. Organizations must carefully evaluate the return on investment of AI initiatives and consider the long-term operating costs and benefits to decide

whether adopting AI aligns with their strategic and financial goals or becomes a financial burden.

- *Bias in algorithms*: AI algorithms utilize historical data, which can perpetuate existing biases in that data, resulting in unfair or discriminatory outcomes in key HR processes. To address this, organizations must continuously implement monitoring systems to identify biases in AI. Additionally, they should use diverse and representative training data and regularly audit algorithms for potential biases (Kaur & Singh, 2023).
- *Need for human oversight*: While AI can automate and enhance many functions of HRM, human involvement remains important for interpreting results and making final decisions (Nyathani, 2023a; Subhadarshini et al., 2024; Varma et al., 2024). AI can automate many tasks to enhance efficiency and support decisions rather than replacing human involvement. A decision must be made while considering human judgment, empathy, and critical thinking. Therefore, it is recommended to maintain a balance between AI automation and human interaction in HR processes (Kaur & Singh, 2023).

HR professionals must strategically incorporate AI in a way that enhances, rather than diminishes, the human aspects of their role. The use of AI should free up more time for HR professionals to build relationships with employees and offer personalized support. HR professionals should avoid over-relying on AI tools without intervening to ensure effective decision-making. Excessive dependence on AI could result in a loss of personal connection and empathy in HR interactions.

- AI implementation requires talent, data, and infrastructure. It depends on the success of the change management process and employee acceptance of the new system (Baabdullah, 2024; Nyathani, 2023b; Wamba-Taguimdje et al., 2020). The successful implementation of change management strategies and providing support from the organization during the change process will significantly enhance employees' expectations of the usefulness of AI, which will impact adoption and overall success (Baabdullah, 2024).
- *Ethical and privacy concerns*: The use of AI raises issues about data privacy, transparency, and potential algorithmic bias (Nyathani, 2023a; Subhadarshini et al., 2024; Varma et al., 2024).

11.7. Case Studies on Real-world Application of AI in HRM

AI is widely used for candidate screening, attrition prediction, and PM. Interpretable algorithms like decision trees are common, and AI is seen as a tool to support – not replace – human judgment in HRM (Gryncewicz et al., 2023; Madanchian et al., 2023; Singh, 2025). Case studies from emerging economies show AI's role in expanding recruitment pools, reducing bias, and supporting employee development. However, adoption remains limited, and many tools lack advanced machine learning capabilities (Fung et al., 2025; Kshetri, 2021).

Several case studies across different sectors were conducted to show the effect of the use of AI on HRM activities as shown in Table 11.1. For example, BigTech

Table 11.1. Case Study Highlights.

Company/Context	AI Application Area	Key Outcomes/ Challenges	Citations
BigTech Services (IT MNE)	Chatbots, talent bots, analytics	Enhanced engagement, productivity, and time savings	Malik et al. (2022)
Leap.ai, Baidu (China)	Recruitment, training	Personalized matching, efficient learning	Jia et al. (2018)
Healthcare Center (Dubai)	HR process automation	Improved performance, limited generalizability	Li et al. (2023)
Indian Companies (various)	Recruitment, analytics	Leadership, data, and ethics are key; barriers remain	Singh and Pandey (2024)
Emerging Economies (Global South/Asia)	Recruitment, retention	Reduced bias, limited adoption	Fung et al. (2025) and Kshetri (2021)
General Industry	Screening, attrition, performance	Interpretable AI, human–AI collaboration	Gryncewicz et al. (2023), Madanchian et al. (2023), and Singh (2025)

Source: Author's creation.

Services, a multinational IT consulting firm, implemented a digitalized HR system with AI-assisted applications such as chatbots for employee queries, talent bots for competency mapping, and analysis dashboards. The study showed that those tools lead to improved employee experience, engagement, and productivity. Moreover, it leads to increasing efficiency by saving thousands of human hours annually and enabling real-time insights into workforce trends (Malik et al., 2022). Another study in China was conducted in a recruitment platform, Leap.ai, which integrated AI to match candidates with jobs based on skills and preferences. Another company, Baidu, applies AI for online employee training. These cases demonstrate how AI can personalize recruitment and learning, making HR processes more efficient and tailored to individual needs (Jia, Guo, Li, Li, & Chen, 2018).

Another study was conducted in a healthcare institution in Dubai. This institution is a Lebanese International Healthcare Center operating in Dubai, has adopted AI tools for HRM, leading to improved financial and operational performance. AI supported several HRM activities such as recruitment, PM, and workforce planning, though the study notes that results may not be universally generalizable (Li et al., 2023). Another study was conducted in Indian companies in three different sectors: software, E-commerce, and FMCG. The three prominent Indian companies at different stages of AI adoption reported that digital leadership, reliable HR data, and ethical frameworks were key to successful AI integration. Barriers included challenges in employee–digital expert collaboration and ethical concerns (Singh & Pandey, 2024).

These cases show that AI in HRM is being used for recruitment, employee engagement, training, and analytics across diverse industries and regions. Success depends on leadership, data quality, and ethical frameworks, while challenges include adoption scale, collaboration, and responsible use.

11.8. Success Stories of AI Integration in HR Functions

This section examines various AI applications in HR, highlighting how top companies have successfully leveraged AI in areas such as recruitment, onboarding, PM, and employee engagement. Several examples demonstrate the implementation of AI in recruitment and talent acquisition. For instance, Unilever has transformed its hiring process by utilizing AI-powered video interviews that assess candidates' facial expressions, tone of voice, and word choice, resulting in a 75% reduction in initial screening time (Booth, 2019; Nieve Consulting, 2024). Additionally, RingCentral partnered with Findem's Talent Search Solution, which leverages extensive internal and external data to automate candidate matching and outreach, resulting in a 40% increase in their pipeline and a 40% boost in interest from underrepresented groups (AIHR, 2025). Another example is Mastercard, which used Phenom's Intelligent Talent Experience platform, including AI scheduling, achieving an 85% increase in interview scheduling, with 88% of interviews scheduled within 24 hours of the request (VKTR, n.d.). Hilton adopted AI tools for resume screening, shortlisting, and interview scheduling, resulting in a 75% reduction in the time required to fill positions (Nieve Consulting, 2024).

PepsiCo invested in AI tools for candidate assessments, utilizing gamified tests and AI-powered chatbots to guide candidates through the application process, resulting in improved candidate experiences and a more efficient hiring process (Nieve Consulting, 2024). Brother International Corporation saw a 140% increase in completed applications and a 25% reduction in time-to-fill after adopting new AI recruiting tools (Blehar, 2025).

Onboarding: IBM deployed an AI-powered chatbot called "Watson" to handle HR questions from employees, including new hires, giving instant answers to common inquiries about benefits, payroll, and company policies (Nieve Consulting, 2024). CloudApper hrGPT is transforming employee onboarding by providing a personalized, efficient, and engaging experience for new hires, streamlining procedures, and ensuring compliance (Bennett, 2024).

PM: General Electric (GE) utilizes AI to analyze employee performance data and deliver personalized feedback, resulting in a 10% increase in employee productivity (Cubeo AI, 2024). Deloitte leverages AI to review employee data and spot potential turnover risks, allowing them to proactively address issues and implement targeted retention strategies (Nieve Consulting, 2024). Truvelop offers AI-powered analytics and automation to help HR leaders gain deeper insights into PM and refine their strategies (Truvelop, 2024).

Learning and development: Accenture has implemented an AI-powered learning platform, Accenture LearnVantage, which recommends personalized training programs based on employees' current skill levels and career aspirations, resulting in a 30% increase in employee skills (Cubeo AI, 2024). Walmart utilizes AI to forecast staffing needs and optimize scheduling, resulting in a 15% reduction in labor costs (Cubeo AI, 2024). Kuehne+Nagel leveraged an intelligent talent marketplace powered by AI to connect employees with internal job opportunities and learning resources, increasing their internal candidate conversion rate by 22% and reducing their time to fill internal requisitions by 20% (Blehar, 2025).

Employee engagement: Microsoft utilizes AI to analyze employee feedback and engagement data, enabling targeted interventions that have resulted in a 15% improvement in overall employee satisfaction (Cubeo AI, 2024). IBM's Watson chatbot not only assists with onboarding but also manages ongoing HR queries, improving response times and boosting employee satisfaction (Nieve Consulting, 2024). Manipal Health Enterprises employed Leena AI's service delivery and engagement software to develop MiPAL. This virtual assistant automatically responds to employee queries, resulting in a reduction in new hire attrition of up to 5% annually and significantly decreasing the average time required to resolve employee cases (VKTR, n.d.).

11.9. Ethical Considerations: Ensuring Responsible AI Adoption in HR

The integration of AI into HR requires a strong emphasis on ethical issues, such as ensuring fairness, transparency, and privacy in AI-driven HR processes, which is essential (Nyathani, 2023a; Qamar et al., 2021).

- *Data privacy concerns*: The use of AI in HR raises significant data privacy concerns because it involves managing large amounts of sensitive employee information, including payroll details, performance data, and personal information. The risk of data breaches and information misuse increases; therefore, organizations must prioritize data security by adopting robust cybersecurity practices, encrypting data, and adhering to relevant data protection laws. Additionally, companies should obtain informed consent from employees for the collection and use of their data.
- *Ensuring transparency and explainability*: HR professionals must provide explanations and be transparent on how AI systems function. Employees will be provided with an understanding of the advantages of AI-driven decision-making, including how these decisions are made and how they impact their careers, such as through PM and career planning.
- Transparency with employees about what data is collected and how it is used is also essential for maintaining trust. Organizations can provide awareness sessions, workshops, and training courses about the benefits of AI applications and how decisions are made using AI data. By fostering open communication with employees regarding any concerns, we aim to build trust and confidence, enabling them to utilize AI tools effectively.

- *Maintaining accountability and oversight*: HR professionals are advised to supervise and direct the design, development, and use of AI applications. Although AI can automate tasks, human supervision remains crucial for interpreting data, making informed decisions, and ensuring that these tools support and augment human expertise.

11.10. Conclusion

The future of HR, when applied with AI tools and technology, primarily supports human expertise and enhances its performance. AI supports HR professionals by enabling them to be more strategic business partners and driving organizational success. HR professionals must enhance their competency by learning and developing new skills to cope with the changes, thus being more efficient, effective, fair, and creating an engaging work environment. The transformation of HR using AI is a continuous journey that will continue to provide data-driven, personalized, and strategic versions of the HR function.

References

AIHR. (2025, March 12). *AI in HR: A comprehensive guide*. Retrieved June 26, 2025, from https://www.aihr.com/blog/ai-in-hr/

Albert, E. T. (2019). AI in talent acquisition: A review of AI applications used in recruitment and selection. *Strategic HR review*, *18*(5), 215–221.

Arora, M., & Mittal, A. (2024). Employees' change in perception when artificial intelligence integrates with human resource management: A mediating role of AI-tech trust. *Benchmarking: An International Journal*, *32*(6), 1884–1908.

Baabdullah, A. M. (2024). The precursors of AI adoption in business: Towards an efficient decision-making and functional performance. *International Journal of Information Management*, *75*, 102745.

Bennett, M. (2024, October 15). *AI-powered HR: Revolutionizing employee onboarding*. CloudApper. Retrieved April 15, 2025, from https://www.cloudapper.ai/ai-in-hcm/ai-powered-hr-revolutionizing-employee-onboarding/

Bhandare, V. (2024). The role of artificial intelligence in learning and development. *International Journal of Scientific Research in Engineering and Management*, *8*(5), 1–5. https://doi.org/10.55041/ijsrem34968

Bharadwaj, V. (2024). Integrating artificial intelligence in human resource management: A comprehensive overview. *Journal of Management (JOM)*, *11*(3), 71–78.

Bhatt, P., & Muduli, A. (2023). Artificial intelligence in learning and development: A systematic literature review. *European Journal of Training and Development*, *47*(7/8), 677–694.

Blehar, M. (2025, May 13). *7 examples of companies successfully using an AI recruiting platform*. Phenom. Retrieved April 15, 2025, from https://www.phenom.com/blog/examples-companies-using-ai-recruiting-platform

Booth, R. (2019, October 25). *Unilever saves on recruiters by using AI to assess job interviews*. The Guardian. https://www.theguardian.com/technology/2019/oct/25/unilever-saves-on-recruiters-by-using-ai-to-assess-job-interviews

Budhwar, P., Malik, A., Thedushika, M., Silva, D., & Thevisuthan, P. (2022). Artificial intelligence – Challenges and opportunities for international HRM: A review and research agenda. *The International Journal of Human Resource Management*, *33*, 1065–1097. https://doi.org/10.1080/09585192.2022.2035161

Cubeo AI. (2024, October 10). *10 use cases of AI in HR with real-world case studies*. Retrieved April 15, 2025, from https://www.cubeo.ai/10-use-cases-of-ai-in-hr-with-real-world-case-studies/

Ejjami, R. (2024). The future of learning: AI-based curriculum development. *International Journal for Multidisciplinary Research*, *6*(4), 1–31.

Faqih, M., Sukistini, A. S., Asrianto, A., & Nggandung, Y. (2024). The impact of AI on talent acquisition: Opportunities and challenges in modern HR practices. *Global International Journal of Innovative Research*, *2*(11), 2626–2638.

Fung, C., Tiwari, S., & Voon, K. (2025). A preliminary review of artificial intelligence adoption in human resource management: Evidence from Asia. *International Journal of Service Management and Sustainability*. https://doi.org/10.24191/ijsms.v10i1.24222

Gryncewicz, W., Zygala, R., & Pilch, A. (2023). AI in HRM: case study analysis. *Preliminary Research*, 2351–2360. https://doi.org/10.1016/j.procs.2023.10.226

Huang, C. K., & Lin, J. S. (2025). Firm performance on artificial intelligence implementation. *Managerial and Decision Economics*, *46*(3), 1856–1870.

Jatobá, M., Ferreira, J., Fernandes, P., & Teixeira, J. (2023). Intelligent human resources for the adoption of artificial intelligence: A systematic literature review. *Journal of Organizational Change Management*. https://doi.org/10.1108/jocm-03-2022-0075

Jia, Q., Guo, Y., Li, R., Li, Y., & Chen, Y. (2018). A conceptual artificial intelligence application framework in human resource management.

Kadirov, A., Shakirova, Y., Ismoilova, G., & Makhmudova, N. (2024). AI in human resource management: Reimagining talent acquisition, development, and retention. In *2024 international conference on knowledge engineering and communication systems (ICKECS)*, (Vol. 1, pp. 1–8). IEEE.

Kaur, P., & Singh, S. (2023). The impact of artificial intelligence on human resource management: A review of challenges and opportunities. *International Journal of Human Resource Management*, *34*(11), 2261–2283.

Kaushal, N., Kaurav, R. P. S., Sivathanu, B., & Kaushik, N. (2023). Artificial intelligence and HRM: Identifying future research agenda using systematic literature review and bibliometric analysis. *Management Review Quarterly*, *73*(2), 455–493.

Kshetri, N. (2021). Evolving uses of artificial intelligence in human resource management in emerging economies in the Global South: Some preliminary evidence. *Management Research Review*. https://doi.org/10.1108/mrr-03-2020-0168

Li, P., Bastone, A., Mohamad, T., & Schiavone, F. (2023). How does artificial intelligence impact human resources performance? Evidence from a healthcare institution in the United Arab Emirates. *Journal of Innovation & Knowledge*. https://doi.org/10.1016/j.jik.2023.100340

Madanchian, M. (2024). From recruitment to retention: AI tools for human resource decision-making. *Applied Sciences*, *14*(24), 11750.

Madanchian, M., Taherdoost, H., & Mohamed, N. (2023). AI-based human resource management tools and techniques: A systematic literature review. *Procedia Computer Science*. https://doi.org/10.1016/j.procs.2023.12.039

Madhumita, G., Diana, P. D., Kiran, P. N., Aggarwal, S., & Nargunde, A. S. (2024, April). AI-powered performance management: Driving employee success and organizational growth. In *2024 5th international conference on recent trends in computer science and technology (ICRTCST)* (pp. 204–209). IEEE.

Malik, A., Budhwar, P., Mohan, H., & Srikanth, N. R. (2022). Employee experience – The missing link for engaging employees: Insights from an MNE's AI-based HR ecosystem. *Human Resource Management*. https://doi.org/10.1002/hrm.22133

Malik, A., Budhwar, P., Patel, C., & Srikanth, N. R. (2020). May the bots be with you! Delivering HR cost-effectiveness and individualized employee experiences in an MNE. *The International Journal of Human Resource Management*, *33*, 1148–1178. https://doi.org/10.1080/09585192.2020.1859582

Marinakou, E., Giousmpasoglou, C., & Papavasileiou, E. F. (2024). The use of artificial intelligence (AI) in talent acquisition: The case of Greek luxury hotels. *Strategic Change*, *34*(4), 533–543.

Msambwa, M. M., Wen, Z., & Daniel, K. (2025). The impact of AI on the personal and collaborative learning environments in higher education. *European Journal of Education*, *60*(1), e12909.

Muridzi, G., Dhliwayo, S., & Isabelle, D. A. (2024). Artificial intelligence in transforming HRM processes within organizations. *International Journal of Innovation Management*, *28*(09n10), 2440006.

Natarajan, D. S., Subbaiah, B., Dhinakaran, D. P., Kumar, J. R., & Rajalakshmi, M. (2024). AI-powered strategies for talent management optimization. *Journal of Informatics Education and Research*, *4*(2), 1526–4726.

Nieve Consulting. (2024, June 3). *AI in HR: 10 success stories that prove the future is now*. Nieve Consulting. https://www.nieveconsulting.com/blog/ai-in-hr-10-success-stories-that-prove-the-future-is-now

Nyathani, R. (2023a). AI in performance management: Redefining performance appraisals in the digital age. *Journal of Artificial Intelligence & Cloud Computing*, *2*(4), 2–5. https://doi.org/10.47363/jaicc/2023(2)134

Nyathani, R. (2023b). AI-enabled learning and development: HR's new paradigm. *Journal of Marketing & Supply Chain Management*, *2*(2), 5.

Okatta, C. G., Ajayi, F. A., & Olawale, O. (2024). Navigating the future: integrating AI and machine learning in hr practices for a digital workforce. *Computer Science & IT Research Journal*, *5*(4), 1008–1030.

Pan, Y., & Froese, F. (2023). An interdisciplinary review of AI and HRM: Challenges and future directions. *Human Resource Management Review*, *33*(1), 100924. https://doi.org/10.1016/j.hrmr.2022.100924

Pereira, V., Hadjielias, E., Christofi, M., & Vrontis, D. (2023). A systematic literature review on the impact of artificial intelligence on workplace outcomes: A multi-process perspective. *Human Resource Management Review*, *33*(1), 100857.

Qamar, Y., Agrawal, R., Samad, T., & Jabbour, C. (2021). When technology meets people: The interplay of artificial intelligence and human resource management. *Journal of Enterprise Information Management*, *34*, 1339–1370. https://doi.org/10.1108/jeim-11-2020-0436

Singh, A., & Pandey, J. (2024). Artificial intelligence adoption in extended HR ecosystems: enablers and barriers. An abductive case research. *Frontiers in Psychology*, *14*. https://doi.org/10.3389/fpsyg.2023.1339782

Singh, P. (2025). Artificial intelligence for human resource management: A comprehensive review. *Brixton Scholarly Review*. https://doi.org/10.3126/bsr.v2i1.78171

Stone, R. J., Cox, A., Gavin, M., & Carpini, J. (2024). *Human resource management*. John Wiley & Sons.

Subhadarshini, S., Nayak, A., & Sukanya Nisitgandha Biswal, D. S. C. (2024). The future of performance management: Leveraging AI for better feedback and coaching. *Journal of Informatics Education and Research*, *4*(2), 39–45.

Tang, K. Y., Chang, C. Y., & Hwang, G. J. (2023). Trends in artificial intelligence-supported e-learning: A systematic review and co-citation network analysis (1998–2019). *Interactive Learning Environments*, *31*(4), 2134–2152.

Tay, C. E., Ying, C. Y., Yeo, S. F., & Cheah, C. S. (2024). Revolutionizing recruitment: The rise of artificial intelligence in talent acquisition. *PaperASIA*, *40*(6b), 191–199.

Truvelop. (2024, April 4). *Harnessing the power of AI: Revolutionizing performance management for HR leaders*. Retrieved April 15, 2025, from https://www.truvelop.com/harnessing-the-power-of-ai-revolutionizing-performance-management-for-hr-leaders/

Tyagi, P. K., Singh, V. J., Singh, A. K., Saxena, A., Tyagi, P., & Mehta, P. (2023, December). The impact of artificial intelligence-based human resource management systems on organizational efficiency. In *2023 10th IEEE Uttar Pradesh section international conference on electrical, electronics, and computer engineering (UPCON)* (Vol. 10, pp. 1727–1731). IEEE.

Varma, A., Pereira, V., & Patel, P. (2024). Artificial intelligence and performance management. *Organizational Dynamics*, *53*(1), 101037.

VKTR. (n.d.). *5 AI case studies in HR*. https://www.vktr.com/ai-disruption/5-ai-case-studies-in-hr/

Wamba-Taguimdje, S. L., Fosso Wamba, S., Kala Kamdjoug, J. R., & Tchatchouang Wanko, C. E. (2020). Influence of artificial intelligence (AI) on firm performance: The business value of AI-based transformation projects. *Business Process Management Journal*, *26*(7), 1893–1924.

Zawada, M. (2024). The impact of artificial intelligence on human resource management: challenges, opportunities, and future directions. *System Safety: Human-Technical Facility-Environment*, *6*(1), 239–250.

Žibret, K. (2024). The transformative role of artificial intelligence in human resources. *Mednarodno inovativno poslovanje* [*Journal of Innovative Business and Management*], *16*(1), 1–15.

Chapter 12

Integrating AI for Strategic HR Efficiency: Empirical Insights from Emerging Digital Ecosystems

Anisha P. Gopal[a], *V. Mohana Sundari*[a] *and Syed Ahmed Salman*[b]

[a]*SRM Institute of Science and Technology, India*
[b]*Lincoln University College, Malaysia*

Abstract

The use of artificial intelligence (AI) in human resource management (HRM) is now an imperative method of enhancing the efficiency of operations and strategic alignment in digital-first businesses. In this research, the mediating effect of AI in facilitating essential human resource (HR) functions among IT firms in Chennai, a fast-emerging digital ecosystem in India, is explored. This study relies on a conceptual framework of six core antecedents AI-enabled strategic workforce planning, proactive management support, smart recruitment, data-driven training, competitive forces, and performance analytics to examine how AI facilitates the transition from traditional HR practices to agile, effective, and evidence-based HRM. An organized survey of 172 managerial staff and HR professionals was undertaken, and the information was analysed by applying SPSS for descriptive statistics, reliability, regression, and correlation. Structural equation modelling (SEM) is applied to verify the refereeing effect of AI on the relationship between antecedents recognized and the HR effectiveness. The results have shown that the use of AI significantly enhances recruitment accuracy, personalizes employee development, and enhances performance management systems. Organizational support and competitive market forces reinforce AI's transformative potential in HR. This chapter contributes to existing HRM literature by presenting empirical knowledge from an emerging economy and underscores the strategic imperative of AI adoption in developing adaptive, forward-looking

Nurturing AI-Powered HR Analytics and Virtual Reality in Employee Psychology and Workplace Happiness, Part A, 199–213

Published under exclusive licence by Emerald Publishing Limited
doi:10.1108/978-1-80686-125-520261012

HR systems. It offers practical recommendations for HR professionals, digital strategists, and policymakers seeking to align human capital strategy with technological advancement in competitive environments.

Keywords: Artificial intelligence; strategic human resource management; HR efficiency; digital transformation; AI integration; information technology sector

12.1. Introduction

AI discusses to the simulation of human aptitude in computers that are designed to reason, learn, and perform activities typically subject to human cognitive capacity, thereby enhancing decision-making and operational efficiency (Nweke, 2025). Integration of smart machines (AI) into SHRM, or strategic HRM, is now crucial for enhancing operational efficiency in the rapidly changing world of new digital ecosystems (Roy et al., 2025).The bid of AI in managing HR is a significant step towards optimizing strategic efficiency, as this chapter demonstrates empirical findings from new digital settings to establish the fact that AI can transform organizational performance and staff management (Madhumithaa et al., 2025). This is a transformative approach that enhances strategic efficiency, simplifies processes, facilitates data-driven decision-making, and facilitates businesses to manage workforce complexity in an increasingly digitalizing world (Okatta et al., 2024). AI has arisen as a transformative supremacy in HR, enhancing strategic efficiency through optimized recruitment, enhanced employee development, and configuration of HR practices with business tactics in Industry 4.0 (Kulshrestha, 2024). The use of AI in HRM simplifies business processes and enhances the effectiveness of strategic decision-making, allowing businesses to manage effectively with the varying dynamics of the personnel (Malik et al., 2023).

12.1.1. The Impression of AI on HR Efficiency

HR administration using AI will most likely increase the operation efficiency by automating operations like recruitment, training, and employee engagement, which further allows organizations to make more rational and fair decisions (Ooi et al., 2025). AI significantly enhances the effectiveness of HR by automating hiring, providing performance management data, and personalizing training modules, thereby allowing organizations to make enhanced strategic decisions, as well as enhancing employees' experience (Mabrouk, 2024). AI significantly enhances HR effectiveness through automating repetitive functions, simplifying the recruitment process, as well as providing customized training and development, thus allowing HR professionals to work on deliberate decision-making and improving employee morale (Stone et al., 2024). It also enhances HR effectiveness via processes such as candidate filtering and analytics, empowering HR managers to make more effective and informed decisions via deep data-driven insights from humongous data sets (Ragavendran, 2024). AI enhances HR effectiveness by reducing repetitive activities and increasing decision-making activities, allowing HR practitioners to devote more time to strategic activities that enhance organizational performance (Kaushal et al., 2023). Application of AI technology for automating HR processes, improving the performance of employees, and facilitating data-driven insights for administrative tenacities and for enhancing firm performance (Biliavska et al., 2022).

12.1.2. Research Gap

There is a lack of inclusive frameworks that examine the mediation role of AI integration between linking HR antecedents (e.g., training, recruiting, and strategic planning) and HR effectiveness, in terms of organizational support and competitive pressures. This research fills knowledge gaps by introducing empirical evidence on AI-based HRM. Although current literature emphasizes the revolutionizing nature of AI in HRM, including process automation, enhanced decision-making, and workforce management optimization, empirical research among IT companies in emerging digital hotspots such as Chennai, India, remains inadequate. Most studies observe the overall bearing of AI on HRM or concentrate only on developed economies, hence without the proper understanding of how AI adoption affects HR effectiveness in the specific socio-economic and technological context of an emerging country's IT sector. Chennai's IT industry clarifies how AI goes between HR practices and the success of an organization in a rapidly digitizing environment.

12.1.3. Objectives of the Research

The purposes of this research are as follows:

1. To evaluate the impact of the AI recruiting tools on improving the accuracy and effectiveness of candidate selection processes in IT organizations in Chennai.
2. To determine how predictive analytics based on AI enhances strategic staff planning by anticipating talent needs and linking them with corporate goals.
3. To investigate the effect of AI on tailoring staff development and training programs to improve skill acquisition and career growth in Chennai's IT industry.
4. To analyse the effect of external competitive forces on the application and success of AI technology in the development of HR services.
5. To assess the effect of AI-based performance management tools on decision-making with data and improving employee motivation in IT companies.

12.2. Literature Review

This review of literature looks at how AI can enhance HR effectiveness by automating tasks, using data to make decisions, and aligning with corporate objectives. AI streamlines recruitment, tailors training, and eases performance management, but concrete data on developing economies' IT sector is limited. This review consolidates AI-informed HRM evidence on six key antecedents: AI-informed strategic planning, anticipatory management assistance, sophisticated hiring, formal training, competitive pressures, and evidence-based measurement of performance. The review synthesizes these factors in elucidating how AI integration impacts HR effectiveness and its real-world implications for Chennai IT businesses in a competitive digital economy.

12.2.1. Strategic HR Planning

Strategic HR planning means aligning the management of human capitals with the strategic goals of the organization for ensuring the best personnel deployment to facilitate on-time fulfilment of goals (Paroli, 2025). Strategic HR planning with respect to integration with AI means the strategic alignment of HRM with the strategic use of AI technology to improve HR, improve the efficiency in talent sourcing, and improve worker performance through data led decision making (Dolapo & Kehinde, 2025) Strategic HR planning in AI integration is the alignment of HR objectives with sophisticated AI technologies to improve workforce management and decision-making and improve a responsive organizational culture that can engage and respond to present and even future business requirements (Sarumathi et al., 2025). It is the integration and alignment of the processes to use HRM with AI technologies to enhance organizational productivity, scale workforce capabilities, and assist in complying with strategic initiatives, while ensuring that HR has the capacity to develop in relation to technology growth (Petrika-Lindroos, 2022).

12.2.2. Smooth Recruitment and Selection Process

An effective recruitment and selection method indicates a process that is highly systematic, that achieves the timely attraction, assessment, and recruitment of desirable candidates, resulting in an overall reduction in wait times and a positive experience for all candidates (Sisneros, 2025). AI tools can enhance outreach, evaluation, review, and candidate management that will maximize the chances for selection of candidates with the appropriate knowledge, skills, and ability to contribute significantly to the organization (Parveen et al., 2025). The recruitment and selection procedure with AI is a timely, efficient, and data-driven process that enhances applicant matching and alleviates bias, ultimately resulting in stronger HRM outcomes (Lodra et al., 2024).

12.2.3. Planned Training and Development

Training and development strategically designed utilize employee's skills, abilities, knowledge, and productivity to enhance a business or provide quality services (Sathakathulla, 2025). Specifically, training and development strategically designed with AI; applied AI denotes to the intentional employment of AI technologies to customize the learning experience, analyse employee performance data, and create customized training planning that offered a path to meet employee's career goals and the objectives of the organization that ultimately provided greater employee competency and performance (Ghedabna et al, 2024).

Intentional use of AI in training and advance is purposeful utilization of AI tools and techniques to design, implement, and evaluate training, to ensure staff development opportunities are customized, effective, and relevant to organizational goals in order to develop a competent workforce (Ali et al., 2023).

12.2.4. Tactical Performance Appraisal

Tactical performance appraisal is a structured appraisal system aimed at assessing employee performance in terms of strategic measures and objectives, relating individual efforts to organization goals for the enhancement of total productivity and performance (de Araújo et al., 2024). It assesses and enhances employee performance in accordance with organizational objectives through the identification of major capabilities and behaviours (Maina et al., 2024). Incorporation of AI into performance tactical review enables companies to leverage predictive modelling and data-based decisions in order to enhance employee evaluation, fairness, and a culture of continuous feedback and development (Nyathani, 2023).

12.2.5. Management Support

Management support encompasses the process of providing guidance, counsel, and encouragement from top to enable employees in the successful attainment of organizational objectives, fostering innovations, and improving overall performance while creating an optimal workplace (Hock-Doepgen et al., 2025). Management support for AI encompasses utilizing digital intelligence technology to improve decision-making, optimize resource utilization, and promote strategic planning and execution in a business (Narne et al., 2024). Application of AI in administration support enhances fact-based decision-making, the effectiveness of operations, and the intricate issues of organizational dynamics (Shwedeh et al., 2024).

12.2.6. Competitive Pressure

Competitive pressure is the external forces applied by competing organizations operating in the same industry that push organizations to improve their performance, innovate, and evolve with shifting market trends in order to retain or increase their market share (Akhtar et al., 2024). Competitive pressure in the context of AI is defined as market forces beyond an enterprise that push businesses to implement AI technology as a means of increasing operational efficiency and remaining competitive in the market (Suki, 2024). It is an increasing pressure and requirement for companies to transform and acclimate to the fast pace AI technology development, thus shaping market trends and competitive status in different sectors (Horowitz et al., 2022).

12.2.7. Integration of AI

The AI raises to the imitation of human intellect in computers for decision-making, learning, and reasoning as human brain activities to enhance decision-making and working efficiency in the majority of industries (Mohsen et al., 2024). AI refers to human astuteness simulation, where computers can think, learn, and solve problems as the human brain, and thus improve decision-making and working efficiency in various industries (Vishwanath & Vaddepalli, 2023). The intersection of AI with best HR practices is strategic application in AI and learning expertise to HR processes for more informed decision-making, improving efficiency, and constructing effective talent management through compliance and stakeholder collaboration (Votto et al., 2021).

12.2.8. Efficient HR Practices

Good HR practices entail strategic application of procedures and resources, enhancing workforce management, enhancing operations, and optimizing employee participation in corporation goals (Mabrouk, 2024). Good HR practices are strategic methods and actions that increase employee performance, employee engagement, and job satisfaction, hence impacting the organization's objectives and targets (Nawaz et al., 2024). Successful HR practices involve the use of technology and strategic approaches for enhancing recruiting, employee involvement, and planning for employees, thereby ensuring congruence with corporate goals (Alaghbari et al., 2024).

12.2.9. Conceptual Research Framework

The conceptual framework demonstrates the mediation function of AI integration in connecting essential HR determinants with efficient HR practices in IT firms.

According to Fig. 12.1, the conceptual framework demonstrates the mediation function of AI integration in connecting essential HR determinants with efficient HR practices in IT firms.

12.3. Research Methodology and Hypothesis

This study employments a quantitative slant in investigating the strategic deployment of AI in HRM for IT firms in the Chennai. Primary data were gathered by means of an organized questionnaire filled out by 172 managing and HR professionals. Purposive sampling was employed as the sampling method with participants having corresponding experience with AI-based HR procedures. The research investigates the influence of AI on recruitment, planning for success, training, performance appraisal, and the effects of outside forces of competition. The analysis of data utilized SPSS, that is, descriptive statistics, reliability tests, and regression and correlation calculations to examine the relationship between the variables. Hypothesis testing was employed to confirm the postulated study hypotheses. The statistical method of analysis guarantees empirical richness and offers intuitions into the impact of incorporation with AI and HR effectiveness. Method conveys the study's objective to investigate AI's revolutionary role in enhancing efficiency, decision-making, and competitiveness for HR services.

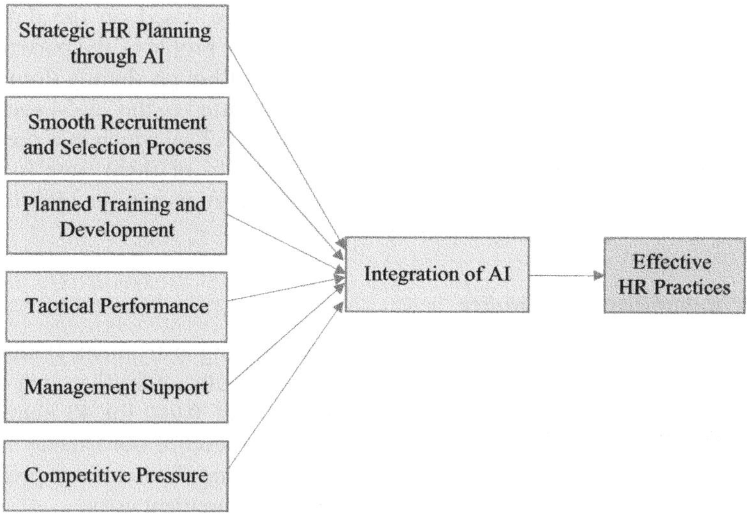

Fig. 12.1. Conceptual Research Framework. *Source*: Developed by the author (2025).

12.3.1. Hypothesis

The subsequent hypotheses are established to empirically investigate the influence of incorporation of AI on multiple facets of management of HR inside Chennai's IT sector.

> *H1.* AI recruiting tools significantly improve the accuracy and effectiveness of candidate selection.
>
> *H2.* AI significantly enhances strategic staff planning.
>
> *H3.* AI significantly affects the tailoring of staff development programs to improve skill acquisition and career growth.
>
> *H4.* External competitive forces significantly influence the application and effectiveness of AI in HR services.
>
> *H5.* AI-based performance management tools significantly affect data-driven decision-making and employee motivation.
>
> *H6.* AI-based performance management tools significantly affect data-driven decision-making and employee motivation.

12.4. Results

12.4.1. Demographic Profile

The demographic characteristics of the respondents, providing an overview of their age, gender, marital status, educational credentials, employment status, organizational size, and years of working knowledge based on the data collected from the fieldwork survey. It shows demographic profile of the participants ($N = 172$) is relatively evenly distributed in gender, although slightly dominated by females (54.1%). The majority of the participants fitted to the 25–34 age range (54.7%) and possessed at least a bachelor's degree (76.7%), which is a predominantly youthful and educated population. Most 62.2% of them were full-time personnel in various organizations with significant experience in the IT field, particularly in the 1–3 years category (37.8%).

12.4.2. Reliability and Validity

Reliability is the consistency and stability of a measuring instrument. It describes the degree to which the instrument provides equal results under the same conditions. The reliability test bent a Cronbach's Alpha of 0.960 for 40 items with overall sample size of 172, reflecting an outstanding level of consistency for the scale used in the research. High reliability supports that the items are precise in measuring the underlying concept with minimal measurement error.

12.4.3. Descriptive Statistics

The descriptive statistics is a collection of statistical measures applied in summarizing, tabulating, and describing the essential properties of a dataset in a concise and understandable manner. It enables the researcher to understand general patterns and distribution of data without making conclusions beyond the sample.

Table 12.1 shows the descriptive statistics also reveals that all variables possess highly comparable mean and median scores ranging from 19 to 20, thereby reflecting a typically high and uniform level of respondent agreement. The low standard deviations and narrow ranges across variables indicate negligible change, demonstrating stable views on AI-based HR processes and strategic effects, compiled from primary data by the author (2025).

12.4.4. Correlation Test

The correlation test was conducted to scrutinize the direction, strength of linear relationships amongst the key variables by using Pearson's correlation coefficient, the analysis helps determine whether and how strongly pairs of variables are related, providing insight into the degree of association between AI-driven HR practices and corresponding organizational outcomes.

Table 12.2 shows correlation matrix manifests strong positive and statistically significant correlations between all the variables, with correlation coefficients ranging from 0.636 to 0.860. The highest correlation rate of 0.860 is observed between Planned Training and Development (PD) and Smooth Recruitment and Selection (SS), manifesting a strong connection between these HR activities. The double asterisk (**) denotes that the correlation is statistically significant at the 1% level ($p < 0.01$). This means there is less than a 1% probability that the observed relationship between the two variables has occurred due to random

Table 12.1. Descriptive Statistics.

Variable	Mean	Median	Mode	Std. Deviation	Range
Strategic HR planning through AI	19.35	20	18	3.46	15
Smooth recruitment and selection process	18.98	20	20	3.99	17
Planned training and development	19.20	20	121	3.61	16
Tactical performance	19.34	20	19	3.35	15
Management support	19.06	20	20	3.19	15
Competitive pressure	19.47	20	19	3.29	15
Integration of AI	19.28	20	20	3.40	15
Effective HR practices	19.52	20	20	3.30	16

Source: SPSS (Data collected by the author).

Table 12.2. Correlation Analysis.

	SP	SS	PD	TP	MS	CP	IA	EHR
SP	1	0.749**	0.787**	0.665**	0.636**	0.734**	0.715**	0.705**
SS	0.749**	1	0.860**	0.712**	0.734**	0.828**	0.755**	0.770**
PD	0.787**	0.860**	1	0.745**	0.766**	0.810**	0.780**	0.795**
TP	0.665**	0.712**	0.745**	1	0.752**	0.751**	0.720**	0.710**
MS	0.636**	0.734**	0.766**	0.752**	1	0.774**	0.735**	0.740**
CP	0.734**	0.828**	0.810**	0.751**	0.774**	1	0.765**	0.785**
IA	0.715**	0.755**	0.780**	0.720**	0.735**	0.765**	1	0.790**
EHR	0.705**	0.770**	0.795**	0.710**	0.740**	0.785**	0.790**	1

Source: SPSS (Data collected by the author).

chance. The findings illustrate a high level of interaction between operational and strategic aspects of HR, affirming the combined role of AI in enhancing effective HR practices.

12.4.5. Regression

Regression analysis is employed to evaluate predictive relationship flanked by independent and dependent variables, allowing for an assessment of the level to which AI-driven HR practices stimulus key organizational outcomes. This statistical method helps quantify the impact of various AI components on factors such as recruitment effectiveness, strategic planning, employee development, and performance management. The model summary reflects high predictive correlation with an R value of 0.902 reflecting high correlation of independent variables with effective HR practices. An R Square of 0.814 reflects that about 81.4% of the variation in HR effectiveness could be accounted for by combined influence of strategic planning, recruitment, training, achievement, management support, workplace competition, and adoption of AI. The ANOVA findings confirm that adopted regression model is significant at F-value 128.32 and $p < 0.001$ level of significance. This confirms that all the combined predictors strategic planning, recruitment, training, performance, management support, competitive pressure, and AI integration are significant in affecting effective HR practices, Compiled from primary data by the author (2025).

According to Table 12.3, regression coefficients indicate that all the seven predictors SP, SS, PD, TP, MS, CP, and IA all significantly contribute towards the expected outcome of workforce behaviour with p-values < 0.05 and positive normalized beta coefficients, which indicate a positive contribution. The Tolerance and VIF values for all the predictors are all within acceptable ranges, which reflect the absence of serious multicollinearity problems and establish the validity of the model estimates.

12.4.6. SEM Analysis

To advance a deeper thoughtful interrelationship among the variables and validate the conceptual framework, a SEM approach was applied. This model tests

Table 12.3. Regression Table – Coefficients.

Coefficients[a]								
		Unstandardized Coefficients		**Standardized Coefficients**	t	**Sig.**	**Collinearity Statistics**	
Model		B	**Std. Error**	**Beta**			**Tolerance**	**VIF**
1	(Constant)	1.132	0.587		1.928	0.056		
	SP	0.172	0.054	0.182	3.192	0.002	0.357	2.8
	SS	0.158	0.051	0.174	3.098	0.003	0.323	3.1
	PD	0.146	0.058	0.165	2.517	0.013	0.345	2.9
	TP	0.121	0.049	0.138	2.470	0.015	0.385	2.6
	MS	0.134	0.055	0.145	2.436	0.016	0.370	2.7
	CP	0.129	0.053	0.140	2.434	0.016	0.400	2.5
	IA	0.143	0.052	0.154	2.750	0.007	0.385	2.6

Source: SPSS (Data collected by the author).

Note: [a]Dependent variable: Workforce behaviour.

both the direct and mediated pathways linking HR antecedents to effective HR practices through the integration of AI. The visual representation of model is presented in Fig. 12.2.

According to Fig. 12.2, the structural model reveals several meaningful insights. All six independent constructs Strategic HR Planning (SP), Planned Training and Development (PD), Tactical Performance (TP), Management Support (MS), Smooth Recruitment and Selection (SS), and Competitive Pressure (CP) demonstrate statistically significant and positively weighted paths to the mediating construct, integration of AI (IA), with standardized coefficients ranging from 0.14 to 0.18. This indicates that foundational HR strategies and environmental enablers meaningfully contribute to espousal and assimilation of AI in HR processes. Most notably, integration of AI exhibits a strong and significant influence on Effective HR Practices (EHR), with a standardized path coefficient of 0.79. This finding reinforces the central role of AI as a transformational enabler that bridges traditional HR activities with enhanced performance outcomes. The model fit indicators, such as low residual variances (e1 = 4.53; e2 = 6.20), further support the robustness of the model and its explanatory power. The SEM analysis aligns closely with the study's hypothesis framework and confirms that AI not only complements but strategically elevates core HR functions when supported by organizational readiness and competitive drive. This empirical validation provides a strong case for structured AI integration in HRM within IT organizations in emerging digital ecosystems like Chennai.

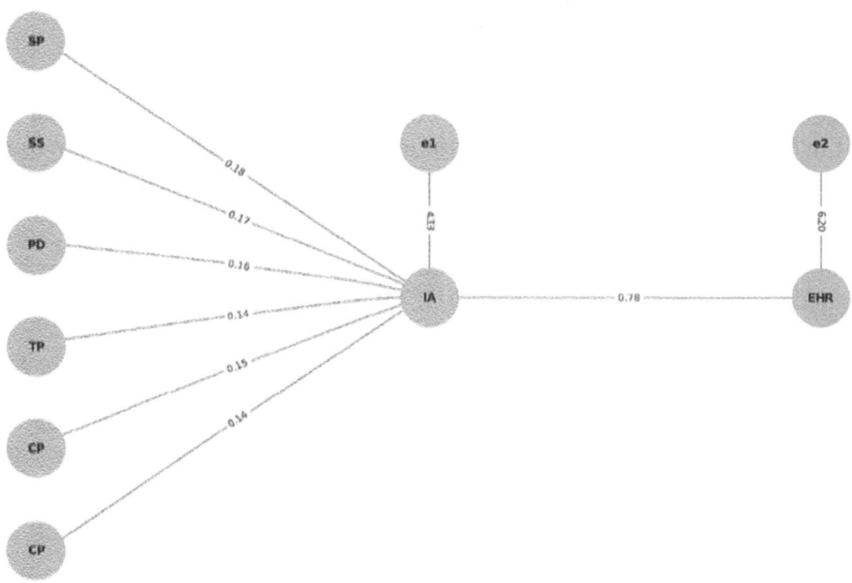

Fig. 12.2. SEM Analysis. *Source*: Compiled by the author (2025).

12.5. Discussion

This research's conclusions clearly highlight the revolutionizing role of AI on enhancing key HR practices among IT corporations in Chennai. The strong correlation results reveal that all the variables under examination, that is, strategic planning, recruitment, training, performance appraisal, motivation from management, and economic pressure are strongly related with the use of AI. Regression analysis confirms the correlations by demonstrating that HR activities based on AI are good predictors of best HR practice. This affirms the value that AI adds in optimizing business operations, decision-making, and employee satisfaction in HR activities. Moreover, the SEM test confirms the mediating function of AI integration to close HR antecedents and successful HR outcomes. The model confirms that AI is a strategic enabler that maximizes recruitment effectiveness and personalizes employee development and aligns performance management systems. Competitive pressure and management support confirm the need for a positive organizational climate for AI implementation. These findings validate the literature that demonstrates AI improves HR performance through automating mundane processes, complementing data-driven insights, and facilitating strategic alignment. The evidence gathered in the current study fills a significant research gap, particularly for nascent digital platforms in poor economies. The paper confirms that policymakers and HR professionals must invest in AI competency and construct agile organizations that enable the convergence of intelligent technologies. Organizations can develop stronger, robust, and visionary HR systems as they become digital-friendly.

12.6. Future Directions

Future research should extend this study by examining the longitudinal impact of AI in HRM to understand its long-term insinuations on employee performance, retention, and organizational adaptability. This research was limited to IT companies in Chennai; therefore, comparative studies across different cities, industries, or nations particularly other emerging digital economies would add more generalizability. Further research is necessary to investigate the ethical implications, worker attitudes, and prejudice in AI-based HR systems. Qualitative methods such as interviews or focus groups can provide detailed accounts of people's experiences of HR practices mediated by AI. In addition, future models can learn from analysing mediators or modifiers like digital preparedness, AI literacy, or resistance to change. Ultimately, expanding interdisciplinary approaches that involve technology management, behavioural sciences, and organizational theory will advance the development of inclusive, flexible, and responsible AI-HR ecosystems.

12.7. Conclusion

This research recognizes AI as a key driver for HR practice change in IT firms operating in emerging digital economies. Empirical data from the IT industry of Chennai shows that AI-based interventions enhance critical HR functions such as talent attraction, workforce planning, training tailoring, and performance management. The empirically supported structural model evokes AI as a mediator function, bridging conventional HR antecedents to measurable HR effectiveness. The presence of strong management support and external competitive forces further strengthens the implementation and impact of AI in HR operations. These results also highlight the crucial role of organizational readiness and contextual facilitators for leveraging AI for strategic HR purposes. This research puts AI integration not just in the guise of a technological upgrade but as a driver of structural and behavioural change, offering critical insights for HR directors, technology architects, and policy makers. HRM designed for the future needs to be inherently linked to AI, data-sensitive, and adaptive-aligned to ensure organizational agility in digitally competitive landscapes.

References

Akhtar, S., Tian, H., Iqbal, S., & Hussain, R. Y. (2024). Environmental regulations and government support drive green innovation performance: Role of competitive pressure and digital transformation. *Clean Technologies and Environmental Policy, 26*(12), 4433–4453. https://doi.org/10.1007/s10098-024-02857-4

Alaghbari, M., Ateeq, A., Alzoraiki, M., Milhem, M., & Beshr, B. (2024). Integrating technology in human resource management: Innovations and advancements for the modern workplace. In *2024 ASU international conference in emerging technologies for sustainability and intelligent systems (ICETSIS)* (pp. 307–311). IEEE. 10.1109/ICETSIS61505.2024.10459498

Ali, N. A. A., Hamdan, A., Alareeni, B., & Dahlan, M. (2023). Artificial intelligence in the process of training and developing employees. In B. Alareeni, A. Hamdan, R. Khamis, R.E. Khoury, (Eds.), *Digitalisation: Opportunities and challenges for business* 620 (pp. 558–568). Springer. https://doi.org/10.1007/978-3-031-26953-0_50.

Biliavska, V., Castanho, R. A., & Vulevic, A. (2022). Analysis of the impact of artificial intelligence in enhancing the human resource practices. *Journal of Intelligent Management Decision, 1*(2), 128–136. https://doi.org/10.56578/jimd010206

de Araújo, M. L., Caldas, L. S., Barreto, B. S., Menezes, P. P. M., Silvério, J. C. S., Rodrigues, L. C., Serrano, A. L. M., Neumann, C., & Mendes, N. (2024). How to evaluate the effectiveness of performance management systems? An overview of the literature and a proposed integrative model. *Administrative Sciences, 14*(6), 117.

Dolapo, B., & Kehinde, L. (2025). *Business management with SAP: Strategic planning, implementation, and performance evaluation.*

Ghedabna, L., Ghedabna, R., Imtiaz, Q., Faheem, M. A., Alkhayyat, A., & Hosen, M. S. (2024). Artificial intelligence in human resource management: Revolutionizing recruitment, performance, and employee development. *Nanotechnology Perceptions, 20*, 52–68.

Hock-Doepgen, M., Montasser, J. S., Klein, S., Clauss, T., & Maalaoui, A. (2025). The role of innovative work behavior and organizational support for business model innovation. *R&D Management, 55*(1), 7–26. https://doi.org/10.1111/radm.12671

Horowitz, M. C., Allen, G. C., Kania, E. B., & Scharre, P. (2022). *Strategic competition in an era of artificial intelligence*. Center for a New American Security.

Kaushal, N., Kaurav, R. P. S., Sivathanu, B., & Kaushik, N. (2023). Artificial intelligence and HRM: Identifying future research agenda using systematic literature review and bibliometric analysis. *Management Review Quarterly, 73*(2), 455–493. https://doi.org/10.1007/s11301-021-00249-2

Kulshrestha, D. S. (2024). Quantitative assessment on investigation on the impact of artificial intelligence on HR practices and organizational efficiency for Industry 4.0. *Journal of Artificial Intelligence, Machine Learning and Neural Network*, *42*, 14–21. https://doi.org/10.55529/jaimlnn.42.14.21

Lodra, R. S., Padhana, T., & Kristin, D. M. (2024). The impact of artificial intelligence on recruitment and selection for human resource management: A systematic literature review. In *2024 international conference on ICT for smart society (ICISS)* (pp. 1–6). IEEE.

Mabrouk, A. (2024). Human resource management in the age of artificial intelligence: Concepts, tools and steps. *Solo International Collaboration and Publication of Social Sciences and Humanities*, *3*(1), 1–12. https://doi.org/10.61455/sicopus.v3i01.216

Madhumithaa, N., Sharma, A., Adabala, S. K., Siddiqui, S., & Kothinti, R. R. (2025). Leveraging AI for personalized employee development: A new era in human resource management. *Advances in Consumer Research*, *2*(1), 134–141.

Maina, G. K., Kamau, D. R., Kenei, D. R., & Thinguri, D. R. W. (2024). Evaluation of the effectiveness of teacher performance appraisal on professional documentation in public secondary schools in Gatanga Sub-County, Murang'a County, Kenya. *Irish Interdisciplinary Journal of Science & Research*, *8*(4), 83–99. https://doi.org/10.46759/iijsr.2024.8411

Malik, A., Budhwar, P., Mohan, H., & Srikanth, N. R. (2023). Employee experience – The missing link for engaging employees: Insights from an MNE's AI-based HR ecosystem. *Human Resource Management*, *62*(1), 97–115. https://doi.org/10.1002/hrm.22133

Mohsen, S. E., Hamdan, A., & Shoaib, H. M. (2024). Digital transformation and integration of artificial intelligence in financial institutions. *Journal of Financial Reporting and Accounting*. https://doi.org/10.1108/jfra-09-2023-0544

Narne, S., Adedoja, T., Mohan, M., & Ayyalasomayajula, T. (2024). AI-driven decision support systems in management: Enhancing strategic planning and execution. *International Journal on Recent and Innovation Trends in Computing and Communication*, *12*(1), 268–276.

Nawaz, N., Arunachalam, H., Pathi, B. K., & Gajenderan, V. (2024). The adoption of artificial intelligence in human resources management practices. *International Journal of Information Management Data Insights*, *4*(1), 100208. https://doi.org/10.1016/j.jjimei.2023.100208

Nweke, O. (2025). Utilizing AI driven forecasting, optimization, and data insights to strengthen corporate strategic planning. *International Journal of Research Publication and Reviews*, *6*(3), 4260–4272. https://doi.org/10.55248/gengpi.6.0325.1209

Nyathani, R. (2023). AI in performance management: Redefining performance appraisals in the digital age. *Journal of Artificial Intelligence and Cloud Computing, SRCIJAICC-146*, 134–135.

Okatta, C. G., Ajayi, F. A., & Olawale, O. (2024). Navigating the future: Integrating AI and machine learning in HR practices for a digital workforce. *Computer Science & IT Research Journal*, *5*(4), 1008–1030.

Ooi, K.-B., Tan, G. W.-H., Al-Emran, M., Al-Sharafi, M. A., Capatina, A., Chakraborty, A., Dwivedi, Y. K., Huang, T.-L., Kar, A. K., Lee, V.-H., Loh, X.-M., Micu, A., Mikalef, P., Mogaji, E., Pandey, N., Raman, R., Rana, N. P., Sarker, P., Sharma, A., & Wong, L.-W. (2025). The potential of generative artificial intelligence across disciplines: Perspectives and future directions. *Journal of Computer Information Systems*, *65*(1), 76–107. https://doi.org/10.1080/08874417.2023.2261010

Paroli, P. (2025). Exploring the role of psychology in strategic human resource management: A qualitative perspective with literature review. *Golden Ratio of Human Resource Management*, *5*, 71–82.

Parveen, M., Suganya, G., Noorul Ayisha, M. L., & Pooja Batt, M. R. (2025). The role of artificial intelligence in modern recruitment and selection process. *Cuestiones de Fisioterapia*, *54*(2), 630–648. http://cuestionesdefisioterapia.com/index.php/es/article/view/779

Petrika-Lindroos, I. (2022). *Unlocking the power of AI in HR: How artificial intelligence can elevate the HR strategy in knowledge-based organizations*. https://urn.fi/URN:NBN:fi:amk-2022112824604

Ragavendran, V. A. (2024). An application framework for conceptual artificial intelligence in human resource management. *Educational Administration: Theory and Practice*, *30*(4), 9116–9120. https://doi.org/10.53555/kuey.v30i4.3168

Roy, S. K., Dey, B. L., Brown, D. M., Abid, A., Apostolidis, C., Christofi, M., & Tarba, S. (2025). Business model innovation through AI adaptation: The role of strategic human resources management. *British Journal of Management*. https://doi.org/10.1111/1467-8551.12894

Sarumathi, S., Gowthaman, R. L., Sabareesh, M. B., & Sultana, A. (2025). AI-enhanced HR interview simulation for realistic candidate assessment. In *2025 3rd international conference on intelligent data communication technologies and internet of things (IDCIoT)* (pp. 1089–1095). IEEE.

Sathakathulla, A. A. (2025). An empirical study on training and development as tool to operational excellence in Dubai electricity and water authority. *Shanlax International Journal of Management*, *12*(3), 12–24. https://doi.org/10.34293/management.v12i3.8387

Shwedeh, F., Nour, M. A., & Akour, I. (2024). Optimizing augmented reality adoption in higher education: A comprehensive analysis of factors impacting data management efficiency. *Journal of Infrastructure Policy and Development*, *8*(9), Article 6232. https://doi.org/10.24294/jipd.v8i9.6232

Sisneros, K. R. (2025). The impact of recruitment and selection strategies on organizational performance and employee productivity. Scholars Crossing. https://digitalcommons.liberty.edu/doctoral/6422/

Stone, D. L., Lukaszewski, K. M., & Johnson, R. D. (2024). Will artificial intelligence radically change human resource management processes? *Organizational Dynamics*, *53*(1), 101034. https://doi.org/10.1016/j.orgdyn.2024.10103

Suki, M. (2024). Mediating role of AI adoption between the relationship of leadership vision, change management capability, competitive pressure, trading partnerships, and SME performance. *Pakistan Journal of Commerce and Social Sciences (PJCSS)*, *18*(4), 872–892.

Vishwanath, B., & Vaddepalli, S. (2023). The future of work: Implications of artificial intelligence on HR practices. *Tuijin Jishu/Journal of Propulsion Technology*, *44*(3), 1711–1724.

Votto, A. M., Valecha, R., Najafirad, P., & Rao, H. R. (2021). Artificial intelligence in tactical human resource management: A systematic literature review. *International Journal of Information Management Data Insights*, *1*(2), 100047. https://doi.org/10.1016/j.jjimei.2021.100047

Chapter 13

Future Trends of Artificial Intelligence and VR for Human Resources

Pradeep Kumar[a], Sanjeev Kumar[b] and Dina Darwish[c]

[a]*Department of Mathematics, Lovely Professional University, India*
[b]*School of Hotel Management and Tourism, Lovely Professional University, India*
[c]*Artificial Intelligence Department, Computer Science and Information Technology Ahram Canadian University, Egypt*

Abstract

Nowadays, artificial intelligence (AI) and virtual reality (VR) play an important role in human resource management (HRM), and they are changing traditional human resource (HR) practices.. AI also plays a vital role in the recruitment and selection process. It effectively sorts resumes and, through chatbots, scans candidates' details and provides accurate information to HR without delay. This helps save time and also reduces human bias in the hiring process.. In addition, AI prepares and maintains individual candidate profiles, tracks employee growth and performance management, and anticipates workforce planning needs.. Through VR technology, employee experience is transformed by enabling a more immersive onboarding process. It also provides training simulations and various tools that help HR overcome many workplace challenges. The synergy of AI and VR has the potential to create improved working environments, enhance decision-making, and promote innovation in talent management. There are various challenges such as ethical issues, privacy of data, cost of implementation, and the need for digital skills to harness their effectiveness. This study will focus on trends and opportunities of AI and VR in HR to improve the quality of work, refine the employee experiences, and generate business success.

Keywords: Artificial intelligence; virtual reality; human resource management; recruitment; employee training workforce; employee engagement

Nurturing AI-Powered HR Analytics and Virtual Reality in Employee Psychology and Workplace Happiness, Part A, 215–228

doi:10.1108/978-1-80686-125-520261013

13.1. Introduction

HR practices used in the personnel management, payroll management, conformity, job hiring, and staff relations have changed with the fast-paced nature of technology over the last 10 years, which has elevated the role of HR to a strategic component of performance of the organization. AI and VR are two of the most disruptive technologies that are used in the HR practices. The revolutionary technologies, AI and VR, are redefining the practices of the HR industry by allowing it to deploy data analysis and make informed decisions as well as streamline the experience of its employees. The AR is used in the HR department for various activities such as resume parsing and predictive analytics, performance tracking, and employee engagement. On the other hand, AI platforms track various resumes within minutes and maintain records of job performance, culture adaptability, and career potential which reduces the burden on HR. AI technology also provides individual training roadmaps, forecasts employee turnover, and makes staffing decisions mathematically, enabling HR specialists to make strategic decisions based on evidence. VR technology focuses on computer-generated environments where personnel may engage with real simulations or work collaboratively in virtual space. VR now explores in more areas of HR like onboarding, training, and engagement. VR software also provides trainings through virtual modes, allowing employees to engage with others and experience the working environment (Garg & Agrawal, 2020). The mixture of AI and VR provides potential that can further complement HR processes. AI processes provide different information and suggestions, whereas VR enhances learning and interaction experiences, resulting in innovations that can revolutionize the hiring process, training, and employee experience. Collectively, these technologies reflect a transition to technology-enabled and employee-centric HR that uses technology to augment human judgment based on insights and immersive experiences (Jooss et al., 2022).

The role of AI and VR in the HR field cannot be reduced to greater efficiency. These technologies can potentially transform the employee lifecycle by solving long-standing issues such as discrimination, less engagement, and skill deficiencies in the workforce, as well as challenges in remote collaboration. One of the greatest advantages of AI is that it helps to eliminate human prejudices in hiring and talent management. Conventional recruitment methods are based on subjective assessments, and they are always susceptible to prejudice. The use of AI can ensure that assessments of the candidates are made on the basis of their competencies and to identify areas of disparity in decision-making. The main value of VR is maximizing learning and experience (Saxena et al., 2021). In a distributed workforce or a hybrid workforce, VR allows employees to interact and train in immersive environments that are matching the real-life jobs (Melo & Machado, 2018). In one case, VR simulations could familiarize workers with high stakes interaction (e.g., customer, leadership, emergency response) without putting them at risk.

AI and VR can improve employee satisfaction and retention by creating the virtual environments where employees feel comfortable in the working environment.

Tailor-made learning plans, engaging training activities, and customized career pathways with different plans and tools help employees feel recognized and supported, leading to more engagement (Tambe et al., 2019). The ability of employers to utilize advanced technologies makes them appear more progressive and modern, which improves their employer branding and helps attract talent. Using new strategic analysis, the combination of AI and VR will allow planning scenarios and objective-based HR decision-making (O'Brien et al., 2025). The advanced analytics allows a leader to recognize his/her work force behavior, forecast performance results, and maximize team composition. The immersive VR experiences can become more insightful and can be transformed into an intervention and build a responsive, adaptive, and resilient workforce. The aim of the study is to identify future trends of AI and VR in HR and analyze their possible implications to change HR practices. The study will do the comprehensive analysis of the benefits, difficulties, and opportunities that come along the way of adopting these emerging technologies (Deepa et al., 2024). The AI will help in recruitment and talent acquisition to understand how VR will transform employee training and experience and identify how AI and VR can be used in HR practices. Various challenges and ethical issues are involved in the use of AI and VR while accomplishing different goals; this study aims to provide a roadmap for HR leaders to utilize AI and VR to improve workforce performance, workforce engagement, and overall organizational success. These technologies, when used in HR as tools and facilitators, transform the way the work is experienced, managed, and optimized in the digital age (Yadav et al., 2023).

13.2. AI and Recruitment and Talent Acquisition

Automation (Resume Screening and Parsing) is one of the most important uses of AI in the HRM. Traditionally, the HR professionals have to manually assess hundreds or thousands of resumes per job posting, a time consuming and subjective process (Vedapradha et al., 2023). However, AI-powered systems use natural language processing (NLP) and machine learning models to parse resumes, extract data, and identify matching skills, experiences, and qualifications to rank resumes based on the suitability of skills to the job. Automated resume parsing works by extracting the important information –education, work experience, technical skills, certifications, and awards – in varying formats and standardizing the details into a database that structures them (Zehir et al., 2020). This will enable recruiters to narrow and shortlist candidates on commend coined limitations within a short period of time. To illustrate, AI-based platforms such as HireVue, LinkedIn Talent Insights, and Pymetrics have the capability to process thousands of job applications in a couple of minutes, leaving the HR professionals with a list of high-quality candidates. The AI helps to prevent errors in processing data and maintain standards of evaluation, and the AI gives the HR teams the potential to concentrate on the strategic initiatives like candidate engagement (Ranawat et al., 2024), employer branding, and workforce planning. Additionally, automated systems can support mass recruitment campaigns, seasonal hiring surge, or world-wide talent search processes without having to incur excessive costs. However, there exist challenges. Under-trained algorithms can miss potential talent by ignoring non-conventional career paths or resumes that are not seen as normal. Organizations have no other choice but to constantly update and supervise their models of AI to guarantee precision and diversity (Bhanumathi, 2025). AI-driven candidate shortlisting is shown in Fig. 13.1.

Over and above parsing resumes, AI has the potential to revolutionize the recruitment process to become more data-driven and strategic in selecting the right candidates. Predictive analytics is the use of historical hiring data, performance measures, and behavioral data to aid in the formation of rules or models to predict and determine which job applicants have a higher probability of being successful at the company (Johnson et al., 2021). As an example, HR teams can use AI-driven insights to assess a combination of skills, education, and past experiences that correlate with high-performing employees in a target role or department. Based on such findings, HR teams can be given the insights on who is most likely to attain a high-performance level without hiring a mismatched candidate and leaving them jeopardized. The predictive analytics focus on predicting candidate retention likelihood, cultural fitness and promotion chances (Pillai & Sivathanu, 2020). AI-powered insights are leveraged by HR leaders; they can predict the future talent shortages, locate areas of skill gaps, and create proactive employee recruitment campaigns. These analytics show the need for data scientists in the organization, allowing HR to consider making such hires. The predictive analytics has many advantages, but it also raises the ethical and practical issues (Paramita et al., 2024). AI-enhanced systems improve data accuracy, system transparency, and reduce the system bias, helping to ensure that AI-driven predictions are reliable. The organizations should set up governance systems and monitor through the AT technology and validate their result with humans. AI-enabled chatbots have become successful in many organizations to communicate

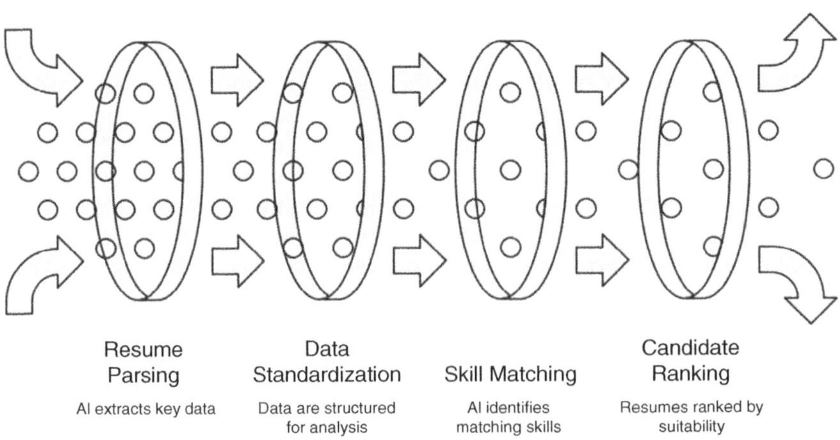

Fig. 13.1. AI-driven Candidate Shortlisting. *Source*: Authors' creation.

with candidates in real time, as well as to guide and provide the feedback on time to improve the performance of the candidates. Chatbots also help in the initial screening, interview dates, and sending automated notifications which reduces the workflow of recruitment. Chatbots also become fruitful day by day, as they can handle many tasks at the same time and reduce the burden on the HR department. Some popular chatbots, such as Mya, Olivia, and XOR, are widely used to improve candidate engagement and application completion. However, chatbots are designed with human touch in mind, especially when it comes to sensitive communication like rejecting a candidate or sending messages on negotiation (Opada et al., 2024).

Excessive use of automated answers without human control can produce unpleasant experiences for candidates and affect employer branding. Human prejudice is always a bonus of concern in the hiring process, and subjectivity, subconscious stereotyping, and variability in assessment criteria could all lead to negative candidate experiences and detrimental employer branding. The way to diminish these biases, offered by us, is to standardize the assessments, concentrate on objective figures, and anonymize candidates' data in the first rounds of screening (Vedapradha et al., 2024). As an example, AI programs are capable of stripping relevant personal information such as name, gender, age, and ethnicity out of resumes so that their analysis and decision-making process can be based on skills, experience, and qualifications only. Using ML, any trained model can be used to spot and flag biased language in a job posting and take the necessary steps to ensure that biased language use in job posts does not occur. In another instance, if the past hiring data represents a gender or racial bias, then inadvertently AI will tend to favor candidates who are likened to those who had been hired earlier (Roppelt et al., 2024). As such, organizations have to conduct bias audits, implement algorithmic transparency, and track systems to make AI-driven recruitment fair.

In addition, AI has to be used to assist human judgment rather than substitute it. Automation minimizes subjective biases; however, human professionals remain critical in assessing cultural fit, emotional intelligence, and subtle interpersonal competences – skills that AI is unable to evaluate. By integrating objective, AI-based solutions with human decision-making, firms can design an effective recruitment process, which is faster, more efficient, and fairer. This practice (1) is a better experience to the candidate, (2) results in overall improved quality of hire, and (3) increases the diversity and inclusion of workforces. These apps save time and cost and result in quality recruits and the ability of the HR members to spend their time in strategic workforce planning. Organizations should be very careful when applying AI as it should be practiced ethically, transparently, and controlled by human beings.

13.3. AI in Employee Development and Performance Management

AI is also playing an increasingly transformative role in employee development and employee performance management. Organizations can transform their current, anti-personal, one-size-fits-all approach to HR into highly individualized, empirical, proactive HR policies that empower employees to grow and lead to high organizational productivity. AI makes it possible to create highly customized, dynamic, and individualized learning experiences, which suit the needs, preferences, and career ambitions of each employee (Thirunagalingam et al., 2024). Sophisticated AI algorithms are capable of evaluating skills shortages, learning behaviors, and performance history, to prescribe personalized courses, webinars, and on-the-job learning programs. Coaching platforms, AI-assisted simulations, and gamified learning experiences further enhance the learning experience, making it more engaging and knowledge retention-friendly. Customized learning paths are not only effective in helping employees develop their skills but also enhance staff satisfaction and automatically increase staff retention rates because of their tangibility and investment in an individual in a manner that is objective, consistent, and unbiased as seen in the traditional performance appraisal process. Performance evaluation tools enabled by AI offer data-driven and objective evaluations and feedback that is continuous. Leveraging numerous data points on task completion rates, teamwork, communication channels, and project results, AI systems may determine high performers, reveal improvement areas, and uncover potential (Madhumita et al., 2024). These insights can underpin fair promotions, merit-based rewards, and development interventions, as well as drive transparency and trust in performance management. AI also enables an HR team with strategic workforce planning and predictive analytics. Reading historical and real-time data, AI models can predict future skills needs, employee turnover rates, and even anticipated skill deficiencies. This empowers organizations to carry out proactive talent pipeline workforce, optimize their resources, and align business aspirations with workforce capabilities. Predictive HR analytics makes succession planning, risk mitigation, and sound decision-making easy, thus making the organization gain competitive advantage in a dynamic business environment (Talukder et al., 2025). AI applications in employee development and performance management are shown in the following sections.

13.3.1. AI-driven Performance Evaluation

AI plays an important role in modern performance evaluation by enabling continuous monitoring and analysis of employee performance. Through data analysis of daily tasks, collaboration patterns, and productivity metrics, AI systems can generate predictive performance scores. This allows organizations to assess performance more objectively and reduce human bias. As a result, employees receive fairer rewards and promotions, while managers gain actionable insights to support employee development and improvement.

13.3.2. Workforce Planning and Predictive HR Analytics

AI is also used in workforce planning through predictive HR analytics. By analyzing historical and real-time data, AI can forecast future talent needs, predict employee attrition, identify skill gaps, and support succession planning. These insights allow organizations to manage their workforce proactively, allocate resources more efficiently, retain top talent, and ensure that HR strategies are aligned with overall business goals.

13.4. VR in Employee Experience and Training

What is more, VR has transformed the way of looking at employee onboarding as these immersive experiences that have proven to be much more than traditional orientation programs. New workers tend to have problems in grasping the company culture, workflows, and in adjusting to the organizational setup. VR onboarding solutions overcome these problematic issues, as they enable employees to test virtual offices, communicate with team members, and participate in the everyday activities of business environments in a secure, harmless environment (Zawadzki et al., 2020). As an example, VR platforms are able to recreate office arrangements, production plants, or stores, ensuring its employees have a sense of location and the chance to physically practice standard operating procedures and safety measures. One of the more successful uses of VR onboarding is its implementation across companies like Walmart and Accenture that need to train thousands of their employees on a regular basis across wider areas (Singh & Kumar, 2024). Increasing interaction and knowledge retention, VR onboarding would help minimize anxiety, speed up productivity, and ensure that the remote employees are acclimated to the same level and in the same spirit as the on-site staff. Besides onboarding and simulation-based training (Saeed et al., 2024), VR also enables employees to train with a degree of real-world circumstances, allowing them to practice in risk-free and controlled environments. VR onboarding improves employee integration, as shown in Fig. 13.2.

This training is most useful when it involves high risk or technical jobs or for difficult interpersonal situations. In health, VR simulations allow medical practitioners to practice surgical operations, emergency care, and patient response, without jeopardizing the health of patients. In production and the building industry, workers have the possibility to train in handling machinery, accident

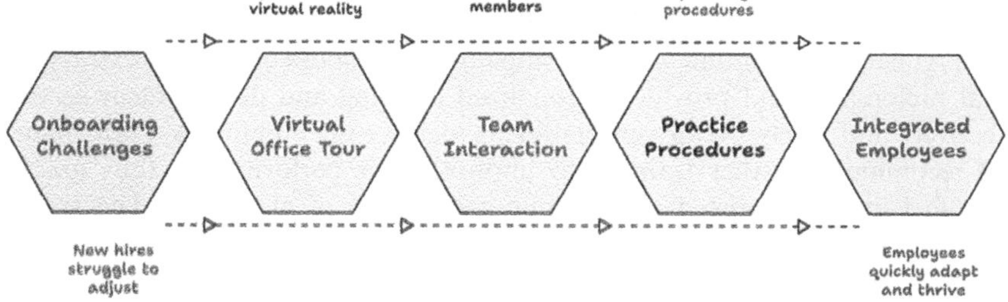

Fig. 13.2. VR Onboarding Improves Employee Integration. *Source*: Authors' compilation.

hazard awareness, and crisis handling (Kravchuk et al., 2024). VR-based roles also facilitate communication, conflict resolution, and problem-solving skills by the customer service teams. Among the benefits of simulation-based training, are a safe learning environment, better knowledge retention, ability to scale locations, and performance tracking based on data. Firms such as UPS have resorted to VR simulation of driver safety training, and it has shown results in the measurable improvement of skills, compliance, and confidence. VR can make helping people develop into an evidence-based process that is proactive. As hybrid and remote work increase in popularity, traditional solutions such as video conferences and collaboration cannot meet the level of engagement (and team building) they bring. VR provides immersive virtual collaboration environments where the staffs can interact, brainstorm, and solve the problems within a shared space without being physically in the same place. Teams can use virtual platforms to conduct meetings in a virtualized office or creative space, manipulate 3D objects, visualize information, and collaboratively use a shared digital whiteboard in real-time. Spatial, MeetinVR, and Horizon Workrooms are primary tools to effectively run a workshop, design thinking session, and strategic planning with stronger creativity and involvement (Yadav, 2025). The collaboration in VR can create an inclusive environment to empower cross-border teams to participate on an equal footing, enhance and bring coherence to organizational culture, and minimize travel. Although VR is facing difficulties, including hardware, digital literacy, and potential discomfort related to the long-term use of VR, the technology has opened new possibilities in terms of enhancing the employee experience and engagement, as well as collaboration (Bayero et al., 2025). These apps drive visibility, knowledge retention, inclusivity, and minimize risk and costs of operation. With the expansion of hybrid models of work, VR can be used to overcome physical distances and build cohesive and effective teams. VR becomes particularly useful when compounded with AI-based analytics capabilities: this can provide individualized, dynamic experiences that increase learning, performance, and organizational HR strategy. Companies which utilize VR in the training of the workforce and collaboration have a better edge in retaining a talented and motivated workforce that is digitally empowered as well (Morrissey et al., 2023).

13.5. Integration of AI and VR in HR

The AI and VR in HR practices transformed the process of employee engagement. AI helps to maintain various companies' data about employees extract personal preferences and provide personalized learning and development services effectively and safely. AI-driven platforms identify the employees' performance and recommend further training to improve their performance, thus making them feel more supported and encouraged (Aydin et al., 2024). The trained employee can then train others and share their experiences that they learned during the period of training and improve the performance of the company. In the real simulations, virtual workshop exercises, and gamified training experiences, the employees are able to participate actively. VR and AI work together to help

HR create an employee-centric environment that enhances satisfaction, productivity, and overall engagement with staff members (Alaghbari et al., 2024). AI and VR also help create positive and eco-friendly work environments. These are the important tools for recruitment by AI which reduce the presence of HR. Through the VR technology, HR can find the suitable candidate geographically and do the effective collaboration and improve the efficiency of the work. For example, VR enables virtual meetings and training simulations, giving remote staff equal opportunities to participate in learning and career development (Dewangan & Kumar, 2024). The use of AI and VR in the organizations creates the positive impact on diversity, inclusivity, and fairness in hiring, development, and engagement. These technologies, AI and VR, also support talent management by bringing innovation through data-driven approaches and practical learning. Using workforce data, AI collects and analyzes it to identify patterns, areas of skill gaps, and trends in performance (Subrahmanyam, 2024). VR also offers different platforms to encourage immersive training, mentoring, and team-building activities. Implementation of AI–VR in talent management improves employee involvement, promotes inclusiveness in the workplaces, and develops innovation in HRM (Madanchian et al., 2023).

13.5.1. Data Privacy and Security Issues

One of the major challenges of using AI in organizations is ensuring the privacy and security of employee data. AI systems require the collection, storage, and processing of sensitive personal and professional information. If not managed properly, these data can be exposed to breaches or misuse. To address this challenge, organizations must implement strong cybersecurity measures, strictly follow data protection regulations, and maintain transparency with employees about how their data are collected and used.

13.5.2. Cost and Resource Implications

The adoption of AI technologies often involves high initial costs related to purchasing AI tools, building supporting infrastructure, and ongoing maintenance. These financial and resource demands can be challenging, especially for smaller organizations. To manage this effectively, companies should plan their budgets carefully, choose scalable AI solutions that can grow over time, and invest in staff training and technical support to maximize the return on investment.

13.5.3. Digital Skills and Workforce Adaptation

Successful implementation of AI requires employees to understand and effectively use AI-based tools. However, many employees may lack the necessary digital skills or feel resistant to technological change. Organizations can overcome this challenge by offering continuous digital upskilling programs, structured change management initiatives, and hands-on training sessions. This helps employees adapt smoothly and increases acceptance of AI in the workplace.

13.6. Challenges and Ethical Considerations

One of the most important obstacles to the use of AI and VR in HR is privacy and security of the data about the employees. The AI systems are based on very large amounts of personal data (resumes, performance data, engagement, and behavioral patterns). Similarly, VR platforms can generate data on user interactions, movements, and his/her engagement levels. Organizations are therefore required to establish impervious cybersecurity mechanisms such as encryption, secure storage, and access. Moreover, they must adhere to data protection laws, including the General Data Protection Regulation (GDPR) and be more transparent with how their workforce information is gathered, analyzed, and managed. The implementation of AI and VR technologies in HR is a very costly labor-intensive process that entails investments into hardware, software, employee training, and constituent maintenance. The cost of VR headsets, simulation software, AI-driven analytics platform, and cloud infrastructure can be high, especially for small- and medium-sized companies. Behind the one-time spending, organizations have to set aside funds to integrate the systems, provide technical assistance, and update the systems constantly in order to retain the effectiveness and security thereof. Unless properly planned, the financial cost may be bigger than the gains and it may become prohibitive to some organizations. It is affected by the digital literacy of HR specialists and employees, as well as their ability to cope with changes brought by AI and VR in HR. This challenge can be alleviated by making strategic investments, cost-benefit analysis, and phased adoption of AI and VR in HR to ensure long-term value. HR teams will have to be able to know how to use complex API analytics tools, process data outputs, and manage VR-based training. Employees, in their turn, must move around virtual space, interact with interactive simulations, and adjust to AI performance feedback. Such changes can be resisted and adoption hampered because of a lack of training or fear of technology. AI and VR provoke serious moral dilemmas in the horizon of HR decision-making. ML algorithms have the potential to reinforce bias when fed on historical data that represent discriminatory tendencies. For example, AI recruitment systems can potentially discriminate against a particular demographic group if in case the base hiring pattern was biased.

13.7. Future Trends and Opportunities

The influence of AI will fuel a revolution in workforce by supporting data-driven HR practices, predictive decision-making, and personalized employee experience. The direction provided by the AI will not only carry out mechanical HR procedures but also predict the requirements of the workforce, skill deficiencies, and will rationalize talent distribution. The analytics of HR professionals will be able to predict employee turnover, succession planning, and career growth more accurately, and proactively manage human capital. AI will support each and every individual in terms of learning patterns and performance management systems and create a dynamic workforce with constant innovation. The use of effective AI will find higher levels of productivity, employee engagement, and workforce that can adapt to the changing business environments

(Hassan & Kumar, 2024). The new trends in VR include immersive leadership development program, scenario-based judgment and decision-making simulation, and cross-functional virtual project environments. HR incorporates AI to deliver adaptive learning experiences, where artificial scenarios change and improve the performance of the employee in different situations. The smart use of AI and VR will enable HR to shift from one level to another level which creates the positive impact on talent management, organizational innovation, and competitive advantages.

13.8. Conclusions and Recommendations

The AI and VR bring tremendous changes in the HR department and factors in HRM. AI has been able to perform various tasks like administrative duties, recruitment process, and anticipating workforce requirements in HR. AI can be used to conduct other tasks which include resume screening, predictive candidate selection, and chatbot exchanges, where human bias will be reduced and also save time and increase the efficiency of the entire recruitment process. AI will also help to make strategic decisions using data and do the analysis properly. VR enhances the capabilities of AI which offer immersive and interactive experiences that engage more employees with effective learning and collaborations. The VR technologies also enable a new employee to explore working areas and get familiar with organizational culture and provide professional training before joining the organization. VR training creates simulation-based experiences for employees and trains them effectively to use these technologies. Combined with AI, VR will be able to adapt the learning modules and provide customized experiences and improve the skills and performance. The mixed use of AI and VR would help to create an inclusive and even more equitable workplace. AI and VR systems also save the data security and privacy of the organization. Companies must install an effective cybersecurity measures and follow the international laws like GDPR. To develop the digital skills of the employee, organizations must provide VR and AI equipments that HR can use effectively and maintain properly. It is important to be aware of these challenges in order to build responsible, effective, and sustainable HR technology strategies. To take the advantage of AI and VR, different strategic approaches must be implemented effectively. On the other hand, companies must adopt transparent AI algorithms, perform frequent audits to identify bias and keep human control over decisions of the AI. Formal and informal learning programs, training seminars, and change management processes can be implemented to develop a technologically competent workforce that can adapt to workflows integrated with new technologies. Collaboration with other departments such as IT, operations, and learning and development departments is important for HR teams to successfully integrate AI and VR. Cross-functional teamwork ensures the innovative design of solutions that are scalable, eco-friendly, and aligned with organizational goals. Collaborations with technology providers and institutions of higher learning can also be a source of information on new trends, best practices, and novel use cases with the potential to drive workforce performance and engagement.

References

Alaghbari, M. A., Ateeq, A., Alzoraiki, M., Milhem, M., & Beshr, B. A. H. (2024). Integrating technology in human resource management: Innovations and advancements for the modern workplace. In *2024 ASU international conference in emerging technologies for sustainability and intelligent systems (ICETSIS)* (pp. 307–311). IEEE. https://doi.org/10.1109/ICETSIS61505.2024.10459498

Aydin, O., Karaarslan, E., & Narin, N. G. (2024). *Artificial intelligence, VR, AR and metaverse technologies for human resources management (Version 1)*. https://doi.org/10.48550/ARXIV.2406.15383

Bayero, S. A., Manoharan, G., & Kumar, S. (2025). Machine learning in finance: The revolutionized fusion. In F. Ghosn, G. Awad, & K. Darwich (Eds.), *Advances in computational intelligence and robotics* (pp. 43–72). IGI Global. https://doi.org/10.4018/979-8-3373-0129-7.ch002

Bhanumathi, P. (2025). Human resource management in the 5.0 era. In P. Nakpathom, K. Kankaew, S. Khetjenkarn, A. S. Musallam Jaboob, & A. M. Baawain (Eds.), *Humanizing the hyperconnected workplace* (pp. 103–136). IGI Global. https://doi.org/10.4018/979-8-3693-8171-7.ch004

Deepa, R., Sekar, S., Malik, A., Kumar, J., & Attri, R. (2024). Impact of AI-focussed technologies on social and technical competencies for HR managers – A systematic review and research agenda. *Technological Forecasting and Social Change*, *202*, 123301. https://doi.org/10.1016/j.techfore.2024.123301

Dewangan, S., & Kumar, S. (2024). AI and Big Data Analytics revolutionizing Industry 5.0: Unlocking the power of smart manufacturing and beyond. In D. Darwish (Ed.), *Advances in business information systems and analytics* (pp. 398–410). IGI Global. https://doi.org/10.4018/979-8-3693-0413-6.ch016

Garg, V., & Agrawal, R. (Eds.). (2020). *Transforming management using artificial intelligence techniques* (1st ed.). CRC Press. https://doi.org/10.1201/9781003032410

Hassan, S. C., & Kumar, S. (2024). Safe green hydrogen: Production and storage as an emerging source of energy for sustainable future. In M. S. Raboaca, S. Djohra, O. Moussaoui, T. C. Mihaltan, & M. Koussa (Eds.), *Advances in chemical and materials engineering* (pp. 143–153). IGI Global. https://doi.org/10.4018/979-8-3693-1014-4.ch008

Johnson, R. D., Stone, D. L., & Lukaszewski, K. M. (2021). The benefits of eHRM and AI for talent acquisition. *Journal of Tourism Futures*, *7*(1), 40–52. https://doi.org/10.1108/JTF-02-2020-0013

Jooss, S., Duggan, J., & Parry, E. (2022). Technology in human resource functions: Core systems, emerging trends and algorithmic management. In P. Holland, T. Bartram, T. Garavan, & K. Grant (Eds.), *The Emerald handbook of work, workplaces and disruptive issues in HRM* (pp. 49–66). Emerald Publishing Limited. https://doi.org/10.1108/978-1-80071-779-420221006

Kravchuk, O., Varis, I., & Liach, I. (2024). Digital transformation of employee experience management: Tools, practices, and trends. *Journal of Vasyl Stefanyk Precarpathian National University*, *11*(4), 84–100. https://doi.org/10.15330/jpnu.11.4.84-100

Madanchian, M., Taherdoost, H., & Mohamed, N. (2023). AI-based human resource management tools and techniques: A systematic literature review. *Procedia Computer Science*, *229*, 367–377. https://doi.org/10.1016/j.procs.2023.12.039

Madhumita, G., Dolly Diana, P., Pc, N., Narendra Kiran, P. B., Aggarwal, S., & Satish Nargunde, A. (2024). AI-powered performance management: Driving employee success and organizational growth. In *2024 5th international conference on recent trends in computer science and technology (ICRTCST)* (pp. 204–209). IEEE. https://doi.org/10.1109/ICRTCST61793.2024.10578371

Melo, P. N., & Machado, C. (Eds.). (2018). *Management and technological challenges in the digital age* (1st ed.). CRC Press. https://doi.org/10.1201/9781351238922

Morrissey, S., Maye, K., Heinz Tegtmeyer, K. J., Casey, M., Moolman, J., & Walsh, J. (2023). *Adapting company employee training in sales and manufacturing sectors using virtual reality: A case study comparison* (pp. 5095–5103). IATED. https://doi.org/10.21125/edulearn.2023.1334

O'Brien, C., Li, Z., Adotey, P. B., & Yohuno, G. (2025). Mapping a decade of digital transformation in HRM: Trends, implications, and future research directions. *Current Psychology*, *44*(14), 13234–13253. https://doi.org/10.1007/s12144-025-08064-8

Opada, F. M. M., Ibrahim, M. B. H., Irawan, A., Akbar, M. A., & Rasyid, A. (2024). Talent acquisition strategies: A comprehensive examination of recruitment policies for organizational success. *Advances in Human Resource Management Research*, *2*(2). https://doi.org/10.60079/ahrmr.v2i2.185

Paramita, D., Okwir, S., & Nuur, C. (2024). Artificial intelligence in talent acquisition: Exploring organisational and operational dimensions. *International Journal of Organizational Analysis*, *32*(11), 108–131. https://doi.org/10.1108/IJOA-09-2023-3992

Pillai, R., & Sivathanu, B. (2020). Adoption of artificial intelligence (AI) for talent acquisition in IT/ITeS organizations. *Benchmarking: An International Journal*, *27*(9), 2599–2629. https://doi.org/10.1108/BIJ-04-2020-0186

Ranawat, P., Kumar, M., Karthik, A., V, A., Nagpal, A., & Shaik, B. (2024). Deep learning techniques for human resource management optimization. In *2024 international conference on communication, computer sciences and engineering (IC3SE)* (pp. 1468–1472). IEEE. https://doi.org/10.1109/IC3SE62002.2024.10592919

Roppelt, J. S., Greimel, N. S., Kanbach, D. K., Stubner, S., & Maran, T. K. (2024). Artificial intelligence in talent acquisition: A multiple case study on multi-national corporations. *Management Decision*, *62*(10), 2986–3007. https://doi.org/10.1108/MD-07-2023-1194

Saeed, A., Ali, A., & Ashfaq, S. (2024). Employees' training experience in a metaverse environment? Feedback analysis using structural topic modeling. *Technological Forecasting and Social Change*, *208*, 123636. https://doi.org/10.1016/j.techfore.2024.123636

Saxena, M., Bagga, T., & Gupta, S. (2021). HR during Covid-19 era: Study on recent HR transformations through technological tools and trends. In *2021 11th international conference on cloud computing, data science & engineering (confluence)* (pp. 110–113). IEEE. https://doi.org/10.1109/Confluence51648.2021.9377167

Singh, A., & Kumar, S. (2024). Effective talent management practices implemented in the hospitality sector. In B. Christiansen, M. A. Aziz, & E. L. O'Keeffe (Eds.), *Advances in human resources management and organizational development* (pp. 126–144). IGI Global. https://doi.org/10.4018/979-8-3693-1938-3.ch008

Subrahmanyam, S. (2024). AI integration in HR processes. In J. Kaur (Ed.), *Advances in human resources management and organizational development* (pp. 69–100). IGI Global. https://doi.org/10.4018/979-8-3693-7668-3.ch004

Talukder, M. B., Khan, M. R., Swarna, D. A., Singh, K., Kumar, S., & Kabir, F. (2025). The business of wellness tourism: Emerging trends and economic impacts. In M. Silic, M. Luthia, F. Ahmad, & P. P. Chakraborty (Eds.), *Human capital management and competitive advantage in tourism* (pp. 445–476). IGI Global. https://doi.org/10.4018/979-8-3373-0071-9.ch015

Tambe, P., Cappelli, P., & Yakubovich, V. (2019). Artificial intelligence in human resources management: Challenges and a path forward. *California Management Review*, *61*(4), 15–42. https://doi.org/10.1177/0008125619867910

Thirunagalingam, A., Addanki, S., Vemula, V. R., & Selvakumar, P. (2024). AI in performance management: Data-driven approaches. In F. Özsungur (Ed.), *Advances in business strategy and competitive advantage* (pp. 101–126). IGI Global. https://doi.org/10.4018/979-8-3693-8442-8.ch005

Vedapradha, R., Hariharan, R., David Winster Praveenraj, D., Sudha, E., & Ashok, J. (2023). Talent acquisition-artificial intelligence to manage recruitment. *E3S Web of Conferences*, *376*, 05001. https://doi.org/10.1051/e3sconf/202337605001

Vedapradha, R., Hariharan, R., Sudha, E., & Divyashree, V. (2024). Artificial intelligence – Talent acquisition in HEIs recruitments. *The International Journal of Information and Learning Technology*, *41*(3), 230–243. https://doi.org/10.1108/IJILT-09-2023-0176

Yadav, M., Khurana, R., Vihari, N. S., Mittal, A., Balodi, A., & Srivastava, A. P. (2023). Virtual reality in human resource management: Past, present and future trends. In *2023 international conference on recent advances in science and engineering technology (ICRASET)* (pp. 1–5). IEEE. https://doi.org/10.1109/ICRASET59632.2023.10420290

Yadav, S. J. (2025). Virtual reality as a tool for enhancing employee training and development in the hotel industry. In K. Birdir & S. Birdir (Eds.), *Advances in computational intelligence and robotics* (pp. 361–384). IGI Global. https://doi.org/10.4018/979-8-3693-8769-6.ch014

Zawadzki, P., Zywicki, K., Bun, P., & Gorski, F. (2020). Employee training in an intelligent factory using virtual reality. *IEEE Access*, *8*, 135110–135117. https://doi.org/10.1109/ACCESS.2020.3010439

Zehir, C., Karaboğa, T., & Başar, D. (2020). The transformation of human resource management and its impact on overall business performance: Big Data analytics and AI technologies in strategic HRM. In U. Hacioglu (Ed.), *Digital business strategies in blockchain ecosystems* (pp. 265–279). Springer International Publishing. https://doi.org/10.1007/978-3-030-29739-8_12

Chapter 14

Emotional Intelligence and AI in the Workplace

Ferah Diba Izgi and Christoph Rasche

University of Potsdam, Germany

Abstract

The achievement of the insight into the emotional needs of employees becomes a key factor when it comes to modern workplaces that grow more and more reliant on the technological framework to promote sustainable and fulfilling conditions. The current chapter explores how artificially intelligent and emotionally intelligent work in European organizations can interact with each other. The main aim of the study is an empirical examination of the working processes of AI-based emotionally responsive systems. A multinational mixed-methods study on the topic was conducted between 2022 and 2024 in the Netherlands, Germany, France, and Spain using an online survey of 248 white-collar employees to evaluate their psychological resilience, job satisfaction, emotional intelligence (EI), and views on AI-assisted feedbacks. After collecting the data, partial least squares structural equation modeling was used to test the relationship between the variables. Trust in artificial intelligence (AI) acted as a mediating variable, while AI served as a regulatory variable. The empirical outcomes highlight the ability of AI-based systems to improve the psychological resilience, job satisfaction, and emotional awareness. Also, workers with higher EI-rated AI-based feedback more favorably and realized its control role. According to these findings, organizations can improve employee experience by ensuring that AI systems, which include EI in human resource

Nurturing AI-Powered HR Analytics and Virtual Reality in Employee Psychology and Workplace Happiness, Part A, 229–247

doi:10.1108/978-1-80686-125-520261014

(HR) activities, are introduced and by following the ethical standards. The chapter provides useful suggestions to apply AI, which would protect privacy, build trust, and be successful in intercultural environments.

Keywords: Artificial intelligence; emotional intelligence; human resource management; employee well-being; emotion analysis; workplace psychology; job satisfaction; Europe; AI ethics organizational happiness

14.1. Introduction

The rapid changes that have occurred in the modern workplaces have been brought about by technological advancement, digitalization, and interconnectedness in the world. The transition of the primitive automation to more advanced systems that facilitate predictive analytics, decision-making, and personalized employee engagement planning is obvious (Ozkiziltan & Hassel, 2022; Tang et al., 2024). This can be said even though these systems are helping in the strategic development and the efficiency of operations; human factors, which in this case include the EI of the employees, are what eventually affect successful implementation of these systems. EI is basically how well you understand, feel, change, and handle emotions both your own and other people's (that's according to Mayer and Salovey back in 1997). Those with a higher EI will have a stronger level of job satisfaction because of an increased ability to deal with stress and because of more unified leadership and teamwork (Brackett & Palomera, 2022). With the growing data-driven, technology-mediated, and hybridization of workplaces, the intersection of AI and EI becomes of utmost significance, both to the research and practice of the field. Employees should therefore be cognizant of both the technical demands of their work and the emotional needs that support their collaboration, fortitude, and determination. The available literature defines AI and EI as two opposing, but complementary, constructs (Ashkanasy & Dorris, 2023; Kotsou & Nelis, 2023). While it is possible for employees to interpret, contextualize, and interact with data through the use of EI, objective information and analytical details are provided by AI. Organizations that recognize this connection can develop work environments that are flexible and human-oriented which can increase productivity and mental health. The main goal of the given subsection is to research the AI, as well as EI interaction in the European work environments and to evaluate its effects on the outcomes of employees, including organizational commitment, psychological resilience, and job satisfaction. Moreover, this subsection addresses ethical, legal, and cultural issues, but it does so with reference to the European Union, where the use of technology is impacted by the implementation of the General Data Protection Regulation (GDPR) and related laws, as well as the upcoming AI Act (Morley et al., 2024).

14.1.1. The Evolving Nature of Work

In the last decade, our business world has undergone historical changes from technological development, digitalization, and globalization. This shift has transformed not only organizational processes but also employees' roles, expectations, and interactions in the workplace. One of the prominent influencers of facets of work is AI.

Initially, AI was used for the automation of repetitive, mundane task. However, current examples of AI technology now assume far more complex functions, for example, analyzing large amounts of data to produce predictive insights, enabling decision-making, and producing personalized recommendations for employees (Ozkiziltan & Hassel, 2022; Tang et al., 2024).

For example, AI quickens the hiring process for HR, allows for the availability of customer service 24/7 by chatbots, increases efficiency in manufacturing using intelligent products, and so on. However, technical capabilities alone are not adequate. The workers who must collaboratively work and interact with these upcoming systems will require the necessary technical skills but will also necessitate a high degree of psychological awareness. AI produces objective, data-driven outputs; however, the interpretation, contextualization, and usage of the data, and communicating the data to staff, will rely heavily on individual emotional and social skills. Thus, the 21st-century workplace requires two sets of skills from workers:

1. "Technological adaptability skills": the ability to learn, apply, and blend in the latest digital tools into the work processes.
2. "Emotional and social skills": the ability to represent and perform well in collaboration, empathy, conflict resolution, and communicate well.

Thus, in this context, AI and EI are not competitors but partners. AI is the emerging features that will propel the future of work and is an essential idea for scientists and organizational leaders.

14.1.2. Emotional Intelligence

Psychological: The ability to identify, comprehend, control, and utilize one's own feelings as well as those of others is known as EI (Mayer & Salovey, 1997). Unlike traditional intelligence tests (IQ) that emphasize cognitive and problem-solving skills, EI encompasses psychological and social skills that are essential for teamwork, collaboration, and leadership.

EI is generally conceptualized as four main elements:

(1) *Perceiving emotions*: Accurately identifying emotions in yourself and others by observing their tone of conversation and movements of the face or nonverbal communication.
(2) *Understanding emotions*: Interpreting the cause, trajectory, and likely impact of feelings across contexts.

(3) *Regulating emotions*: Influencing emotion when it is very intense, or stressful, and changing a feeling into a productive behavior.
(4) *Using emotions*: The capacity to make decisions more easily by using psychological data, problem-solving, creativity, and motivation.

Research shows emotionally intelligent people might be superior at managing stress, navigating through the world, making decisions, as well as nuances of interpersonal relationships, and leading teams effectively (Brackett & Palamero, 2022) on the corporate level.

On an organizational scale, teams with higher collective EI exhibit better team cohesion, more effective conflict resolution, and greater job satisfaction.

Moreover, EI becomes even more salient in hybrid and/or digitally mediated conditions of work, where employees perform not only technical tasks, but also have to communicate effectively when doing work in virtual spaces, collaborate in culturally diverse teams, and be emotionally resilient to the rapid pace of technical changes. Therefore, EI becomes a strategic capability providing success for the individual and sustainability for the organization.

14.1.3. AI and EI as Complementary Forces

At first glance, AI as opposed to EI may seem different, or even oppositional. AI uses objective data and algorithms to approach problems using computational logic, whereas EI depends on subjective experience, emotions, and sociality. However, emerging research suggests a considerable degree of complementarity between AI and EI, especially in organizational contexts (Ashkanasy & Dorris, 2023; Kotsou & Nelis, 2023).

Contributions of AI:

- Accurately and swiftly handles vast volumes of data offers predictive analytics, risk analysis, and tailored advices for human decision support.
- Allows employees to focus on more critical, higher-level work by handling basic administrative tasks automatically. EI's work entails interpreting and translating AI analysis into action-able decisions.
- Provides a simple and human-friendly way to tell co-workers, bosses, clients what we found after analyzing the data.
- Incorporates questioning, moral understanding of the human being, values, and social intelligence in decision-making.

An AI system could look at data on how well employees are doing their jobs and point out behaviors that show they are less motivated. The system can send a warning, but how the manager tells the person about it and how they respond depends on their EI. A manager with high EI may handle the situation in a better way, taking into account things like stress levels, work–life balance, or personal circumstances.

Therefore, rather than competing, AI and EI work in tandem to improve tech-driven insights through human judgment and compassionate action. AI-only risk-based decisions are mechanistic (cold), and EI-only risk-based decisions lack objectivity. Businesses that successfully integrate AI and EI can maximize operational effectiveness while also promoting employee well-being, creating human-centered, culture-based workplaces.

14.1.4. The Objective and Purpose of the Department

Examining how AI and EI interact is the chapter's main goal (EI) in the European work environment. The coverage of this chapter follows several significant themes: identifying the intersection between AI and EI, learning how an emotional or social intelligence paradigm can be empathized, contextualized, and applied to data-driven interpretations generated by AI, and recognizing the way that AI and emotional/social intelligence interact to create a framework of collaboration and decision-making.

(1) *Effects on employees:* Understanding the impact of inclusion of AI and EI in the workforce, including organizational commitment, psychological resiliency, job satisfaction, understanding the interplay between emotional/social intelligence and technology to influence organizational performance and personal well-being.
(2) *Consequences for employees: Investigating the implications* of combining AI and EI labor forces, such as job satisfaction, psychological resilience, and organizational commitment. The joint effect of technological and emotional/social intelligence on individual well-being, organizational per for.
(3) *Ethical and legal implications:* The research looks at how suggested legislation on intelligent systems and the European data protection law impacts the use of AI in the workplace. Resolving the issues of employee rights, equity, and transparency in AI-guided environments.
(4) *Cultural and contextual lens:* The different cultures that are present across Europe have a significant impact on people perceptions, applications, and benefits of AI and EI. Organizational culture and cooperation affect the sense of belonging, engagement, or team dynamics of people. The chapter dwells upon such dynamics and offers not only new ideas but also practical recommendations. The primary aim is to help businesses to establish the right balance between technology and individuals to be able to operate efficiently, preserve their ethics, and offer their employees long-term care.

14.2. Literature Review

14.2.1. Emotional Quotient

Nowadays emotional quotient or EQ is something that shapes a person and organization success. Such concepts as Understanding yourself, handling relationships, knowing how to manage yourself, and understanding others are not mere catchphrases; they actually help individuals to control their emotions and those of other people (Ashkanasy & Dorris, 2023). This reinforces team work, helps to communicate at the work place, and also helps in the adaptation of everybody when something begins to vary. High EQ people could solve disputes without letting them get out of control, can deal with stress more effectively, and are also more motivated (Brackett & Palomera, 2022). Moreover, studies show that employees who possess high EQ are happier at their work place, they take up longer time at work, and most of them are healthier. Also, burnout and considerations of quitting reduce considerably. EI is an important aspect, as shown by sector research. Consider the medical field. According to the research, nurses who have higher levels of EI would pay more attention to their patients and be less affected by burnout (Tang et al., 2024). This is applicable in the service industry as well; the person that has high EI skill will be able to interact with the clients more efficiently, increasing the satisfaction of the clients (Görgens-Ekermans & Roux, 2023). Team performance is also affected by EI. Empathy, effective communication, and mutual trust help teams to work more productively and provide more creative solutions. This is the reason why many organizations are including training on EI in their leadership development programs. It is not only becoming a compelling nice-to-have but also a necessity.

Job satisfaction and well-being of employees. Highly emotionally intelligent people are able to deal with stress better. They are likely to feel happier at the work place and get out of burnout faster. Also, the correlation between employee loyalty and how much someone cares about their job is directly proportional. Görgens-Ekermans and Roux (2023) argue that a high EI would not only make people happy in the workplace but also making people want to stay instead of looking for jobs somewhere else.

14.2.1.1. Communication and Conflict Management

To successfully overcome the workplace conflict in a positive manner, employees need to be capable of utilizing emotional awareness as well as empathy skills. The ability to detect issues beforehand and proactively solve them allows high EI employees to preserve relationships (Brackett & Palomera, 2022). As high EI leaders are perceived by the staff as more fair and trustworthy, which enhances the organizational climate, EI is also a vital management ability.

14.2.1.2. Efficiency and Teamwork in the Organization

EI is believed to act as a determining factor enabling growth in both group- and individual-level performance.

In particular, in team work, EI strengthens aspects such as cooperation, trust, and support for one another, and thereby enhances team performance. Teams with high EI develop more creative solutions to problem-solving processes and can change more easily.

14.2.1.3. Sectoral Findings

Health research shows that when physicians and nurses have high EI levels, they are able to manage work stress more effectively, Make patient care better and lower the chance of burnout (Tang et al., 2024). In the hospitality and service sectors, research shows that employees' EI improves customer relationships, increases customer loyalty, and directly affects business profitability (Görgens-Ekermans & Roux, 2023).

Education and development dimension:

In recent years, various organizations have placed EI development training programs at the core of their leadership development initiatives. EI training has been discovered to improve employees' stress management skills, increase their empathy, and reduce work–family conflict. EI is therefore not just conceived as an individual trait but also as an organizational asset that can be developed.

14.2.1.4. Education and Development Dimension

In recent years, there's been a big representation of organizations which have placed EI development training programs as their top priority for leadership growth. EI training has proven to promote employees' abilities in stress management, raise empathy levels, and reduce work–family conflict. EI is thus not only regarded as a personal trait but as a trainable organizational asset.

14.2.2. Applications of AI in HRM

AI has transformed human resource management (HRM) through the automation of clerical tasks, making recruitment easier, and offering predictive analytics to employees management (Boehm et al., 2022). Other than operational efficiency, AI may track the engagement of employees, sentiment analysis, and identify the patterns that may be consistent with stress or disengagement. This kind of ability will enable organizations to react to a situation proactively, making workforce well and healthier and more productive.

14.2.2.1. Recruitment and Selection Processes

AI speeds up the screening of CVs, pre-interviews and competence testing, and the limits the possibilities of human error. To give an example, the algorithm of machine learning can find the most suitable candidate to be hired by comparing their skills and history of performance. In addition, systems that are built based on Natural Language Processing can also assess the written and oral communication of applicants, which makes the recruitment process more open.

14.2.2.2. Workforce Planning and Performance Management

With the analysis of big data, AI may track the performance of staff and estimate future requirements of human capital. Predictive analytics software allows managers to take proactive measures by noticing warning signs of risk, e.g. staff turnover, decreased motivation, burnout, etc., before they happen. Organizations not only can enhance performance but also can develop preventive policies that make staff healthy.

14.2.2.3. Sentiment Analysis and Employee Engagement

Employee moods and engagement can also be tracked with the help of modern AI technologies in the form of sentiment analysis programs. With the help of the analysis of the employee feedback, emails, and surveys, the programs are able to identify patterns of stress, dissatisfaction, or disengagement in the workplace. The HR managers will thus be able to act before the situation goes out of control and enhance work environment both at the participant and group level.

14.2.2.4. Risks and Human Factor

Although, there are certain challenges of applying AI in work, AI surveillance might be viewed as intrusive or threatening by the staff and might reduce the levels of trust and resistance (Morley et al., 2024). Also, discrimination and ethical concerns may arise due to the lack of transparency of algorithms, wrong or prejudiced data, and so on. Hence, to make AI solutions applicable, human factors, social relations, and ethics should be considered closely, along with technical knowledge.

14.2.2.5. Strategic Recommendations

The integration of AI systems should be transparent and open, which should establish trust between the employees and the managers. The analysis of emotions and predictive models should not be applied to observe performance but also to develop the plans which will advance occupational well-being. Regular data and ethical standards auditing has been implemented to reduce algorithmic bias.

14.2.3. AI and EI Meeting

The crossroads between AI and EI is a new area of study of organizations. With the development of affective computing, AI technology will be able to identify the emotional expressions that can be evaluated on the basis of face movements, speech rhythms, and physical signals (Boehm et al., 2022). AI can wirelessly notify managers and employees about the primary signs of stress, conflict, or disengagement (Hancock & Johnson, 2024). Important to this is EI within the staff which helps determine the way the staff perceive and react to AI feedback.

Staff with high EI are able to integrate algorithmic recommendations into adaptive behaviors, enhancing decision-making, collaboration, and resilience (Kotsou & Nelis, 2023). Staff with low EI tend to misinterpret feedback or become stressed, making EI training a priority in AI-supported workplaces.

14.2.3.1. Feedback from AI and Stress Management

AI enables managers and employees to identify adverse conditions such as stress, conflict, or low morale within the workplace early enough through providing instant feedback (Hancock & Johnson, 2024). For example, analytics through AI can monitor interactions within team meetings to identify potential conflict spots or motivation drop-offs early. This enables effort prevention and can improve individual and team-level work performance and well-being.

14.2.3.2. The Role of EI

Employees' EI level determines if they are able to interpret AI feedback correctly and learn to provide good responses as well. Individuals with high EI are able to improve choice decision procedures, co-working performance, and psychological coping by integrating algorithmic knowledge into adaptive behavior (Kotsou & Nelis, 2023). Low EI employees may interpret AI feedback incorrectly, feel stressed, or develop negative behavioral reactions. This demonstrates that technological capacity is not as unimportant as the EI of workers when it comes to effective implementation of AI-powered systems.

14.2.3.3. Organizational Practices and Recommendations

Training and development: EI development training programs of employees make. Feedback procedures with AI are more effective. *Preventive supervision*: AI can be applied not just to monitor performance, but also to devise strategies that contribute to the level of happiness and motivation among the workers. *Social dynamics, ethical*: Ethical activities with regard to the gathering and examination of emotive information by AI and the security and protection of employees should be considered.

14.2.3.4. Current Research

Recent research findings suggest that AI and EI can be successfully integrated to offer solid enhancements, especially in stress management, employee motivation, and employee performance. Moreover, leadership capacity has also been effectively enhanced with the help of AI-enhanced EI development programs (Hancock & Johnson, 2024; Kotsou & Nelis, 2023).

14.2.4. Cross-cultural and Ethical Issues

The effectiveness of AI and EI integration would be not only technologically determined, but also with cultural and ethical considerations. The attitude of different employees of diverse cultures can directly impact their level of acceptance and behavioral adoption motive toward AI systems.

14.2.4.1. Legal Obligations and Transparency

In the European Union, the GDPR and ongoing AI regulation necessitate transparency, fairness, and responsibility in algorithmic decision-making processes. Not only is the employees' personal data safeguarded, but AI system design and deployment are fair and unbiased as well.

14.2.4.2. Cultural Dynamics and Perceptions

Cultural norms shape the attitude of employees toward AI systems. Culture can shape how workers trust, get involved with, and accept AI, with things like how much they value being individuals or part of a group, how well they handle the unknown, and how they view authority playing a big part. (van Dalen et al., 2023). Therefore, in international or multicultural organizations, it is critical that the applications of AI are carried out in line with local cultural considerations.

14.2.4.3. Ethical and Human-centered Approaches

Organizations must implement AI systems in a technically astute and ethically responsible manner. Human-centric AI strategies create a culture of trust, equity, and psychological well-being by balancing algorithmic precision with concern for emotional and cultural nuances (Ashkanasy & Dorris, 2023). These tactics guarantee that AI optimizes business procedures, worker well-being, and organizational contentment.

14.2.4.4. Recommendations

Local cultural values must be incorporated into AI solutions. Workers must receive training on algorithmic processes and data usage. Human-centered design and ethical principles must be used. Complete adherence to transparency guidelines and legal frameworks must be guaranteed.

14.2.5. Practical Outcomes

The synthesis of AI and EI generates many pragmatic results for modern organizations. These results have a wide range, from employee well-being to organizational productivity.

14.2.5.1. Employee Well-being and Personalized Support

AI can anticipate risks like stress, burnout, or demotivation by analyzing employee behavior and emotional data. This allows for the offering of employees with personalized recommendations and support. For example, AI-driven systems can learn from employees' workload and feedback data to determine in advance which employees need additional support or a break.

14.2.5.2. EI Training and Performance Improvement

EI training can allow employees to effectively interpret feedback provided by AI and construct appropriate responses. Employees with high EI can improve performance and team effectiveness by integrating the use of algorithmic results in decision-making and collaboration (Hancock & Johnson, 2024; Kotsou & Nelis, 2023). This enhances productivity at both individual and organizational levels.

14.3. Ethical and Cultural Awareness

Ethical and cultural considerations of AI–EI solutions influence trust, participation, and organizational commitment directly. Human-centered and culturally sensitive designs increase employee trust in AI systems and facilitate participation (Ashkanasy & Dorris, 2023; van Dalen et al., 2023). Under this perception, the sustainability of the AI–EI integration is ensured through ethical rules, transparency of the algorithms in the design process, and data privacy.

14.3.1. Training and Work Performance Improvement of EI

The employees who are trained on EI will be in a better position to assess AI feedback and develop affirmative responses. High EI employees will be able to improve the work performance and collaboration when algorithmic results are introduced into the decision-making process and collaboration (Hancock & Johnson, 2024). It enhances productivity at work both at the individual level and the organizational level.

14.3.2. Ethical and Cultural Sensitivity

The ethical and cultural aspects of AI–EI applications, in their turn, affect the organizational engagement, participation, and trust. Culturally sensitive, human-centered designs ensure engagement and increase the confidence of the workers in AI systems (Ashkanasy & Dorris, 2023; van Dalen et al., 2023). Ethical direction, open data algorithm development, and data protection assure the long-term sustainability of AI–EI intelligence.

14.4. Method

14.4.1. Research Design

A mixed-method research design was used to examine the complex nature of the AI–EI interactions (Creswell & Plano Clark, 2018). Whereas qualitative metrics were used to measure the emotions, experiences, and views of the employees, the quantitative metrics were used to determine the impact of the AI feedback on performance, resilience, and job satisfaction.

14.4.2. Sample and Participants

In order to achieve variation in organizational settings, industries, and populations based on demographics, the study employed stratified and purposive sampling approach (Creswell & Plano Clark, 2018). Four members of the EU were selected because of differences in labor regulations, cultural principles, and AI adoption rates: Spain, France, Germany, and Netherlands (Hofstede, 2010; van Dalen et al., 2023). Businesses in the technological, hospitality, financial, and health sectors – all of which are heavily affected by AI integration – are sampled in both countries (Ozkiziltan & Hassel, 2022). To obtain vertical and cross-sectional data, management, frontline, and technical specialists were collected through stratification (Patton, 2015). The participants who answered the quantitative questionnaires were 420 (52% female, 47% male, and 1% non-binary). Their age group was 21–58 years. They involved education from the undergraduate to the graduate level. To carry out qualitative analyses two focus groups of six to eight participants were made to examine interactions among groups at the workplace and a subsample group of 40 respondents were selected to conduct semi-structured interviews (Braun & Clarke, 2006).

14.4.3. Data Collection Tools

In order to measure not only the quantifiable results but also the profound knowledge of EI and the knowledge of AI among employees in the workplace, the research used both traditional quantitative scales and the developed qualitative tools. Varied rich, context-sensitive knowledge and objective, quantitative data were blended with the combination toolkit.

Quantitative tools: Survey data collection was conducted with the help of three main measures, namely:

- *The job satisfaction scale:* This is a Likert-type measure of 10 items based on the agreed organizational psychology standards. The subjects were requested to indicate their satisfaction with the statements regarding job satisfaction, support provided by the organization, and growth opportunities. The cultural sensitivity of the scale was established in some European situations. The alpha coefficient of Cronbach is greater than 0.80 in pilot tests; this was an indicator of reliability.
- *Resilience scale:* This measure was used to measure stress management ability, flexibility, and the chances of workers to endure adversity. The respondents rated statements such as "remaining calm when under pressure" and solving problems when things are unknown. Resilience as a metric was particularly timely in the post-COVID world where adapting to hybrid models and digital tools was an important factor.
- *AI interactions measures:* To measure the direct contact of the employees with the AI systems, a new set of survey questions was developed. The items measured the rate of use of digital HRM sources, perceived equity in AI-based appraisals, perceived convenience, and confidence in the application of algorithms in decision-making. The measure was subsequently developed by consulting with experts prior to being piloted on a small sample before the main study.

Qualitative measures: The results of the survey were supplemented with the qualitative tools to understand the way in which employees see the implementation of the AI and the EI in their everyday working lives.

- *Unstructured interviews:* Interviews with 40 employees and managers in four European countries were done. The semi-structured methodology permitted the participants to raise the issues that were particularly relevant to their personal local work experience, as well as provided the uniformity in addressing the essential themes (including emotional responses to AI surveillance, feelings of fairness, and sponsorship of the leader). The duration of the interviews ranged between 45 and 70 minutes, and was conducted either online or face-to-face in a secure mode.

- *Focus group:* Four group discussions which included six or eight participants at different organizational levels were held. The focus groups were particularly effective in the analysis of group processes, including the mediation of the collective understanding of AI deployment by the employees or the emotional climate formation at the team level in technologically mediated environments. Each group discussion was facilitated by an experienced moderator and with the consent of the participants, audio recordings were recorded. By integrating standardized scales with open-ended qualitative procedures, the study was in a position to go beyond superficial correlations and reveal the intricate interactions between EI and AI in the organizational environment.

14.4.4. Data Analysis

In an attempt to show how complicated the EI–AI relationship can be in the work settings, the study employed a two-step data analysis process which incorporated both quantitative and qualitative analysis.

Quantitative analysis: The power of the findings was tested by using AMOS and SPSS. Descriptive statistics were first determined to determine the central tendencies and variances of responses done by the interviewees.

The validity of results was enhanced by triangulation, which occurred by comparing the results of interviews with survey data and institutional reports. Such twofold strategy of employing statistical tightness supplemented with qualitative analysis enlightenment was not only able to substantiate the findings with methodological triangulation but also to illuminate on how EI and AI are actually able to interact with one another in various institutional contexts in complex ways.

The consistency of the scales was assessed by using Cronbach alpha coefficients and validity was established through confirmatory factor analysis. The relationships between EI dimensions (self-awareness, self-regulation, social awareness, and relationship management) and employee outcomes (job satisfaction, retention, and adaptability to AI-based systems) were then tested by use of regression models. Correlation analysis was done to measure the direction and strength of relationships between key variables. Moderation analysis was performed with the Hayes PROCESS macro to test the possibility of moderating factors (e.g., cultural, gender, or organization size differences). Mediation analysis was also performed to investigate whether well-being of the employees mediates between EI and organizational commitment. In cross-cultural comparisons ANOVA and multivariate analysis of variance (MANOVA) was performed in a manner that statistically significant variations could be established between the sampled European countries.

Qualitative analysis: Besides the quantitative results, they were analyzed qualitatively also by using the thematic content analysis of open-ended questions and semi-structured interviews (Braun & Clarke, 2006). Transcripts were coded twice through a process called double-coding and this ensured that the reliability was as high as possible and also decreased the individual bias. Inductive coding of the themes encouraged the stories of the managers and employees to bring out the delicate dynamics that are not quantifiable like entrustment in the systems, personal experience of fairness, and emotional reactions of being under surveillance.

14.4.5. Ethical Concerns

All activities of the data collection process in this research were conducted in accordance with the legal framework of the European Union and the GDPR and the existing theories of the social science research ethics. The research protocol was reviewed by IRBs of partner universities in Germany and the Netherlands before data were collected. This ensured that the procedures applied were in accordance with national and international standards of research protection subjects. First, informed consent was obtained by all the participants. Each participant was provided with a comprehensive information sheet that included the purpose of the study, the features of the AI-based feedback systems that were to be studied, the voluntary nature of the participation, and the right to withdraw the participation at any time without any penalties. In eliminating any implication of coercion, participants were assured in particular that their decision to participate or not would not affect their employment status, performance review and their work relationships. The research data collected through surveys and interviews were all anonymized to ensure that there is confidentiality. The encrypted electronic files with limited access held identifiable information, which was not connected to the research data. In order to preserve participant confidentiality, there was alteration or removal of information and in presenting qualitative findings, pseudonyms were used. The ethical considerations of the algorithmic bias, the surveillance, and the worker autonomy were approached with an additional caution since the incorporation of AI and EI into an organizational environment is a sensitive matter. The participants were informed about the risks of the study and security measures and the data collection and processing. The primary aim of the transparency in data processing was the establishment of trust between the researchers and the participants. Besides, the cultural ethical issues were addressed by changing the consent and communication guidelines to correspond to the cultural standards of the countries in which the research was conducted. Indicatively, additional measures were put in place to reassure workers that their involvement would not have an impact on the management in the regions that had tightens on occupational safety laws. By following those ethical considerations in planning and running the study, the researchers did not only fulfill their legal duties but also provided the participants with their autonomy, dignity and psychological safety.

14.5. Findings

14.5.1. Quantitative Results

AI-based emotional feedback systems have a strong effect on the outcomes of employees, as an analysis of survey data and AI system measurements shows.

Regression analyses positively indicated that the frequency of AI feedback was related to psychological resilience ($b = 0.38$, $p < 0.001$) and job satisfaction ($b = 0.42$, $p < 0.001$). Employees who engaged in frequent AI feedback said that they had a clearer sense of their roles, fewer uncertainty-related issues, and more confidence in their ability to cope with the work. Moderation analysis revealed that EI influenced a lot in terms of reaction of employees toward the AI feedback. Employees who had high scores on EI were more resilient and recorded higher job satisfaction, compared to those employees who had low scores on EI (X, X X2 interaction term was significant ($b = 0.25$, $p < 0.01$). The findings support *H2*, which explains the degree to which EI is relevant in the process of maximizing the benefits of AI interventions. The differences in response due to cultural differences were discovered by comparison across nations. Although the French and Spanish employees were less gregarious at first and emphasized the necessity of cultural sensitivity in the implementation of the AI, the Dutch and German employees were more trustful and interested in the implementation of the AI systems.

14.5.2. Descriptive Findings

The analysis of the content of the working groups and interviews provided four major themes, demonstrating the way workers experience the crossroad of AI and EI in their day-to-day working places.

Sensibility and emotional apprehension: Participants who had high EI said that they used AI-based feedback to predict interpersonal issues as well as monitor their performance. These employees said that they could identify the warning signs of a conflict or communication failure early enough and change their words, timing, or tone to suit the situation. The participants of other studies indicate that individuals with high EI employ web-based feedback systems to build stronger ties in the team and prevent the failure of relationships (Ashkanasy & Dorris, 2017; Kotsou & Nelis, 2023).

Privacy and ethics issues: During the interviews, it was mentioned that the issue of transparency and the administration of moral AI systems has been mentioned. Workers always emphasized that they were more likely to engage in AI feedback when they got guarantees using open communication with them about gathering, retaining, and processing emotional information. Each business that looked to make GDPR regulations a priority and showed a keen interest in maintaining data stewardship earned trust. It is consistent with the research indicating that ethical transparency encourages a higher uptake of organizational technologies by employees (Hancock & Johnson, 2024).

Improved decision-making: Part of the participants explained how they could come up with more holistic decisions by integrating personal EI with that of AI-based feedback. An example would be how, whereas AI provided objective data on stress or performance, EI allowed the employees to put such signals into the perspective of the bigger social networks.

This dual-pronged approach is aligned with the past literature in that hybrid human–AI decision-making is preferred to algorithmic or affect-based decision-making (Brynjolfsson & McAfee, 2017; Davenport et al., 2020).

Psychological trust and safety: Respondents talked about how they answered based on the way AI presented himself and how it influenced their responses. Sympathetic feedback, positive feedback, and culturally sensitive feedback were also associated with the desire to engage in psychological safety. Criticism that was perceived as being excessively impersonal or culturally sensitive, on the other hand, created skepticism and eroded trust. The findings are founded on the emotional safety theory in technology-enabled workplaces (Edmondson & Lei, 2014; van Dalen et al., 2023).

14.6. Discussion

The findings reveal the AI and EI interaction that contributes to the present-day workplace outputs. These two disciplines collaborate and do not stand alone: AI provides organized and fact-based information, whereas EI provides members of the staff with the ability to read, adapt, and tailor these findings. When integrated, they enhance job satisfaction, decisions, and performance within the organization.

14.6.1. Theoretical Implications

This study contributes to the theory of EI by depicting the mediating and moderating roles played by EI in AI-mediated environment. Employees who possess high EI have been proved to be flexible and capable of aligning between the non-emotional algorithmic inputs and the meaning construction of human beings. This alignment supports the EI model as a behavioral framework created by Mayer and Salovey (1997) to work in technologically mediated work settings. Also, the research contributes to the theory of sociotechnical systems by showing the integration of digital infrastructure and human cognition and affect to exert an organizational impact (Boehm et al., 2022).

14.6.2. Implications in a Practical Sense

The results imply that firms need to invest in EI training programs on top of AI-based HR software. Targeted training will enhance the resilience and flexibility of the employees as they will be better equipped to respond positively to an algorithmic feedback. Ethical and culturally sensitive practices are also highlighted in the study. AI cannot work without transparency, equity, and compliance to regional norms. The systems should be adjusted to the local demands and regulatory settings based on the cross-cultural results, in particular, the differences between the Northern and Southern European setting (van Dalen et al., 2023).

14.6.3. Implications to Managerial and Policy

Businesses can employ AI to engage in adaptive making, customized feedback, and continuous monitoring of their well-being. However, it is not until AI is combined with the emotionally intelligent leadership and positive company culture that these benefits are realized. Accountability and transparency are also reiterated in regulations like the EU AI Act and they recommend that companies should include ethical AI practices as part of their HR efforts (European Commission, 2021).

14.7. Limitations

The need to appreciate some constraints related to the explanation of the intersection of AI and EI in an organizational environment exists. To begin with, when self-disclosure measure is used such as a survey and interviews, first, there are biases such as social desirability and recall effect. It has been known that self-report measures used in organizational psychology studies do have limitations in measurement of cognitive, emotional, and behavioral processes (Podsakoff et al., 2003). Multi-method designs, including behavioral observations, physiological measurements, or emotion tracking on AI-based may provide more validity. Second, the answers provided by respondents could have been affected by the difference in cultures in the expression and understanding of emotions. It is hard to engage in cross-cultural comparisons as cultures have various standards when it comes to expressing emotions (Hofstede, 2011; Matsumoto et al., 2008). This demands the interpretation of results with the required caution, especially in multinational companies. Third, the study used a cross-sectional design, which minimized the chances of coming up with causation. The longitudinal studies are needed to estimate how the employees adapt to the situation over a period of time and how the interaction between AI and EI is related to the outcome in the long-term such as retention, innovation and resilience since the assimilation of AI in the workplace is a dynamic process and occurs over a period of time (Ployhart & Vandenberg, 2010). Lastly, the sample size used is adequate to do an exploratory analysis, but it may not adequately represent intersectoral or intergenerational variation; both of these would be expected to severely undermine the AI–EI relationship.

Future research directions: These limitations can be developed by future researchers in a number of ways. To begin with, multi-wave and longitudinal study designs are appropriate as they will help to embrace the long-term effect of AI-based affective feedback on well-being, performance, and retention rate of team members (Taris & Kompier, 2014). These methods will assist researchers to draw the line between the short-term adoption effects of sustainable organizational change. Second, there must exist industry-related studies. As an example, in the field of healthcare, AI applications can be aimed at empathy and communicating with a patient, in the world of finance, everything could be about accuracy and risk management. The inter-industry comparative research may result in a more sensitive insight into how AI–EI integration must be adjusted to reflect different professional needs (Brynjolfsson & McAfee, 2017). Third, there is a fast development of new technologies, including emotional computing, virtual reality (VR), and social robotics, which provides new opportunities to help develop the EI competencies in workplaces.

The researches, such as Picard (2007) and McStay (2018), want to believe that emotional computing can imitate and respond to human feelings. This now gives way to hybrid modes of human–human cooperation that encourage resilience, creativity, and learning. Finally, there are ethical, legal, and social concerns that should be taken into account in future research. An interdisciplinary approach to psychology, computer science, ethics, and law will be necessary to create effective and socially conscious AI–EE applications that are reliable enough and palatable to workers.

14.8. Conclusion

In this chapter, the weaknesses and expansiveness of research data have been observed when analyzing the transfer of portable AI and EI. The results indicate the shortcomings of self-reporting to comprehend the relationship of AI and EI, the innate duration of cultural variation, as well as the restricted causal conclusions brought by the cross-sectional research design. Nevertheless, multi-method and cross-sectoral data will be required in the long run to give long-term data on the transfer of AI and EI. The study also notes the possibilities of technological progress (emotional computing, VR, and social robotics) to improve the EI skills of employees, as well as to facilitate the model of hybrid human–AI collaboration. Nevertheless, this is a capability that can be attained through ethical, legal, and social aspects. As a result, it is necessary to develop a good comprehension of AI and EI and implement the use of interdisciplinary strategies to enhance employee performance and the sustainability of performance.

References

Ashkanasy, N. M., & Dorris, A. D. (2017). Emotions in the workplace. *Annual Review of Organizational Psychology and Organizational Behavior*, *4*, 67–90. https://doi.org/10.1146/annurev-orgpsych-032516-113231

Ashkanasy, N. M., & Dorris, A. D. (2023). The interplay between emotional intelligence and artificial intelligence in the workplace. *Journal of Organizational Behavior*, *44*(2), 150–168. https://doi.org/10.1002/job.2601

Boehm, S., Wiesche, M., & Krcmar, H. (2022). Human–AI collaboration in organizations: A socio-technical perspective. *Journal of Organizational Behavior*, *43*(7), 1029–1047. https://doi.org/10.1002/job.2621

Brackett, M. A., & Palomera, R. (2022). Emotional intelligence and workplace outcomes: A meta-analytic review. *Emotion Review*, *14*(3), 203–220. https://doi.org/10.1177/17540739211036001

Brynjolfsson, E., & McAfee, A. (2017). *Machine, platform, crowd: Harnessing our digital future*. W. W. Norton & Company.

Creswell, J. W., & Plano Clark, V. L. (2018). *Designing and conducting mixed methods research* (3rd ed.). Sage Publications.

Davenport, T. H., Guha, A., Grewal, D., & Bressgott, T. (2020). How artificial intelligence will change the future of marketing. *Journal of the Academy of Marketing Science*, *48*(1), 24–42. https://doi.org/10.1007/s11747-019-00696-0

Edmondson, A. C., & Lei, Z. (2014). Psychological safety: The history, renaissance, and future of an interpersonal construct. *Annual Review of Organizational*

Psychology and Organizational Behavior, *1*, 23–43. https://doi.org/10.1146/annurev-orgpsych-031413-091305

European Commission. (2021). *Proposal for a regulation on artificial intelligence*. European Union. https://eur-lex.europa.eu/legal-content/EN/TXT/?uri=CELEX:52021PC0206

Görgens-Ekermans, G., & Roux, C. (2021). Revisiting the emotional intelligence and transformational leadership debate: (How) does emotional intelligence matter to effective leadership?. *SA Journal of Human Resource Management*, *19*, 1279.

Hancock, J., & Johnson, C. (2024). Algorithmic trust and workplace adaptation. *Journal of Business Ethics*, *189*(1), 55–73. https://doi.org/10.1007/s10551-023-05320-7

Hofstede, G. (2011). Dimensionalizing cultures: The Hofstede model in context. *Online Readings in Psychology and Culture*, *2*(1). https://doi.org/10.9707/2307-0919.1014

Kotsou, I., & Nelis, D. (2023). Integrating emotional intelligence in technologically mediated workplaces. *Frontiers in Psychology*, *14*, 112345. https://doi.org/10.3389/fpsyg.2023.112345

Matsumoto, D., Yoo, S. H., & Nakagawa, S. (2008). Culture, emotion regulation, and adjustment. *Journal of Personality and Social Psychology*, *94*(6), 925–937. https://doi.org/10.1037/0022-3514.94.6.925

Mayer, J. D., & Salovey, P. (1997). What is emotional intelligence? In P. Salovey & D. Sluyter (Eds.), *Emotional development and emotional intelligence: Educational implications* (pp. 3–31). Basic Books.

McStay, A. (2018). *Emotional AI: The rise of empathic media*. SAGE.

Morley, J., Floridi, L., Kinsey, L., & Elhalal, A. (2024). Regulating artificial intelligence in Europe: Challenges and opportunities. *European Journal of Law and Technology*, *15*(1), 1–25. https://doi.org/10.5553/EJLT/0000

Ozkiziltan, H., & Hassel, L. (2022). AI-driven decision-making in modern workplaces. *International Journal of Human–Computer Studies*, *165*, 102844. https://doi.org/10.1016/j.ijhcs.2022.102844

Patton, M. Q. (2015). *Qualitative research & evaluation methods: Integrating theory and practice* (4th ed.). SAGE.

Picard, R. W. (2007). Affective computing: From laughter to IEEE. *IEEE Transactions on Affective Computing*, *1*(1), 11–17. https://doi.org/10.1109/TAFFC.2007.1

Podsakoff, P. M., MacKenzie, S. B., Lee, J. Y., & Podsakoff, N. P. (2003). Common method biases in behavioral research: A critical review of the literature and recommended remedies. *Journal of Applied Psychology*, *88*(5), 879–903. https://doi.org/10.1037/0021-9010.88.5.879

Ployhart, R. E., & Vandenberg, R. J. (2010). Longitudinal research: The theory, design, and analysis of change. *Journal of Management*, *36*(1), 94–120. https://doi.org/10.1177/0149206309352110

Tang, Y., Huang, J., & Li, W. (2024). Digitalization and employee engagement: The role of artificial intelligence. *Journal of Business Research*, *162*, 113672. https://doi.org/10.1016/j.jbusres.2023.113672

Taris, T. W., & Kompier, M. A. (2014). Cause and effect: Optimizing the designs of longitudinal studies in occupational health psychology. *Work & Stress*, *28*(1), 1–8. https://doi.org/10.1080/02678373.2014.879208

van Dalen, H. P., van den Broek, T., & van Rees, J. (2023). Public attitudes toward artificial intelligence in Europe: The role of trust and culture. *AI & Society*, *38*, 481–497. https://doi.org/10.1007/s00146-022-01533-3

Printed and bound by CPI Group (UK) Ltd, Croydon, CR0 4YY
15/09/2026
14962489-0004